Maximizing Corporate Value through Mergers and Acquisitions

Founded in 1807, John Wiley & Sons is the oldest independent publishing company in the United States. With offices in North America, Europe, Australia and Asia, Wiley is globally committed to developing and marketing print and electronic products and services for our customers' professional and personal knowledge and understanding.

The Wiley Finance series contains books written specifically for finance and investment professionals as well as sophisticated individual investors and their financial advisors. Book topics range from portfolio management to e-commerce, risk management, financial engineering, valuation and financial instrument analysis, as well as much more.

For a list of available titles, visit our Web site at www.WileyFinance.com.

Maximizing Corporate Value through Mergers and Acquisitions

A Strategic Growth Guide

PATRICK A. GAUGHAN

WILEY

Published by John Wiley & Sons, Inc., Hoboken, New Jersey.
Published simultaneously in Canada.

For general information on our other products and services or for technical support, please contact our Customer Care Department within the United States at (800) 762-2974, outside the United States at (317) 572-3993 or fax (317) 572-4002.

Wiley publishes in a variety of print and electronic formats and by print-on-demand. Some material included with standard print versions of this book may not be included in e-books or in print-on-demand. If this book refers to media such as a CD or DVD that is not included in the version you purchased, you may download this material at http://booksupport.wiley.com. For more information about Wiley products, visit www.wiley.com.

Library of Congress Cataloging-in-Publication Data:

ISBN 9781118108741 (Hardcover)
ISBN 9781118224229 (ePDF)
ISBN9781118262351 (Mobi)
ISBN 9781118237335 (ePub)

Printed in the United States of America

10 9 8 7 6 5 4 3 2 1

Contents

CHAPTER 5
Horizontal Integration and M&A   117

CHAPTER 11
Valuation and Merger Strategy 291

Mergers and acquisitions (M&A) are an integral component of the growth strategy of many corporations. M&A often allows companies to achieve more rapid growth relative to what they would experience through internal or organic processes. However, that growth comes with a price.

The risks that come with M&A are often poorly understood and underestimated. Too often only the potential benefits of a deal are considered while the risks tend to be downplayed. This leads to companies overvaluing targets and paying premiums that are too high.

For many companies M&A has been the key to their success. For example, Cisco and Johnson & Johnson would not be the great successes they are without their M&A programs. In addition, because these companies have done so many deals, they have sharpened their ability to identify valuable targets and to integrate them into the overall company after the deal. However, even for such experienced acquirers there are significant M&A failures.

M&A is one of the most researched fields of finance. A rich body of high-quality, pragmatic research studies have explored all aspects of M&A. For example, many studies have explored the impact of M&A on acquirers and targets and have shed light on which types of deals are value enhancing and which are wealth destroyers. Another large body of research literature has explored many aspects of corporate governance as it relates to M&A success or failure. These are just a couple of examples of the bountiful supply of research that is available to practitioners. Amazingly, however, the bridge between the corporate world of practitioners and dealmakers and the academic researchers has yet to be firmly put in place. This is surprising, as in other areas of finance, such as investments, practitioners have aggressively taken advantage of relevant studies to enhance the value of their work.

While M&A has been used very successfully to facilitate the growth of many companies, there are a troublingly high amount of major M&A failures. Amazingly, some companies seem to be unable to learn from their mistakes and repeat their M&A failures—sometimes on an ever-larger scale. Some boards seem to lack the ability to discern between a value-enhancing M&A and ones that will result in a significant loss of shareholder wealth.

This book explores the various ways that M&A can successfully help companies enjoy profitable growth. It seeks to identify the keys to successful M&A while also highlighting some of the pitfalls and ways that M&A can backfire and stunt growth. In doing so, the book seeks to take a step toward building that bridge between practitioners and researchers. It attempts to summarize many of the pragmatic research studies that shed light on the types of M&A that build corporate value as well as the aspects of deals that tend to destroy value.

In addition to focusing on M&A, we also analyze the circumstances when less-expensive alternatives, such as joint ventures and strategic alliances, can achieve some of the same strategic goals as M&A. For deals that did not work out, we explore the positive shareholder wealth effects of downsizing. Various downsizing alternatives exist, including divestitures, equity carve outs, and spinoffs. Research shows that each typically generates positive shareholder wealth effects while they differ in the circumstances in which one would better fit shareholder needs.

We adopt a frank approach to accessing deals that turned out poorly. Too often, CEOs propose deals that cause shareholders to lose the value of their equity but the CEOs are able to avoid blame. In a troubling number of cases, CEOs get rewarded for doing deals yet incur no penalties when these deals turn out badly. Boards are often reluctant to blame the CEO while also refusing to blame themselves for a company's M&A failures. Hewlett-Packard's board is a perfect example. We explore the failure of the corporate governance system while also emphasizing the types of governance that results in M&A that enhances growth rather than destroy value.

CHAPTER 1

Merger Growth Strategy

Mergers and acquisitions (M&A) can accelerate a company's growth probably more than most other means within its arsenal. This is particularly true of larger deals. However, as we discuss, the track record of M&A success is spotty at best. The key is determining *a priori* the deals that will be winners and the ones to avoid. The problem is further complicated by the fact that management may sometimes seek to pursue M&A for their own personal benefit, which may work against the interests of shareholders.

As we discuss at length in this book, there is a large body of research on the effectiveness of M&A and the impact that M&A has on shareholder wealth. In fact, M&A is one of the most researched topics in the field of finance. There is a large body of high quality pragmatic studies that scrutinize M&A decisions and the impact they have on the shareholders. These researchers, primarily academics, have devoted considerable time and effort to trying to determine the answers to questions such as "Do diversifying deals or M&A outside of a company's established expertise have positive or negative effects on the wealth of their shareholders?" This is one example of an important question that M&A decision makers could answer better if they were aware of the relevant research. However, one of the surprising facts of the field of M&A is that decisions makers, CEOs, and their boards of directors, generally have no awareness of this large body of quality research and make no effort to try to look into it further. As we discuss throughout this book, the answer sometimes lies in the fact that they have their own agenda and are not interested in uncovering facts and evidence that would not be supportive of that agenda.

We explore the different kinds of M&A with an eye toward determining which ones work better than others. The unfortunate part of M&A, though, is that so much of the *strategy*, ironically, does not appear to be very strategic. There is a troublesome volume of major M&A that make you want to scratch your head and wonder how could these deals really be based on a well-thought-out strategy. Unfortunately, it seems clear that many of them were

1

based on motives other than the furtherance of shareholder wealth. Indeed, some of them, such as the Citigroup one-stop-shop financial supermarket that was formed in the years prior to 2000, clearly did not serve consumers or shareholders. In fact, it mainly served Citigroup's CEO Sandy Weill's ego and bank account.

STRATEGY AND M&A

As we reiterate in Chapter 2, companies need to develop a growth strategy. Historically, the bulk of the return on equities comes from capital gains not dividend income. For there to be capital gains, the earning power of the company needs to rise. In other words, there should be growth. Therefore, companies need to create a strategic plan for how they are going to achieve such growth. Only secondarily do we inquire if M&A can facilitate that strategy. Sometimes it will be clear that M&A will play an integral part in the path to growth. In other instances, it may play only a minor role or no role at all.

The problem with many M&A is that sometimes they clearly are not a part of a well-thought-out strategic plan. Some seem haphazard such as deals that come up when dealmakers, such as investment bankers, approach a company with a brilliant idea that will make the bankers money but may have questionable value for the buyer. While such non-strategic motivations may be responsible for many M&A failures, there is reason to believe that most M&A do have some kind of a strategic basis even though that basis may be questionable. As an example, we consider the highly questionable M&A history of American Express in the case study that follows.

CASE STUDY: AMERICAN EXPRESS AND ITS STRANGE M&A HISTORY

We are all very familiar with American Express. It is the world-renowned credit card company that has enjoyed decades of success in the industry. In fact, the company can trace its roots back to the mid-1880s. However, like so many companies, it was unsatisfied with its great success in the business that it excelled at—credit cards—and aspired to broaden its reach into areas where it possessed no expertise at all. In 1981, American Express acquired the major brokerage firm Shearson Loeb Rhoades for $900 million ($3.3 billion in 2013 dollars). Shearson was the second-largest U.S. brokerage firm after

(*continued*)

Merrill Lynch and was crafted by CEO Sandy Weill through a series of 15 different M&A.

One has to wonder what could be the commonalities between credit cards and buying and selling shares of stock and bonds? Could it possibly be that when you call Shearson for a stock purchase you tell the broker "please charge it on my AmEx" and then perhaps you would get a discount for keeping it all in the family? Not really.

Undaunted at this absurd combination, American Express went out to create a financial supermarket—a one-stop company that markets a variety of financial services. In fact, that would not be the only major financial services company to try to create a financial supermarket that consumers did not want. Citigroup would outdo them years later.

In 1984, American Express acquired the investment bank Lehman Brothers for $360 million ($1.12 billion in 2013 dollars). Now, we have to wonder what these synergies could be? Perhaps someone who has a credit card with American Express could call up the Lehman Brothers unit and ask could they underwrite an offering of bonds and perhaps put that as well on his or her AmEx card? We can see there may be, and I mean *may* be, some synergies between the brokerage operation and the investment banking business. The reason why we say *may be* is that the tension between these two units would cause a great deal of consternation at Lehman years later where Lew Glucksman, from the rougher brokers' side of the business, forced out the investment banker Pete Peterson for the leadership of the firm. Peterson went on to be the very successful founder of the Blackstone Group while Lehman would eventually fall into bankruptcy under the leadership of Glucksman's protégé Dick Fuld.

Not a company to leave bad enough alone, in 1984, American Express went on to buy the Ameriprise financial planning business. Again, all the businesses involve money in some way so perhaps that would be the source of the synergy? It did not work out that way.

In 1988, the brokerage firm E.F. Hutton merged with Shearson Lehman, and the name was changed in 1990 to Shearson Lehman Hutton. This became the largest brokerage firm in the United States. In 1993, Shearson was sold to Primerica (Sandy Weill) for $1.15 billion. In 1994, American Express then spun off Lehman Brothers but not before it had to inject $1.1 billion to keep it viable. This is a business it acquired roughly a decade earlier for $360 million. Clearly American Express was great at running a credit card business but terrible at strategic planning and M&A.

(*continued*)

(*continued*)

The company would hold on to Ameriprise, a financial planning business that was a combination of different financial planning and asset management businesses, starting with its acquisition of IDS Financial Services from Alleghany Corporation in 1984. American Express owned this business for years, and actually added to it through other acquisitions, such as London-based Threadneedle Asset Management Holdings in 2003, even though it also offered no synergies. In 2005, American Express spun it off but not before it had to give Ameriprise a $1 billion infusion. While this is clearly terrible M&A planning, there have been even worse deals.

INTRODUCTION TO M&A

The field of M&A has grown greatly over the past half century. At one time M&A was mainly a U.S. phenomenon but starting in the fifth merger wave of the 1990s, M&A volume in Europe rivaled that of the United States. When we say that the United States was for many years the leader in M&A, this should not be construed to be as a good thing necessarily. While some M&A deals are great, there are all too many that are outright terrible.

By the 2000s, M&A had become a commonly used corporate expansion strategy for companies worldwide. By the 2000s, Asia, including rapidly growing China and India, had joined the ranks of the major participants in M&A. They have also been joined by South and Central American as well as Australian companies. Indeed, M&A is truly a global phenomenon.

While we have been mentioning just M&A, it is corporate control deals in general that have grown dramatically across the globe. These include M&A but also restructurings, such as divestitures and spinoffs. Indeed, one company's divestiture may be another's acquisition. Joint ventures and strategic alliances have grown comparably as well.

In this book, we analyze how M&A can be used to facilitate a company's growth. We will also see that an M&A can be a double-edged sword, which sometimes bestows great benefits and other times yields high costs and few benefits. The trick, so to speak, is to find out in advance which deals can help companies facilitate growth and which ones should be passed on. As the large number of merger failures will attest to, this is no easy task. For this reason, we spend almost as much time examining the causes of M&A failures as we do on the benefits from successful deals. Many of the failures have some common elements that should have enabled the dealmakers to identify them in advance. There is also a large body of very pragmatic and useful research that could help M&A decision makers, but all too often, they are totally unaware of this valuable knowledge base.

Before we begin such discussions, it is useful to discuss some general background information and cover the basic terminology we use throughout.

BACKGROUND AND TERMINOLOGY

A *merger* is a combination of two corporations in which only one corporation survives. The merged corporation typically ceases to exist. The acquirer gets the assets of the target but it must also assume its liabilities. Sometimes we have a combination of two companies that are of similar sizes and where both of the companies cease to exist following the deal and an entirely new company is created. One of the classic examples of this occurred in 1986, when UNISYS was formed through the combination of Burroughs and Sperry. However, in most cases, we have one surviving corporate entity, and the other, a company we often refer to as the *target*, ceases to officially exist. For statistical purposes deals are recorded with the larger company being treated as the acquirer and the smaller one as the target—even when the two companies call it a merger.

Most M&A are friendly transactions in which two companies negotiate the terms of the deal. Depending on the size of the deal, this usually involves communications between senior management of the two companies, in which they try to work out the pricing and other terms of the deal. Along the way, the boards of each company track the progress of the negotiations. For public companies, once the terms have been agreed upon, they are presented to shareholders of the target company for their approval. Larger transactions may require the approval of the shareholders of both companies. Once shareholders approve the deal, the process moves forward to a closing. Public companies have to do public filings for major corporate events, and the sale of the company is obviously one such event that warrants a filing by the target.

HOSTILE TAKEOVERS

While most deals are friendly in nature, some are outright hostile takeovers. The hostile takeover started to become popular in the 1980s during the fourth merger wave—a period known for its colorful hostile deals and also for the many leveraged buyouts that took place. While we had hostile deals for many years in the United States prior to the fourth merger wave, it was during that time period that hostile takeovers of major companies became more common.

In addition, it became acceptable for major companies as aggressors to embark upon such bids. Today, these types of transactions are common all over the world.

Hostile takeovers refer to the taking control of a corporation against the will of its management and/or directors. Taking over a company without the support of management and directors does not necessarily mean it is against the will of its shareholders. The way the takeover process works, shareholders usually do not get to express their views directly during a takeover battle and rely on management to do this for them. The situation may be different if the company has some large aggressive shareholders such as hedge funds. Such large investors are in a better position than smaller shareholders to get management and the board of directors to listen to their views on the deal. It may even be the case that the hedge funds are the one pushing the deal forward—possibly even in opposition to management. They may do this if they believe that current management is not optimizing the value of the company and that the quickest way to enhance the firm's value is to put it up for sale.

The main reason why a bidder pursues a hostile, as opposed to a friendly takeover, is that the deal is opposed by the target's management and board. Bidders usually want to do friendly deals because hostile deals typically are more expensive to complete. The greater expense comes from the fact that the bidding process may result in a higher premium as other bidders push up the price. It also may mean that the bidder has to keep raising the price to overcome the target's resistance. Hostile deals also may increase investment bankers' fees and legal costs. For the bidder, going hostile means that there is less assurance that a deal will go through compared to friendly deals, which have a much higher percentage of completion.

One of the main tools used to complete a hostile takeover is the *tender offer*. Tender offers are bids made directly to shareholders, bypassing management and the board of directors. If a company were pursuing a friendly deal, the logical place to start would be to contact the target company management. If this contact is rejected, then there are two other alternatives: (1) go to the board of directors or (2) go directly to shareholders. When bidders make an offer directly to the board of directors, this is sometimes referred to as a *bear hug*. It is mainly a hostile tactic because it carries with it the implied, and sometimes stated, threat that if the offer is not favorably received, the bidder will go directly to shareholders next.

If a friendly overture or a bear hug is not favorably received, then one of the next alternatives is a tender offer. Here the bidder communicates the terms of its offer directly to shareholders, hoping they will accept the deal. In the United States, the Williams Act (1968), a law that was an amendment to the Securities Exchange Act of 1934, provides specific regulations to which tender offers must adhere. Bidders cannot immediately purchase shares that are tendered to them but have to wait 20 days. During the 20-day offer period, other bidders may make offers. The first bidder may have put the target company *in play* and may then find itself in a bidding contest. Target company shareholders then get to consider both offers and possibly even others. This usually works to their advantage because they tend to receive higher premiums when there are multiple bids.

For bidders, however, it usually means they either will have to pay a higher price for the target or will have to drop out of the process. Shrewd bidders know where to draw the line and step back. Others, sometimes consumed by hubris, will bid on in an attempt to "win" the contest. Often what they end up winning is the *winner's curse*, where they pay more than the company is worth. As we discuss in a case study in Chapter 11, this was the case in 1988 when Robert Campeau, having already acquired Allied Stores, went on to make an offer for Federated, which would give him the largest department store chain in the world. Unfortunately for him, Macy's stepped into the bidding process, and CEOs Edward Finkelstein and Robert Campeau went head-to-head, increasing the premium until finally Campeau "won out." The ultimate winning bid was $8.17 billion (equity, debt, and total fees paid), but the acquisition saddled the combined company with billions of dollars in new debt. Unable to service the debt, and unable to sell off units at favorable prices in an M&A market that sharply cooled after the completed the deal, Campeau was forced to file for Chapter 11 bankruptcy not that long after the successful completion of the takeover. As we will see, this is not an isolated incident. All too often tightly fought bidding contests force takeover prices too high thereby eliminating the chance to realize net gains from the takeover.

A deal that may have been a good strategic fit can become less appealing if the offer ends up being a hostile takeover. If the process turns hostile, the bidder may (not always) end up overpaying. This may create a situation where the higher price offsets the initially perceived strategic value. If this is the case the bidder needs to back away and adjust the strategy. What is a "good" strategic fit at one price can be a bad one at another.

Another alternative to a tender offer is a *proxy fight*. This is where the bidder tries to use the corporate democracy process to garner enough votes to throw out the current board of directors and the managers they have selected. They would either try this at the next corporate election or call a special election. The *insurgent*, as such bidders are now called in this context, then presents its proposals and/or its slate of directors in opposition to the current group. In the 2000s, proxy battles became a popular method used by hedge funds to bring about changes in companies they had amassed stakes in. Such hedge funds would seek out undervalued targets, which they believed could benefit from specific changes such as replacing management, using cash for larger dividend payments, selling off assets, and so forth. Often the goal of hedge funds is not to take over a target but to enable them to realize short-term gains on their investment.

When a proxy fight is used to facilitate a takeover, bidders often find that it is a costly and uncertain process. It is often unsuccessful, although again, success depends on how you define it. If the bidder is trying to bring about changes in the way the target company is run, this process often does accomplish that. For hedge funds, such changes might be selling off assets or even an outright sale of the entire firm. If the goal, however, is to get shareholders to outright reject the current board and then go so far as to accept a bid for the company against management's recommendation, then this process often does not work. That is, bidders also find themselves having to expend significant sums for an outcome that often does not work in their favor—at least in the short run. Hedge funds, though, have been enjoying some success in acquiring equity positions in undervalued companies and then agitating to bring about changes that will uplift the value of their, and other shareholders', equity investments. In fact, in the 2000s, many hedge funds specialize in this activity. At times these hedge fund strategies can work to be benefit of shareholders who find themselves stuck with an overpaid and intransient management who are unwilling to make necessary changes to uplift shareholder values.

TAKEOVER DEFENSE

The hostile takeover process is somewhat like a chess match, with the target company being pitted against the hostile bidder. The methods used became much more sophisticated in the fourth merger wave of the 1980s, when hostile takeovers suddenly became commonplace. Targets, while initially slow to respond with effective defenses, eventually developed somewhat effective means of thwarting some bidders and extracting greater gains for their shareholders from others. We are now a quarter of a century after that fourth merger wave and many of the tactics developed in that period remain close to being state-of-the-art. Moreover, the laws, including case laws, have refined which techniques are legal and which are not. Many of the laws regulating defensive and offensive hostile takeover methods, which originally developed in the United States when M&A was mainly a U.S. phenomenon, have been copied and adapted into the securities laws of nations all across the world.

There are two types of takeover defenses. *Preventive takeover defenses* are put in place in advance of any specific takeover bid. They are installed so that the bidder will not attempt a takeover. *Active takeover defenses* are deployed in the midst of a takeover battle where a bidder has made an offer for the company. Although there are a variety of both types of defenses, many of them are less effective than when they were initially created.

The most effective preventive takeover defense is a *poison pill*. Poison pills are also called *shareholders' rights plans*. Rights are short-term versions of warrants. Like warrants, they allow the holder to purchase securities at some specific price and under certain circumstances. Poison pills usually allow the rights holders to purchase shares at *half-price*. This is usually worded as saying the holder can purchase $200 worth of stock for $100.

Poison pills are an effective defense because they make the costs of a takeover very expensive. If the bidder were to buy 100 percent of the outstanding shares, it would still have to honor the warrants held by the former shareholder, who would then be able to purchase shares at half-price. Because this usually makes an acquisition cost prohibitive, bidders seek to negotiate with the target to get it to dismantle this defense. Sometimes the bidder makes direct appeals to shareholders, requesting them to take action so they can enjoy the premium it is offering, which management and the board may be preventing them from receiving. Target management and directors, however, may be using the protection provided by the poison pill to extract a suitable premium from the bidder. Once a satisfactory offer is received, they may then dismantle this defense. This can usually be done easily and at low cost to the target company.

Corporate governance advocates have put pressure on companies to remove their poison pills. They are concerned that companies use this potent defense to insulate management from the corrective pressure of the takeover market. This is why in the 2000s, many companies chose to not renew these plans, which often are in effect for 10-year periods. The other reason is that these same companies know that if they needed to they could implement a new one in very short order. For example, Netflix did just that in November 2012, when Carl Icahn's presence as a 9.9 percent shareholder became a cause of concern for them.

Other types of preventive takeover defenses involve different amendments of the corporate charter. One such defense is a staggered board, which alters the elections of directors so that only a limited number of directors, such as one-third, come up for election at one time. If only one-third of the board could be elected at one time, then new controlling shareholders would have to wait for two elections before winning control of the board. This hinders bidders who make an investment in the target and then cannot make changes in the company for a period of time. Such changes may be a merger with the bidding company or the sales of assets, which might be used to help pay off debt the bidder incurred to finance the acquisition of the target's stock. Today these kind of boards are less common than they were years earlier.

Other common corporate charter amendments are supermajority provisions, which require not just a simple majority but a higher percentage, before certain types of changes can be approved. If a group of shareholders will not vote with the bidder, such as managers and some employees who are worried about their jobs, then a bidder may not be able to get enough shares to enact the changes that it needs to take full control of the company.

Other corporate charter–based defenses include dual capitalizations. These feature different classes of stock, which afford different voting rights and dividend entitlements to holders of the shares. They often involve one class of super voting rights stock, which usually pay very low dividends. These shares are usually distributed to all shareholders, but those who are interested in augmenting their control, such as managers, may retain it while others may accept a follow-up offer by the company to exchange these shares for regular voting and dividend-paying stock. The end result of such a stock offering/dividend distribution is that increased control is concentrated in the hands of shareholders who typically are more *loyal* to the corporation and who would be less likely to accept an offer from a hostile bidder. The Securities and Exchange Commission (SEC) and stock exchange rules limit the extent to which companies can issue and trade such shares.

A target company can take several steps when it is in receipt of an unwanted bid. Drawing on the defense that has been used for many years, it could file a lawsuit. Unless there are important legal issues it could argue, this often is not enough to stop a takeover. It may, however, provide time, which may enable the target to mount other defenses. This may include selling to a more favored bidder—a *white knight*. It may also involve selling shares to a more friendly party. This can be done in advance of an offer or as an active defense. The buyer in such sales is referred to as a *white squire*.

Targets may also restructure the company to make it less attractive to a bidder, or it may make some of the same changes that are being suggested by a bidder, thereby taking this recommendation away from the bidder. Restructuring the company may involve both asset sales and purchases. The company may also restructure its capitalization to increase its debt, making it more leveraged. Capital structure changes may have some impact by making the company less attractive and by reducing the amount of debt that can be raised by a bidder to finance the target's own takeover.

LEVERAGED TRANSACTIONS

Leveraged deals are those that use debt to finance takeover. They are sometimes referred to as highly leveraged transactions (HLTs). One well-known version of HLTs is a leveraged buyout (LBO). An LBO is an acquisition that uses debt to buy the target's stock. When people refer to an LBO, however, they are often referring to a transaction in which a public company is bought using debt and then is taken in private. For many years the largest LBO of all time was that of RJR Nabisco in 1988 for $24.8 billion. Using a 2.8 percent annual inflation adjustment factor this equates to just under a $50 billion deal in 2013 dollars!

RJR Nabisco was bought by the well-known buyout firm of Kohlberg Kravis and Roberts (KKR). Although many of KKR's deals have been successes, this buyout was not part of that notable group. This was the case for many reasons including overpaying, as well as not being able to anticipate the changes in the economic climate—even though these changes, such as economic expansions coming to an end after a certain time period, are the norm. The takeover was, nonetheless, quite colorful and became the subject of a successful book and movie.[1]

One of the risks that LBOs in general have is that the buyer takes on substantial debt, which leaves the company with a high degree of financial leverage. This carries with it all of the risk that high financial leverage imposes. This comes in the form of fixed charges for the increased debt service. Buyers of companies in leveraged transactions often plan on reducing this leverage with asset sales where the proceeds from those sales can be used to pay down the debt and reduce the debt service. In Robert Campeau's leveraged takeover of Federated Stores, the market soured after the acquisition and he was not able to sell off divisions at prices that reflected the value he paid when he overpaid for the overall company using borrowed funds whose debt he could not continue to service. Not overpaying is one key to takeover success. Related to that, avoiding bidding contests and overly hostile deals, which often cause the bidder to come away with the *winner's curse*, is also very important.

One of the other ways to reduce the pressures imposed by the debt incurred in an LBO is to implement cost structure changes and increased efficiencies, which will lower the company's overall costs and enable it to service the debt. Even here there may be problems. If a company sacrifices needed capital expenditures to reduce costs, such as what Campeau had to do and what Sears/Kmart did after their combination, this leaves the company in a weakened competitive position.

Buyers of companies in LBOs usually have a plan to reduce the debt over a period of time while they make various changes at the company. Many of these dealmakers plan on doing a *reverse LBO* sometime after the original LBO. In a reverse LBO, the private company that was bought out in the LBO goes public again. This can be done all at once or in stages, as it was done in the case of RJR Nabisco. In the RJR Nabisco deal, KKR sold percentages of the company to the public and used these proceeds to pay down the mountain of debt it had assumed. One of the reasons why this deal was not a success has to do with the bidding contest that occurred as part of the buyout. RJR received a lowball offer from a group led by then CEO Ross Johnson. KKR entered the fray with its own offer, knowing that the Johnson group's offer was low. However, a bidding contest ensued, and KKR won, but it really bore the winner's curse.

The winner's curse that the RJR Nabisco bestowed on its buyers was nothing compared to what became the largest LBO of all time—the 2007 $43 billion acquisition of electricity provider TXU by KKR and TPG Capital. This was a commodity-based business that was greatly affected by the price of natural gas, which, in turn, was greatly depressed by the glut of natural gas that came on the U.S. market after the LBO. It is amazing that we have this very famous private equity firm, KKR, pursuing these big mega-LBO flops. It is equally amazing that they, and another famous private equity firm, TPG Capital, did not consider that maybe a company that could be greatly affected by volatile commodity prices would not be a good candidate for great leverage and the high fixed payments that such debt requires.

Reverse LBOs are quite common following private equity LBOs. Private equity buyers acquire what they consider to be undervalued targets. They then seek to "flip" them—but only after they have extracted whatever gains they can such as through what are called dividend recapitalizations. When these buyers sell the acquired entity it is sometimes hard to find one buyer willing to pay a higher price than the private equity buyer did—especially after the private equity owners may have loaded the company up with debt and then used the debt proceeds to pay themselves dividends—what is known as *dividend recapitalizations*. When they cannot sell the now debt-laden company to one buyer, they often unload it to the market in an IPO. IPO buyers tend to be more naïve then other buyers—such as other private equity firms. Anyone unsure of the naïveté of IPO buyers need only think back to the Facebook IPO for confirmation.

RESTRUCTURINGS

Mergers and acquisitions are but one form of corporate restructuring. One form of restructuring that is the opposite of M&A is sell-offs. In a *sell-off*, a company sells part of itself to another entity. This can be done in several ways. The most common way is a divestiture, where a company simply sells off part of itself to another entity. However, downsizing can be accomplished in other ways, such as through spin-offs, where parts of a company are separated from the parent. Shares in the spun-off entity are given to shareholders of the parent company, who then become shareholders in two, as opposed to one, company. We discuss these types of transactions in Chapter 10 because they can be a way of *reversing the error*. Another way that a division of a parent company, perhaps one that was acquired in a deal that is now being viewed as a failure, can be separated from the parent company is through an equity carve-out. Here shares in the divisions are offered to the market in a public offering. In Chapter 10, we discuss the shareholder wealth effects of these different types of transactions. However, we can point out now that, in general, the shareholder wealth effects of these various forms of downsizing tend to be positive. A careful review the research convincingly reveals this to be true over an extended time period.

Another form of corporate restructuring on which we do not focus in this book but which is related to the world of M&A is restructuring in bankruptcy. Bankruptcy is not just an adverse event in a company's history that marks the end of the company. There are various forms of bankruptcy, and some of them are more of a tool of corporate finance where companies can make changes in their operations and financial structure and become a better company. Such restructurings can come through a Chapter 11 filing. The Chapter 11 filing refers to the part of the U.S. Bankruptcy Code that allows companies to receive protection from their creditors—an automatic stay. Other countries have bankruptcy laws that allow for restructuring, but many, such as Great Britain and Canada, are more restrictive on the debtor than the United States.

While operating under the protection of the bankruptcy court, the *debtor in possession*, as the company that did the Chapter 11 filing is called, prepares a reorganization plan, which may feature significant changes in the debtor company. These changes may provide for a different capital structure, one with less debt and more equity. It may also provide for asset sales, including sales of whole divisions, which supplies a cash infusion and may be used to retire some of the debt that may have led to the bankruptcy.

In the 1990s, many of the companies went through LBOs in the fourth merger wave, were forced to file for Chapter 11 protection. Returning to our Campeau Corporation example, it became a very different company after it emerged from bankruptcy protection. As with most Chapter 11 reorganizations, the equity holders, which included the dealmakers who dreamed up this highly leveraged acquisition, incurred significant losses as the market penalized them for their poor financial planning. Part of the focus of this book is to determine how such merger failures can be prevented. One of the options available for companies that have made poor deals is to proactively make some of the needed restructuring changes without having to go down the bankruptcy road. Sometimes, however, the situation is such that the pressure of the laws of the bankruptcy court is needed to force all relevant parties, including different groups of creditors who have different interests and motivations, to agree to go along with the proposed changes.

Bankruptcy presents many M&A opportunities. Shrewd bidders can find "great buys" in the bankruptcy process. This can be the case especially if the company is generally solid but has specific problems that can be remedied by the bankruptcy process. For example, if the company has valuable products and services and is only in bankruptcy due to too high leverage that was brought on by LBO artists, then this could be "fixed" in Chapter 11. Buyers in the Chapter 11 process may be able to acquire the valuable aspects of the company without the burden of all of its debt.

TRENDS IN MERGERS

Some volume of M&A always exists, but there have been several periods when a very high volume of deals was followed by a period of lower deal volume. These periods of intense M&A volume are referred to as *merger waves*. There have been six merger waves in the United States. The first merger wave occurred during the years 1897 to 1904. It featured many horizontal M&As. Many industries started the period in an unconcentrated state with many small firms operating. At the end of the period, many industries became much more concentrated, including some being near monopolies. This was ironic because the Sherman Act, as previously discussed, was specifically passed to prevent such an industry structure. The first wave ended when the economy and the market turned down. During the slow economy there was less pressure to do deals. This changed in the 1920s, when the economy started to boom. The vibrant economic conditions led to a second merger wave, which was concentrated during the 1916 to 1929 period. This wave featured many horizontal deals but also featured many vertical transactions. Deals were especially concentrated in specific industries. When the stock market collapsed in 1929 and the economy went into a prolonged and deep recession in the 1930s, the merger wave ended. We did not have another major merger period until the end of the 1960s. The decade of the 1950s was an up and down economy that had intense, if not absurd, antitrust enforcement.

The third merger wave was an interesting period in that it featured many conglomerate M&A because of the intense antitrust enforcement of that time period. The Justice Department was aggressive in its opposition to M&A and saw many deals, which would be approved immediately today, opposed on antitrust grounds. For this reason, companies that were acquisition-minded were forced to do deals outside of their industry to avoid the wrath of the Justice Department and the FTC—the two antitrust regulators in the United States. Many large conglomerates, such as ITT, LTV, Gulf & Western, Teledyne, and Textron were built during that period. While the 1960s featured a booming economy for much of the decade, both the economy and the market turned down at the end of the decade. Like the prior merger wave, it ended when the economic and financial pressures to expand subsided.

The 1970s featured a more modest number of M&As but did have many others forms of restructurings as companies, which may have been acquired during the third merger wave and were sold off as the firms adjusted to the slower economic conditions. Shareholders questioned some of the deals they had made when the economy was booming. The judgment of the company's managers may have been clouded by dreams of wealth that never materialized. As companies felt the economic pressures of a deep recession in the middle of the decade, they implemented management changes, and some of those changes helped bring about the various restructuring and sell-offs we saw during that period.

The 1980s proved to be the longest post-war economic expansion until we got to the following decade, which featured an even longer growth period. The 1980s provided the colorful fourth merger wave, which had many interested facets including the megamerger (see Figure 1.1). As noted earlier, some of these deals were highly levered and the fuel for these highly leveraged deals was provided by the junk bond market, which also boomed in response to the deal-related demand for this form of capital. The fourth wave also featured many hostile deals as companies, including major corporations, found themselves the target of unwanted suitors. Hostile bids certainly occurred before this period, but they were mainly offers by relatively smaller companies for other smaller companies. Before that period, it was unusual to hear of a hostile offer for large companies. It was even less common to have major reputable companies taking part in hostile takeovers. All of that changed in the late 1970s, and this set the stage for many of the hostile takeovers that occurred in the fourth merger wave of the 1980s.

The fourth merger wave ended when the economy slowed at the end of the decade and the junk bond market collapsed, in part as a function of weak economic conditions but also as a result of specific problems with that part of the bond market, including the indictment of Michael Milken and his investment bank—Drexel Burnham Lambert.

In 1990 to 1991, there was a mild recession in the U.S. economy, which recovered slowly initially and then with the rebound, picked up steam. As with many prior expansions, companies looked to grow, and the fastest way to expand is to buy whole companies as opposed to building such a business internally. To some extent, this makes sense as expanding economic

(a)

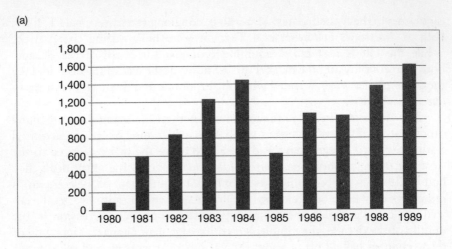

(b)

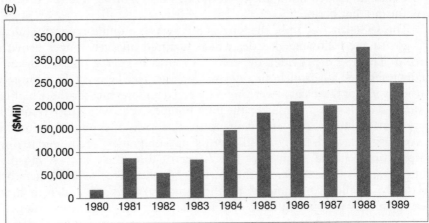

FIGURE 1.1   (a) Number and (b) Value of U.S. M&A in the 1980s
Source: Thomson Financial Securities Data.

conditions create market opportunities that companies may need to react to quickly in order to take full advantage. The problem occurs when dreams of economic riches cloud the judgment of management causing them to not make the most enlightened decisions. Another problem with booming economic conditions is that they can mask poor management. Increased demand can lead to higher sales and profits even for some companies that are not that well managed. When this occurs, shareholders and the board may credit management with gains that they did not bring about. This may lead them to go along with acquisition proposals that they may not scrutinize carefully enough. Management may get a pass, so to speak, until, for some of the less astute managers, their acquisition schemes blow up in their face. However, for those who made well-thought-out deals, they may be able to advance the company and take advantage of competitive opportunities in the marketplace.

The fifth merger wave was precedent-setting in terms of the total volume of mergers as well as the size of the deals that took place (see Figure 1.2). While many mega mergers took place in the fourth wave, some of the deals

(a)

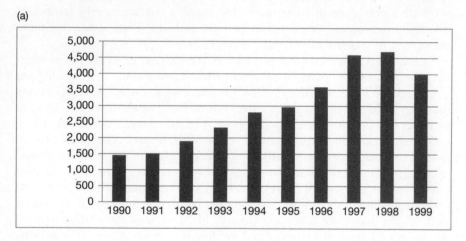

(b)

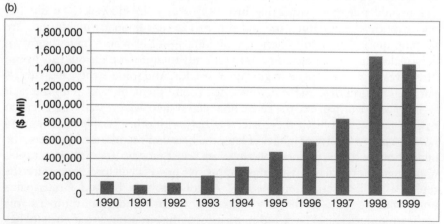

FIGURE 1.2 (a) Number and (b) Value of U.S. M&A in the 1990s
Source: Thomson Financial Securities Data.

that took place in the fifth wave made the fourth wave deals seem ordinary. Later in this book, we examine many of these leading deals that were simply flops—megaflops. M&A such as the AOL-Time Warner *merger of equals* were failures that left certain Time Warner shareholders incensed. Others, such as the Warner Lambert acquisition by Pfizer or the merger between Exxon and Mobil, clearly were major successes. The difference between successful and failed deals is discussed throughout the rest of this book.

The fifth merger wave was truly an international one with M&A volume in Europe rivaling that of the United States. The Europeans had drunk the American's M&A Kool-Aid and were off to the dealmaking races. In many ways, this was a needed change as for many years some very inefficient corporate structures had existed in Europe, and M&A was a way for these economies to create more efficient enterprises.

Like the merger waves that preceded it, the fifth merger wave ended when the economy turned down. Hot sectors such as the dot coms and the telecoms collapsed. However, like the 1990 to 1991 recession, the 2001 recession was relatively mild and only eight months in duration. The recovery was initially slow but low interest rates helped to boost certain sectors, such as real estate and construction, and a real estate bubble ensued. Alan Greenspan, the chairman of the Federal Reserve (Fed), basked in the glow of the praise bestowed upon him by those benefiting from the low interest rates he maintained. Not one to believe that one of his responsibilities as chairman of the Fed was to regulate lending in the country, he virtually ignored major producers of debt such as the mortgage lending industry. He also was a big supporter of deregulating banks, as he felt confident they would never engage in actions that would put these venerable institutions at risk. However, he did not understand human nature and did not realize that financial institutions are nothing more than a collection of individuals—all of whom have their own personal agendas. This agenda was to take advantage of the various short-term incentives that were in place to gain great wealth. And some of these individuals put their institutions, and everyone else around them, at risk. With the tacit support of Greenspan and the Fed, a financial system was created where certain employees can win big if they place big bets with other people's money and never have to give any of it back if later the bets don't work out.[2] In effect, the institutions become a casino—playing with house money. If some have scruples not to engage in such behavior, the competitive process will force them out to be replaced by less scrupulous people. All of this was beyond Greenspan's understanding, who to this day refuses to accept responsibility for his role in the subprime crisis.[3] The troubling aspect of this situation is that not a lot has changed in the years following the subprime crisis.

The subprime crisis and the Great Recession that followed brought an end to the sixth merger wave. After a short hiatus, deal volume continues at a

(a)

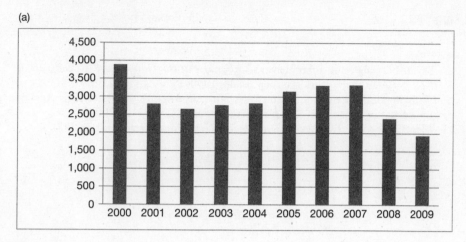

(b)

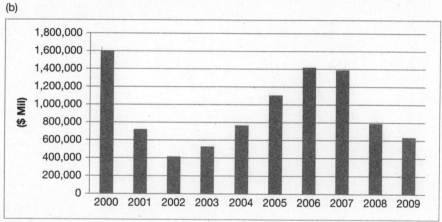

FIGURE 1.3 (a) Number and (b) Value of U.S. M&A in the 2000s
Source: Thomson Financial Securities Data.

good pace but featuring somewhat smaller deals (see Figure 1.3 (a)). Low interest rates make deal capital cheap even though the weak economic environment raises the risk profile of many deals. An intense M&A period has traditionally needed a robust economic and market expansion to take off. The weak U.S. recovery, followed by stagnation in Europe and weakness in China and much of Asia, has put a damper on M&A volume. Nonetheless, M&A continues, as it is an integral part of corporate growth strategy. This leaves us to explore how this strategy can be maximized.

NOTES

1. Bryan Burrough and John Helyar, *Barbarians at the Gate: The Rise and Fall of RJR Nabisco* (New York: Harper Trade, 1990).
2. William Fleckinstein and Frank Sheehan, *Greenspan's Bubbles: The Age of Ignorance at the Federal Reserve* (New York: McGraw-Hill, 2008).
3. Alan Greenspan, *The Age of Turbulence* (New York: Penguin Press, 2007).

CHAPTER 2

Growth through Mergers and Acquisitions

Companies are under continual pressure to grow. Corporate growth allows companies to pay increased dividends and to have shareholders realize increases in their equity investments. Management at companies would have a difficult time telling shareholders that their long-term goal is to stay at the same level and not grow. If they did, shareholders and directors would cry for a replacement management team that could achieve growth. So it is widely accepted that growth is required as part of management's strategy. However, this assumption, although widely accepted, should be critically evaluated and reexamined.

The pursuit of growth has led many companies to go astray and adopt strategies that fail to achieve such goals and may even cause the companies to incur significant losses. Pressure from securities markets forces management to pursue the growth that investors demand. One of the fastest ways that growth can be achieved is through mergers and acquisitions (M&A). Unfortunately, M&A can be risky. All too often it results in losses. The key is to determine which deals will lead to bona fide growth and which ones should be avoided. The long and inconsistent track record of M&A successes and failures underscores the fact that *a priori* identification of which proposed deals will be successful is a great challenge.

IS GROWTH OR INCREASED RETURN THE MORE APPROPRIATE GOAL? THE CASE OF HEWLETT-PACKARD

It is virtually taken without question that a major goal for a company's management and board is to achieve growth. While the advisability of this goal is often unquestioned, managers need to make sure that the growth strategy is one that will generate good returns for shareholders. Too often management may be able to generate acceptable returns by keeping a company at a given size, but instead they choose to pursue aggressive growth, which may put those steady returns at risk. Boards need to critically examine the expected profitability of the revenue derived from growth and determine if the growth is worth the cost. Consider the case of Hewlett-Packard (HP) in the post-Fiorina era. Having made a highly questionable $19 billion mega-acquisition of Compaq in 2002, HP found itself managing several business segments in which it is a leader in only one—printers. The company had revenues in excess of $80 billion. If, as an example, its goal was to grow at 10 percent per year, it would have to generate approximately $8 billion in new revenues each year. In effect, it would have to create another large company's worth of revenues each year to satisfy management's growth goals. When we consider the fact that a significant portion of its business comes from the highly competitive PC market with its weak margins coupled with steady product price *deflation*, one has to wonder where the growth will come from and at what price. Would the company be better off downsizing and having separate, but more manageable and focused, businesses? Would it be better off leaving the PC business, as the founder of the business, IBM, did in mid-2005 when it sold its PC division to Chinese computer manufacturer Lenovo? The Compaq acquisition enabled HP to claim it was the world's largest PC maker. However, its dissatisfaction with this business led it to announce in 2011 that it was getting rid of the PC business only to retract this statement following still another change of CEO. Leo Apotheker announced he was stepping down after his ill-fated 2011 $11.7 acquisition of Autonomy at an 80 percent premium! The market was shocked (and probably the sellers to) that HP was willing to pay such a premium. In Chapter 11, we will discuss this acquisition in the contest of poor due diligence and valuation analysis. The fact that HP's analysis was terrible was underscored when it announced in November 2011 that it was taking an $8.8 billion charge—largely due to the Autonomy deal. The failure of this deal is but one more blow to the company in addition to flat sales, low profit margins, and declining shareholder equity (see Figure 2.1).

HP has been really bad at M&A for many years. It still can't rival AT&T, however, for the title of the worst company at M&A in history. AT&T, which has gone through many transformations in its history, has that title locked up. But give HP credit, it keeps trying, and maybe one day it can wrest this auspicious title from AT&T. One has to wonder if Mark Hurd would have made such a bad financial decision. We will never know; he was forced out by the board following a situation where a former employee filed a lawsuit seeking money from him. The board ultimately found that he did not violate any major rule or laws but forced him out anyway. Rival Oracle CEO

(a)

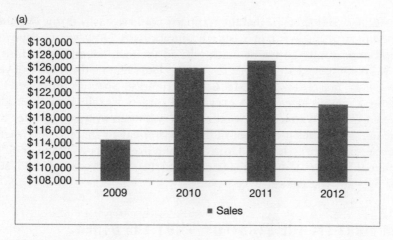

(b)

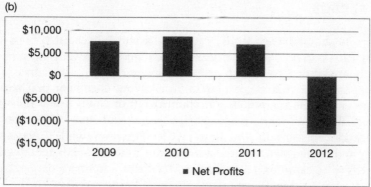

(c)

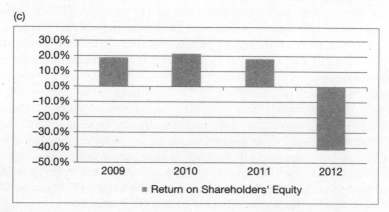

FIGURE 2.1   HP (a) Revenues, (b) Net Income, and (c) Shareholder Equity
Source: Value Line, January 4, 2013; WSJ Market Data, March 8, 2013.

Larry Ellison was shocked that the company could so easily throw out one of the best managers it ever had over such a minor issue. However, not one to let a good opportunity go by, he quickly hired the then-unemployed Hurd.

We don't mean to imply that companies like HP, and the AT&T of years gone by, do not create great M&A opportunities. They certainly do. They serve as a source of gains for overvalued targets to sell themselves to an unwitting and rich buyer who is more than willing to overpay them for their companies. From the perspective of the sellers and their shareholders, there is a very special place in the world for companies like this. For HP shareholders, they should be irate at their management and their board, which has a history of being very dysfunctional.

M&A MUST FIT THE STRATEGY—NOT THE OTHER WAY AROUND

A company should have a strategy for how it will deliver value to its share-holders. This strategy should be clearly articulated, approved, and supported by the board of directors. Each proposed merger or acquisition needs to fit into that strategy. A strategic plan is an evolving document that naturally needs to change and adjust to a marketplace and an economy that is also evolving. In recent years, the world economy and many industries have become more volatile and difficult to predict. However, while the company's strategy and related plan need to have a certain amount of inherent flexibility, one needs to be cautious if a proposed M&A deal requires a major strategic change for the acquirer. Such proposals should raise red flags for the board.

To consider this, we can go back to our HP example. HP has different divisions including the personal computer business and the printer business. For many years the personal computer business had been challenging for the whole industry—not just HP. It has been characterized by stagnant and sometimes falling prices that were the product of intense competition from lower-cost entrants. In addition, many of the U.S. PC companies faced certain rising cost increases thus squeezing margins. This was a tough business, in which HP was not a leader. Its printer business, however, had been a mainstay, and HP was a market leader in that business. Its board, however, should not have been surprised when Carly Fiorina proposed that HP do a $25 billion acquisition of one of its chief rivals—Compaq. Instead of expanding in areas where it was strong, printers, it was seeking to use M&A to expand more in the challenging PC business. When we consider that Fiorina was hired by HP from AT&T, which we have noted was a company that for many years had the absolute worst track record in M&A, we should not be surprised that she would suggest a poorly conceived M&A strategy. We will revisit HP's multiple M&A failures in Chapter 11.

STRATEGY SHOULD NOT BE JUST M&A

M&A can play a role, sometimes even a major role, in a company's strategy. However, there has to be a lot more to a company's growth strategy than just M&A. While this seems obvious, there have been many prominent examples where the only meaningful attempts at growth for a company was its M&A strategy. Probably one of the best (but from shareholders' perspective, it was really one of the worst) examples of this was the Worldcom debacle (see case study that follows a little later in this chapter). Here, management, mainly CEO Bernie Ebbers, was great at M&A and incapable of managing the huge company he created through dealmaking. A somewhat similar situation occurred at Tyco under the leadership of Dennis Kozlowski. He also built the company through a very aggressive M&A program. Indeed, many of his deals fell below the size reporting threshold, which, as the company grew, meant larger and larger deals could be done without significant reporting to the markets. It is ironic that the CEOs of both companies went to jail for extended prison terms. Ebbers' wrongful acts played a major role in the largest U.S. bankruptcy as of that time. In the case of Kozlowski, while he was certainly very piggish about extracting compensation and absurd perks, the company actually did fine during his tenure. He suffered from being pursued by the government in the wake of Enron and Worldcom.

ORGANIC GROWTH OR GROWTH THROUGH M&A

When companies are seeking to grow, they have two not mutually exclusive alternatives. They can grow internally using the resources that the company has available within it. This may end up being a slower process. It also is often (certainly not always) less expensive than external growth through mergers and acquisitions. With external growth through M&A, the company usually has to pay a transaction cost and a premium for the target and then also incur significant, and often difficult to measure, post-acquisition integration costs. These latter costs can be more or less predictable depending on how often the company pursues M&A and is required to implement integration. It is a kind of "practice makes perfect" situation. If a company rarely does M&A, it is likely that its managers are not in a good position to anticipate what the real integration costs will be. This does not mean that the solution is to do a lot of M&A so that when you need to do a deal, you will be better able to anticipate the integration costs. Companies have to figure out ways to measure such costs without having to live through many failed deals to do so. Ironically, some companies never learn. Post-divestiture AT&T was a great example of this. It used M&A to enter the highly competitive computer industry, which it eventually exited after losing substantial sums. Not one to learn from its costly mistakes, it would later use M&A to overpay for an entrée into the cable industry, which it also eventually exited after significant losses.

Sometimes markets force a company's hand. A firm may be inclined to pursue internal growth and avoid the higher costs associated with M&A. However, if markets are rapidly changing and the competitive environment is intense, waiting for slower internal growth to bear fruit may not be an option. The speed of market changes may force a company's hand. It may have to decide to become a player, or try to maintain its market share, or to risk falling behind the competition, which may be aggressively pursuing growth through M&A.

John Chambers, the CEO of Cisco, described this process as follows:

> *In periods when the industry ran slower, and different business models worked, the vast majority of product development came from internal teams. As the market begin to accelerate, you can't keep up with the customers' requirements; everything moves too rapidly. . . . Companies who are going to be leaders will have to have a new focus totally on acquisitions as a core competency.*[1]

Cisco is a great example of this process and of how a company was very successful for a long time in dealing with this dilemma. It is one company that can attribute much of its success to properly managing M&A. It is in an industry that has been rapidly changing. The industry requires participants to constantly develop new products to meet the rapidly changing needs of the marketplace. While Cisco profited greatly from its very successful M&A program, we will also see that it encountered some major stumbling blocks along the way. Experience helps a lot but it is no guarantee of M&A success.

ACQUISITION AND DEVELOPMENT VERSUS RESEARCH AND DEVELOPMENT

In rapidly changing industries, such as high-tech industries, it is often difficult for companies to keep up with the pace of innovation. Large bureaucratic enterprises are often not the best places to achieve innovation. As we will see, big companies can do many things small enterprises cannot. Size also is a byproduct of success. However, such size has its own costs and stifling innovation and creativity can be one of them.

Technologies that seem promising can quickly be eclipsed by rivals who are more innovative. Companies need to invest in specific technologies, and it is difficult to predict how successful these efforts will ultimately be. The same is true of other industries such as the pharmaceutical industry. Here, the ability of companies to develop new blockbuster drugs, drugs that have sales in excess of $1 billion, has been limited.[2] In the United States, fewer drugs are being approved by the Federal Drug Administration (FDA). Part of the problem is that many of the easier-to-cure illnesses have been dealt with by pharmaceutical treatments. The industry is left with much more complex, yet pervasive, illnesses such as Alzheimer's disease and several troublesome forms of cancer, which have proved to be very difficult to deal with. This has led many companies to invest considerable sums over many years in different lines of research that have proved fruitless.

The challenges of the pharmaceutical industry have been further compounded by the fact the drugs that are approved but have been the product of expensive research often require manufacturers to charge high prices to try to recoup their considerable investment. U.S. pharmaceutical companies are now finding insurers reluctant to reimburse companies for the latest high cost medicines.

The above problems of drug companies, which have certain elements in common with the computer and networking industry, have led companies to move away from research and development (R&D) and to pursue *acquisition and development* (A&D). Cisco, for example, has focused on companies where the target has already developed and validated the technology, and where consumers have convincingly demonstrated a demand for it. It would then pay the necessary premium to acquire such technologies through acquisitions. One of the benefits of this strategy is that it allows the market to weed out the unsuccessful technology developers and to focus on more successful targets. These targets then may receive an *offer they cannot refuse* in that it includes a premium to compensate them for having absorbed the risk of development failure and achieved success.

This strategy that Cisco used successfully in so many acquisitions is more difficult to implement in other industries such as the pharmaceutical industry. A&D is certainly used in acquisitions of biotech firms as well as of even large pharmaceutical companies. In the pharmaceutical industry, however, the process of development for blockbuster drugs has grown to be so long, often 10 years, and so costly, often over $1 billion with no assurance of Food and Drug Administration (FDA) approval or even market success, that there is not an abundance of lower-cost smaller firms developing blockbuster medicines. For many years, however, Cisco's success came from it having the luxury of being surrounded in Silicon Valley by a plethora of budding high tech firms filled with many promising technologies that are close to being very successfully marketed. Pharmaceutical companies, on the other hand, often have to either focus on R&D or acquisitions where the target's returns are much more distant and, therefore, uncertain.

CASE STUDY: CISCO'S ACQUISITION STRATEGY

One company that enjoyed good success with a growth through M&A strategy was Cisco. It had such great success even though high technology is an area that possesses great M&A risks given its inherent unpredictability. In fact, during the period where Mark Volpe ran the M&A process at Cisco, the company became the model for how M&A should be done and how post-M&A integration should proceed. Unfortunately, in the period 2009 to 2011, the wheels started to come off the cart.

It is not surprising that Cisco would rely on M&A to find growth during the economically weak post-subprime crisis period. M&A worked in the past to vault the company onto a successful growth path—why would it not do the trick during these tough times? One obvious answer to that question lies in the types of deals to which Cisco resorted. When we look at a company that is considering a particular deal, we have to ask—is this deal in an area that the company knows? Is it within its field of expertise, or is it venturing out of what it does best? For Cisco, it was the latter.

Cisco had a long history of M&A within its general area of expertise. It excelled at growth through M&A within this area. Presumably, because it ran out of valuable targets, and more importantly, could not achieve true organic growth with the maze of massed acquisitions that it had assembled into a company, it resorted to M&A outside of its expertise. It did this in 2003 through a $500 million acquisition of home networking company Lynksys and a $6.9 billion acquisition of cable box maker Scientific Atlanta in 2006. While the relevance of these deals is questionable, the $590 million acquisition of Flip camera business in 2009 was even more questionable.

As with many failed deals outside the area of a company's expertise, the attempt to integrate the poor acquisitions partly contributed to Cisco's loss of business in the switching field to more nimble rivals such as Juniper Networks. This is a common danger of failed M&A. This forces the company to devote considerable efforts to fixing the failed M&A as opposed to growing the business.

While Cisco is known more for its M&A successes, its failures are more common than one would think. In a study of large gain and loss acquisitions, including 2,297 transactions over the period 1996–2008, Fich, Nguyen, and Officer found that Cisco had 22 large loss deals producing dollar losses for its shareholders of $316 billion compared

(continued)

to 33 large gain deals producing gains of $352 billion (all 2008 dollars).[a] So we see the market does not take it for granted that Cisco's deals will work to the benefit of its shareholders.

The real question is—why did Cisco not concentrate on improving the business it had but instead moved into such unrelated fields as Flip phones? Even more fundamental a question is when management first proposed these strategically far-flung deals to Cisco's board, why did they not raise the stop sign? They were the gatekeepers and instead of saying this makes no sense and let's not proceed with the deals, presumably they gave management the go-ahead.

In spite of these M&A failures involving forays into unrelated fields, Cisco has had a long-term track record of more corporate success than failures. The recent failures were certainly not the only ones it had. For example, during the Internet boom of the 1990s, Cisco paid just under $10 billion for three networking companies and derived very few benefits from them. However, Cisco's M&A failures have been far fewer than its successes.

A well-managed company that has been successful in the past will usually make changes when it sees it is moving in the wrong direction. Following its experience with some recent M&A flops, Cisco seems to have righted the ship. The world's largest maker of computer networking equipment reported good results in 2012, despite weakness in Europe, which is a factor that affected companies all over the world. It did this with strong sales in Asia, which also have been growing more slowly than in the recent past. In addition, like many companies, Cisco continued to become more efficient through cost cutting and reductions in labor costs. More importantly, Cisco wised up and stopped doing foolish M&A. Rather than buy companies outside of its expertise to try to fuel M&A-related growth, it took some of its cash flows and returned them to shareholders through stock repurchases (see Figure 2.2). In addition, in 2013 it sold Linksys to Belkin. This shows that the company and its CEO, John Chambers, are sensitive to their obligations to shareholders. If a great deal comes down the road and they have to redirect future earnings to M&A, then they can cut

---

[a] Eliezer M. Fich, Tu Nguyen, and Micah Officer, "Large Wealth Creation in Mergers and Acquisitions," paper presented at the American Finance Association Meetings, San Diego, January 2013.

(continued)

(continued)

back on stock repurchases. In the meantime, the company returned money to shareholders rather than wasting it on bad deals. This is a lesson for managers around the globe.

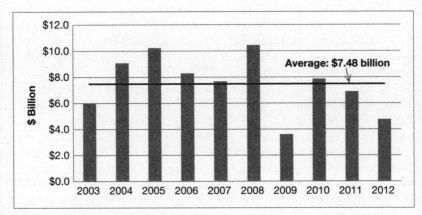

FIGURE 2.2   Cisco's Share Repurchases: 2003–2012
Note: For fiscal years ending in July.
Source: Cisco annual reports.

CAN M&A BE EFFECTIVELY USED TO BUY GROWTH?

Companies that have had trouble growing the business or businesses they already have often look to acquire other fast-growing businesses to jump-start their own growth. The reasoning is that if we acquire a fast-growing company, at a minimum, the weighted average growth rate should be higher—or so we hope. This raises some obvious questions about why the acquirer's current business is slow growth. However, the answer could be simply that it is a mature low-growth business in a low-growth sector, which may not leave many organic growth options.

One obvious question is: How effective are such *buying growth* strategies? The track record of such M&A is pock-marked with failures. One reason is that if you are buying a business that has perhaps shown steady growth, the present value of these fast-growing cash flows should be built into the price. More often than not, the buyer is *prepaying* for this growth. If it turns out this is the case, then the real value will have to come from synergies that generate even greater growth than what the target would have enjoyed on its own. This may certainly be the case in a lot of deals but as we discuss in Chapter 3, synergistic gains are much easier to talk about than to achieve.

SUCCESS IN CORE BUSINESS DOES NOT ALWAYS TRANSLATE TO SUCCESS WITH M&A STRATEGY: FOCUS ON MICROSOFT

We have discussed how Cisco was able to achieve so much of its success through its highly successful M&A strategy. Given the nature of its industry, it would be hard to conceive of how Cisco could have enjoyed comparable success if it had not completed so many very successful M&A. However, just because a company is very successful does not mean it will be successful doing M&A deals. A great example was Microsoft's 2007 $6.3 billion all cash acquisition of aQuantive. This was part of the very successful company's failed attempt to develop an Internet division that could compete with Google. One would think that Microsoft had good knowledge of this related business, but its performance belies that notion. Microsoft developed an excellent search engine, Bing, but it could not get this product to generate significant profits. In July 2012, the company announced a $6.2 billion charge, which basically wiped out all the company's profits for the prior quarter.

Microsoft paid handsomely for aQuantive and poured millions into its failed effort to develop an Internet division. It would seem reasonable to believe that having such a business would not be such a stretch for the highly successful software company. However, in spite of its prior success and great financial resources, Microsoft was a failure at using M&A to extend its reach into Google's domain.

GROWTH THROUGH BOLT-ON ACQUISITIONS

Bolt-on acquisitions are acquisitions that fit in naturally with a company's existing line of business. They are sometimes referred to as *add-on* or *tuck-in* acquisitions. Some private equity professionals often consider this a term they invented but it has been around a long time—even before they changed the name of their own businesses from leveraged buyout (LBO) firms to private equity firms to avoid the connotation associated with the many debt-laden bankruptcies of the 1980s.

A bolt-on target could be a company that has a product line that complements the buyer's existing product line and could be sold by the same sales staff. In the private equity context, a private equity firm might acquire a target and merge it into a company they had already acquired to make that company more robust and marketable when they got around to exiting the investment. That greater marketability may come from having a broader product line. One of the ways this could be done would be to have the private equity–owned firm acquire some other companies and thereby grow its overall size and product line. This could make the combined business more appealing and easier to market in an initial public offering or other sale process. In that sense, the private equity buyers could create actual value. Too often, they merely extract value and then flip their acquisitions.

The term *bolt-on* has vague meanings and is subject to the interpretation of the users. However, it does come with the implication that the *bolts* fit well and that the companies are a complementary fit. Being complementary implies that there may even be synergistic benefits that flow back and forth from the acquirers to the target. Fich, Nguyen, and Officer found that some of the deals that created the greatest wealth for the shareholders of acquirer's were bolt on deals where the target was small relative to the acquirer.[3]

One company that has grown very well in the medical products and pharmaceutical field is Johnson & Johnson. We discuss its successful acquisition strategy in the case study that follows.

CASE STUDY: JOHNSON & JOHNSON—GROWTH THROUGH A BOLT-ON ACQUISITIONS STRATEGY

Johnson & Johnson (J&J) is a manufacturer and marketer of a wide range of health care products. Over the period 1995 to 2011, the company engineered over 70 significant acquisitions as part of its growth through acquisitions strategy (see Table 2.1). This strategy is similar to that pursued by companies in other rapidly changing, innovation-filled industries such as the computer software industry. Rather than internally try to be on the forefront of every major area of innovation, J&J, a $68 billion company, has sought to pursue those companies who have already developed successful products. In doing so, it tries to not waste time with unsuccessful internal development attempts and only goes after those products and companies that have demonstrated success. However, the company has to pay a premium for such deals. This strategy has sometimes simply meant that J&J would buy its competitors rather than try to surpass them using internal growth. For example, in 1996, it acquired Cordis in the medical stent business for $1.8 billion. When this deal failed to place

(continued)

J&J in the lead in this market segment, Johnson & Johnson resorted to M&A again by its $25.4 billion bid (initial bid) for market leader Guidant. This acquisition would have been the largest deal in J&J's long history of M&A. However, J&J lowered its bid when Guidant's litigation liabilities became known and then was outbid by Boston Scientific. Following the collapse of the Guidant deal, the cash-rich J&J acquired Pfizer's consumer products division for $16 billion.

The result of this process is that we have a dominant and successful company that is an assemblage of multiple acquisitions that have resulted in a huge corporate entity that includes over 250 subsidiaries. Clearly, J&J is a company that has very successfully used M&A to become a world leader.

TABLE 2.1 Johnson & Johnson: Growth through Acquisitions Strategy: Sample Acquisitions

Company Acquired	Primary Focus	Date	Size in Billions
Synthes	Trauma devices	2011	19.7
Pfizer Consumer Healthcare	Consumer healthcare	2006	16.6
Alza	Drug delivery	2001	12.3
Centocor	Immune-related diseases	1999	6.3
Depuy	Orthopedic devices	1998	3.6
Scios	Cardiovascular diseases	2003	2.4
Crucell	Biotech	2011	2.3
Cordis	Vascular diseases	1996	1.8
Inverness Med. Tech.	Diabetes self-management	2001	1.4
Mentor Corporation	Medical products	2008	1.1
Cougar Biotechnology	Cancer drug development	2009	1.0
Neutrogena	Skin and hair care	1994	0.9
Micrus	Stroke devices	2010	0.5
Omrix Biopharmaceuticals	Biosurgery products	2008	0.4
Closure	Topical wounds	2005	0.4
Peninsula Pharmaceuticals	Life-threatening infections	2005	0.3

(continued)

(*continued*)

It is ironic that while M&A, including the large acquisition of Pfizer's consumer products division, helped J&J grow its top line revenues (see Figure 2.3), the resulting $65 billion company was not without problems. The company's consumer products division, which features huge brands such as Band-Aid and Tylenol, has been beset with a series of embarrassing product recalls, manufacturing problems, and government inquiries. It had to recall hundreds of millions of packets of Motrin, Tylenol, and Benadryl due to defects or bad labeling. Sales in the consumer products business suffered. J&J had to replace the head of this unit and lay off many workers.

One can only wonder: Did the increasing size of the overall company, accomplished through a successful M&A program, result in a hugely diverse health care behemoth that is simply too difficult to manage well? When J&J acquired Pfizer's consumer products division, it took its already successful McNeil Consumer Products unit and moved it away from the more closely related pharmaceutical division of the company and toward the more market oriented (less quality control oriented) consumer products unit it acquired from Pfizer. Since then, quality control has become a problem for J&J.

Was the movement further into the consumer products submarket with the Pfizer consumer products acquisition a wise one? In addition

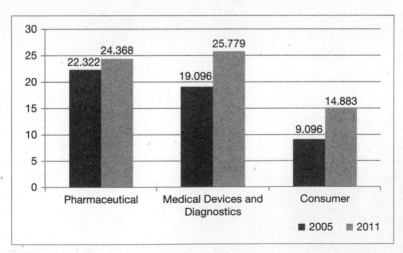

FIGURE 2.3   J&J Sales by Division
Source: Johnson & Johnson annual reports.

(*continued*)

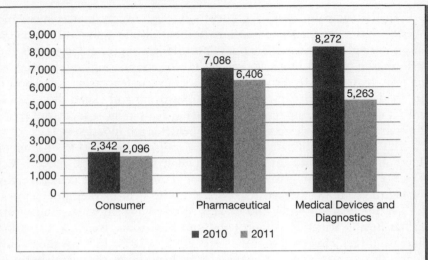

FIGURE 2.4 J&J Operating Profit by Division
Source: Johnson & Johnson annual reports.

to the quality control problems, the increased movement into the lower margin consumer products business lowered the average profitability of the overall business. This was due to the much lower margins on consumer products compared to pharmaceuticals, medical devices, and diagnostics (see Figure 2.4). One cannot help but think that this is one of the reasons why Pfizer got rid of that business. J&J was also hurt by the fact that 2011 proved to be an overall challenging year with margins in all three segments falling—especially in medical devices and diagnostics.

One also wonders: Would shareholders be better off separating the company into more focused units? Are there really any synergies between consumer products and pharmaceutical and medical devices? Instead, perhaps the company has gotten so large through M&A that it is losing its ability to manage what is now the second-largest medical products company in the world. M&A has enabled the company to achieve a critical mass in each of its three major business segments, which could now possibly be more efficient if each were on its own.

KNOWING WHEN TO EXIT A BUSINESS

In Chapter 10, we discuss *demerging* or downsizing through divestitures and selloffs. However, when we discuss growth through a program of many M&A, it is important to note the role that selloffs can play in this program.

When a company grows aggressively through M&A, management and investors have to understand that not all the deals are going to be winners. This is normal as markets change and it is difficult to predict the actions and performance of competitors. We can see this by considering how Johnson & Johnson (J&J) used M&A to become a leader in the stent business and how it later had to accept that it had become an *also ran* and exited the business while it used the freed-up resources to pursue deals in more successful areas. Stents are tiny metal devices that prop open clogged blood vessels.

The 1996 $1.8 billion acquisition of Cordis enabled J&J to be a major player in the promising and rapidly growing stent business. Indeed, J&J played a major role in getting stents to be more used in medicine, thereby helping to create the market. J&J's share in the stent market grew impressively in the first half of the 2000s. This reversed a trend when competitors such as Boston Scientific, Abbott Labs, and Medtronic, were taking market share from J&J. However, over the years 2005 to 2010, J&J saw these same competitors again eat away its market share. In addition, the overall business itself began to decline. This was a bad combination.

J&J had to come to the realization that while the stent business was promising at one time, 15 years after its 1996 acquisition, many things had changed. Some medical research implied that stents might be overused. Other research seemed to imply that the incidence of heart attacks and the related use of significant heart procedures to deal with such medical events had declined. In addition, when the growth of competitors actually increased in this stagnant market, the business was no longer promising.

Rather than be discouraged by declines in one market, in 2011 J&J cut its losses and exited the stent business and aggressively moved in the same year to pursue its largest acquisition—the $19.7 billion acquisition of Synthes. Exiting a no-growth business frees up resources to pursue other high-growth areas. At one time the stent business was a high-growth market. However, developments in medical research are difficult to predict. Early on, such research implied stents had a great future. Fifteen years later, the research had turned in the opposite direction. J&J adapted to the changing marketplace, accepted the gains it had enjoyed, but when the market turned down, it cut its losses and shifted its focus to higher-growth areas.

FROM GROWTH THROUGH M&A TO GROWTH THROUGH ORGANIC EXPANSION

Certain industries require that companies be a certain size in order to be meaningful *players* in the industry. Telecommunications is a great example. U.S. consumers want to use a telecommunications company that can allow them to call anywhere in the country at competitive prices. In fact, globalization has expanded this range to anywhere in the world. Small telecom companies who lack their own network may not be able to provide competitive rates, which they need to be able to do to attract consumers away from the major carriers. Therefore, smaller and medium-size companies are faced with slow organic growth of their networks using their internal cash flows and what they can access in securities markets. The other alternative is to use M&A to grow more rapidly.

Companies in many other industries face a similar dilemma. Those who are able to use M&A to grow rapidly may be able to show securities markets their rapid, M&A-driven growth and parlay this into additional capital, which they can use for more M&A and internal investment. One of the problems companies can encounter is that at some point management may need to slow down or turn off the M&A "spigot." There are certain managerial skills that are especially important for companies that have grown mainly through M&A, and there are other managerial skills that are needed to run normal day-to-day operations of a company to bring about organic growth. Some companies have been successful at doing both. Cisco is a good example. For many years, it was able to successfully grow mainly through M&A but was also able to successfully use the acquired entities to facilitate its own organic growth. Only in recent years did it have trouble due to poor M&A target selection.

The case study that follows, Worldcom, is a great example of a company that was led by a manager who was a great dealmaker but a terrible overall manager. When the company reached a sufficient size, the reins needed to be turned over to a real manager, but the board of directors did not do their job, and the rest is history.

CASE STUDY: WORLDCOM—CASE OF FAILING TO TURN OFF THE M&A PROCESS

One classic example of a consolidation acquisition program was the acquisitions of WorldCom, formerly LDDS, over the second half of the 1980s and 1990s. WorldCom, based in Jackson, Mississippi, was formed through a series of more than 40 acquisitions, culminating in the $37 billion acquisition of MCI in 1998. Many of these deals were acquisitions of regional long-distance telecommunication resellers, which added more minutes to WorldCom's market clout while bringing a regionally based sales force to service the acquired market. It is

(continued)

(*continued*)

ironic that WorldCom was a telecommunications business owned by ITT that was later acquired by LDDS. ITT was a conglomerate that underwent a series of downsizing transactions, whereas LDDS went on to grow horizontally to become the second-leading long-distance company in the U.S. market. In paying a high price for MCI, which enabled it to outbid British Telecom, WorldCom asserted that it would realize significant cost savings from combining these two long-distance companies.

WorldCom is a classic example of a company run by a CEO, Bernie Ebbers, who was a good dealmaker but a bad manager. The company's board was asleep at the wheel and allowed its CEO to pursue deals when the company was already of a sufficient size. They also allowed him to continue to run the company when he was clearly out of his element. He tried to continue dealmaking, but the company became so large that meaningful deals, such as the proposed acquisition of Sprint, were halted by antitrust regulators. Management even resorted to illegal means to try to manufacture profits that it could not otherwise achieve. The end result of this acquisition program was an inefficient company that spiraled into the largest bankruptcy of all time. For his part in the illegal activities, Bernie Ebbers was sentenced to a long prison term.

CONTROLLING THE RUNAWAY DEALMAKER CEO

We saw in the Worldcom case study how the dealmaking CEO can play a very important role for some companies in helping the firm reach the necessary size to have a chance to be successful in the marketplace. When that size is reached, the control of the company needs to be turned over to other managers who can optimize the company's business. It may not be the case that the dealmaking CEO is also the best day-to-day manager. For years, this was the case at Cisco. Clearly at Worldcom, Bernie Ebbers should have been let go well before the company's demise. Such decisions have to be done by the board. In order for the board to do their job, they themselves need to be competent and also independent of the CEO. On both fronts, this was not the case at Worldcom.

A great example from corporate history of a company that was very successful in making the change from the M&A dealmaker to the successful manager was General Motors (GM)—during its more formative years.

CASE STUDY: GENERAL MOTORS AND WILLIE DURANT—KNOWING WHEN TO TURN OFF THE M&A PROCESS

General Motors was initially built by Willie Durant, who was the consummate dealmaker. In the years 1909 to 1916, Ford was the major player in the U.S. car market and the Model T dominated. One problem the Model T had was that each year the car looked the same. However, Henry Ford was great at quality control and efficiency—so much so that he was able to offer automobiles at lower and lower prices. This was great for furthering his dream of making cars affordable to the *common man*. It did not thrill Ford's investors including the Dodge brothers, Ford parts suppliers, who went on to form their own successful car manufacturer.

New competitors began to crop up and they offered more product differentiation including different styles and colors. The problem many of these competitors had was that it was difficult to compete with Ford's manufacturing processes and facilities as well as its expansive dealer network. This created an opportunity for Willie Durant to combine companies, such as Chevrolet and Oldsmobile, into one large auto company that could rival Ford itself.

The dealmaking CEO can rankle other managers who want to focus on a product's quality, efficiency, and in the case of automobiles—better engineering. This was the case when Willie Durant knocked heads with Walter Chrysler—a master of engine design. Walter could not handle wheeling and dealing Willie and left to start his own company— Chrysler, which was very successful for many years.[a]

When GM's performance started to flag, one member of the board who was also a large shareholder, Pierre DuPont, began to lose patience with Willie. Like Bernie Ebber's, Willie's answer to every company problem seemed to be to do another deal. DuPont, of the DuPont chemical company fame, knew this was wrong and used his equity position and clout on the board to throw Willie out of the company he had formed. Pierre DuPont sought out a real manager who could closely monitor the bottom line of the business. He settled on the accountant Albert Sloan (for whom the Sloan School at MIT is named). This proved to be the best possible choice, as Sloan mastered the art of corporate management.[b] Under his leadership, the company thrived and eventually displaced Ford as the leading automaker in the world. Willie Durant did not enjoy such success after leaving GM. While he was at one time wealthy, he died penniless as he kept throwing his

(continued)

(*continued*)
wealth into one failed deal after anoter. If he had not been fired by DuPont, odds are that GM would have suffered a similar fate.

---

[a] Vincent Curcio, *The Life and Times of an Automotive Genius* (New York: Oxford University Press, 2000).

[b] David Farber, *Sloan Rules: Alfred E. Sloan and the Triumph of General Motors* (Chicago: University of Chicago Press, 2000).

USING M&A TO ACHIEVE GROWTH IN A SLOW-GROWTH INDUSTRY

As noted, corporate managers are under constant pressure to demonstrate successful growth. This is particularly true when the company and the industry have achieved growth in the past. However, when the demand for an industry's products and services slows, it becomes increasingly difficult to continue to grow. When this happens, managers often look to M&A as a way to show growth. It often is hoped that such acquisitions will lead not only to revenue growth but also to improved profitability through synergistic gains. Unfortunately, it is much easier to generate sales growth by simply adding the revenues of acquisition targets than it is to improve the profitability of the overall enterprise. In fact, one can argue that although acquisitions bring with them the possibility of synergistic gains, they also impose greater demands on management, which now runs an even larger enterprise. Management needs to make sure that the greater size in terms of revenues has brought with it commensurate profits and returns for shareholders. If not, then the whole growth through M&A strategy has not improved shareholder's position and investors would have been better off if management had resigned themselves to be a slower-growth company. Think back to J&J's recent M&A history. M&A was a key to the establishment of J&J as one of the leading health care companies in the world. However, its further expansion into consumer products with its acquisition of Pfizer's consumer products unit was the start of a process that gave the company many problems.

SQUEEZING OUT GROWTH IN A SLOW-GROWTH INDUSTRY USING MULTIPLE OPTIONS

Given that securities markets are constantly looking for growth and are impatient with firms that appear to be in a slow-growth mode, companies often feel pressured to generate growth even when their industry is not growing. When that is the case, there arc a few options. One is to try to squeeze more profits out of flat revenues by cutting costs and becoming more efficient. U.S. corporations have become quite good at this following the subprime crisis when they were forced to become more efficient and increase profits with weak revenue growth.

When an industry has been in a slow-growth mode for some time it may be the case that efficiency gains have already been realized leaving fewer opportunities to generate growth. Sometimes the solution may be to expand to other higher-growth, geographical markets. For example, a company that has maximized sales in the large U.S. and European markets, both mature and slow growing, may seek to expand to high-growth markets such as China and India as well as Brazil. We discuss cross-border deals in more detail in Chapter 7. However, another alternative is to try to use M&A in your home market.

A good example of this was the flavor and fragrance industry, which slowed significantly in the 1990s. Companies in this industry sell products to manufacturers and marketers of various other products. When they found the demand for the end users' products slowed, the demand for intermediate products such as flavors also slowed. Food manufacturers rely on various suppliers, including flavor developers, to come up with new or improved products. The frozen food business is a case in point.

In order to understand the growth dilemma of the flavor and fragrance industry, it is important to know about its history with growth. The advent of the microwave oven gave a boost to the industry's growth. This is similar to the impact of products like the VCR in the consumer electronics industry in the 1980s. However, when the proliferation of microwaves reached its peak, the growth in the frozen food business also slowed. Companies that sold to frozen food manufacturers experienced the impact of this slowing demand in the form of a slower demand for their products and increased pressure was placed on them by manufacturers for price concessions that would enable the manufacturers to improve their own margins. Faced with the prospect of slow growth, and unable to squeeze out significant revenues from the mature market it was serving, International Flavors and Fragrances, Inc. (IFF), one of the largest companies in this industry, acquired competitor Bush Boake Allen, which was about one-third the size of IFF. On the surface, however, the acquisition of Bush Boake Allen increased the size of IFF by one-third, giving at least the appearance of significant growth in this slow-growth industry.

The acquisition of Bush Boake Allen gave IFF some growth while the overall industry in the United States consolidated. However, given that the U. S. and European markets were mature, further M&A in these markets would not be a solution to the growth problem. Therefore, the company had to look elsewhere for growth. They did this by later focusing on emerging markets. Specifically, the company was able to enjoy real growth in Asia and Latin America, which helped offset the fact that sales were flat in the United States.

DEALING WITH A SLOW-GROWTH BUSINESS AND INDUSTRY

Executives can get themselves in trouble sometimes by not accepting reality. Sometimes there are powerful overriding forces that render the industry a slow-growth industry. An example is banking in the U.S. economy. Banking profitability is driven by several factors including the state of the economy. If the economy is in a slow-growth period, then the demand for loans and other banking services will also be slow. The basic banking model involves taking in deposits and paying depositors interest while lending out most of these funds at high enough rates to cover the bank's expenses and giving shareholders a reasonable return. The problem is that bank managers are often unwilling to accept such a boring business and seek to expand into the more exciting areas of finance such as proprietary trading and investment banking.

During the years after the Great Recession of 2008 to 2009, the U.S. economy struggled to achieve growth above 2 percent. In addition, the fallout from the subprime crisis left banks leery of lending to nonprime borrowers. In such situations, management can either accept this or can try to move the bank into other areas that offer a higher return. Normally, higher return means higher risk. There are all too many examples of such managerial blunders.

One example was Citigroup during the 2000s. When Robert Rubin brought his expertise to the Citigroup board of directors, he urged the bank to take on more risk. They did and invested in higher-return assets such as subprime mortgages, and the rest is history. It is ironic that when confronted with the fact that he advised the bank to take such steps, Rubin's defense was that he actually did not do the trades himself, so he should not be held responsible. Surely Corporate America can get better leaders. Rubin's role in the financial crisis is best summarized by Professor Nassim Nicholas Taleb, author of the *The Black Swan* and *Fooled by Randomness*, who said of Rubin, "Nobody on this planet represents more vividly the scam of the banking industry." "He made $120 million from Citibank, which was technically insolvent."[4]

A more recent example of an executive pushing his institution into riskier activities is MF Global Holding Ltd and its recent CEO Jon Corzine. Corzine had been ousted from his position at Goldman Sachs and then moved into politics using the considerable wealth he amassed at Goldman to fund his campaigns. He enjoyed some success and became a U.S. senator and governor but was ousted again, this time by the electorate of the state of New Jersey. He then took over the reins of MF Global, even though at the time he professed to know little about the firm—not a good sign. He then directed the company's investment managers to take on more risk, such as European debt. The market for such securities then collapsed, and this, in turn, brought about the collapse of MF Global. In retrospect, MF Global would have been better off with a less highly paid and less well-known executive who was willing to pursue only modest growth that could be realistically and safely achieved. MF Global made a mistake by going after the big name manager who already had a track record of taking risks that caused big losses, such as what occurred when he was head of the fixed income department at Goldman Sachs.[5]

Perhaps Corzine felt that he, the new high-profile CEO, fresh from his political failures, needed to make a splash to justify the company confidence in him. If so, then he made it more about him and less about the profitable growth of the company. In addition, Corzine, being absent from the securities industry while he pursued a political career that ultimately ended in failure, may not have been on top of his game. In addition, his leadership basically supplanted the investment and risk management of the company. However, if markets are weak and there are few growth opportunities, a company's board needs to make sure that a newly appointed CEO, recently back in the game, does not bet on the company pursuing a risky strategy in order to achieve. In retrospect, the company would have been better off pursuing a less risky, less *all in* strategy during an unsettled market period, and accepting that growth was going to be modest for a while.

There are a number of other examples of companies that pursued high growth and were unwilling to accept the fact that their business was a slow-growth, albeit steady, business. One is Vivendi, run by the empire-building Jean Marie Meissier. We discuss this case in further detail in Chapter 4. Another instructive, yet almost hard to believe case, is that of Montana Power. It seems unbelievable as it is difficult to accept that management would recommend, and that a board would accept a recommendation, to basically leave the safe but slow-growth main business that Montana Power was in for many years, and then move into a business that was high flying and risky. Nonetheless, this is what the all-knowing management and board of Montana Power did.

CASE STUDY: MOVING INTO UNFAMILIAR BUSINESS AREAS TO PURSUE RISKY HIGH GROWTH

So often it is a prescription for disaster—moving into business areas that you really do not know anything about. The risk of such ventures seems so obvious that it is a wonder they are even suggested by

(continued)

(*continued*)

management and approved by a board of directors. However, this is what happened in the utility industry in the 1980s and 1990s. Spurred on by deregulation, many power utilities decided to try to spice up their corporate lives by taking the capital generated by the boring utility business and investing it in more exciting areas and possibly higher-growth areas. Such was the case in 2001 when Montana Power decided to enter the high-flying telecommunications business.

On the surface, the decision might have displayed some merits. The fact that the power utility business was slow growth and generally dull was well known. In February 2001, Montana Power announced that it was spinning off its utility entity, Montana Power, to concentrate on the telecommunications entity it controlled—Touch America. Montana Power was not a newcomer to the utility business. The company was founded in 1912. It moved into oil and gas in the 1930s and then expanded into coal in the 1950s. Its first move into the telecommunications business began in the 1980s when it took advantage of the breakup of AT&T. It slowly began to expand its position in the telecommunications business by laying more fiber and building more of its own network.

In spite of its extended track record in the power utility business, the combined company eventually sold off its stodgy power utility for $1.3 billion and invested the proceeds into the high-flying telecommunications business.

The energy distribution business was sold to NorthWestern Corporation for $612 million in cash plus the assumption of $488 million in debt.[a] The monies from the sale were invested in Touch America's telecommunications business. In August of 2000, PanCanadian Petroleum Ltd agreed to purchase Montana Power's oil and gas business for $475 million.[b] This acquisition increased PanCanadian's oil field capacity by providing it with properties in Alberta, Colorado, Montana, and Colorado. It was indicated by PanCanadian that the acquired fields had reserves of 550 billion cubic feet of gas and 20 million barrels of crude oil.

For a while, Touch America was a rapidly growing telecommunications company. In the summer of 2000, it entered a deal with Quest to buy its in-region long distance network. Due to regulatory constraints, Quest had to divest this part of its business pursuant to an agreement related to its acquisition of U.S. West. U.S. West was one of

(*continued*)

the seven superregionals that were formed in the breakup of AT&T. In the sale, Quest gave Touch America its long distance operations in a 14-state area for $200 million.[c] This acquisition gave Touch America a business with sales of approximately $300 million and 250,000 customers.

After the selloff of the power utility, Montana Power changed its name to Touch America Holdings, Inc. The company was traded in the New York Stock Exchange. For a while, the company was highly touted by the market and the industry.[d] Touch America started off as a growing company in a growing industry while being largely debt-free. Initially, it seemed that the combination of rapid growth without debt pressures made Touch America seem highly desirable.

However, all was not well in the telecom industry and Touch America's fate went down with the industry. In just one year after its impressive 2001 performance, the company was in trouble. By the second and third quarters of 2002, the company lost $32.3 million and $20.9 million. This occurred even though revenues actually increased from $73.6 million to $76.6 million.

Part of Touch America's problems stemmed from a billing dispute it had with Quest where Touch America claimed that Quest owed it $46 million.[e] However, on March 27, 2003, an arbitrator ruled that Touch America owed Quest $59.6 million plus interest. The stock fell to $0.53 per share and was then delisted by the New York Stock Exchange.[f] To put this collapse in equity values in perspective, we need to be aware that at the time that Montana Power had sold off its nontelecommunications assets, the stock traded at $65 per share.

Touch America's capital investment strategy calls to mind a slight variation on the mysterious advice given to Kevin Costner's character in *Field of Dreams*: Build it and they will come. Telecom managers throughout the United States invested heavily in network expansion and fiber-laying throughout the 1990s and early 2000s. Billions of dollars were spent on laying fiber optic cable as telecom and non-telecom companies expanded. The result was that 360 networks held over 87,000 miles of fiber-optic cable linking urban areas in North America, Asia, and South America.[g] Touch America was one such company. "Renamed Touch America, the company's fiber network will span 26,000 route miles by year end, making it one of the largest and highest capacity long haul networks in the United States."[h]

(*continued*)

(continued)

In June 19, 2003, Touch America finally filed for Chapter 11 bankruptcy protection and its assets were put up for sale. Clearly, its shareholders would have been better off if the company had stayed in the basic utility business.

---

[a] "Montana Power and Northwestern in $612 Million Deal," *New York Times*, October 3, 2000.

[b] "PanCanadian Will Acquire Oil and Gas Assets," *New York Times*, August 29, 2000.

[c] "Unit of Montana Power Is Buying Quest Phone Business, *New York Times*, March 17, 2000.

[d] Steve Skobel, "Rising Starts," *Telecom Business*, July 1, 2001.

[e] "Touch America Says Quest Owes It $46 Million," *Reuters Limited*, January 23, 2003.

[f] Matt Gouras, "Touch America Trading Suspended; Company Made Disasterous Move Into Telecommunications," Associated Press Newswires.

[g] Lucy I. Vento, "Who Will Profit From the U.S. Fiber Network Glut?" *Business Communications Review*, September 1, 2001.

[h] Ibid.

GEOGRAPHICAL EXPANSION THROUGH M&A

Another example of using M&A to facilitate growth is when a company wants to expand to another geographic region. It could be that the company's market is in one part of the country but it wants to expand into other regions. Alternatively, perhaps a company has a strong market share in its national market but seeks to tap the markets of other nations, such as South America or Asia. In many instances, it may be quicker and less risky to expand geographically through acquisitions than through internal development. This may be particularly true of international expansion, where many characteristics are needed to be successful in a new geographic market. The company needs to know all of the important nuances of the new market. It needs to recruit new personnel and circumvent many other hurdles such as language and custom barriers. Internal expansion may be much slower and more difficult. Mergers, acquisitions, joint ventures, and strategic alliances may be the fastest and lowest-risk alternatives.

INTERNATIONAL GROWTH AND CROSS-BORDER ACQUISITIONS

In the 1990s and more so in the 2000s, European and American companies increasingly recognized that growth opportunities in their *home* geographical markets were harder to achieve, while growth opportunities in emerging markets provided much greater potential. In many industries, growth and increased market share are difficult and costly to achieve when markets are mature. In such industries there may be only a few major companies, and gaining additional market share is expensive and comes at great effort. However, when a company's products can be introduced to a growing international market, gains *may* be less costly and easier to achieve.

Emerging markets present great opportunities for established companies seeking to enter these markets. It is often the case that companies with established brands who have achieved significant success in their home markets can take advantage of much of the work that went into developing their position in their home markets. Such companies might have advantages over newer companies in the emerging markets, which might be trying to take advantage of the growing demand in their own markets. There are numerous examples of this but one of the best is the British distiller Diageo. We discuss this company in Chapter 7 when we explore growth opportunities through emerging market M&A.

TAKING ADVANTAGE OF CURRENCY FLUCTUATIONS TO PURSUE HIGH-GROWTH M&A

Fluctuating currencies can present opportunities or obstacles to successful M&A. They can create obstacles for companies in countries that have declining currencies. On the other hand, they can create opportunities for companies whose currencies have risen in value. This was the case in 2011, when the Japanese yen rose in value. Given the export orientation of the Japanese economy, this is normally not good news for many Japanese companies. However, given the years of economic stagnation that Japan has had to deal with, many Japanese firms looked to expand outside their island nation economy.[6]

One major example of a company taking advantage of the rising value of its currency occurred in May 2011, when Takeda Pharmaceutical reached agreement to buy Nycomed of Switzerland for 9.6 billion euros ($13.7 billion). Like many of the other pharmaceutical mergers across the world, it was partly motivated by the difficulties drug companies have had to develop new major

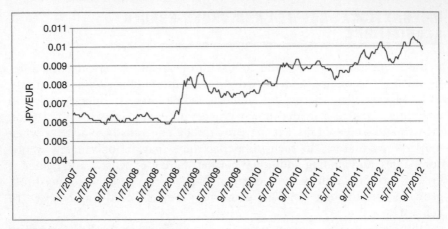

FIGURE 2.5   Yen/Euro 2007–2012
Source: Oanda Forex Trading.

drugs and to deal with competition from generics. By buying Nycomed, Takeda
was able to add to its Nycomed treatments for gastric, respiratory, and
inflammatory disorders. However, due to the rising value of the yen relative
to the euro (see Figure 2.5) it was able to do so at a bargain price. This deal was
one of the largest overseas acquisitions by any Japanese company. In fact,
Nycomed had already done a mega-deal in 2008 when it acquired the American
Biotechnology company Millenium for $8.8 billion in 2008.

Like most major pharmaceutical companies, Takeda had difficulty
developing new blockbuster drugs. Generics have been a drag on its sales
and then the rise of the yen made it even to tougher to expand sales outside
Japan. However, rather than wallow in its tough position, Takeda made the
most of a bad situation by using the rising yen to significantly expand
the position of the company in the global pharmaceutical market.

Other examples of Japanese companies taking advantage of the rising
value of the yen were Pola Orbis Holdings, the fourth-largest cosmetics maker
in Japan, buying the Australian skin care products company, Jurlique
International Pty Ltd, in 2011 for approximately Australian $300 million
(which in 2011 was approximately the same value in U.S. dollars). The
Jurlique acquisition gave Pola Orbis access not just to the high-growth
Australian market but also the Hong Kong and Chinese markets where
Jurlique had a good presence.

Also in 2011, Japanese beer maker Asahi Group Holdings acquired
Australian mineral water company Mountain H2O for an undisclosed

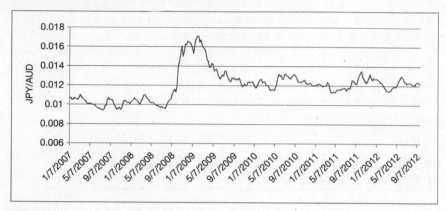

FIGURE 2.6   Yen versus Australian Dollar: 2007–2012
Source: Oanda Forex Trading.

amount. This deal announcement followed Asahi's announcement of its intention to buy New Zealand's Independent Liquor for $1.3 billion. The yen had been generally rising against the Australian dollar since April 2011 (see Figure 2.6).

These are a few examples of Japanese companies looking outside their own troubled economy to pursue growth. However, a key element in these decisions was the favorable variation in the respective currency values, which lowered the acquisition costs and enabled the company to pursue growth in higher-growth markets.

FINDING GROWTH IN HIGH-GROWTH MARKETS

As discussed when a business has *tapped out* the growth potential in a given market, and when many competitors are aggressively competing for the same market, achieving real growth can be a challenge. Often it takes increasing expenditures on marketing just to achieve modest growth or even just to maintain a company's current business volume. This was the case in the 1990s and 2000s for many U.S. and European as well as Japanese companies. In the case of the U.S. auto industry, the situation was even worse. The major U.S. automakers struggled with quality problems and a competitive disadvantage caused by having to assume the burden of high labor costs imposed by an inflexible union—the United Auto Workers (UAW). The case study on

GM in Chapter 7 features a sick company that found success and growth in the fastest-growing market in the world—China.

In Chapter 7, we discuss the leading high-growth markets that present M&A opportunities for companies in slower-growth developed markets. In that same chapter, we also discuss the opportunities that are available to companies from high-growth markets to acquire valuable companies in slower-growth developed countries.

CYCLICAL COMPANIES ACHIEVING GROWTH IN RECESSED MARKETS

Many companies provide products and services that have a highly cyclical demand. Examples include heavy equipment and aircraft manufacturers. These companies can be well managed but show poor performance when the economy goes through a prolonged downturn. For example, aircraft manufacturers will find many orders that were made in a stronger economic periods get cancelled when the economy goes into a recession. Heavy equipment manufacturers can see the *bottom fall out* when the economy enters such a period. When this happens, it puts management under intense pressure as often profits become negative and the return in equity collapses.

Management has often pursued various strategies to deal with such contingences. However, too often they have used M&A to enter very different fields well beyond their core competency just to achieve a different economic variability. For example, a company that faces a very cyclical demand may try to acquire targets that are much less cyclical or who are even countercyclical. There are really not many truly countercyclical companies—companies whose demand rises when the economy turns down and falls when it rises.

From a corporate finance perspective, acquisitions into such diverse fields are highly questionable. In effect, management is pursuing an expensive strategy to try to make their results look less volatile. However, shareholders can adjust their portfolio much less expensively than corporations can when they pursue costly acquisitions. In addition, each investor can select each of their securities while considering the nature of their cyclical variability. Does this rule out M&A as a solution to the problem of cyclicality? The answer is clearly *no*.

One of the many beneficial effects of globalization is that we have a global economic system in which not all companies face the same cyclicality. Two of the biggest markets in the world are the United States and Europe. At one time, U.S. investors could achieve significant diversification benefits by investing in Europe. However, partly through M&A, the returns of U.S. and European companies exhibit a much greater degree of covariation. In fact, when there are problems in one market they quickly spread to the other. Examples include the U.S. mortgage market and the subprime crisis as well as the European debt crisis of 2010 to 2012. The European debt crisis and recession also helped slow the growth of China, for which Europe is a large market for the export-oriented Chinese economy. Nonetheless, managers can still look to other markets to try to offset some of their cyclical variation.

While globalization has meant that a downturn in one market may be felt in markets geographically far away from their own market, the extent of the impact can vary considerably. For example, high-growth markets in China, India, and Brazil can certainly have their own *recessions* and are also affected by slowdowns in other parts of the world. However, the fact that these economies are growing so rapidly can have great ramifications for companies in mature markets, which are slow growing in good times and have negative growth during recessions. For example, for a number of years China had been growing in the 9 to 11 percent range. One might consider a 6 percent growth rate for China to be a recession. In fact, in 2010 and 2011, the Peoples Bank of China raised interest rates and increased its required reserve ratio to as high as 27.5 percent in an effort to slow down an economy that was exhibiting inflationary pressures. Ironically, the slowdown in Chinese export markets such as Europe reduced some of these inflationary pressures enabling the Chinese central bank to ease monetary policy somewhat, as the main problem became slower growth and there was less concern about inflation.

If companies in slower-growing markets can tap into the buying power of fast-growing markets through M&A, they can allow even highly cyclical companies to enjoy significantly faster growth by taking advantage of the different cyclical variation of the faster-growing market.

When developed countries in markets such as the United States and Europe enter a recession, they may slow their purchases of products from fast-growing countries such as China. This will have adverse feedback effects for the Chinese economy. However, these adverse effects will be greatly offset by the inherent growth of the Chinese economy. This is also very much the case in India and Brazil. These nations may still grow impressively when the world economy is in stagnation.

Even when they slow a little, as China did in 2012, the market was still growing relatively rapidly compared to many of the comparatively stagnant Western and Japanese economies. Companies in slow-growth markets can seek to tap into the high-growth markets and share in their very different cyclical variation as a way of avoiding slowing down significantly when their economy *turns south*.

This was very much the case with the heavy equipment maker Caterpillar. The Great Recession of 2008 to 2009 took a heavy toll on its business. Revenues in 2009 dropped a shocking 39 percent, which was its largest single decline in over half a century. However, the truly impressive part of the story was its 31 percent increase in revenues in 2010. There were many reasons for the rebound but one of them is the fact that the company was able to generate over two-thirds of its revenues from outside the United States. Part of the reason it was able to do that was its use of M&A, which enabled Caterpillar to become a truly global company and market its well-known brands and high-quality products all over the world. No longer does the company go up and down in unison with the U.S. business cycle. Rather it faces a much broader cyclical variation, which does not move in lockstep with the U.S. economy. The pursuit of growth through M&A in fast-moving markets on distant shores did not go smoothly for Caterpillar. As we will discuss later in the book, Caterpillar stumbled mightily with its money-losing acquisition of Siwei. It eventually had to write off most of the $700 million it paid for the entity due to alleged fraud on the part of the target. This underscores the risks that come with trying to extract growth from markets far from a company's home base.

NOTES

1. Ed Paulson, *Insider Cisco: The Real Story of Sustained M&A Growth* (New York: John Wiley & Sons, 2001), 78.
2. Joseph A. Demasi, Ronald W. Hansen, and Harry Grabowski, "The Price of Innovation: New Estimates of Drug Development Costs," *Journal of Health Economics* 22 (2003): 151–185.
3. Fich, Nguyen and Officer, 2013.
4. William D. Cohan, "Rethinking Robert Rubin," *Bloomberg Businessweek*, September 30, 2012.
5. William D. Cohan, *Money and Power: How Goldman Sachs Came to Rule the World*, (New York: Doubleday) 2011, 328–330.
6. The case of the rising yen in a climate of economic stagnation is a good example of how currency values are controlled by more than just basic economic fundamentals.

CHAPTER 3

Synergy

So many mergers and acquisitions (M&A) are justified on the grounds of achieving proposed synergies. This usually sounds great. In addition, it is hard to refute as it refers to benefits that may occur in the future—possibly many years down the road. Sometimes this occurrence or lack of occurrence is long after the CEO who came up with the brilliant idea has departed the scene. Given that it is common for many of these proposed synergies to fail to appear, and given that mechanisms to hold CEOs and their boards financially accountable when they do not (such as through give-backs of compensation) are almost always not in place, it is important that there be a more rigorous analysis *a priori* so that an objective evaluation can be made. Deal decision makers need to be able to critically evaluate proposed synergies and determine how likely they will be. Fortunately, there is useful research that can shed some light on such synergies. Unfortunately, few deal decision makers are aware of any of this research. Even worse, some don't want to know about it in case it implies that a proposed deal may not yield the benefits they say it will. There is little more to say about the latter group, but we attempt in this chapter to add to the information set of those who would find such relevant knowledge useful.

WHAT IS SYNERGY IN THE CONTEXT OF M&A?

In the context of M&A, *synergy* refers to the combination of two companies that create an overall entity that is more valuable than the separate values of the two individual companies. The term is often associated with the physical sciences rather than with economics or finance. It refers to the type of reactions that occur when two substances or factors combine to produce a greater effect together than the two operating independentlywould produce. For example, a synergistic reaction occurs in chemistry when two chemicals combine to produce a more potent total reaction than the sum of their separate effects.

In M&A, a synergistic deal is one where $2 + 2 = 5$. It refers to the ability of a corporate combination to be more profitable than the individual companies that were combined. Right away, though, as every beginning elementary school student knows, $2 + 2 = 4$, so doubts and suspicions about this new math should be in the forefront of one's mind. We will see that sometimes it is possible that $2 + 2 = 5$, but all too often it does not. Even more troubling, in M&A, sometimes $2 + 2 = 3$. In this chapter, we explore the reasons for these curious arithmetic results.

The anticipated existence of synergistic benefits allows firms to justify incurring the expenses of the acquisition process and still being able to afford to give target shareholders a premium for their shares. Synergy may allow the combined company to appear to have a positive *net acquisition value* (NAV).

$$NAV = V_{AB} - [V_A + V_B] - P - E \qquad (3.1)$$

where: V_{AB} = the combined value of the two firms
V_A = the value of A
V_B = the value of B
P = premium paid for B
E = expenses of the acquisition process

Reorganizing equation 3.1, we get:

$$NAV = [V_{AB} - (V_A + V_B)] - (P + E) \qquad (3.2)$$

The term in the brackets is the *synergistic effect*. This effect must be greater than the sum of $P + E$ to justify going forward with the merger. If the bracketed term is not greater than the sum of $P + E$, the bidding firm will have overpaid for the target. One of the problems of evaluating this simple equation is that not only is the measurement of the synergistic effect difficult to get a handle on, sometimes even the expenses, E, can be hard to measure. Sometimes targets bring with them hidden liabilities that may not be known until long after the deal closes. For now, our focus is on synergy.

What are these synergistic effects and when we do a deal, how do we know if they will exceed $P + E$? Synergy is sometimes defined broadly and includes changes such as the elimination of inefficient management by installing the more capable management of the acquiring firm.[1] Although we could adopt such a broad definition, we will opt for a narrower and better quantified definition. This approach is consistent with the more common uses of the term *synergy*.[2]

ACHIEVEMENT OF SYNERGY: A PROBABILISTIC EVENT

When we hear the prognostications of management when they announce another acquisition, they downplay the possibility that the synergies will never materialize. The fact that they often do not is one reason why the market responds to M&A announcements by lowering the value of the bidder.

It has to be recognized that the achievement of significant synergies is an uncertain outcome. For companies that do many M&A, such as Cisco (leaving out some of their more recent M&A flops), there are more data points that can be used to evaluate the likelihood of success. Even when the bidder has not done many M&A, the success rate in the industry can provide some information.

Evaluators need to recognize that the achievement of synergy is uncertain and for some companies and industries, this uncertainty is greater than others. If a company is acquiring a target outside its industry, the probability of realizing significant synergies usually will be lower than for deals within the industry. As we see in Chapter 4, there is some convincing research evidence on the track record of diversifying deals to support this assertion.

CASE STUDY: ALLEGIS—SYNERGY THAT NEVER MATERIALIZED

The case of the Allegis Corporation is a classic example of synergistic benefits that had a seemingly reasonable expectation to occur but that failed to materialize. The concept of Allegis was the brainchild of CEO Richard Ferris, who has risen through the ranks of United Airlines.

Ferris's dream was to form a diversified travel services company that would be able to provide customers with a complete package of air travel, hotel, and car rental services. Accordingly, United Airlines paid $587 million for Hertz Rent-a-Car ($1.3 billion in 2013 dollars) from RCA in June 1986—a price that was considered a premium. In addition to buying Pan American Airways' Pacific routes, Ferris bought the Hilton International hotel chain from the Transworld Corporation for $980 million ($2.2 billion in 2013 dollars). The Hilton International purchase on March 31, 1987, was also considered expensive.

(continued)

(continued)

United Airlines had already acquired the Westin International hotel chain in 1970 for only $52 million ($280 million in 2013 dollars). On February 18, 1987, United Airlines changed its name to Allegis Corporation. In fact, United paid over a $1 million ($2.2 million in 2013 dollars) to come up with the short-lived name.[a]

Allegis' strategy was to offer customers one-stop travel shopping. With one telephone call they could book their air travel, hotel reservations, and car rental within the same corporate umbrella. Allegis hoped to weave the network together through a combination of cross-discounts, bonus miles, and other promotional savings and the introduction of a new computer system called Easy Saver. With Easy Saver, customers could check prices and book reservations through the Allegis network. All travel services could be charged on an Allegis credit card. Travel agents using United Airlines' Apollo computer reservation system, the largest at that time in the airline industry, would pull up Allegis' air, hotel, and car services before any other competitor's products.

Despite the concept's appeal to Ferris, customers, particularly business customers to whom the program was mainly targeted, failed to respond. One of the numerous problems with the deal was that there were many cities that business people wanted to go but where United did not fly to, and there were also numerous cities that did not have a Westin hotel. Even if United flew to the desired city, the flight times might not work, or maybe the Westin hotel that might have been in the city was not conveniently located relative to where the person needed to be.

Even though Ferris was very experienced in the business travel market, he totally failed to understand these problems. He did not recognize the requisite scale that United would have to reach to be a truly effective one-stop shop. To really offer such a service, it would have to be a much larger airline and a far larger hotel chain. When Ferris assumed office, he ran a United Airlines that competed against many other airlines. With the advent of Allegis, the new company then was competing against a much broader travel industry.

While Ferris was fooled by the problems of making the concept work, it is doubtful that others in United's management were also fooled. More likely, they were afraid to even broach the topic and

(continued)

---

[a] Michael Tracey, *Double-Digit Growth* (New York: Portfolio Publishers, 2003), 175.

tell the boss that his big idea, the biggest idea he ever had, was poorly thought out. It is much easier to say—"Wow what a brainstorm, boss. You are brilliant. I guess that is why they pay you the big bucks (and I hope you recommend a big bonus and raise for me before this whole crazy scheme blows up)."

At a time when the stock market was providing handsome returns to investors, the Allegis stock price fell; in February 1987, its stock price was in the low-to-mid-$50 range. The market did respond, however, when Coniston Partners, a New York investment firm, accumulated a 13 percent stake in the travel company. Coniston planned to sell off the various parts of the Allegis travel network and distribute the proceeds to the stockholders. On April 1, 1987, Allegis announced a large recapitalization plan proposal that would have resulted in the company's assuming $3 billion worth of additional debt to finance a $60 special dividend. The recapitalization plan was intended to support the stock price while instilling stockholder support for Allegis and away from the Coniston proposal. The United Airlines Pilots Union followed up Allegis' recapitalization plan proposal with its own offer to buy the airline and sell off the nonairline parts.

The pressure on Chief Executive Officer Ferris continued to mount, leading to a pivotal board of directors meeting. According to Chairman of the Board Charles Luce, the board "thought the market was saying that Allegis was worth more broken up and that the current strategy should be abandoned." Although the outside directors had supported Ferris during the company's acquisition program, they now decided that Ferris was an obstacle to restructuring the company. "There comes a point," said Luce, "when no board can impose its own beliefs over the opposition of the people who elected it." Investors must have been saying, "No kidding, Einstein. Where were you when Ferris hatched this plot?" Ferris was replaced by Frank A. Olsen, chairman of Allegis's Hertz subsidiary.[b]

Allegis is one of many examples of management wanting to create a one-stop shop for consumers that the market failed to embrace. Sears' diversifying acquisitions (see Case Study—Sears: A Failed Diversification Strategy) and Citicorp's related acquisitions are other examples of such failures. Boards that should know better seem to be too passive and allow managers to waste resources on these failed empire-building efforts.

---

[b] Arthur Fleisher Jr., Geoffrey C. Hazard Jr., and Miriam Z. Klipper, *Board Games: The Changing Shape of Corporate America* (Boston: Little, Brown, 1988), 192.

TYPES OF SYNERGY

The two main types of synergy are operating synergy and financial synergy. Operating synergy comes in two forms: revenue enhancements and cost reductions. These revenue enhancements and efficiency gains or operating economies may be derived in horizontal or vertical mergers. Financial synergy can come in different forms but one of the most common is when a deal results in a lowering of the cost of capital and/or an increase in the availability of capital by combining one or more companies.

Revenue-Enhancing Operating Synergy

Revenue-enhancing operating synergy is usually more difficult to achieve than cost reduction synergies. It may come from new opportunities that are presented as a result of the combination of the two merged companies.[3] There are many potential sources of revenue enhancements, and they may vary greatly from deal to deal. They could come from cross-marketing where each merger partner sells its products and services to the other merger partner's customers. Perhaps they could come from having a broader product line, which could expand selling opportunities but also yield competitive advantages and help insure customer retention.

Cross-marketing has the potential to expand the revenue base of each merger partner, thereby enabling each partner to quickly realize greater revenues. Perhaps the larger company markets a major brand and has great market awareness. This can lend increased credibility to a smaller acquired company. Sometimes, the acquirer has a major name, such as Procter & Gamble, but the name is not really a product name as it stands for a collection of other brand names. Does such an acquirer really benefit when it takes over another company, such as Gillette, which itself was already very well known in the marketplace as a market leader and whose name is directly associated with the product as opposed to the Procter & Gamble name?

Does anyone really buy a product because it is under the Procter & Gamble umbrella? For example, does anyone buy Charmin bathroom tissue because the brand it is owned by Procter & Gamble, or are sales due to the advertising of Charmin and the quality of the product? However, there are other synergistic benefits that come from being in the Procter & Gamble network. That corporate entity has huge market clout and can command advantages such as shelf space in major stores that individual brands struggle to get access to. On the other hand, when a company such as Gillette, which was acquired by Procter & Gamble in 2005, already has such a position in retail stores, what are the synergistic benefits?

The multitude of ways in which revenue-enhancing synergies may *possibly* be achieved defies brief descriptions. It can come from one company with a major brand name lending its reputation to an upcoming product line of a merger partner. Alternatively, it may arise from a company with a strong distribution network merging with a firm that has products of great potential but questionable ability to get them to the market before rivals can react and seize the period of opportunity. Still another example could be a larger company providing broader management expertise and financial resources that a smaller target lacked.

Although the sources of synergies may be great, revenue-enhancing synergies are sometimes difficult to achieve. Such enhancements are tough to quantify and build into valuation models. This does not mean that deal promoters, such as investment bankers, are reluctant to incorporate these potential gains into their valuation models. It is just that they may, at times, be hard to justify—especially based upon past experience with such purported gains.

This is why cost-related synergies are often highlighted in merger planning, whereas the potential revenue enhancements may be discussed but often are not clearly defined. It is easier to say we have certain specific facilities that are duplicative and can be eliminated than to specifically show how revenues can be increased through a combination of two companies. Potential revenue enhancements often are vaguely referred to as merger benefits but they tend to be hard to reliably quantify. Their quantification may be built into valuation models but the reliability of these quantified amounts may be suspect.

This is one reason some deals fail to manifest the anticipated benefits. The source of the problem can be traced to poor premerger planning and insufficient critical research on the proposed revenue enhancements. Probably the most dramatic example of such vague and generally poor merger planning is one of the largest deals of all time—the disastrous 2002 merger of AOL and Time Warner. The talk of the two CEOs of AOL and Time Warner at the time of the deal was that it was a merger of content (Time Warner) and new distribution methods via the Internet (AOL). How it all would work out to increase revenue was left very vague and undefined. This should have raised many warning flags. It was no surprise that there were no revenue enhancements and Time Warner ended up giving away their company to AOL shareholders in exchange for the temporarily overvalued AOL shares. It is testimony to what is wrong with corporate governance that Time Warner's CEO did not have to give back a large part of the compensation he took from Time Warner for leading the company into such a horrendous deal. Instead, he walked off into the sunset with plenty of shareholders' money in his pocket. We will further explore this disastrous deal in the AOL–Time Warner Merger case study that follows.

CASE STUDY: AOL–TIME WARNER MERGER— BIGGEST FLOP IN M&A HISTORY

On January 20, 2000, AOL's CEO Steve Case and Time Warner's CEO Gerald Levin announced what they called a "strategic merger of equals." Nothing could be further from the case.

In their announcement of the deal the companies stated the merger would combine the valuable brands and assets of Time Warner with "American Online's extensive Internet franchises, technology, and infrastructure, including premier online brands, the largest community in cyberspace, and unmatched e-commerce capabilities."[a] They were right about Time Warner's brands and assets and could not be more wrong about AOL and its assets. Time Warner included *Time* magazine, *Sports Illustrated,* and *Fortune*, as well as CNN, Warner Brothers, HBO, and many other valuable assets.

It is well known now that AOL's market valuation far exceeded its true value. Steve Case did a great job in exchanging very overinflated AOL shares for valuable Time Warner shares. In 1999, his total compensation was reported to be $1.6 million before stock compensation. From AOL shareholders' perspectives, he earned this money. Steve Levin was reported to have earned a mind-boggling $152.6 million in total compensation in 2000.[b] In 2002, Levin decided to quit his post. Richard Parsons was president of Time Warner and was reported to have received $4.4 million in 1999 as compensation prior to stock awards. Ironically, Parsons was allowed to stay on for years after this disastrous deal. Interestingly, Parson was on the board of Citigroup during this disastrous run up to its collapse, following the subprime collapse. It is good to know that he saved his sage advice for only the biggest flops.

In 2002, AOL–Time Warner reported an incredible $54 billion goodwill write down! This underscores that this was one of the worst cases of horrible M&A due diligence in history, and these top managers/directors, especially Levin and Parsons, have to carry much of the blame. There is plenty of other blame to go around. Time Warner hired Morgan Stanley to advise the company on the deal. Morgan Stanley had Internet analyst Mary Meeker giving very bullish reports on the Internet industry.[c] Having this firm advising on the deal clearly was not

(continued)

---

[a] AOL–Time Warner Press Release, January 10, 2000.
[b] Dan Ackman, "Back to the Future," *Forbes*, January 7, 2002.
[c] Alec Klein, *Stealing Time: How Steve Case, Jerry Levin and the Collapse of AOL Time Warner* (New York: Simon & Schuster, 2003), 91.

a help. It brought a famous name to the deal table, but what value did they provide? Did they in any way question how the synergistic benefits would materialize? Or did they just keep quiet and count the dollars they received in payment?

At the time the deal, Levin explained his beliefs about the benefit of AOL and the Internet, which he said would "create unprecedented and instantaneous access to every form of media and unleash immense possibilities for economic growth, human understanding, and creative expression."[d] If there ever was a CEO who could not understand the future ramifications of a merger it was Levin. Levin went on to explain the negotiation process. "Steve and I met at a hotel for several hours. The idea was not to talk about any transactional detail but to talk about philosophy and values, and it was several hours. I took away the fact that he had good values, which was important to me—that his company was a real company."[e] Impressive. This is real M&A due diligence.

Analysts at the time of the deal talked about both revenue-enhancing and cost-reducing synergies. Lehman Brothers and Salomon Smith Barney analysts talked about potential cross-selling, which they thought might increase advertising revenues. The company also talked about growing subscription revenues. What you did not hear was any enlightened discussion of how the industry could change and why there was reason to believe that AOL was in the forefront of these changes. In reality, it was in the forefront of the industry declines.

Time Warner knew that the demand was shifting away from typical print media and into electronic forms. However, the company did not have any great ideas of how to profitably move into electronic media on a large scale. It knew AOL at the time was profitable and that many Internet companies at the time were not. What it did not anticipate was that AOL's business model, which depended on subscription revenues in exchange for customers being able to access the Internet, was a model that would quickly die as consumers could access the Internet for free. In effect, AOL was a one trick pony and it did not have a business model that showed it what to do when consumers shifted to free Internet access.

(continued)

---

[d] Tim Arango, "How the AOL–Time Warner Merger Went So Wrong," *New York Times*, January 10, 2010.
[e] Ibid.

(continued)

Lehman Brothers also discussed how AOL could leverage Time Warner's distribution channels to promote the AOL's online business.[f] This would not be the first time that Lehman Brothers would fail to understand a business it was analyzing. In fact, Lehman Brothers' failure to understand its own business is one of the main reasons why that once storied investment bank no longer exists.[g]

The main lesson of the AOL–Time Warner disastrous merger is that vague and unclear synergies cannot be a basis for an M&A. If the path of how the synergies are going to materialize is vague and unclear, then the probability of their not happening has to be very high. Another lesson of this deal is how a CEO can take huge compensation from a company and its shareholders while leading them into a disastrous deal and then have the gall to walk away with an exorbitant amount of the company's money in his pocket while doing a disgraceful job. One of the problems we have with corporate governance is that boards will not try to make any efforts to get bad performing CEOs to give back some of the money they clearly did not earn.

---

[f] Lynda M. Applegate, "Valuing AOL-Time Warner Merger," Harvard Business School Case Study, 2002.

[g] In fairness to the many bright people who were employed at Lehman Brothers, many of whom questioned Lehman's investment decisions, the blame has to lie with the most senior managers such as CEO Dick Fuld and his sycophant reportee Joe Gregory who extracted huge compensation from this storied investment bank, while providing it with terrible leadership as they took it on a path to destruction.

Cost-Reducing Operating Synergies

Cost-reducing synergies are usually much easier to realize and predict than revenue-enhancing synergies. These cost reductions may come as a result of *economies of scale*—decreases in per-unit costs that result from an increase in the size or scale of a company's operations. The consolidation of the steel industry with mergers such as those orchestrated by Lakshima Mittal are an example of lower per-unit cost gains from larger, more efficient plants and elimination of less-efficient plants. When dealmakers such as Mittal say they can realize certain cost reductions, these words come with certain credibility as he has done many cost economies–based deals in the past.

Manufacturing firms, especially capital-intensive ones, typically operate at high per-unit costs for low levels of output. This is because the fixed costs of operating their manufacturing facilities are spread out over relatively low levels of output. As the output levels rise, the per-unit costs decline (see Figure 3.1). This is sometimes referred to as *spreading overhead*. Some of the other sources of these gains arise from increased specialization of labor and management and the more efficient use of capital equipment, which might not be possible at low output levels. This phenomenon continues for a certain range of output, after which per-unit costs may rise as the firm experiences diseconomies of scale. Diseconomies of scale may arise as the firm incurs higher costs and other problems associated with coordinating a larger-scale operation. The extent to which diseconomies of scale exist is a topic of dispute among many economists. Some economists cite as evidence the continued growth of large multinational companies, such as Exxon and General Electric. These firms have exhibited extended periods of growth while still paying stockholders an acceptable return on equity.[4] Others contend that such firms would be able to provide stockholders a higher rate of return if they were smaller, more efficient and focused companies.

A conflict can arise if CEOs pursue revenue and size gains to generate personal financial and psychic income for themselves. At some point, companies can become too big to be efficient, thereby moving up the average cost curve in the diseconomies of scale range (see Figure 3.1). Where on this curve are the ever-growing, too big to fail, large U.S. banks?

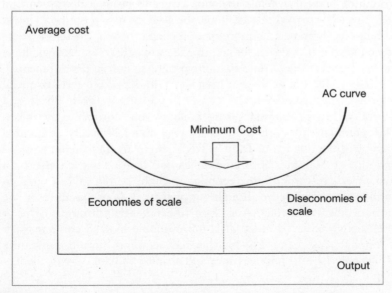

FIGURE 3.1 Average Costs and Economies and Diseconomies of Scale

CASE STUDY: PFIZER'S PURSUIT OF COST ECONOMIES IN WYETH ACQUISITION

In 2010, Pfizer began the process of integrating Wyeth into Pfizer. One of the key elements of that process was cost cutting at the combined company's facilities, which would ultimately yield significant synergies. This included closing eight manufacturing sites in Ireland, Puerto Rico, and the United States.[a] Additionally, it included a 6,000-worker reduction in the company's global workforce. Pfizer further indicated that as many as six other facilities could also be closed. While Wyeth added important blockbuster drugs to Pfizer's product line, both companies had some similar manufacturing facilities, thus creating the opportunity for eliminating redundant overhead. This is an example of how a combination of businesses can create a greater value for the combined company than the values of the companies as independent businesses.

The reduction of costs and the achievement of cost economies are critical to the financial performance of big pharmaceutical companies. Big pharma has not been good at developing new blockbuster drugs and most of the *easy-to-cure* illnesses have been addressed. Many prior blockbusters, such as Pfizer's Lipitor, have come off patent protection. Very complicated medical conditions, which affect increasingly large numbers of the population, such as Alzheimer's, continue to confound the pharmaceutical industry. While the industry is working furiously to find solutions to these medical questions, the need for new products to boost earnings has become even more of a pressing problem. Therefore, some companies, such as Pfizer, looked to M&A to achieve improvements in financial performance while awaiting progress on drug development.

Using M&A to achieve at least short- and medium-term financial improvement makes a lot of sense. For example, both Pfizer and Wyeth had large manufacturing facilities and corporate overhead. The redundant parts of these cost areas could be easily eliminated thereby generating gains. Even in R&D, there are gains from consolidation. For example, both companies had major research efforts in Alzheimer's research. Some economies might be realized in consolidating these efforts even though big pharma does not seem to be the most productive arena to produce research breakthroughs. This is often better achieved at smaller, more nimble biotech companies. It is for that reason that big pharma has acquired biotech companies or has entered into joint venture and strategic alliances with them.

---

[a] "Pfizer Global Manufacturing Announces Plans to Reconfigure Its Global Plant Network," Pfizer Press Release, May 18, 2010.

INDUSTRIES' PURSUIT OF COST ECONOMIES

The pursuit of cost economies can sometimes be an industry phenomenon. Sometimes it is inspired by regulatory factors such as the deregulation that occurred in the banking industry that gave rise to two decades of M&A that even continues today. Corporate CEOs, while they like to pretend they are all-knowing and very confident in their strategic plans, often play follow-the-leader when it comes to mimicking the strategy of competitors. Just think back to the acquisitions by pharmaceutical companies of pharmacy benefit managers such as the failed acquisition of Medco by Merck. Roche did their own acquisition of a pharmacy benefit manager when they acquired Syntex Corp for $5.3 billion, and Eli Lilly bought PCS Health Systems for $4.1 billion. The deals were not well thought out and did not perform well.

In certain industries, we see trends of companies doing M&A because their competitors are doing M&A. Other times, it is a product of widespread factors such as the globalization of an industry. For example, the globalization of the beer industry was an outgrowth of the industry's effort to sell beer brands across the world and take advantage of the benefits a truly global marketer like Inbev can lend to a company such as Anheuser-Busch and Modelo. The U.S.-centric Anheuser had done a poor job extending the reach of their hugely successful Budweiser and Michelob brands outside of the United States Inbev's Brazilian investment bankers took over control of the combined Interbrew, which sported brands such as Stella Artois and Becks, and AmBev, which had a dominant position in the South American brewing market. Later in this chapter, we discuss InBev's pursuit of cost economies through its acquisition of Anheuser-Busch.

Other times, industry-wide gains can come from synergies such as cost economies as well as economies of scope. This was the case in the U.S. cruise line industry. This industry was at one time relatively fragmented, which is unusual given the high capital costs associated with acquiring a cruise ship and the expensive costs of national and international marketing programs. We discuss this in detail in the case study that follows.

CASE STUDY: CONSOLIDATION IN THE CRUISE INDUSTRY AND THE PURSUIT OF ECONOMIES AND OTHER SYNERGIES INCLUDING DEMAND-EXPANDING SYNERGIES

Several examples of mergers and acquisitions (M&A) motivated by the pursuit of scale economies have occurred in the cruise industry, which has undergone a series of consolidating M&A. This process

(continued)

(continued)

started years ago in the late 1980s. Examples include the 1989 acquisition of Sitmar Cruises by Princess Cruises and the 1994 merger between Radisson Diamond Cruises and Seven Seas Cruises, which enabled the combined cruise lines to offer an expanded product line in the form of more ships, beds, and itineraries while lowering per-bed costs. The cruise industry has learned that a sales force of a given size can easily market a greater number of ships and itineraries. As cruise lines combine, they find that they do not need to maintain the same size administrative facilities and sales forces. For example, for years, each cruise line had its own network of district sales managers who would call on travel agencies within a geographical area. When one cruise line buys another, one company's sales force may be able to service the combined itineraries of both groups of ships. In fact, the acquirer can select the most productive salespeople from both sales forces, thereby possibly enjoying productivity gains.

One of the acquirer's goals is to purchase the target's projected revenues while assuming only part of the target's historical cost structure. Over time, the marketing of cruises has changed with travel agencies disappearing and the cruise lines using the Internet to directly market to consumers thus saving on commissions. In fact, airlines had much earlier left the travel agencies behind thus saving on the 10 percent commission these agencies got from the airlines. In the cruise industry, this commission was as high as 20 percent. The loss of these two main sources of business is why we used to see many travel agencies and now they have largely disappeared.

Another example of scale economies related to these cruise mergers is the use of marketing expenditures. Partly because of the size of its fleet, Princess Cruises was able to maintain a national television advertising campaign. A cruise line needs to be of a certain minimum size for a national television advertising campaign to be feasible. By buying Sitmar in 1988, which offered similar cruises and was of similar size, Princess was better able to market its "Love Boat" theme nationally based on the television show that featured their ships. They were also able to expand capacity quickly through this acquisition while at the same time ordering new ships to be built. When the new ships arrived, Princess sold off some of the older Sitmar ships, replacing them with much more modern vessels. The Sitmar acquisition served its purpose by providing an avenue for quick expansion to take advantage of a window of marketing opportunity.

(continued)

In the cruise industry, the smaller cruise companies have difficulty competing with the bigger lines because they are not large enough to be able to spread out the costs of a national and print television campaign across a large enough number of ships to make such marketing costs effective. They then are relegated to other forms of marketing that do not have the same effectiveness as television in generating consumer awareness. They also are forced to incur large costs such as senior management compensation and administration facilities including a reservation system and staff. Therefore, acquisitions are one way to develop a larger revenue base to support the use of the more expensive marketing media used by larger competitors and to spread out certain necessary overhead costs. The marketing advantages combined with cost economies help explain the consolidation-through-mergers phenomenon we have witnessed in this industry over the 1980s and 1990s. This consolidation has resulted in three large rivals in the U.S. market—Carnival and Royal Caribbean and Norwegian Cruise Line (partially owned by Star Cruises).

Carnival, originally a low-priced, mass-market cruise line, has become the largest company in the industry through a broad acquisition program. Interestingly, it has been able to acquire upper-end cruise lines, such as Seaborne, without experiencing any negative effects on the quality and reputational integrity of the high-price cruise brand. This was possible because Carnival marketed the brands somewhat and did not significantly change the way they were marketed or the quality of the product, after they were acquired. The synergistic benefits were accrued to Carnival in a behind-the-scenes manner that was seamless to the traveler.

The 2003 merger of P&O's Princess Cruises and Carnival firmly placed the combined company in the leadership position of this industry. This is why Royal Caribbean, the number-two company in this industry, fought hard to outbid Carnival for this valued target. The resulting Carnival also includes a number of significant acquisitions such as Cunard Line Costa Cruises, Holland American, Seaborne, Windstar, and Princess. Basically, Carnival offers the full range of *price points and quality* in the industry while allowing these brands to enjoy the economies of scale in management, its reservation system, purchasing, and so on (see Figure 3.2). These economies of scale appear seamless to the consumer.

Royal Caribbean was able to acquire Celebrity in 1997, but it was much less active in M&A than Carnival. Instead, it grew organically

(*continued*)

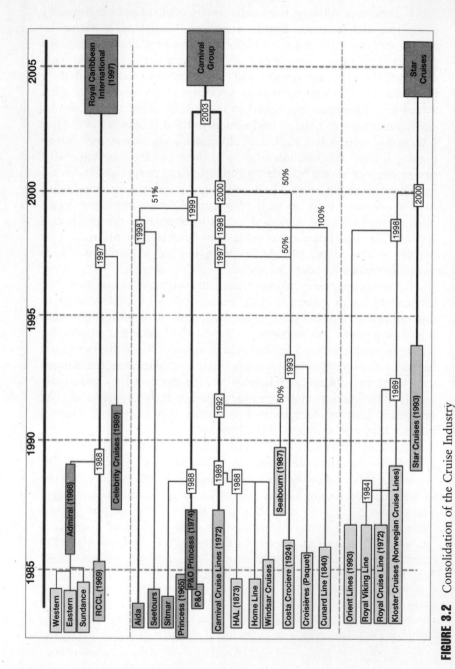

FIGURE 3.2 Consolidation of the Cruise Industry

Source: Gisnas, H., Holte, E., Rialland, A. and Wergeland, T. (2008), "Cruise market industry analysis", Visions Project, MARINTEK.

through the slower process of building a number of truly impressive ships with high capacity.

The achievement of synergies and cost economies using M&A has enabled the industry to grow. This growth enabled it to provide more targeted product offerings to consumers that were not their typical consumers. In the past, the typical cruiser was older and often retired with a lot of time on her hands and looking for long vacations. If this is your clientele, you are limited—even with the aging of the overall U.S. population. Indeed, perhaps the most luxurious cruise line in history, Royal Viking, acquired by NCL, basically disappeared—more or less coinciding with when its client list became deceased.

With the advent of the *full service* cruise company, companies such as Carnival can offer a cruise line for every prospective cruiser. If you want relatively inexpensive party boats, you can take the traditional Carnival vessel. However, if you want something more upscale, you can go to Holland American or Princess, or even go all the way up the price point scale to Seaborne. In addition, the company offers other alternatives in between such as Winstar's large sailing ships, which offer good quality and reasonable prices. So many cruisers are now working full-time and seeking short trips that are cost effective. Royal Caribbean and NCL (Star Cruises), as well as Carnival, are able to service this large market with some of their mega-ships. The industry has been able to expand its market and grow impressively while using its scale to make sure this revenue growth is profit growth as well.

M&A is not a panacea. Obviously, it will not fix all the problems of an industry. The industry continues to be cyclical, and when the economy slows, its revenues and profits weaken. In addition, profits are sensitive to the levels of key costs such as fuel. However, using M&A to be as cost efficient as possible enables the industry to lessen the effects of the economic and commodity price storms.

RESEARCH ON OPERATING ECONOMIES IN M&A

Given how often synergies, and in particular cost-related economies, are cited as a reason for pursuing various M&A, it is useful to examine the research on whether such synergies actually occur. What is the empirical evidence available to support such bases for M&A?

Fortunately, there is empirical support spanning a long time period for the assertion that M&A are at times effectively used to achieve operating economies. For example, Lichtenberg and Siegel detected improvements in the efficiency of plants that had undergone ownership changes.[5] In fact, they found that those plants that had performed the worst were the ones that were most likely to experience an ownership change. There is also somewhat more recent research that supports these findings. Shahrur examined the returns that occurred around the announcement of 463 horizontal mergers and tender offers over the period 1987 to 1999. He noticed positive combined bidder/target returns and interpreted these findings to infer that the market saw the deals as efficiency enhancing.[6] These results are also consistent with the market reactions (positive return of 3.06 percent over a three-day window) detected in Fee and Thomas's analysis of a large sample of 554 horizontal deals over the period 1980 to 1997.[7]

It should not, however, be concluded that simply because some evidence exists that mergers that were included in the samples of certain studies were associated with operating economies, mergers are the best way to achieve such economies. That proposition is not supported by economic research.

ECONOMIES OF SCOPE

Another concept that is closely related to and sometimes confused with economies of scale is *economies of scope,* which is the ability of a firm to utilize one set of inputs to provide a broader range of products and services. A good example of scope economies arises in the banking industry. In the banking industry, scope economies may be as important as economies of scale in explaining M&A.[8] The pursuit of these economies is one of the factors, although probably second behind economies of scale, that help explain the consolidation within the banking industry that occurred in the fifth merger wave of the 1990s.

When financial institutions merge, they can share inputs to offer a broader range of services, such as a trust or wealth management department, consumer investment products unit, or economic analysis group. An example of a large expansion of a wealth management business occurred when the financial supermarket, Bank of America, acquired U.S. Trust in 2007 for $3.3 billion. The goal was to greatly expand Bank of America's presence in this business through an acquisition of one of the leading companies in field—the 104-year-old storied wealth management firm—U.S. Trust. Whether this high-end firm would mesh well in the supermarket culture of Bank of America was another issue.

Smaller banks might not be able to afford the costs of some of the various capabilities that large banks offer. Whether enhancing these capabilities is either the true reason or a sufficient reason for the increased number of banking mergers that have taken place in the post-deregulation period is a very different issue.[9] The many bank mergers that occurred during the fourth merger wave resulted in a new breed of bank in the industry—the superregional bank. The acquisition of other regional banks largely accounts for the growth of the superregional banks of the 1980s. These superregional banks, such as the Bank One Corporation, Barnett Bank, and NationsBank, grew to the point where they were competitive with the larger money center banks in the provision of many services. Other banks, such as the Bank of New England, expanded too rapidly through acquisitions and encountered financial difficulties.

In the 1990s, the superregionals NationsBank and First Union continued to expand and became two of the largest banks in the United States. However, in the fifth wave, the banking industry in the United States continued to consolidate and the superregionals were merged with or acquired by even larger banks. First, Union Bank acquired First Fidelity in 1996 at a time when it was acquiring several other mid-sized banks. Between 1997 and 1998, NationsBank acquired Boatman's Bank, Signet Banking Corp., and Barnett Banks, Inc. Later in 1998, NationsBank itself merged with Bank of America and assumed the better-known Bank of America name.

In 2001, First Union merged with Wachovia in a $13.6 billion deal. However, M&A would prove to be Wachovia's undoing as it could not digest subprime mortgage issuer Goldenwest Financial, which was the largest such issuer in the western and southwestern United States.

Wachovia's initial success with M&A as a valuable synergistic growth tool was mirrored by Washington Mutual. Through M&A, CEO, Kerry Killinger, built a small northwestern thrift into a leading nationwide bank. Like so many other exclusively M&A growth stories, the CEO did not know how to turn off the acquisition engine and manage the huge bank he had created. Mismanagement and greed took over, and the institution incurred huge losses on its loan portfolio, which led to a bank run.[10] Controls on lending fell by the wayside while the bank continued to focus on M&A. When its loan losses became known to the market, a run on the bank occurred, and regulators had to step in and arrange an acceptable merger partner. The opportunistic JPMorgan Chase quickly gobbled up the bank and the branch network it had built. For JPMorgan Chase, this was a boon as it ended up acquiring a branch network in large markets such as Florida, where it had lacked a presence.

After the failure of the largest thrift Washington Mutual, Wachovia, which was beset with similar mortgage-related problems, saw its stock price collapse, and it was forced to sell to Wells Fargo for $15 billion in December 2008. We discuss the use and misuse of M&A by Wachovia in a separate case study that follows. It features many lessons but principally how companies and their CEOs can get so enthralled with M&A that they fail to recognize when to turn off the M&A spigot. If you are good at M&A and you get fast growth from doing deals, doing more M&A can be the easiest thing to do. It often is a lot harder to stop the M&A-growth process and manage the company you have. Managers who are not confident of their managerial skills will keep pushing the M&A process until they destroy the company. Managers who were competent managing a medium-size company may be outside of the limits when it comes to managing a very large company. Boards need to be aware of these issues and recognize when a change in management is needed. However, if the CEO exercises too much influence over the board, this may be hard to accomplish.

Banking is not the only industry where these types of failures have occurred. Looking at the telecom industry, this was the case with Worldcom. We have discussed how the company's CEO Bernie Ebbers was really only good at M&A and should have been asked to step down long before the company became the largest bankruptcy in U.S. history until Lehman Brothers' management destroyed that historic investment bank to become the largest U.S. bankruptcy.[11] M&A also played a role in Lehman Brothers' problems, as the bank used M&A to make major investments in the mortgage industry and to acquire large amounts of real estate at the peak of the market, paying peak prices, just prior to the subprime crisis. We would be remiss if we did not note that the senior management of Lehman Brothers supposedly possessed great financial expertise, as that was their business. Instead, they lacked true expertise but tried to make up for their ignorance with arrogance. There were a lot of highly skilled and knowledgeable financial experts at Lehman but the few people at the top, most principally its CEO, the arrogant Dick Fuld, successor to the equally arrogant Lew Glucksman, refused to listen to them. Therefore, the company pursed an M&A strategy, which was one factor that helped cause the demise of the storied investment banks. As with virtually all such disasters, all of these very senior managers remain very rich men and refuse to accept responsibility for their actions.

SCOPE ECONOMIES AND THE ONE-STOP SHOP

A number of CEOs seem determined to provide their customers with a one-stop shop regardless of whether or not they really want it. On the surface, it seems that being able to offer consumers more of the products and services they will definitely consume would enable them to save on search costs. Consumers, however, may not want to purchase one type of product or service from a supplier who they associated with that one product or service but not with others. There are many examples of this but a classic one-stop shop flop was the dysfunctional Citigroup that Sandy Weill formed. It was a dysfunctional financial supermarket that the market never wanted and that did not further shareholders' interests; it only served CEO Sandy Weill and his managers' personal financial interests. We discuss Citigroup in the case study below.

CASE STUDY: CITIBANK—FINANCIAL SUPERMARKET THE MARKET DID NOT WANT

The subprime crisis underscored the concern about financial institutions that are too big to fail. Banking M&A result in larger financial institutions that impose risks on the whole financial system. When a medium-sized financial institution fails, the exposure to the rest of the system is limited. When a large financial institution fails, the impact of its failure can be far reaching. When we have several such types of institutions taking similar risks, such as risk, that is directly or indirectly related to mortgage-backed securities, then the exposure of the banking system as a whole is greatly magnified. In addition, when banks, such as Citigroup, became very large and diversified this resulted in increased managerial demands, which they could not handle. When Sandy Weill created the Citigroup financial conglomerate based on a failed growth strategy, and then handed off the management of the giant bank to Charles Prince, an attorney by training and a man poorly equipped to understand and manage such a complex financial institution, it was only a matter of time before problems would manifest themselves. This was exacerbated when one of its directors, the politically savvy Robert Rubin, encouraged the bank to take more risks as a way to elevate its returns. This is just what the bank did, and the rest is history.

Regulators were asleep at the wheel while Weill used M&A to build a super-bank based on a strategy that made little sense. Laws designed to limit the growth of banks into non-banking businesses were disassembled to allow aggressive growth and risk taking. Regulators were even more asleep when they allowed such an institution to take on so much leverage and invest in risky assets, jeopardizing depositor's assets.

There are many lessons to be learned from Citigroup's failed growth through M&A strategy. However, the history of M&A tells us that such lessons will be quickly forgotten.

Source: Adapted from Patrick Gaughan, *Mergers, Acquisitions, and Corporate Restructurings,* 5th edition (Hoboken, NJ: John Wiley & Sons, 2010).

COPYCAT FOLLOWING OF ANOTHER FIRM'S FOOLISH M&A STRATEGY

We have already discussed how often one company will pursue a failed M&A strategy and competitors will blindly follow with a comparable, ill-thought-out strategy. In the 1990s to 2000s, it was not just Citigroup that pursued a failed one-stop shop financial services strategy. One key element of this strategy was the combination of banking and insurance. This combination made little sense. Just think about it. If you have a bank account at a given financial institution, and if it offers life and property casualty insurance, are you more likely to purchase such insurance simply because the bank where you have your accounts owns one of the insurance companies that offers insurance in that highly competitive market? How about if the bank also owns a brokerage firm? Are you more likely to open a brokerage account at a firm that is owned by the bank where you have your checking account? How about if we add to the question the fact that the businesses were not effectively integrated and the cross-marketing was at best a joke?

In 1988 Credit Suisse acquired a 44 percent stake in First Boston as part of a "bailout" of one of the leading investment banks in the United States that got stuck being unable to refinance bridge loans in the Ohio Mattress, the maker of Sealy mattresses, buyout. The deal has become known as the "burning mattress." The junk bond market collapsed and First Boston, this leading M&A "advisor," did not seem to be able to advise itself on market conditions. Credit Suisse gained at First Boston's expense. It eventually acquired the rest of First Boston and later did away with the famous First Boston name. However, Credit Suisse would soon prove that it also did not seem to know much about its industry and the damaging role that M&A can play in it. In 1997 Credit Suisse acquired Winterthur Insurance. It then began the process of marketing itself as a "diversified financial services company"—whatever that means. In 2006, Credit Suisse sold off Winterthur Insurance. So much for the combination of banking and insurance. These M&A flops are pretty funny when these well-known banks hold themselves as M&A experts and have made significant amounts of money from marketing such services.

Citigroup and Credit Suisse were not the only incompetent acquirers in the financial services industry. Not to be outdone by the aggressive banks moving into the insurance industry, the giant German insurance company, Allianz, the largest European insurer, acquired Dresdner, the number-three bank in Germany, in 2001 for $38 billion. This was an expensive acquisition but the successful Allianz could afford it—or at least its shareholders could—couldn't they? Like the other financial services miscues we have discussed, Allianz had a terrible, but expensive, merger strategy. It counted on being able to cross-sell services. Instead, it acquired a company with hulking mortgage-related liabilities. This is another example of how the costs of an M&A can be hard to measure in advance. In 2008, Allianz announced it was selling off Dresdner for $14.3 billion—less than half of what it paid for it. As always, it was never management's fault. It was circumstances that could not be foreseen.

COST ECONOMIES IN BANKING MERGERS: UNITED STATES VERSUS EUROPE

While we devote significant time to discussing M&A failures with an eye toward devising a way to avoid such costly blunders, we also need to focus on the numerous M&A successes. The banking industry has had a long history of such successes.

An example of successful cost reductions was the acquisition of Manufacturers Hanover Trust by Chemical Bank in 1991. When the deal was announced, the companies declared that they anticipated savings of approximately $650 million (1.1 billion in 2013 dollars). However, the actual savings derived from closing unnecessary branches and eliminating redundant overhead proved to be approximately $100 million greater. The success of this deal was one factor that led Chemical Bank to merge with Chase Manhattan in a $13 billion deal in 1995 (22.1 in 2013 $). This bank would continue to merge with other major financial institutions to create one of the biggest banks in the world. In September 2000, J. P. Morgan and Chase Manhattan combined. Just four years after that, in 2004, J. P. Morgan Chase merged with Bank One to form the banking institution we now know as JPMorgan Chase.

The banking industry has consolidated significantly over the past 25 years since the industry was deregulated. The question arises: When banks engage in M&A programs do they realize cost economies and at what point, after doing a number of deals, do the cost economies disappear—and possibly diseconomies appear?

Studies of fourth merger wave bank mergers do not show significant gains from combining banks. For example, Houston and Ryngaert analyzed 152 bank mergers over the period 1985 to 1991, and found average bidder announcement returns of –2.25 percent, while target returns were 14.77 percent.[12] A later study by the same authors, using 184 mergers over the period 1985 to 1992, found –0.24 percent and 20.4 percent for bidder and target returns respectively.[13] While evidence from the fourth merger wave is not impressive, there is more recent evidence that bank mergers do realize synergistic gains and that mergers in this industry do not take place just to create empires for chief executive officers (CEOs). For example, Becher analyzed 558 U.S. bank mergers over the period 1980 to 1997.[14] Over the full time period, he found that bidder returns were not dramatically different from zero while shareholders of target banks enjoyed positive returns. However, over the 1990s, the fifth merger wave, the picture improved and both bidder and target returns were positive. He concluded that these banking industry deals brought real benefits to shareholders of both companies and not just to the CEO.

There have been several studies that have found that European banks may be more successful than their U.S. counterparts at realizing cost economies following mergers. Using event studies, Cybo-Ottone and Murgia found positive abnormal returns for European bank merger announcements.[15] This implies that the markets see benefits, and the most obvious benefits from bank mergers would be cost economies. More directly, however, Vander Vennett found evidence of falling average operating costs in 492 European Union bank mergers over the period 1988 to 1993.[16] Other studies have focused on specific European countries. For example, Humphrey and Vale found a 2 percent reduction in operating costs following Norwegian bank mergers.[17] Resti found somewhat similar benefits for Italy while Hayes and Thompson did the same for England.[18] Some studies found few benefits from Spanish bank mergers.[19] While Valverde and Humphrey generally found the same type of neutral results for 22 Spanish bank mergers over the period 1986 to 2000, they did detect the presence of cost benefits for larger deals and deals where the bank had more prior experience from mergers.[20] This implies that in this market there is more of a learning effect when banks *learn by doing*. The Valverde and Humphrey result is interesting when we consider that many studies of U.S. bank mergers found lower gains for the 1980s, while finding greater benefits for the 1990s. This may also imply some learning effect in the U.S. market.

The pursuit of scope economies can certainly lend great benefits to companies. However, at some point a company may have used M&A to attain an optimal level of scope in its product line or services offerings, and it then becomes time to end the M&A process and work with the capabilities that a company has. However, sometimes this gets lost on corporate managers, and they seem to instinctively keep on doing M&A. Wachovia is an excellent example of a company that used M&A to broaden its scope and then continued to do M&A until it ended up bringing the company down.

As we discuss in Chapter 9 on corporate governance, one of the concerns we have with M&A programs is agency costs and the risk that the CEO will be doing the deals to pursue his or her own personal benefits. Another risk is that when management is able to achieve growth, albeit non-organic growth, they will succumb to continuing M&A programs long past optimality. If they end up creating a huge institution that is too big for them to effectively manage, they can put shareholders' interests at risk. The way financial systems are set up, however, depositors are protected by insurance, such as the FDIC insurance, and ultimately taxpayers will pay for the excesses of managers running institutions that are too big to fail. Unfortunately, in banking there are incentives for management to continue M&A programs for their own personal benefits. From their point of view, they have few risks, as no one will ask them after the fact to give back their ill-gotten gains, even if they destroy the institution and shareholder value. Fortunately, these managers are the minority. However, there are too many very prominent examples of such bank managers, such as Citigroup's Weill and Washington Mutual's Killinger. In the case study that follows, we discuss another prominent example of corporate failure caused by unchecked M&A.

CASE STUDY: WACHOVIA—SUCCESSFUL PURSUIT OF SCOPE ECONOMIES IN 2005, FOLLOWED BY A DISASTROUS PURSUIT OF SIZE IN 2006

As discussed, over the past 20 years, the bank we now know as Wachovia grew from a medium-sized bank to the fifth-largest bank in the United States. By 2005, Wachovia commanded a huge base of depositors but not the product line width of some of its large competitors. With its large depositor base, Wachovia had a great amount of capital to lend but not enough business opportunities, such as consumer loans, to lend these monies out. In 2000, the Charlotte, North Carolina–based bank had sold off its credit card and mortgage divisions due to their poor performance. They used the monies from the sale of these business units to help finance Wachovia's $13.6 billion merger with First Union in 2001. However, they still needed to be able to offer customers services that other major banks offered—credit cards and mortgages. In order to do that, Wachovia entered into agreements with MBNA for credit cards and Countrywide Financial Corp. for mortgages.

In late 2005, Wachovia elected not to renew its five-year agreement with MBNA and started to offer credit cards directly. In September 2005, Wachovia decided to use merger and acquisition (M&A) to accelerate its returns to the consumer finance business by buying Westcorp, Inc., for $3.9 billion (Westcorp. has a significant auto lending business). This acquisition quickly transformed Wachovia into the ninth-largest auto lender in the United States—a position more consistent with its overall size in the market. At the same time, Wachovia also internally expanded its own mortgage lending business while acquiring AmNet, a small West Coast mortgage company, for $83 million.[a]

(continued)

---

[a] David Enrich, "Wachovia Re-Enters the Consumer Finance," *Wall Street Journal* (December 14, 2005): B3B.

(continued)

Through a combination of internal development and M&A, Wachovia quickly was able to achieve valuable economies of scope.

The acquisition of Westcorp is a relatively modest deal when compared to the bold acquisition of MBNA, the largest credit card issuer in the United States, by the Bank of America in June 2005 for $35 billion. While Wachovia had pursued some negotiations for MBNA, a company with which it was familiar and therefore somewhat comfortable, the price tag of this deal was more than Wachovia wanted to pay for a business that is much more risky than traditional banking. Up to that point, Wachovia had acquired a number of smaller companies. In doing so, it acquired the expertise it needed in specialized areas, such as Westcorp's skills in auto lending, while not risking the capital needed to do a megadeal. With these moves, Wachovia had achieved a broader product line without all of the risk that the Bank of America assumed with its MBNA deal.[b]

Unfortunately, Wachovia's CEO changed his strategy in 2006 when Wachovia acquired Golden West Financial, the parent company of thrift World Savings for $25.5 billion. Golden West was the largest issuer of subprime mortgages in the West and Southwest. It boasted a 285-branch network spanning 10 states. Its owners, Marian and Herb Sandler, who bought Golden West in 1964 for $4 million, smiled when they sold the bank at the top of the market to Wachovia, whose CEO referred to Golden West as his "crown jewel." His pursuit of size through M&A proved to be the bank's undoing. He was eventually fired, and *all of Wachovia* was sold to Wells Fargo in 2008 for $15 billion (just $1 billion more than what Wachovia paid for Golden West alone). Wachovia's failed M&A strategy carries many lessons. Relatively smaller, strategic deals can often fuel profitable growth and steady expansion. However, the aggressive pursuit of size through M&A is fraught with peril. Managers have to be able to recognize when to stop M&A and when to manage the company to achieve organic growth. M&A growth can be the easiest to achieve—especially for managers who are not good at running the big corporations they may have created through M&A. M&A-fueled growth can present to the market a false image of a growing company and can buy management time to extract more benefits from the now larger company while not really serving shareholders' interests.

---

[b] Exposure to credit card losses would come back to haunt Bank of America in 2010.

INTERNATIONALIZATION THEORY OF SYNERGY AND INFORMATION-BASED ASSETS

The internalization theory of synergy has been discussed in microeconomics, and in the subfield of industrial organization, for many years.[21] The internalization theory of synergy states that companies with information-based assets acquire other companies to take advantage of these assets that they possess. This can lead them to acquire firms in different fields and to, at times, pursue a diversification strategy where they acquire companies that seem to be in unrelated fields. However, according to this theory, the relatedness comes from their ability to leverage their information-based assets to exploit potential and competitive advantages of these assets in these other fields.

Information-based assets include unique know-how, which a company can apply in different ways. Two proponents of this theory, Randall Morck and Bernard Yeung, cite as an example the 3M Corporation, which has used its ability to apply substances to tape-like materials to move into several fields. They applied glue to tape to make their famous Scotch tape. However, they also were able to market other tape-like products such as VCR tapes, which were quite popular before they became extinct with the advent of the CD. This makes sense but clearly at this point 3M is a highly diversified conglomerate and has moved way beyond extending its ability with adhesives to other related products.

Morck and Yeung's definition of an information-based asset is broader than one might think. It is more than just know-how. They include market capabilities and managerial skills, as well as intellectual property such as brand names. For example, they cite well-known brand names such as Calvin Klein and the ability of that company to extend the Calvin Klein brand from jeans to underwear and even to jewelry. Buyers usually believe that they will get a stylish, designer brand product as well as the quality associated with the brand. In that sense, they are purchasing *insurance* of a certain level of quality. This is why owners of such brands are very protective of their quality control in production so that no product they put their name on will reflect badly on their much larger business.

Information-based assets can even explain geographical diversification. For example, companies in developed economies such as in the United States, Europe, and Japan, have brought their know-how to undeveloped markets to exploit competitive advantages that they possess relative to indigenous firms. When they successfully do so, they are able to achieve growth that would not be as easily achievable in their home markets, which may be growing slowly and where they may even have to compete against local competitors who have comparable information-based assets.

It may be more efficient for a company with information-based assets to acquire targets than to try to market their assets. Such assets may be subject to inappropriate uses when not protected; thus other market solutions, such as licensing or strategic alliances, may not be effective. When this is the case, then the best way to exploit these assets is to simply acquire a target and then allow the now acquired entity to have use of the assets. That is, the best way to utilize such assets may be to internalize them under one unified corporate umbrella.

Morck and Yeung tested this hypothesis by looking at companies that diversified.[22] They found that firms that had substantial information-based assets increased their shareholder value when they diversified. Firms that did not possess such assets, however, failed to uplift their shareholder value when the pursued diversifying acquisitions.

Morck and Yeung's research also had some other interesting results. Consistent with their theory, they found that companies that pursued geographical diversification had increased values when they had information-based assets but not when they did not. Companies that got bigger did not grow shareholder value unless they possessed information-based assets. Of the information-based assets, intangibles related to research and development seemed to be the ones that had the greatest impact on shareholder value.

They also looked at potential targets and tried to determine if there was a relationship between companies that possessed information-based assets and those that were more likely to be taken over. They found that companies that had such assets, but that had not diversified or engaged in geographical expansion, were more likely than others to become takeover targets. This is the same synergy but in reverse. Here, the potential targets have the valuable synergistic assets, which potential bidders may lack but also are able to generate even greater values when they can more quickly apply them to other fields or geographical markets.

The internalization theory is a very interesting explanation of why some companies are able to achieve synergistic benefits from M&A and others cannot. For example, Morck and Yeung point to very diversified companies from the late 1970s. They compared the one time huge quintessential conglomerate ITT to 3M. In 1978, ITT operated in 12 different industries but had a Tobin's q of 0.57 while 3M operated in 11 different industries but had a Tobin's q of 2.02.[23] When we flash forward we should not be surprised that ITT went through several restructurings and has all but disappeared, while 3M continues to thrive after all these years and changes in the marketplace.

Synergy and Acquisition Premiums

Acquisition premiums typically, although not always, are paid in control share acquisitions. This premium is a value in excess of the market value of a company that is paid for the right to control and proportionately enjoy the profits of the business. Bidders often cite anticipated synergy as the reason for the payment of a premium. Given the track record of some acquisitions that have not turned out as anticipated, the market sometimes questions the reasonableness of this synergy, especially when it is used as the justification for an unusually high premium. Synergy requires that the bidder receive gains, such as in the form of performance improvements, that offset the premium.[24] It is hoped that these gains will be realized in the years following the transaction. In order for the premium payment (P) and true deal expenses (E) to make sense, the present value of these synergistic gains (SG) must exceed this amount. This relationship is expressed as follows:

$$P + E < [SG_1/(1 + r) + SG^2/(1 + r)^2 + \ldots + SG_n/(1 + r)^n] \qquad (3.3)$$

where r = risk-adjusted discount rate and n = number of periods.

One of the complicating factors in rationalizing the payment of a significant premium is that the premium is usually paid up front, with the uncertain gains coming over the course of time. The further into the future these gains are realized, the lower their present value. In addition, the higher the discount rate that is used to convert the synergistic gains to present value, the more difficult it is to justify a high premium. If the bidder also anticipates that there will be a significant initial period before the gains begin manifesting themselves, such as when the bidder is trying to merge the two corporate cultures, this pushes the start of the gains further into the future. If a bidder is using a high discount rate and/or does not expect gains to materialize for an extended period of time, it is hard to justify a high premium. Moreover, the higher the premium, the more pressure the combined company is under to realize a high rate of growth in future synergistic gains.

The best situation is when the business is able to realize both revenue enhancement and cost reduction. When a bidder has paid a significant premium, it implicitly assumes more pressure to realize greater revenue enhancement and more cost reductions. The higher the premium, the greater the need for both.

Throughout the process, the bidder needs to be aware of the actual and anticipated response of competitors. Enhanced revenues may have come at the expense of competitors' revenues when the market is not expanding. It may not be realistic to assume that they will stand still and watch a competitor improve its position at their expense through acquisitions. When a company can demonstrate such performance improvements through M&A, competitors may respond with their own acquisition programs. We have discussed how such copycat M&A is not uncommon. Once again, the myriad different responses may be somewhat difficult to model, but they, nonetheless, need to be carefully considered. Although it has already been mentioned, it is so important that it is worth mentioning again how easy it is to build a financial model that shows whatever result one wants to see. Assumptions can be built into the valuation models that are developed in Chapter 11 to show both revenue enhancement and cost reductions. As the merged business takes steps to realize the theorized financial gains, it may discover that the financial model building process was the easiest part, whereas working through all the other steps necessary to realize the actual gains proves to be the most difficult task.

Financial Synergy

Financial synergy refers to the impact of a corporate merger or acquisition on the costs of capital to the acquiring firm or the merging partners. The extent to which financial synergy exists in corporate combinations, the costs of capital should be lowered. Whether the benefits of such financial synergy are really reasonable, however, is a matter of dispute among corporate finance theorists.

As noted, the combination of two firms may reduce risk if the firms' cash flow streams are not perfectly correlated. If the acquisition or merger lowers the volatility of the cash flows, suppliers of capital may consider the firm less risky. The risk of bankruptcy would presumably be less, given the fact that wide swings up and down in the combined firm's cash flows would be less likely.

Higgins and Schall explain this effect in terms of *debt coinsurance*.[25] If the correlation of the income streams of two firms is less than perfectly positively correlated, the bankruptcy risk associated with the combination of the two firms may be reduced. Under certain circumstances one of the firms could experience conditions that force it into bankruptcy. It is difficult to know in advance which one of two possible firms could succumb to this fate. In the event that one of the firms fails, creditors may suffer a loss. If the two firms were combined in advance of financial problems, however, the cash flows of the solvent firm that are in excess of its debt service needs would cushion the decline in the other firm's cash flows. The offsetting earnings of the firm in good condition might be sufficient to prevent the combined firm from falling into bankruptcy and causing creditors to suffer losses.

The problem with the debt-coinsurance effect is that the benefits accrue to debtholders at the expense of equity holders. Debtholders gain by holding debt in a less risky firm. Higgins and Schall observe that these gains come at the expense of stockholders, who may lose in the acquisition. These researchers assume that the total returns that can be provided by the combined firm are constant (R_T). If more of these returns are provided to bondholders (R_B), they must come at the expense of stockholders (R_S):

$$R_T = R_S + R_B \qquad (3.4)$$

In other words, Higgins and Schall maintain that the debt-coinsurance effect does not create any new value but merely redistributes gains among the providers of capital to the firm. There is no general agreement on this result. Lewellen, for example, has concluded that stockholders gain from these types of combinations.[26] Other research, however, fails to indicate that the debt-related motives are more relevant for conglomerate acquisitions than for nonconglomerate acquisitions.[27] Studies have shown the existence of a coinsurance effect in bank mergers. Penas and Unal examined 66 bank mergers and looked at the effects of these deals on 282 bonds.[28] They found positive bond returns for both targets (4.3 percent) as well as acquiring banks (1.2 percent). One explanation that may play a role is that larger banks may be *too big to fail*, as regulators would not want to allow a larger bank to fail outright and would step in to provide assistance.

Billet, King, and Mauer examined the wealth effects for target and acquirers' returns in the 1980s and 1990s.[29] They found that target company bonds, which were less than investment grade prior to the deal, earned significantly positive announcement period returns. In contrast, acquiring company bonds earned negative announcement period returns. They also found that these announcement period returns were greater in the 1990s compared to the 1980s. These results support the coinsurance effect.

Higgins and Schall show that the stockholders' losses may be offset by issuing new debt after the merger. The stockholders may then gain through the tax savings on the debt interest payments. Galai and Masulis have demonstrated this result.[30] The additional debt would increase the debt-equity ratio of the post-merger firm to a level that stockholders must have found desirable, or at least acceptable, before the merger. With the higher debt-equity ratio, the firm becomes a higher risk–higher return investment.

As noted previously, a company may experience economies of scale through acquisitions. These economies are usually thought to come from production cost decreases, attained by operating at higher capacity levels or through a reduced sales force or a shared distribution system. As a result of acquisitions, *financial* economies of scale are also possible in the form of lower flotation and transaction costs.[31]

In financial markets, a larger company has certain advantages that may enable it to have a lower cost of capital compared to smaller firms. It may enjoy better access to financial markets, and it tends to experience lower costs of raising capital, presumably because it is considered to be less risky than a smaller firm. Therefore, the costs of borrowing by issuing bonds are lower because a larger firm would probably be able to issue bonds offering a lower interest rate than a smaller company. For many years, this was one of the benefits that GE bestowed upon many of its targets. In addition, there are certain fixed costs in the issuance of securities, such as Securities and Exchange Commission (SEC) registration costs, legal fees, and printing costs. These costs would be spread out over a greater dollar volume of securities because the larger company would probably borrow more capital with each issue of bonds.

The analysis is similar in the case of equity securities. Flotation costs per dollar raised would be lower for larger issues than for smaller issues. In addition, the selling effort required may be greater for riskier issues than for less risky larger firms. It is assumed in this discussion that larger firms are less risky and bear a lower probability of bankruptcy and financial failure. If a larger firm, which might result from a combination of several other firms, is so inefficient, however, that profits start to fall, the larger combination of companies could have a greater risk of financial failure. Levy and Sarnat have developed a model to show the diversification effect that occurs when two or more imperfectly correlated income streams combine to lower the probability of default. This lower risk level induces capital holders to provide capital to the combined firm or conglomerate at lower costs than they would have provided to the individual, premerger components. Their analysis presents the financial synergistic benefits as an economic gain that results from mergers.

Financial Synergy and Acquisitions Followed by Divestitures

In Chapter 10, we discuss research, such as that of Kaplan and Weisbach, which shows how a large percentage of acquisitions were subsequently divested.[32] As Kaplan and Weisbach note, not all the acquisitions that were acquired and subsequently divested should be considered failures. There can be an explanation for why a company may want to acquire another firm and then, perhaps less than 10 years later, sell it off. In the view of Fluck and Lynch, one explanation could be that larger companies with strong balance sheets and financing capabilities may acquire smaller targets, which have marginally successful projects that they cannot finance due to weak balance sheets and sketchy cash flows.[33] The larger companies, perhaps ones that are struggling to find profitable projects to pursue with their bountiful financing capability, may acquire these targets and finance their marginally profitable projects. With the larger companies and their lower cost of capital, the net present value of these projects may be higher than what it would be for smaller and financially weaker companies.

Larger companies that pursue these types of acquisitions tend to be less valuable than other large companies. This can help explain why, most of the time, conglomerates sell at a discount. It also can explain why large companies will try to realize gains from selling off the acquired entities and with them their now realized, but still marginally profitable projects.

CASE STUDY: SEARS ROEBUCK'S BIZARRE PERCEPTION OF SYNERGY

In 1992, Sears Roebuck and Co. announced that it was ending its costly *synergistic* diversification strategy and would be selling off its financial services operations. In order to understand the company and its decision to enter the financial services business, it helps to know a little of its history and how it got to be one of the leading retail merchants in the United States. The company was formed in 1886 by Alvah Roebuck and Richard Sears. At the turn of the twentieth century, the company formed a financial services division that would handle some of the credit needs of customers seeking to purchase products from Sears. As it built its retail empire, the company continued to move further into financial services. In the 1930s, it started an insurance division, Allstate, which marketed automobile insurance. In the 1950s, the company formed Sears Roebuck Acceptance Corporation, which focused on short-term financial management for the company. It also began its own credit card operation at that time. So, when we say Sears Roebuck's movement into financial services in the 1980s was part of a diversification strategy, it is important to keep in mind that this was not a totally new area for the company. However, the part of the financial services business that it moved into in the 1980s was different from the part with which it had been previously involved. With the exception of automobile insurance, the other parts of its financial services business were complementary to its retail operations. For example, credit cards could enhance credit sales to

(continued)

(*continued*)

its customers, especially those who might not be eligible for credit from other companies.

However, the movement into automobile insurance was a move away from its core operations. This was not the only initial move away from core activities. The company moved into mutual fund operations and purchased California Financial Corporation, a large savings and loan company. The moves demonstrated a tendency on the part of Sears to move away from its core businesses. In later years it would take this tendency and move it to a new level.

The seeds of the movement away from its core businesses can be traced partially to weaknesses in its retail operation, which were partially related to the difficulties Sears had in competing with Walmart. Sears was losing ground to other retail rivals who were willing to use aggressive price competition to attract customers away from Sears while weakening the margins of the retail giant. At a point like this, the company can move in two different directions: fix the problem in its core business or invest resources elsewhere by trying to find a more attractive business. Sears took the latter route, and it proved to be a failure.

In 1981, Sears bought Coldwell Banker, the largest real estate brokerage company in the United States, for $175 million in stock and cash. It then purchased Dean Witter Reynolds, a large securities brokerage company, for $600 million in stock and cash. These deals were acquisitions of leading companies in their respective businesses. What were the gains that Sears saw? That is, how could Sears sell real estate and securities more advantageously than these two companies were currently selling them for? Remember that when one acquires a target company, you are usually paying a value that reflects their projected profitability and cash flow—generating capability. Unless you bring something new to the table or can create value-enhancing synergies, the deal may not be accretive. Sears saw such synergies through taking advantage of its large retail network and regular customer base to sell them new products—homes and stocks, and maybe a bond or two.

The Sears strategy is not a new one. It goes by several names, and some would say it is based on cross-selling the acquirers and target products and services to their respective customer bases. Sears had a large network of retail stores throughout the United States and a

(*continued*)

regular flow of customers. It also had a long history of credibilty with consumers who knew the company as one that offered high quality products that it stood behind. However, to put the strategy in perspective, consider a hypothetical discussion between two Sears' customers. Say, for example, a husband is going to Sears to buy some lawn-mowing equipment. Or perhaps a wife is going to Sears for a new dishwasher (excuse the sexist nature of this example). One spouse says to the other, "Hi, honey, I'm off to Sears to buy that new lawn mower/dishwasher." The spouse responds, "Oh, great, but could you pick me up a house while you're there? And how about 100 shares of Microsoft as well? I heard the company is doing well; maybe you can ask for some financial advice from the appliance salesman?" While somewhat humorous, the absurdity of this exchange under-scores the flaws in Sears' strategy. These products simply do not go together, and when that is the case, it does not matter if you are one of the biggest retailers in the world; you are not going to make this combination work.

Sears' management was convinced that the strategy would be successful. The market thought otherwise. In particular, institutional investors, who typically command a majority of the shares of most large public companies, questioned Sears' strategy as well as its inability to solve the woes of the retail business. Finally, after intense pressure from institutional investors, who clearly saw that the strategy was not working, Sears decided to spin off Dean Witter and Coldwell Banker in 1992 and refocused its efforts back onto its core business that had continued to decline over the prior decade. In that same year, Walmart passed Sears in total sales. Walmart was not distracted by poorly conceived M&A and used Sears' acquisition problems to surpass Sears. When Sears refocused, it began to capitalize on its strengths and grow again. However, it was not until 2003 that it finally came to the realization that its credit card business was a drain and sold it to Citigroup.

Gillan, Kensinger, and Martin described the insurrection brought about by institutional investors, which were led by Robert Monks of the LENS fund.[a] Sears was a case of an entrenched management team

(*continued*)

---

[a] Stuart Gillan, John W. Kensinger, and John Martin, "Value Creation and Corporate Diversification," *Journal of Financial Economics* 56, no. 1 (January 2000): 103–137.

(continued)

that also dominated the board of directors. Management held almost a majority of the board seats, and some of the board members sat on different boards together. The close relationship between management and the board did not facilitate objectivity. Management was not responsive to dissent by its shareholders, particularly knowledgeable institutional investors.

The lessons from the failed Sears diversification strategy are threefold. First, just because you are good at one business does not mean that you can extend the assets and managerial resources of your organization to another very different business. The second lesson is that forays into more exciting business categories in which you have not demonstrated any expertise can be expensive and a losing proposition. It is often better to simply stay with the same old boring business that you are good at and learn ways to improve your performance. It is much easier to make small but meaningful improvements in a business in which you have established success than to move to a totally different business area. The third lesson is that so often, the one-stop shop does not work. If customers are not of a mindset to buy products from you that they normally do not associate with your business, then adding such business activities may not work. You may be doing the customers a favor they do not want.

In 2004, Sears still lagged behind Walmart along with another retail giant—Kmart. Kmart, fresh from being acquired in Chapter 11 by cost-cutter Eddie Lampert and his hedge fund, merged with Sears. Sears had 1,100 stores while Kmart had 1,504 stores. Sears/Kmart continued to struggle while competitors, such as Target, gained market share at Sears/Kmart's expense. Knowing that Lampert's strategy is to cut costs to try to wring profits out of acquisitions, competitors such as Target used this as an opportunity to invest in upgrading their stores. Many of the Sears stores became shabby looking, as if they were in need of capital expenditures to uplift their appearance. As of the end of 2012, Sears/Kmart continues to struggle.

Source: Derived from original case study that appeared in Patrick A. Gaughan, *Mergers: What Can Go Wrong and How to Prevent It* (Hoboken, NJ: John Wiley & Sons, 2005), 86–89. This case study updated the events since that book was published.

NOTES

1. Paul Asquith, "Merger Bids, Uncertainty and Stockholder Returns," *Journal of Financial Economics* 11, nos. 1–4 (April 1983): 51–83; and Michael Bradley, Anand Desai, and E. Han Kim, "The Rationale behind Interfirm Tender Offers: Information or Synergy?" *Journal of Financial Economics* 11, nos. 1–4 (April 1983): 183–206.
2. Michael Jensen and Richard Ruback, "The Market for Corporate Control: The Scientific Evidence," *Journal of Financial Economics* 11, nos. 1–4 (April 1983): 5–50.
3. Mark N. Clemente and David S. Greenspan, *Winning at Mergers and Acquisitions: The Guide to Market-Focused Planning and Integration* (New York: John Wiley & Sons, 1998), 46.
4. Even though it sported a long and impressive performance record, GE paid a heavy price for its foray into financial services when the subprime crisis took hold in 2007 to 2008.
5. Frank Lichtenberg and Donald Siegel, "Productivity and Changes in Ownership of Manufacturing Plants," *Brookings Papers on Economic Activity* 3 (1987): 643–683.
6. Husayn Shahrur, "Industry Structure and Horizontal Takeovers: Analysis of Wealth Effects on Rivals, Suppliers and Corporate Customers," *Journal of Financial Economics* 76 (2005): 61–98.
7. C. Edward Fee and Shawn Thomas, "Sources of Gains in Horizontal Mergers: Evidence from Customer, Supplier, and Rival Firms," *Journal of Financial Economics* 74 (December 2004): 423–460.
8. Loretta J. Mester, "Efficient Product of Financial Services: Scale and Scope Economies," *Review, Federal Reserve Bank of Philadelphia* (January/February 1987): 15–25.
9. Patrick A. Gaughan, "Financial Deregulation, Banking Mergers and the Impact on Regional Business" (*Proceedings of the Pacific Northwest Regional Economic Conference, University of Washington*, Spring 1988).
10. Kristen Grind, *The Lost Bank: The Story of Washington Mutual—The Biggest Bank Failure in American History* (New York: Simon & Schuster, 2012).
11. Lawrence C. McDonald and Patrick Robinson, *A Colossal Failure of Common Sense: The Inside Story of the Collapse of Lehman Brothers* (New York: Crown Business, 2009).
12. J. F. Houston and M. D. Ryngaert, "The Overall Gains from Large Bank Mergers," *Journal of Banking and Finance* 18: 1155–1176.
13. J. F. Houston and M. D. Ryngaert, "Equity Issuance and Adverse Selection: A Direct Test Using Conditional Stock Offers," *Journal of Finance* 52: 197–219.
14. David Becher, "The Valuation Effects of Bank Mergers," *Journal of Corporate Finance* 6 (2000): 189–214.
15. Alberto Cybo-Ottone and Maurizio Murgia, "Mergers and Shareholder Wealth in European Banking," *Journal of Banking and Finance* 24 (2000): 831–859.
16. R. Vander Vennett, "The Effects of Mergers and Acquisition on Efficiency and Profitability of EC Credit Institutions," *Journal of Banking and Finance* 20 (1997): 1531–1558.

17. D. B. Humphrey and B. Vale, "Scale Economies, Bank Mergers and Electronic Payments: A Spline Function Approach" (Working Paper, 2002, Central Bank of Norway, Oslo, Norway).

18. A. Resti, "Regulation Can Foster Mergers. Can Mergers Foster Efficiency?: The Italian Case" *Journal of Economics and Business* 50: 157–169; M. Hayes and S. Thompson, "The Productivity Effects of Banking Mergers: Evidence from the U.K. Building Societies," *Journal of Banking and Finance* 23 (1999): 825–846.

19. J. L. Raymond, "Economias de Escala y Fusiones en el Sector de Cajas de Ahorros," *Papeles de Economia Espanola* 58 (1994): 113–125; I. Fuentes and T. Sastre, "Mergers and Acquisitions in the Spanish Banking Industry: Some Empirical Evidence" (Working Paper 9924, 1999, Bank of Spain, Madrid, Spain).

20. Santiago Carbo Valverde and David Humphrey, "Predicted and Actual Costs from Individual Bank Mergers," *Journal of Economics and Business* 56 (2004): 137–157.

21. Richard Caves, "International Corporations: The Industrial Economics of Foreign Investment," *Economica* 38 (February 1971): 386–405; Peter Buckley and Mark Casson, *The Economic Theory of the Multinational Enterprise* (London: Macmillan, 1976).

22. Randall Morck and Bernard Yeung, "Why Firms Diversify: Internalization vs. Agency Behavior," in John Hand and Baruch Lev, eds., *Intangible Assets* (Oxford, UK: Oxford University Press, 2002).

23. Ibid., 1.

24. See Mark L. Sirower, *The Synergy Trap* (New York: Free Press, 1997), 44–81.

25. Robert C. Higgins and Lawrence C. Schall, "Corporate Bankruptcy and Conglomerate Mergers," *Journal of Finance* 30 (March 1975): 93–113.

26. Wilbur G. Lewellen, "A Pure Rationale for the Conglomerate Merger," *Journal of Finance* 26, no. 2 (May 1971): 521–545.

27. Pieter T. Elgers and John J. Clark, "Merger Types and Shareholder Returns: Additional Evidence," *Financial Management* 9, Issue 2 (Summer 1980): 66–72.

28. Maria Fabiana Penas and Haluk Unal, "Gains in Bank Mergers: Evidence from the Bond Markets," *Journal of Financial Economics* 74 (2004): 149–179.

29. Matthew T. Billet, Tao-Hsien Dolly King, and David C. Mauer, "Bondholder Wealth Effects in Mergers and Acquisitions," *Journal of Finance* 59, no. 1 (February 2004): 107–135.

30. Dan Galai and Ronald W. Masulis, "The Option Pricing Model and the Risk Factor of Stock," *Journal of Financial Economics* 3, nos. 1/2 (January/March 1976): 53–81.

31. Haim Levy and Marshall Sarnat, "Diversification, Portfolio Analysis and the Uneasy Case for Conglomerate Mergers," *Journal of Finance* 25, no. 4 (September 1970): 795–802.

32. Steven Kaplan and Michael Weisbach, "The Success of Acquisitions: Evidence from Divestitures," *Journal of Finance* 47 (March 1992): 107–138.

33. Zsuzsanna Fluck and Anthony Lynch, "Why Do Firms Merge and Then Divest? A Theory of Financial Synergy," *Journal of Business* 72, no. 3 (July 1999): 319–346.

CHAPTER 4

Diversification

D iversification means growing outside a company's current industry category. Many companies pursue diversification to varying degrees. In this chapter, we examine pros and cons of a merger and acquisition (M&A) diversification strategy. In doing so, we look at the performance of companies that have pursued diversifying acquisitions.

In Chapter 3, we discussed synergy and companies' efforts to derive synergistic benefits from M&A. Can companies derive similar synergistic benefits from diversifying acquisitions? This is a question we will explore. We will also explore the troubling instances where diversification destroys value. This may be surprising to readers, as we will see that companies across the developed and less developed world have a long history of creating very diversified companies. If, and it is a big *if* that we want to explore in detail, diversification does not add to corporate value, and if it sometimes destroys value, then why does it occur? We will see that the question is a complex one that requires lengthy exploration.

While we regularly see examples of companies doing diversifying acquisitions, one time period in the United States, the late 1960s, provides many examples of large companies built through diversifying acquisitions. Thus, it makes sense to begin our discussion of such deals with a look back at the *conglomerate era*.

DIVERSIFYING M&A IN THE CONGLOMERATE ERA

The 1960s in the United States provide us with numerous examples of large-scale diversification. The 1950s and 1960s in the United States were a period of intense antitrust enforcement. Companies that wanted to expand through M&A found that the Justice Department and the Federal Trade Commission challenged many horizontal and even vertical M&A. During this period, deals were challenged that would have quickly qualified for early approval today. Companies that wanted to expand were forced to pursue M&A totally outside their own industry. The absurd antitrust regulatory policies of the U.S. government, policies that regulators would laugh at now, prevented large companies from doing meaningful synergistic acquisitions. Ironically, the government eliminated the possibility of being able to realize synergy on a large scale. The absurdity of such policies is amusing. While we still have poor regulatory policies throughout the world, at least we no longer have such policies in the United States.

The 1950s was an up and down economy with a major war (the Korean War), so the issue of major M&A expansion programs was moot. The 1960s, however, featured an extended economic expansion, and as with many expansions, companies sought rapid growth to take advantage of the growing aggregate demand through M&A, which is usually faster than the slower organic growth.

Thus during the 1960s, the only alternative was M&A outside of the company's main lines of business. This gave rise to what has become known as the conglomerate era. Henri Servaes used a large sample of such firms to show that while in 1961, 55 percent of the firms he studied operated in only one business segment, by 1976 that number had declined to 28 percent.[1] Over that same time period, the percentage of companies that operated in four or more business segments increased from 8 to 30 percent.

Companies made numerous acquisitions across many different industry categories to form highly diversified companies called conglomerates. These companies became some of the largest companies in the United States. Examples include ITT, LTV, Litton Industries, Gulf and Western, Tenneco, Teledyne, and many others. Conglomerates are the extreme form of diversification in that the company includes many businesses that often have little in common with each other.

The track record of the conglomerates of the 1960s is not very impressive. The market turned down by the end of the decade and investors soured on the conglomerates. In addition, the economy slowed dramatically in the 1970s and fell into a deep recession. The conglomerates responded with asset sales and many began the process of *deconglomerization*.

MODERN-DAY U.S. CONGLOMERATES

While many of the huge conglomerates of the 1960s have been dissembled, we still have several very big and largely successful conglomerates operating today. Perhaps the leading example is GE—formerly General Electric. Contrary to what the original name implies, for many years now GE has no longer been merely an electronics-oriented company. Through a pattern of acquisitions and divestitures, the firm has become a diversified conglomerate with operations in insurance, financial services, television stations, plastics, medical equipment, and so on.

During the 1980s and 1990s, at a time when the firm was acquiring and divesting various companies, earnings rose significantly. The market responded favorably to these diversified acquisitions by following the rising pattern of earnings. However, this all came to an end with the subprime crisis, which left the company with large losses in its capital division. Since then the company has been trying to navigate the difficult waters of a serious recession in the United States and a weak recovery while at the same time dealing with a recessed European economy. As a result, many have questioned the company's conglomerate model and the benefits of being in so many diversified industries.

Even with a slow recovery from the Great Recession, and with stagnation in Europe and slower growth in three of the high-growth BRIC countries, China, India, and Brazil, some conglomerates continue to expand and be more diverse. One example is United Technologies. As Figure 4.1 shows, in 2011, no one business area accounted for as much as a quarter of total revenues with Pratt & Whitney comprising 23 percent and Otis Elevator 21 percent of total revenues.

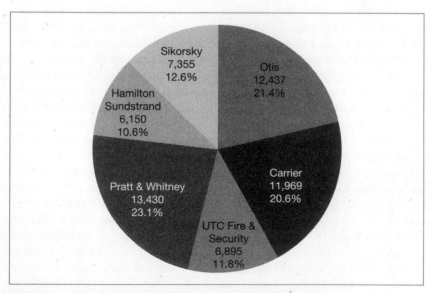

FIGURE 4.1 United Technologies Sales by Segment ($ in Millions)
Source: 2011 annual reports.

United Technologies can trace its roots to the aerospace industry. It was created through the breakup of a company that was formed by William Boeing in 1929. When that entity was broken up in 1934, United Airlines, Boeing, and United Technologies were formed. However, the company expanded outside of aerospace with acquisitions in the 1970s of Otis Elevator and Carrier Refrigerator.

When we look at Figure 4.1, we have to wonder what could be the synergies between Otis Elevator, for example, and Pratt & Whitney or Sikorsky. In addition, how does Carrier Air Conditioning fit with these other very different companies? Having said that, we have to give credit to the overall management of each well-performing unit that has shown decent financial performance in a difficult economy, where most of the component businesses are somewhat cyclical in their earnings pattern.

The market has (belatedly in most cases) voiced its disapproval of several large conglomerates. Some of the companies were forced to break into smaller, more focused units. Tyco and Sara Lee are some examples. However, United Technologies has moved in the opposite direction. While some other conglomerates are admitting that it is likely that the parts will be worth more than the whole and are *deconglomerizing*, UTI has taken the opposite approach, believing a larger diverse conglomerate will better maximize value. Toward that end, in 2012, the company announced that it was acquiring Goodrich Corp. for $16.4 billion in cash.

UTI's argument is that Goodrich will mesh well with its three other aerospace units: Pratt & Whitney (engines), Hamilton Sundstrand (aircraft control systems), and Sikorsky (helicopters). This deal expands the role of aerospace in the company's structure with over half of the revenue of the company coming from aerospace. It also could allow UTI to better compete with large rivals in aerospace such as Honeywell and French supplier Safran SA. The deal does, however, raise questions about what these aerospace units have in common with an elevator or air conditioning business. History tells us that unless the market expresses its disapproval through weak stock prices, that conglomerate structure will likely remain.

Goodrich itself is an interesting story in corporate transformation. It was long known as one of the major tire manufacturers in the United States as well as a major manufacturer of industrial rubber products. This was the case until about 1977. Tires are a cyclical business that is naturally tied to the auto industry. Changes in tire manufacturing and consumption, including a shift to longer-lasting radial tires, meant a slowdown in sales and revenues. Ironically, not unlike the PC segment of the computer industry, technological advancement and the improvement of products have resulted in *lower* long-run profits. That resulting slowdown left this cyclical industry too crowded and a natural candidate for consolidation.

Goodrich of that time period was not well managed and decisions to vertically integrate and make some of its own raw materials (polyvinyl chloride) did not work out well. In Chapter 6, we see that often, vertical integration does not work out. This was the case for Goodrich. The company expanded into this business and incurred much debt to do it. Eventually, it was forced to exit the tire business altogether after one of its biggest competitors, Uniroyal, was taken private. That private entity was then merged with Goodrich's tire business in 1986 in a deal that gave Goodrich 50 percent of the joint venture that combined the two firms. The business still remained troubled, and in 1988 Goodrich sold its stake in the venture thus becoming a non-tire company. It then expanded into various other fields including aerospace. Thus, the company so many people associated with automobile tires has long had nothing to do with tires. Such is the world of corporate *growth*.

PORTFOLIOS OF COMPANIES

In the conglomerate era of the 1960s, it was common for large companies to own many diverse entities and to manage them as though the overall company was a portfolio of many distinct subunits. Harold Geneen, the former CEO of ITT, the quintessential conglomerate, was a master of this art. For many years, he was the most famous CEO in the United States. He was followed by Jack Welch of GE, who enjoyed great success at GE managing its diverse units. However, one has to question how the shareholders of the diverse entity really benefit from investing in a corporate entity that itself is a conglomeration of many other companies. It raises the question: Why is the overall corporation doing the diversification for shareholders when they can do such diversification in a more cost-effective manner themselves? That is, shareholders can choose to purchase shares in some but not all of the companies within the corporate umbrella. Given this is the case, what benefits is management really giving them when they do the *stock picking* for the investors?

Another example of a recent conglomerate, a kind of mini-GE, was Tyco. Run by deal-a-day CEO, Dennis Kozlowski, Tyco combined many acquisitions to form a very large conglomerate that operated in four main business segments: (1) security and electronics, (2) fire protection and flow control, (3) health care and flow control, and (4) financial services. Clearly, financial services has little to do with health care or security and fire protection. The market initially liked Tyco's acquisition program, although accounting issues, such as doing many small acquisitions that were below the 10 percent materiality reporting threshold, may have clouded the true volume of Tyco's deals. Tyco sold off its CIT financial services business shortly after it was acquired. By January 2006, the company had a market capitalization of $62 billion but a weak stock price. It finally succumbed to market pressures and announced that it was selling off its electronics and health care businesses, thus breaking up the conglomerate. As we have previously mentioned, Kozlowski was convicted of stealing corporate wealth and served a long prison sentence, even though during his tenure at Tyco the company he did relatively well—unlike other companies run by convicted CEOs of his era, such as Bernie Ebbers of Worldcom, who pushed their companies into bankruptcy causing shareholders to lose massive amounts of money. In fact, Tyco continued to do fine, which raises questions about the Ebbers-like sentence he received.

It is important to remember that when a parent company acquires a target, especially a large target, it is often a risky venture and one that is costly to implement. The acquirer has to pay an acquisition premium and then invest time and money managing and integrating the target. Admittedly with conglomerates there is not as much integration as the overall company may adopt a more stand-off position and merely monitor the target's performance. The target may end up being a component in an overall portfolio of companies. If the target fails to live up to expectations, it can be sold, and the proceeds can be used to acquirer another company.

The ultimate answer to the shareholders' dilemma lies in what returns the conglomerate generates for them. If the returns are superior to the market, on a risk-adjusted basis, then whether the overall corporate structure makes sense is really moot. If the market approves and enables the company to generate good shareholder returns, then shareholders should be satisfied even if some finance professors are not. At times, the market has been keen on companies such as GE. However, some questions have been leveled at GE and other conglomerates. This has caused many of them to trade at a *diversification discount*. We will discuss this in greater detail later in this chapter.

CASE STUDY OF THE HOLDING COMPANY MODEL AS A BIG FAILURE: VIVENDI

Vivendi was a 100-year-old stodgy French water utility. The company selected former investment banker at Lazard—Jean Marie Massier—to run the quiet business and to maintain the status quo of a company that had proudly stood the test of time, and he proceeded to transform it

(continued)

into an international entertainment and communications company. What else would an investment banker do but do deals as opposed to running the company in its main line of business?

Amazingly, through this formerly quiet water utility Meissner was able to live of his dream of being an entertainment executive. He did this by first buying Seagram Universal—itself a foolish combination of a soft drinks company and Universal Entertainment. Seagrams, a world-renowned name in soft drinks, was thrust into the entertainment and movie business when young Edgar Bronfman expanded out of that family firm's core business, soft drinks, and into the more exciting world of movies and entertainment. After it became part of Vivendi, Meissier could now also enjoy the entertainment dream job.

Meisser's diversification strategy did not stop with Seagrams Universal. He then went on to buy Canal Plus—a French cable TV network. He then purchased Barry Diller's USA Networks in December 2001 for $10.3 billion.[a] He also made other big acquisitions, including buying publisher Houghton Mifflin for $2.2 billion. Perhaps thinking he had not fully transformed the water utility, he also bought U.S. Filter Corporation.

Eventually Vivendi's shareholders decided they had enough. The company incurred a lot of debt to finance Meissner's failed dreams. In 2002, they replaced Meissner with chairman Jean-René Fourtou and CEO Jean-Bernard Levy. Initially, Vivendi began to engage in some restructuring by selling off its health and publishing business in 2002, and then sold its Universal Entertainment unit to GE's NBC unit for $14 billion. But then the process stalled and the company then (unbelievably) started to do M&A again. In 2009, it acquired Brazil Telecom company GVT, and then in 2011 it acquired the recorded music division of EMI for $1.87 billion. As of 2012, Vivendi was still one big holding company (see Figure 4.2). Finally, the board had enough (again) and Levy was forced to step down.

There are a few lessons that can be drawn from this grand saga. One is—"Stick to What You Know Even if It Is Boring." Another is "Don't Bring in a CEO with a history of dealmaking if you won't want to do deals and more deals." For Seagrams, perhaps it is "Help the Kids Get a Job But Don't Let Them Run the Company."

HP's hiring of Carly Fiorina from AT&T—the company with the worst M&A history—is another example of a company hiring a CEO who you should be able to expect to want to do M&A deals and, maybe, not good ones. Lastly, another lesson is that if you bring in new

(continued)

(continued)

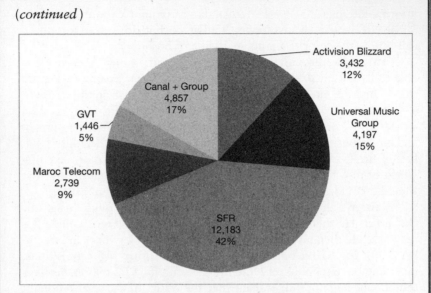

FIGURE 4.2   Revenues by Business Segment (millions of euros): 2011
Source: Vivendi 2011 annual report.

management to downsize and refocus the company, make sure that is what they do. The board should have made sure that the refocusing and downsizing continued and should not have allowed more M&A to go on. We would be remiss if we did not note that GE would later sell off its NBC Universal business to Comcast in two transactions that were completed in 2013. It is pretty funny that the movie business has such an attraction; however, managers should admit that it is much less expensive on shareholders if they simply go to the movie theater on their own once in a while as opposed to asking them to buy the movie producing company.

---

[a] Patrick A. Gaughan, *Mergers: What Can Go Wrong and How to Prevent It* (Hoboken, NJ: John Wiley & Sons, 2004), 115.

THEORETICAL BASIS FOR DIVERSIFICATION

There are several potential benefits from diversification. They include economies of scale benefits. This can occur when companies become bigger through acquisitions. They are then larger enterprises and may realize lower average costs as a result of this greater size. The question becomes: Will the company realize as much in economies of scale when they acquire companies in different business areas as they would from expansion within their main line of business?

Other benefits could possibly come from economies of scope derived from M&A. These economies of scope could come in the marketing of a broader array of products to an expansion group of customers.

Diversification may also provide financial benefits from earnings smoothing. This can occur when companies are acquired that have a different variability in their earnings. When a company has a volatile earnings pattern, such as a firm that markets commodities such as a mining or petroleum company, their earnings may rise and fall mainly as a function of the market price of the commodities rather than the acumen of management. Management may try to offset their natural variability by acquiring companies that have a different variability. We will discuss this further when we consider the *coinsurance* effect of M&A.

Another, more financial, reason for diversification is the attempt to derive benefits from *internal capital markets*. Normally companies finance expansion internally through cash flows or externally through borrowing or the issuance of securities. However, large diversification companies, such as GE, have great financial resources, which they can make available to acquisition targets. This can give the acquired companies a potential competitive advantage—or at least that is the party line. Whether this is the best use of those financial resources is often a more complicated issue.

APPLYING PORTFOLIO THEORY TO CONGLOMERATES?

One possible area of benefits of diversification that has been cited is the *coinsurance effect*. This occurs when firms with imperfectly correlated earnings combine and derive a combined earnings stream that is less volatile than either of the individual firms' earnings stream. The covariance is a statistical measure of the linear association between two variables. If the covariance between earnings of two potential merger candidates is negative, there might be an opportunity to derive coinsurance benefits from a combination of such firms. What the merger partners have to determine is if these coinsurance *benefits* truly provide gains for shareholders beyond what they can achieve on their own. When they purchased their shares in the companies in question, shareholders presumably were aware of the pattern of earnings at the companies. They reconciled the pattern of those earnings, and the investment returns these securities provided, with those of other securities in their portfolio. As we have noted, it is questionable that the managers of the merger candidates are truly providing a benefit for shareholders that they could not achieve on their own and at a lower cost. Mergers motivated by financial diversification may provide benefits for the management who may be then able to demonstrate a less volatile earnings stream. Whether this is truly a benefit for shareholders is a separate issue.

DIVERSIFICATION AND THE ACQUISITION OF LEADING INDUSTRY POSITIONS

Part of the reasoning behind GE's successful diversification strategy has been the types of companies it has acquired. General Electric sought to acquire leading positions in the various industries in which it owned businesses. Leading is usually interpreted as the first or second rank according to market shares. It is believed by acquirers like GE, that the number one or number two position provides a more dominant position, which affords advantages over the smaller competitors. These advantages can manifest themselves in a number of ways, including broader consumer awareness in the marketplace as well as superior distribution networks. Corporations in the secondary ranks, such as numbers four or five, may sometimes be at such a disadvantage that it is difficult for them to generate meaningful returns or to capture much greater market share. Divisions of companies that do not hold a leading position in their respective industry, and which do not have reasonable prospects of cost-effectively acquiring such a position, become candidates for divestiture. The released resources derived from such a divestiture can then be reinvested in other companies to exploit the benefits of their dominant position or used to acquire leading companies in other industries.

CASE STUDY: GE—WHAT TO DO WHEN YOU CAN'T ACHIEVE A LEADING POSITION

While the General Electric Company has enjoyed great success with acquisitions in many different industries, it experienced difficulty turning a profit in the insurance industry. This was underscored in November 2005, when General Electric (GE) announced that it would sell its reinsurance business to Swiss Re for $8.5 billion. GE's CEO at that time, Jeffrey Immelt, successor to the well-known Jack Welch, indicated that the insurance business was "a tough strategic fit for GE" (for a conglomerate the term strategic fit may make one wonder). That business had lost over $700 million in the five years prior to the sale and had required the infusion of $3.2 billion more of GE capital. However, even with the strong financial support of GE, its reinsurance business could

(continued)

not move up in industry rankings relative to leaders Munich Re and Swiss Re. Reinsurance is the part of the insurance industry that provides insurance to insurance companies—hence the term *re*insurance. However, the deal allowed Swiss Re, which would then have total revenues of $34 billion, to overtake Munich Re, which had 2004 sales of just under $29 billion. These two companies are clearly the market leaders as their sales are more than double their nearest rivals, General Re ($10.6 billion) and Hanover Re ($10.1 billion). GE, which marketed its reinsurance business under the name GE Insurance Solutions, had $8.2 billion in total 2004 sales. Munich Re was able to overtake Swiss Re in the years that followed, but both are by far the two leaders in the insurance with Hanover lagging well behind those two leaders.[a]

For GE, this was an admission of failure by a very successful company. GE cut its losses and sold the reinsurance business to another company that was better at insurance than they were. GE has done this before when an acquisition has failed to achieve expected goals. For example, in 1982, it sold off its Trane air conditioning business, which, with its 10 percent market share, was an also-ran by GE standards and was more trouble that it was worth.[b] In many ways, this is a sign of good management as managers need to know when to cut their losses and focus on areas in which they can achieve greater returns rather than continue with a failing business just to avoid having to admit mistakes to shareholders. Given the volume of deals that GE does, all of them are not going to be a success. We also noticed that with J&J—another company partly built using M&A. The key is to quickly recognize and admit mistakes and refocus on the winners. It was good management by Immelt to admit the mistake and move on rather than pour money resources into a company that was not a good strategic fit and was a drain on the overall business. We see some of the same willingness to admit a mistake and change direction at J&J. It is no wonder both companies have been so successful for so long. The problem with GE, however, is it made a very large investment in financial services, which made the company look good in the first half of the 2000s, but which proved to be another major flop. Unfortunately, the GE of the post-Welsh era has had some very large flops.

---

[a] Carrie Burns, "Top Global Reinsurers," *Insurance Networking News*, September 6, 2011.

[b] Patrick A. Gaughan, *Mergers: What Can Go Wrong and How to Prevent It* (Hoboken, NJ: John Wiley & Sons, 2004), 51–52.

ACHIEVING A NUMBER ONE OR TWO RANKING IS NOT A PANACEA

Simply achieving a number one or two ranking in an industry is not sufficient to guarantee success. This was demonstrated in the farm equipment business. In 1994, Case Corp. found itself mired in a distant third position in farm equipment business with little hope of catching the leader, John Deere Corp. The success that companies like General Electric had in using a dominant position in various markets to outpace smaller rivals surely was not lost on the management of Case when it decided to merge with the number two company in the business, New Holland. The 1999 $4.6 billion (8.1 billion on 2013 $) merger created CNH Global—a company with sales of almost $11 billion. These sales would grow to over $19 billion by 2011. However, merely being in the number two position did not prevent the combined company from losing further ground to larger competitors such as John Deere, International Harvester, Caterpillar, and a host of other big companies such as Komatsu. Since the merger, CNH has had trouble generating profits and continues to try to cut costs. The combination did not create a market leader—just a larger version of the two merger partners that still have trouble dealing with the cyclical nature of the industry.

DIVERSIFICATION TO ENTER MORE PROFITABLE INDUSTRIES

One reason management may opt for diversified expansion is its desire to enter industries that are more profitable than the acquiring firm's current industry. It could be that the parent company's industry has reached the mature stage or that the competitive pressures within that industry preclude the possibility of raising prices to a level where extra-normal profits can be enjoyed.

One problem that some firms may encounter when they seek to expand by entering industries that offer better profit opportunities is the lack of an assurance that those profit opportunities will persist for an extended time in the future. Industries that are profitable now may not be as profitable in the future. We saw a great example of this in the case study on Montana Power, which we featured in Chapter 2.

Competitive pressures serve to bring about a movement toward a long-term equalization of rates of return across industries. Clearly, this does not mean that the rates of return in all industries at any moment in time are equal. The forces of competition that move industries to have equal returns are offset by opposing forces, such as industrial development, that cause industries to have varying rates of return. Those above-average-return industries that do not have imposing barriers to entry will experience declining returns until they reach the cross-industry average.

Economic theory implies that in the long run only industries that are difficult to enter will have above-average returns. This implies that a diversification program to enter more profitable industries may not be successful in the long run. The expanding firm may not be able to enter those industries that exhibit persistently above-average returns because of barriers that prevent entry and may be able to enter only the industries with low barriers. When entering the low-barrier industry, the expanding company will probably be forced to compete against other entrants who were attracted by temporarily above-average returns and low barriers. The increased number of competitors will drive down returns and cause the expansion strategy to fail.

EMPIRICAL EVIDENCE ON DIVERSIFICATION

While one can debate the pros and cons of conglomerates, it may be more useful to see the shareholder wealth effects of diversified companies and the market's reaction to the diversifying acquisitions. This will enable us to see the market's assessment, one made through the objective interaction of many buyers and sellers across the world. This does not mean that the reaction is always correct. However, it is an important piece of evidence that needs to be considered.

EMPIRICAL EVIDENCE ON THE ACQUISITION PROGRAMS OF THE 1960s

Given the volume of diversifying deals that took place in the 1960s, coupled with the huge conglomerates that were built at that time, it would be useful to review the research on the shareholder wealth effects of these deals and resulting corporate structures. Schipper and Thompson have analyzed the wealth effects of firms that announced acquisition programs.[2] Specifically, they considered what impact an announcement of an acquisitions program had on the value of the acquiring firm. They examined announcements of such programs before 1967 to 1970, because regulatory changes such as the Williams Act and the Tax Reform Act of 1969 took place in these years. These regulatory changes created certain impediments to the types of acquisitions that occurred in the 1960s. The study found that during this period, acquisition programs were capitalized as positive net present value programs. These results indicate that, at least before the regulatory changes of the late 1960s, the market had a positive view of acquisition programs, many of which involved substantial diversification. The favorable response of the market to the diversifying acquisitions of that time helps explain why the third takeover wave was as significant as it was. Another study by Scherer and Ravenscraft also showed that investors who bought shares of the 13 conglomerates in their sample, which included many of the more notable ones (such as ITT, Gulf & Western, Textron, and Teledyne) prior to the start of the conglomerate boom outperformed the market, but those who purchased them after the merger wave took hold, earned returns below the market.[3] Some point to these results to imply a favorable view of the conglomerates that became so prominent during this time period. Another view, though, was that the market, like the companies themselves, was looking for growth and some accepted, for a period of time, the view that this growth could be profitably achieved by these very diverse and huge conglomerate structures. In addition, the bizarre antitrust policies pursued by the Justice Department basically precluded true synergistic M&A. After the market had more time and data to examine, and after the economy turned down, the market changed this assessment. It is also important to recall that given the strangely intense antitrust enforcement at the time, companies were prevented from engaging on more synergistic deals so those investment options were not available to investors.

Other studies also show positive shareholder wealth effects of conglomerates. For example, Elger and Clark found that returns to stockholders in conglomerate acquisitions are greater than in nonconglomerate acquisitions.[4] The study, which examined 337 mergers between 1957 and 1975, indicated that conglomerate mergers provided superior gains relative to nonconglomerate mergers. The researchers reported these gains for both buyer and seller firms, with substantial gains registered by stockholders of seller firms and moderate gains for buying company stockholders. This finding was supported by later research by Wansley, Lane, and Yang. They focused on 52 nonconglomerate and 151 conglomerate mergers. It was also found, however, that returns to shareholders were larger in horizontal and vertical acquisitions than in conglomerate acquisitions.[5]

While the studies we have cited show some positive shareholder wealth effects of conglomerates, they may really be reflecting an overly optimistic initial assessment. The subsequent undoing of many of these deals, sometimes through bust-up takeovers, spinoffs, and divestitures, has confirmed the questionable nature of this expansion strategy.

HOW LIKELY IS IT THAT DIVERSIFYING ACQUISITIONS WILL END UP BEING SOLD OFF?

In Chapter 10, we discuss the research of Kaplan and Weisbach, who did a study of 271 large acquisitions that took place over the period 1971 through 1982, and which they followed until the end of the 1980s. They found that a total of 43.9 percent of the deals were divested by 1989. In addition, they determined that diversifying deals were four times more likely to be sold off than nondiversifying transactions. Moreover, 38 percent of diversifying deals in their sample were unsuccessful, while only 13 percent of nondiversifying deals were failures.

Other studies, such as one by Michael Porter, actually found an even higher percentage.[6] Porter found that over half of deals that brought the company into new fields were later divested. His study is also noteworthy as his sample included leading companies—ones that the market considered to be well managed. However, the company could be well managed when it comes to their core business and yet have an ill-conceived M&A strategy.

IS THERE A DIVERSIFICATION DISCOUNT?

When diversified companies are formed through diverse acquisitions, does the combination raise value relative to the combined value of the individual businesses, assuming these are not combined? Alternatively, could the combination destroy value? That is, does the fact that the diverse businesses were combined under one large corporate umbrella destroy value? In other words, is there a *diversification discount*?

Using the aforementioned large sample drawn from the 1960s, Henry Servaes compared the Tobin's q of diversified firms to those that were not diversified.[7] Tobin's q, named after the Nobel prize-winning economist from Yale, is the ratio of the market value of a firm, as measured by the market value of its equity and debt, to the replacement costs of its assets. If a company has a Tobin q of greater than one, the market values the company at an amount that is greater than what it would cost to replace the company's assets or *rebuild the firm*.

Servaes found no evidence that diversification increased corporate values. On the contrary, he found that the Tobin's q for diversified firms was significantly lower than those for multisegment companies. Other research has found that the diversification discount was not restricted to the conglomerate era. A study conducted by Berger and Ofek, using a large sample of firms over the 1986 to 1991 sample period, found that diversification resulted in a loss of firm value that averaged between 13 and 15 percent.[8] This study estimated the imputed value of a diversified firm's segments as if they were separate firms. The results found that the loss of firm value was not affected by firm size but was less when the diversification occurred within related industries. The loss of firm value results was buttressed by the fact that the diversified segments showed lower operating profitability than single-line businesses. The findings also showed that diversified firms overinvested in the diversified segments more than single-line businesses. This implies that overinvestment may be a partial cause of the loss of value associated with diversification.

Value-reducing effects of diversification were detected by Lang and Stulz.[9] Using a large sample of companies (in excess of 1,000), Lang and Stulz found that greater corporate diversification in the 1980s was inversely related to the Tobin's q of these firms. These findings are quite consistent with the aforementioned research by Servaes and Berger and Ofek. In spite of this impressive evidence, this conclusion is not universally accepted by finance researchers. Villalonga believes that the diversification discount is merely an artifact of the data used by these researchers.[10] He states that the data used by these researchers were artificially restricted by Financial Accounting Standards Board definition of segments, as well as requirements that only segments that constitute 10 percent or more of a company's business are required to be reported. Using a data source that is not affected by this problem, Villalonga finds a diversification premium, as opposed to a discount. In addition, there are other studies that also not only fail to find a diversification discount but that imply that unrelated deals may at times be superior to related M&As. We will return to this finding in a couple of pages when we compare related to unrelated M&As.

FOCUS HYPOTHESIS

Other studies have tackled the problem differently. Comment and Jarrell analyzed a sample of exchange-listed firms from 1978 to 1989. They found that increased corporate focus or specialization was consistent with shareholder wealth maximization.[11] In addition, they found the companies in their sample that experienced the worst returns were the ones that decreased their focus.

Comment and Jarrell concluded that the commonly cited benefits of diversification, economies of scope, go unrealized and that the access to greater internal capital does not appear to affect the diversified firm's propensity to pursue external capital. One benefit of diversification that was found was that diversified firms tend to be targets of hostile takeovers less frequently than their less diversified counterparts. Given that such hostile takeovers often result in higher premiums for target shareholders, some might consider this a dubious benefit. Nonetheless, diversified firms were more active participants, as both buyers and sellers, in the market for corporate control.

TYPES OF FOCUS INCREASES

A study by Dasilas and Leventi analyzed the types of focus-increasing spinoffs that had the greatest positive shareholder wealth effects.[12] Their research compared spinoffs that increased industrial focus with those that increased geographical focus. Spinoffs that increased industrial focus generated positive shareholder wealth effects, while those that increase geographical focus did not. In addition, the positive market response to increases in industrial focus was greater for U.S. spinoffs than it was for European deals.

FOCUS-INCREASING ASSET SALES RAISE VALUE

When companies notice their market values are below the values that would result from determining the estimated market value of all its major business units as standalone entities, they may look to asset sales to raise their equity price. John and Ofek used several accounting measures of performance, such as operating margins and return on assets, to determine if a company's performance improved after it sold off assets.[13] They compared 321 divestitures that resulted in greater focus with ones that did not. They found that only those firms in their sample that had greater focus after the assets sales showed improved performance. Those that sold assets but did not have an increase in focus failed to show improved performance. Thus, their conclusion is that it is the focus-enhancing effects of the divestitures, not just the simple act of a divestiture, that are the source of the value gains. These value gains can then serve to undo the diversification discount.

EXPLANATION FOR THE DIVERSIFICATION DISCOUNT

On the surface, we may be led to simply conclude that diversification itself destroys value. We can easily think of some very logical explanations for this destruction process. Perhaps it is the greater managerial demands of a diverse and less focused enterprise that limits the potential of diverse companies. Perhaps it is simply wasteful managers who pursue diverse M&A for their own self-interests. For example, the larger diversified company might compensate their senior managers much better and allow them to believe they were great empire builders. However, could it also be the greater analytical demands such enterprises present for market analysts who may be inclined to assign them lower valuations compared to more focused business?

Many analysts specialize in a type of business. For example, in its heyday, Altria was followed by tobacco analysts who covered the Philip Morris part of the business but also food analysts who covered the Kraft side. Investors had to kind of put the two together when accessing the investment prospects of the overall entity. The problem was even more challenging when Altria owned Miller beer and beer industry analysts had to chime in with their thoughts about this relatively weaker business.

An interesting study by Lamont and Polk of a large sample of 2,390 diverse firms, covering the 19-year period of 1979 through 1997, raises some questions regarding a simple explanation for value destruction of diverse companies.[14] Among their various findings was that companies with discounts have *higher* subsequent returns than companies that traded at a premium! Could it be that the market is incorrectly assigning discounts that turn out to be wrongfully assigned when the diverse firms end up generating higher returns than what the discounts implied?

The Lamont and Polk story does not eliminate the challenges to diversified firms. Their analysis focused on just returns and there are many other measures, such as profitability, capital expenditures, and other fundamental measures that may give support for the traditional explanations of the diversification discount such as irrational managers, productivity, corporate waste, and so on. However, for adherents of behavioral finance, of which there have been rapidly growing ranks, one additional explanation for the diversification discount may be that the market irrationally undervalues diverse companies. At a minimum, the Lamont and Polk research shed light on the complexity of the *diversification puzzle*.

RELATED VERSUS UNRELATED DIVERSIFICATION

Diversification does not mean conglomerization. That is, it is possible to diversify into fields that are related to the buyer's business. An example of a related diversification occurred in 1994, when Merck purchased Medco. Merck was one of the largest pharmaceutical companies in the world, and Medco was one of the larger marketers of pharmaceuticals in the United States. The two businesses are different in that one company is a manufacturer and the other company is kind of a distributor. Nonetheless, the two companies are both in the broadly defined pharmaceutical industry, and each has a greater knowledge of the other's business than an outside firm would have. In addition, there may be a more reliable expectation of economies of scale and scope in related diversifications because a buyer may be better able to leverage its current resources and expertise if it stays closer to its current business activities. However, while these two companies were leaders in their respective segments of the drug industry, their combination did not yield synergistic benefits. Merck assumed that with the advent of managed care, owning a company such as Medco would provide it with competitive advantages. Indeed, as we discussed in Chapter 3, shortly after the Merck-Medco merger, in 1994, some of Merck's competitors thought the same, as Roche acquired Syntex Corp. for $5.3 billion and Eli Lilly bought PCS Health Systems for $4.1 billion. Unfortunately, relatedness was not enough to ensure success, and Merck and Medco had to later undo the deal after concluding that they did not understand the regulatory environment that would not allow Medco to influence the usage by physicians and consumers of its drugs. This eliminated certain synergistic benefits. Eli Lilly's acquisition of PCS was also ill fated and Eli Lilly had to write off $2.4 billion of the $4.1 billion, almost 60 percent of what it paid for the company, just three years after the acquisition.[15]

It is not always clear when another business is related. One example we discussed in Chapter 3, which was put forward by Young and Morck, is the 3M Corp.[16] 3M is well known for its brand of Scotch tapes. However, the company branched out a long time ago and extended its expertise to the manufacture and marketing of other related products, such as Post-it Notes and other tape products like VCR tapes. Given the adhesive and tape-related aspects of these products, they seem like product and expertise extensions. However, the modern day 3M is a far cry from the tape manufacturer some people still think of it as. As Figure 4.3 shows, it is a $30 billion company with very diverse business activities.

There is evidence that shows that the track record of related acquisitions is significantly better than that of unrelated acquisitions. Morck, Shleifer, and Vishny found that in their sample, the market punished shareholders in

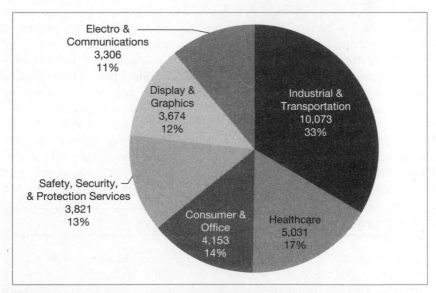

FIGURE 4.3 3M 2011 Revenues by Business Segment ($ in Millions)
Source: 3M 2011 annual report.

companies that engaged in unrelated acquisitions, whereas shareholders in companies that made related acquisitions did significantly better.[17] Their study of 326 acquisitions between 1975 and 1987 presented a more favorable picture of this type of diversification. Rather, a particular form of diversification, unrelated diversification, showed poor results. They measured relatedness by determining if the two firms had at least one of their top three lines of business in the same Standard Industrial Classification (SIC) code. Not all the research on related diversification shows the same results. For example, the result found by Agrawal, Jaffe, and Mandelker was the opposite of the result of Morck, Shleifer, and Vishny. Their findings, obviously using a different data set, showed that unrelated acquisitions outperformed related acquisitions.[18] In addition, a recent study by Aggarwal and Baxamusa showed that nonrelated acquirers experienced higher announcement period returns than related acquirers.[19] Nonrelated acquirers also have better post-deal performance, implying that these deals are value enhancing. Nonrelated acquirers generate these returns and post-M&A performance in spite of the fact that they tended to have a higher costs of capital than unrelated bidders. Aggarwal and Baxamusa postulated that the targets, in an internal capital market, were subsidizing the investments of the acquirers. This leads to a perplexing conclusion that nonrelated acquirers may have trouble funding their own capital investments but not in funding acquisitions. This conclusion is supported by the authors' additional finding that nonrelated acquisitions tend to be stock-financed deals. Perhaps the market is overvaluing the shares of nonrelated acquirers, allowing them to pursue nonrelated targets that, in turn, they use to subsidize the capital needs their other business units.

The key question seems to be: Are the two companies related in a way that will generate greater benefits if they are combined than if they were to remain independent? It is meaningless to defend an M&A by contending that because the companies are related, the M&A will likely yield benefits. While it is true that research shows that the track record of related M&A *may* be better than unrelated, each deal stands on its own. Dealmakers have to show that the relatedness, or others factors, will result in a successful combination. That is, they need to show how the ways in which they are related will yield benefits such as synergies.

CASE STUDY: LVMH—IS LUXURY RELATED?

If the track record of related diversifications is better than unrelated, then how do we define *related*? This is not that obvious and, unfortunately, is open to interpretation. If it is misinterpreted, it

(*continued*)

can result in losses for shareholders. One such example was LVMH's fifth-merger-wave expansion strategy. LVMH, which stands for Louis Vuitton, Moet, and Hennessy, led by its flamboyant CEO Bernard Arnault, seems to see any connection to luxury to be related. The Paris-based company went on an acquisition binge that focused on a wide variety of companies that marketed products or services to upper-end customers. This led them to acquire such major brand names as Chaumet jewelry, Dom Perignon (part of Moet), Fendi, Givenchy, Donna Karan, Loewe leather goods, Sephora, TAG Heuer, Thomas Pink shirts, and Veuve Cliquot champagne. The company has become a clearing-house for luxury products, but the combination of various different acquired companies has provided few, if any, synergies. Many of the acquired businesses, such as Fendi and Donna Karan,while major inter-national brands, generated few profits. In November 1999, LVMH stretched the luxury-related connection by buying fine art auctioneer Phillips De Pury & Luxembourgh for $115 million. However, in doing so, Arnault violated several rules of merger success. First, he acquired a company that was a distant third behind Sotheby's and Christie's. Second, he stretched the definition of *related* so far that there were no possible synergies. Finally, he acquired a company that needed a large cash infusion with little potential for it to be recouped—not a good way to start the integration process. As with many other failed deals, CEO Arnault went unchecked by his directors and shareholders paid the price. LVMH eventually admitted this failure and sold off the art auctioneering company at a loss. Clearly, defining *related* as any luxury good or service was a faulty strategy. Relatedness is a subjective concept and the more narrow the definition, the more likely the deal is to be successful.

WHY ARE *VERY* DIVERSIFIED COMPANIES ALLOWED TO FORM? BEWARE OF THE EMPIRE BUILDERS

Given the questionable track record of many, but not all, diversified compa-nies, the obvious question arises: Why are they formed in the first place? Why does the market allow such corporate structures to be built? There seem to be several answers. One of them is that corporate CEOs love empire building. In Chapter 9, we explore in detail the incentives for CEOs to build empires. Larger empires pay higher compensation than small empires. In addition, larger empires feed the CEO's ego more than small ones. Moreover, a more diversified company will generate less volatile returns, which may lower the probability that management has to report lower returns during certain periods and possibly be forced out.

Another part of the answer seems to be that the market and even the media tend to be somewhat gullible and forgiving. For example, the market and the media were very accepting when Sandy Weill was building his diverse and dysfunctional financial conglomerate of Citigroup. There were few protests when he paid himself up to a quarter of a billion dollars in some years for putting together a dysfunctional financial conglomerate that, along with other highly flawed financial services firms, helped cause the subprime crisis. The market and the media also have been very accepting when other absurd combinations, such as in the case of Sara Lee, have been formed. It is worthwhile considering the diversified businesses that were combined under the Sara Lee umbrella.

CASE STUDY: SARA LEE

Sara Lee's history as a conglomerate is so amazing, it is comical. Through a series of very diverse acquisitions, it assembled a diverse group of businesses that had absolutely nothing in common with each

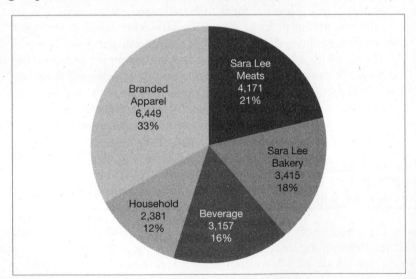

FIGURE 4.4   Sara Lee Sales by Segment: 2004 ($ in Millions)
Source: Sara Lee 2004 annual report.

(continued)

other and looked downright silly. In its heyday of its conglomerateness, the firm fielded businesses ranging from underwear to meats to bakery goods (see Figure 4.4). One would think that its board of directors as well as the market and the media would ask the simple question: What does, for example, men's underwear have to do with high-calorie products like Sara Lee cakes and cholesterol-filled Ball Park franks? Perhaps the strategy was that if the cake division sells more high-calorie foods to men, they will more regularly have to replace their underwear as their waistlines expand? However, even this strategy was a *stretch* (forgive me for that one) that did not bear fruit.

While the market and the media seemed to be very accepting of Sara Lee's structure during the years 1995 to 2004, this started to change in 2005. Finally, a weak stock price forced the company to make some obvious changes. In that year, Sara Lee began the process of disposing of assets. In 2006, it spun off its branded apparel division into a separate, publicly held company that traded under the name Hanesbrands. This company performed relatively well in the market. In that same year, Sara Lee also divested its European Meats business. That left it with the bakery and the U.S. meat businesses—two businesses that still lack strong synergy.

As we will discuss in Chapter 10, it was common that when companies announced plans to break apart major units, the stock price normally got a boost. The market, however, did not jump for joy when Sara Lee started its initial breakup. One of the reasons was that the focusing strategy was only partly done and the remaining units still lacked necessary focus. In addition, a cohesive strategy still had not fully taken hold. Finally, in June 2012, the company announced that it was making the U.S. meat business and the bakery business separate companies. Why this process took so long is a great example of why corporations—sometimes large, diverse corporations—are simply not very efficient business structures.

DO MANAGERIAL AGENDAS DRIVE M&A?

Managers have their own personal agendas and these may differ from that of the company. For managers, and CEOs in particular, it may be to extend their stay in their positions and to continue to receive what in the United States are bountiful compensations and perks. This monetary compensation is on top of the psychic income they receive from being The Big Cheese.

Morck, Shleifer, and Vishny analyzed 326 acquisitions over the period 1975 to 1987. They found that bad deals were driven by the objectives of the managers doing the deals. They found that three types of acquisitions caused lower and usually negative announcement period returns. These were: diversifying M&A, acquiring a rapidly growing target and acquiring a company when the managers have a poor performance track record prior to the deals. Their findings about diversification are further evidence that such a strategy is questionable. However, their results related to rapidly growing targets probably reflects the fact that it is hard to buy growth, and when you do, you will likely be forced to overpay. We saw this in Chapter 3.

Their findings related to having a bad managerial track record are also quite intuitive. If you are bad at running the business you have, adding to it and thereby increasing the managerial demands will only worsen managerial performance. Perhaps managers are good at managing a specific type of focused business. Allowing them to foray into areas beyond their knowledge base may be a prescription for disaster. On the other hand, senior management at companies that have been historically diverse, such as GE, are in the business of managing very diverse enterprises. These management abilities are their skill set. In effect, this is what they do.

NOTES

1. Henri Saerves, "The Value of Diversification During the Conglomerate Merger Wave," *Journal of Finance* 51, no. 4 (September 1996): 1201–1225.
2. Katherine Schipper and Rex Thompson, "The Value of Merger Activity," *Journal of Financial Economics* 11, nos. 1–4 (April 1983): 85–119.
3. David Ravenscraft and Frederick Scherer, "Mergers and Managerial Performance," in John Coffee, Louis Lowenstein, and Susan Rose Ackerman, eds., *Knights, Raiders and Targets* (New York: Oxford University Press, 1988), 194–210.
4. Peter T. Elgers and John J. Clark, "Merger Types and Shareholder Returns: Additional Evidence," *Financial Management* 9, no. 2 (Summer 1980): 66–72.
5. James Wansley, William Lane, and Ho Yang, "Abnormal Returns to Acquired Firms by Type of Acquisition and Method of Payment," *Financial Management* 12, no. 3 (Autumn 1983): 16–22.
6. Michael Porter, "From Competitive Advantage to Corporate Strategy," *Harvard Business Review* (1987): 43–59.
7. Henri Servaes, "The Value of Diversification During the Conglomerate Merger Wave," *Journal of Finance* 51, no. 4 (September 1996): 1201–1225.
8. P. G. Berger and E. Ofek, "Diversification's Effect on Firm Value," *Journal of Financial Economics* 37, no. 1 (January 1995): 39–65.

9. Larry Lang and Rene Stulz, "Tobin's q, Corporate Diversification and Firm Performance," *Journal of Political Economy* 102, no. 6 (December 1994): 1248–1280.

10. Belen Villalonga, "Diversification Discount or Premium? New Evidence from the Business Information Tracking Series," *Journal of Finance* 59, no. 2 (April 2004): 479–506.

11. Robert Comment and Gregg Jarrell, "Corporate Focus and Stock Returns," *Journal of Financial Economics* 37, no. 1 (January 1995): 67–87.

12. Apostolos Dasilas and Stergios Leventi, "Wealth Effects and Operating Performance of Spin-Offs: International Evidence," Working Paper. International Hellenic University, Greece.

13. Kose John and Eli Ofek, "Asset Sales and Increase in Focus," *Journal of Financial Economics* 37 (1995): 105–126.

14. Owen Lamont and Christopher Polk, "The Diversification Discount: Cash Flows Versus Returns," *Journal of Finance* 56 (October 2001): 1693–1721.

15. Michael A. Hitt, Jeffrey S. Harrison, and R. Duane Ireland, *Mergers and Acquisitions: A Guide to Creating Shareholder Value* (New York: Oxford University Press, 2001), 123.

16. Bernard Young and Robert Morck, "When Synergy Creates Real Value," in *Mastering Strategy*, University of Michigan Business School Website paper.

17. Randall Morck, Andrei Shleifer, and Robert Vishny, "Do Managerial Objectives Drive Bad Acquisitions?" *Journal of Finance* 45, no. 1 (March 1990): 31–48.

18. Anup Agrawal, Jeffrey F. Jaffe, and Gershon N. Mandelker, "The Post-Merger Performance of Acquiring Firms: A Reexamination of an Anomaly," *Journal of Finance* 47, no. 4 (September 1992): 1605–1671.

19. Rajesh K. Aggarwal and Mufaddal Baxamusa, "Unrelated Acquisitions, Paper Presented at the American Finance Association Meetings, January 2013, San Diego.

CHAPTER **5**

Horizontal Integration and M&A

Horizontal integration refers to combinations between competitors as opposed to those who have a buyer-seller relationship. Essentially, it means buying or merging with your rivals. There are several reasons why companies might pursue horizontal deals including gaining competitive advantages and market power over their rivals as well as seeking consolidation economies of scale. In this chapter, we explore the evidence that exists regarding the extent to which these types of mergers and acquisitions (M&A) generate benefits. As with other types of M&A, we see that sometimes they yield great benefits and others leave the participants no better off and sometimes even worse. This latter possibility is somewhat surprising in light of the fact that horizontal deals do not have some of the inherent problems as other types of M&A, such as diversifying deals. With horizontal M&A, we are merging two businesses in the same industry. It is reasonable to expect that the likelihood of success should be greater than other types of M&A. This is true, but horizontal deals can still present their own challenges.

ADVANTAGES OF HOLDING THE ONE AND TWO POSITION IN THE INDUSTRY

A horizontal merger between two of the larger companies in an industry may allow the combined entity to attain the number one or two position in the industry. This position by itself may convey competitive benefits over rivals. We have discussed this concept in Chapter 4, where we considered highly diverse companies, such as conglomerates, pursuing a strategy of holding business units in diverse industries that held a number one or two position in their respective industries. In this chapter, we discuss how a focused company can achieve competitive advantages by using horizontal M&A to move into the position of the top two companies in its industry.

We discussed in Chapter 4 how Jack Welch, long-time successful CEO of GE, has often touted the strategy of acquiring the number one or number two position in an industry. Welch's thesis was that being in the number one or two position gave these companies so many advantages that it was difficult for the somewhat smaller rivals to effectively compete. It is always difficult to put forward a general rule that will fit all industries in all geographical markets. However, it is intuitive that the larger firms should possess resources and other advantages that smaller rivals lack.

The number one or number two company in an industry may be able to enjoy greater buyer power when dealing with suppliers. They also have larger market shares, and usually this conveys greater name recognition with consumers. In addition, because they are larger, they can have bigger marketing budgets that allow them to pursue a broader marketing strategy, which may greatly enhance consumer awareness. The smaller rivals, on the other hand, have to struggle to keep up. Suppliers may not be as accommodating to them as they are to the larger rivals. Many attractive marketing options may simply be financially out of reach for the smaller companies. One example is the U.S. cruise line industry, discussed in Chapter 3. At one time, the industry featured many smaller companies. These companies could not afford a national television advertising campaign and could not attract enough interest from travel agents who are major marketers of cruises. When the industry consolidated, larger companies such as Carnival, Royal Caribbean, and Norwegian Cruise Line were able to offer an array of different-priced cruises to cater to the tastes and budgets of a variety of potential cruisers.

In capital-intensive industries, such as the mobile telecom industry, which we discuss later in this chapter, a large customer base is needed to lower average costs. The capital costs of a large mobile network that covers the whole nation and offers dependable service and fewer dropped calls are very expensive. In addition, competitive pressure forces rivals to mount expensive marketing campaigns to maintain market share. Further significant expenditures are needed to expand market share in a process that is a zero sum game as gains come at the expense of rivals who are also spending aggressively to maintain the share they have. As we will see in the following section, this partially explains why Sprint/Nextel, T-Mobile, and Metro PCS failed to enjoy the success of Verizon and AT&T.

In Chapter 2, we discussed how Cisco has very successfully used M&A to grow. The company seeks to have a 50 percent market share in the segment of any subcategory of its industry that it enters. While it considers small acquisitions, in the past it has avoided sectors in which it could not get a 20 percent market share right off the bat.[1] Unless there is a reason to believe that due to being part of Cisco, the target will expand quickly and become a more major player in its segment, Cisco would tend to avoid such deals. This became more the case as the company has grown so much and is now a $46 billion company (year ending July 2012), and smaller deals had less of an impact on it.

BENEFITS OF SIZE: SPOTLIGHT ON THE MOBILE TELECOMMUNICATIONS INDUSTRY

One industry where size really matters is mobile telecommunications. Consider the U.S. mobile market where AT&T and Verizon are the two largest companies (see Figure 5.1). In this industry, mobile providers negotiate with hardware suppliers so as to be able to offer the most innovative products. For example, AT&T secured great advantages over rivals like Verizon by being able to be the first in the United States to offer the iPhone. This enabled AT&T to win away customers from Verizon, which many claimed had better service and coverage at the time. With the large influx of customers, AT&T was able to expand its network and service area coverage, which helped it close the gap in this area with Verizon. In many areas, Verizon had better coverage and fewer dropped calls. However, with the iPhone, AT&T was able to get a leg up on Verizon while it vigorously worked to enhance its network.

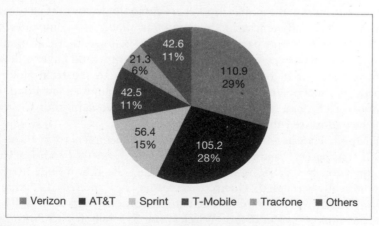

FIGURE 5.1 U.S. Wireless Market by Number of Subscribers

Companies in the mobile telecommunication industry compete not just to be able to offer the latest and most innovative devices; they also compete in offering the fastest networks such as a 4G network. 4G, which stands for fourth generation, offers a speed of service that is comparable to home broadband Internet services that customers are already used to. Smaller rivals, such as Sprint, had lagged behind the larger companies in being able to offer such expensive services. Competitors in their field have to invest significant sums to build out their networks. For the bigger companies like AT&T and Verizon, they bought the spectrum they needed to provide fast services. Companies such as Sprint had to be more innovative and try to accomplish this through alliances and partnerships. For example, in 2008, Sprint entered into a partnership to acquire a large stake in Clearwire, which was a wireless company that had a significant amount of spectrum. Using these resources, Sprint actually became the first company in the United States to offer 4G service. It was also the first one to offer a 4G smartphone. In 2012 Sprint, using cash from the sale of a stake to Japan's Softbank, acquired the remaining part of Clearwire, which they did not own.

The large resources of the two largest players allowed them to overtake Sprint in being the number one 4G service provider. The fourth player, T-Mobile (a company that we discuss separately), basically signaled its frustration in being unable to effectively compete with the other three major players and made an unsuccessful attempt to exit the U.S. market by selling itself to AT&T. Unfortunately for both AT&T and T-Mobile, this merger was opposed by the U.S. Justice department and was abandoned. T-Mobile's pain was greatly lessened by the large breakup fee it received from AT&T.

The challenges in the mobile market are compounded by the fact that there are technological differences in the networks that these companies offer. Providers such as Sprint have to convince the major equipment manufacturers to build devices to fit their network or Sprint would have to devote a significant amount of financial resources to shift to the technology that competitors such as Verizon, which uses a technology called Long Term Evolution (LTE), employ. However, through its acquisition of Clearwire, Sprint has addressed this issue.

T-Mobile USA had been increasingly losing customers to rivals in 2010 and 2011. Its parent, Deutsche Telecom AG, saw the merger with—or rather, the acquisition by—AT&T as a way of exiting the U.S. mobile market in which it really struggled. Duetsche Telecom had entered the large and seemingly lucrative U.S. mobile telecommunications market in 2001 with the acquisition of Voice Stream Wireless for $35 billion and Powertel for $24 billion. The company changed its name to T-Mobile in 2002. These were expensive acquisitions of also-rans, which gave Deutsche Telecom the ability to compete in a highly competitive market against larger and firmly entrenched rivals. It did not work out well at all. It also served to reinforce the idea that the number one and two companies, in this case Verizon and AT&T, usually have great advantages over smaller rivals. It also showed that in capital-intensive industries, these advantages can be even more pronounced.

As we will discuss, the AT&T and T-Mobile deal, which was to be T-Mobile's exit strategy, was opposed by the Justice Department and had to be cancelled. T-Mobile was compensated by a $4 billion breakup fee, but the focus on the merger with AT&T left it even further behind rivals. Once it realized it would be on its own to fight it out with stronger rivals AT&T and Verizon, it then had to resume its focus on being able to offer 4G LTE technology—a great expense it was hoping to avoid. While the breakup fee was a nice benefit of the failed deal, the competitive delay caused by the merger imposed another very sizable cost.

After the failure of the AT&T–T-Mobile combination, Sprint Nextel considered an acquisition of smaller rival MetroPCS. Sprint was facing the costly burden of expanding its network, combined with its expensive Apple, Inc. iPhone deal. Ultimately, in late February 2012, Sprint's board rejected an offer of a 30 percent premium for MetroPCS. Various reasons can explain the rejection of the deal. MetroPCS was using virtually all of its network so it would not help alleviate Sprint's network capacity constraint, although Sprint's network might help with MetroPCS' customers. Sprint was also still smarting from its troubled merger with Nextel in 2005, which was something of a road map for how *not* to do M&A. One lesson the Sprint board learned from that failed deal was that M&A between two troubled companies may not make one untroubled company, unless the underlying problems of the two merger candidates can be fixed through M&A.

The situation changed as we moved later into 2012. T-Mobile, having lost an opportunity to join with AT&T, made a bid to acquire smaller rival MetroPCS Communications. MetroPCS focuses on the low end of the market, which features users with cheaper phones and low-cost contracts, or even no contract, data plans. T-Mobile tended to offer more expensive plans but also service that can accommodate high-speed users. MetroPCS, however, provides service to a large number of prepaid users, thereby allowing T-Mobile to expand in a segment of the market in which it did not previously have as significant a presence.

As T-Mobile and MetroPCS planned their merger, Sprint was left out in the cold. That was until Japan's Softbank made a bid to acquire 70 percent of Sprint, which, in turn, helped enable Sprint to complete a 100 percent acquisition of Clearwire. We discuss the Sprint-Softbank offer in more detail later in the chapter.

MOTIVATION TO INCREASE SIZE

Mobile telecommunications is but one example of an industry in which there are significant advantages to having greater size. Larger companies have more resources and are able to do more things than their smaller competitors. The key issue is how big is big enough? At what point does getting bigger create more inefficiencies and other costs that outweigh the incremental advantages of a larger entity? As we discuss later in this book, CEOs may seek larger size for the psychic benefits that being the head of a large company confers. They also seek the higher compensation and perks that go with running a larger enterprise. The existence of these incentives requires that the board of directors be careful when approving deals to make sure they are being done for the right reasons. We will discuss the responsibilities of directors in detail in Chapter 9.

It is also the case that smaller companies may be able to accomplish things that larger, more bureaucratic enterprises cannot. Smaller companies can often react faster to a changing marketplace and generally may be more nimble. Their layers of management tend to be fewer and decisions can often be made much more quickly. So there are some advantages to being smaller; the best option depends on the industry and the circumstances.

COMPETITIVE PRESSURES OF COMPETITORS' M&A PROGRAM

In the field of M&A, companies naturally react to what competitors are doing. If their competitors are acquiring other companies in the industry, or are becoming more vertically integrated, this may cause other companies to consider doing the same. In Chapter 3, we discussed the case of Merck trying to vertically integrate by buying Medco and how this led Eli Lilly and Roche to do similar deals. We see the same phenomenon with horizontal deals. When two competitors combine and thereby become larger, their rivals sometimes worry that they will lose out when competing with the now-larger company. This may cause them to consider finding their own merger partner. Sometimes this leads to a whole consolidation in an industry.

Whether horizontal deals really provide competitive benefits is an industry-specific and deal-specific issue. It is hard to provide an answer that applies to horizontal deals in general. However, as we will see later in this chapter, the research that exists on this issue tends to raise some doubts about the gains these deals provide.

COMPETITIVE PRESSURES OF M&A PROGRAMS: CASE STUDY OF THE AIRLINE INDUSTRY

In this book, we often discuss the M&A that are value destroyers and how they are often done for the wrong reasons. However, there are many other instances where deals are not only beneficial but also necessary for survival. A good example is the U.S. airline industry. This industry was absurdly regulated for many years, and fares and routes were ultimately determined by a national body called the Civil Aeronautics Board. The United States likes to hold itself out as though it is this great bastion of free market commerce. Unfortunately, the pursuit of free markets in the United States is often corrupted by its faulty political system, which is dominated by lobbyists and politicians all too eager to cater to special interests to garner votes and campaign contributions. This led to many market imperfections and for many years U.S. airfares were the outcome of one such imperfection. Unfortunately, while deregulation often results in competition, where theoretically the most financially sound should survive, the process has not worked out that well in the airline industry. Even as the industry has consolidated, and competitors such as TWA, PanAm, Eastern, Frontier, Ozark, and many others fell by the wayside, the survivors still are not that fiscally sound. Some companies, such as Continental Airlines, were in and out of Chapter 11. Many have been stuck with high labor costs and intransient unions while they are burdened by high, and equally important, volatile fuel costs. In such an environment, only the efficient and the strong survive. In the case of American Airlines, it became noncompetitive and had to go into Chapter 11 to restructure the airline. Ironically, one of the reasons American Airlines ended up in Chapter 11 is that it did not engage in a significant M&A program, while its competitors did.

As of 2012, American Airlines had the highest labor costs in the industry. These costs accounted for 30 percent of the airline's total costs. The other major airlines, such as Delta, or the merged United–Continental have labor costs in the low 20 percent range. This is part of the reason why consumers would pull up American's fares and find that they were often significantly higher than competitors. How did the competitors end up with lower labor costs? The reason is partly due to restructuring through bankruptcy and M&A. Continental, for example, engaged in multiple Chapter 11 reorganizations. Unfortunately,

(continued)

(*continued*)

due to the intransient nature of unions, it is often difficult to receive major cuts in labor costs when dealing with a union outside of Chapter 11. Part of the reason for this is that unions have their own political processes and a president of a union who voluntarily agrees to major wage and benefits costs usually has a very short life as union president. This is why unions and their leaders often refuse to give concessions outside of Chapter 11. When the company is in bankruptcy, union leaders can more readily say to their membership that they were forced to accept them and it was not the result of their just agreeing to do the right thing.

In the case of American Airlines, the failure to get labor costs under control was only one of its many problems. Competitors grew through M&A and gained competitive advantages over American. United merged with Continental, and Delta merged with Northwest. As a result, each expanded their route structures and enhanced their product offerings while American remained stagnant. The M&A programs of American's competitors meant that American even lost ground in key markets such as New York and Chicago, where it was traditionally somewhat strong.

The end result of the competitors' M&A programs, combined with American's reluctance to enter Chapter 11 as a way to lower its burdensome labor costs, left the airline unprofitable while its competitors began to generate some, albeit weak, profits. In this case, the unwillingness of its laborers to accept wage concessions and the company's failure to pursue M&A to become more efficient left American as a weaker rival and a shadow of its former self. In 2013, American Airlines and US Airways announced a $11 billion merger to create the world's largest airline.

HORIZONTAL DEALS: ACQUISITIONS OF COMPETITORS AND THEIR COMPETING BRANDS

When a market features several competitors with some of the companies lagging behind the leaders, there are often incentives for the companies that are not in the number one or two position to merge and try to move up the ranks. There can be some clear gains from doing so. Perhaps significant cost economies can be realized by eliminating duplicate facilities and overhead? Companies that are in the same industry, and who know their competitors' characteristics, should be able to construct a good estimate of these gains. It is always surprising when gains, which should be easier to estimate, are not accomplished at all or take much longer to accomplish than anticipated. This was the case with the Sprint–Nextel merger. Rather than aggressively moving to eliminate redundant facilities, the companies maintained separate corporate headquarters for years after the deal. This merger was a classic example of how not to do post-merger integration.

Another cost that needs to be factored into the deal calculus is the costs of the elimination of competing brands. When AT&T acquired Cingular and when Sprint and Nextel merged, the acquired brands, Cingular and Nextel, were not maintained. They were eliminated, which is a real cost. Significant monies were invested in developing the market awareness of those brands. The price that is paid for targets typically includes the value of the brands. However, this is basically thrown away when the brands are eliminated. Bidders also need to factor in the losses that they will incur when consumers who were attached to the brands that are eliminated do not stay with the combined company. For companies that do many deals in an industry that has consolidated, such as banking, they may be in a better position to measure these costs. In other industries, this process can be more challenging.

SPRINT–NEXTEL HORIZONTAL DEAL: ONE OF THE WORST IN M&A HISTORY

On August 12, 2005, Sprint and Nextel merged, creating Sprint Nextel. The deal was touted as a $36 billion merger of equals, who were leaders in U.S. mobile telecom. The result has been an absolute M&A mess. This was underscored when the company announced a $29.7 billion fourth-quarter goodwill impairment charge in 2007. To put this in perspective, its 2011 total revenues were $40.1 billion.

In horizontal mergers, as well as other types of mergers (but maybe more so with horizontal deals), one of the risk factors is retention of customers or clients. This proved to be a huge problematic issue in the Sprint–Nextel deal. In addition, the management structure was a revolving door. The company was a case study in post-merger chaos.

Figure 5.2 shows the post-merger profitability of the combined entity. Profits tailed down and the company moved into the red right after the merger. The main cause of the losses was the mass customer defections. Following the deal, hundreds of thousands of customers defected to other carriers.

Nextel offered a very different technology from Sprint. This made the integration of the companies' respective technologies difficult. Nextel's "push

(a)

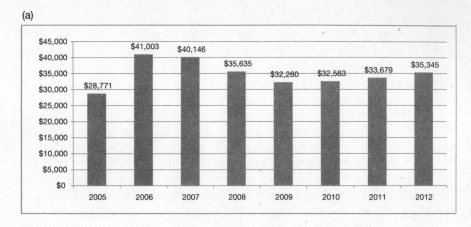

(b)

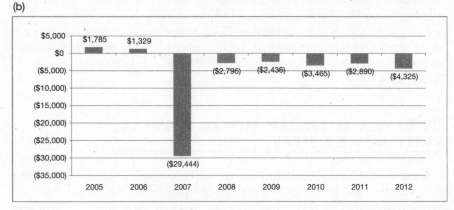

FIGURE 5.2   Sprint Nextel Profitability: 2005–2012 (a) Net Revenues ($ Millions) and (b) Net Profit and Loss ($ Millions)
Source: Sprint Nextel annual reports.

to talk" technology helped the company grow and became closely associated with the brand. Consumers directly associated push to talk, and its walkie-talkie-like mobile phone, with Nextel—and not with any other U.S. carrier. However, consumer tastes changed and this capability became less appealing, thus lowering the value of what Sprint thought it was getting when it merged with Nextel. Sprint then had the challenge of getting Nextel's customers to switch to Sprint's phones while also trying, often unsuccessfully, to get back Nextel's customers who left.

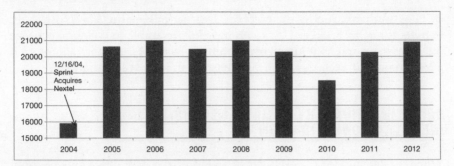

FIGURE 5.3　Sprint Nextel Long-Term Debt ($ in Millions): 2004–2012
Source: Sprint Nextel Value Line, 2012.

When the valuation of Nextel was done prior to the merger, Sprint assumed that it would be able to retain a large percentage of Nextel's customers and its revenues. This proved to be a crucial but very wrong assumption.

Sprint was never really able to utilize the Nextel network to great success. In fact, in the middle of 2012 it announced that it was shutting down the network. So much for the benefits of an intimate knowledge of the industry, from which you expect to achieve success with horizontal M&A.

Following the merger between T-Mobile and MetroPCS, which made a bigger number-four carrier, the pressure started to mount on Sprint. However, Sprint's situation changed when it received a bid from Japan's Softbank to buy a 70 percent stake in Sprint. The acquisition did was structured so that $8 billion of the shares would be purchased directly from Sprint, thus giving it a cash infusion, with the remaining $12 billion to be acquired in the market. This presented some financial synergy benefits for Sprint, as it was heavily indebted—partly from the horrendous acquisition of Nextel.

From Softbank's perspective, the deal would give the Japanese company, already loaded with plenty of its own debt, entrée into the large U.S. telecom market. However, entrée into that market does not mean it can be an effective competitor. Just look at Deutsche Telecom's failure to make a success of its entrance into the U.S. market after it was quite successful in Germany. What it does give Softbank is the right to compete against two large and quite successful carriers with plenty of scale to make life difficult for the Japanese entrant. While being in the number one or two position in an industry may convey great benefits, being a distant number three, Sprint's position, is a challenge. Together, Verizon and AT&T account for about two-thirds of industry revenues and most of its profits.

For Softbank, run by the eccentric Internet billionaire, Masayoshi Son, battling it out with larger U.S. rivals may be preferable to trying to squeeze out gains in the stagnant Japanese economy, which has been stagnant for such a long time that even this challenge may be an improved situation.*

DECLINING INDUSTRY DEMAND NECESSITATING INDUSTRY CONSOLIDATION

When the demand for the products of an industry is high, there may be room for many competitors to supply the products. When an industry declines, we may be left with too many competitors and a shake-out may need to take place. Rather than let the competitive process weed out the less viable competitors, sometimes the managers of the firms in the industry will try to merge so as to reduce overall capacity, while potentially enabling the merger partners to gain from the strengths of each company and avoid being negatively impacted by the weaker elements of each firm.

An example of such a consolidation occurred in the U.S. defense industry in the wake of the Cold War.[2] The firms in the industry lived well while red tensions waged high. When the "Evil Empire" collapsed and the remains of the Soviet Union discovered they could not afford such a large military establishment, the United States looked to save on defense expenditures so that there would be more money available for politicians to fund entitlement programs. It was clear that we did not need so many large defense contractors.

The industry's solution was to consolidate. For example, Boeing purchased a stake in Rockwell in 1996, and in that same year, they merged with McDonnell Douglas. Such M&A was inevitable as the pie had shrunk greatly, and there was not enough demand around to support all the competitors. Thus, this defense industry M&A consolidation was a necessary reaction to changes in the business environment. It was not M&A to expand but rather M&A just to survive. When the industry changes as much as the U.S. defense industry did, companies either have to close up shop, merge, or actually try to outcompete the rest of the industry and excel. Risk-adverse managers, mindful of maintaining their positions and compensation, will tend to go the M&A route.

When an industry consolidates, we naturally expect to experience economies of scale in the form of cost reductions. However, the defense industry, an industry that supplies products to the government using tax dollars, is not a normal purchaser. In the private sector, companies have to report profits to the market, which tends to lower their stock price when

---

*As of the date of this writing, this deal has not been finalized.

profits fall below expectations. The government is run by politicians who are often only concerned with the next election and may not stay up late at night worrying about wasting taxpayer dollars. This helps explain why, for example, after a two-thirds reduction in the number of fixed wing military contractors over the period 1990 to 1998, less than half of the weapons systems experienced a reduction in costs.[3] In addition, Hensel Nayantara found that even though there was a great increase in M&A activity among defense industry contractors, 56 to 61 percent of the per-unit costs of weapons systems were unaffected by the M&A.[4] This result does not lend much support for the ability of M&A to produce economies of scale. However, one also has to keep in mind that this is an unusual industry. Costs are ultimately passed on to taxpayers in a minimally competitive market for which politicians are the ultimate arbiters.

SYNERGISTIC GAINS AND HORIZONTAL M&A

In Chapter 3, we discussed synergistic gains that can possibly, and we mean *possibly*, be realized by M&A. It is important to emphasize in this discussion how some of these gains are much easier to theorize about than to achieve. We further discussed in Chapter 3 how economies of scale are often easier to realize than revenue-enhancing synergies. So we will not repeat that discussion here. However, we do want to emphasize that when we analyze M&A proposals, we need to be cognizant of all the potential costs that can arise with such deals. Certain costs are easier to estimate and measure than others. The price that is paid, and the premium included within it, is only one of the costs of a deal. Other costs can be harder to measure. These include integration costs. They also can include other difficult-to-measure costs such as litigation costs. For example, when Bank of America and its CEO Ken Lewis hurriedly approved the $4.1 billion acquisition of Countrywide Mortgage, they were not in a good position to measure the future potential liabilities they would face from investors who bought mortgage-backed securities from Countrywide. One could argue that given what was known at the time of the troubles in the mortgage market, it was not a stretch to anticipate that they could face significant claims. Instead, Bank of America seemed to focus mainly on the potential revenue-enhancing synergies while closing their eyes to the potential costs. The deal made Bank of America the biggest company in one of the most troubled industries in the United States—hardly an impressive distinction.

At the time of the deal, Bank of America touted its expectation about a reported $670 million in synergistic after-tax savings to be enjoyed by merging the two companies' mortgage operations. However, the bank's post-deal hype contained no comments about the real possibility of large litigation-related losses. The bank incurred numerous billion-dollar losses, including one related to a lawsuit filed by the Justice Department associated with bad loans Countrywide sold to Fannie Mae and Freddie Mac. Bank of America paid $65 million for a settlement of Andrew Mazillo's fraud claim, $2.5 billion to buy back mortgages sold to Fannie Mae and Freddie Mac, $1.6 billion to Assured Guarantee, which insured mortgages sold to investors, $8.5 billion to settle investors claims, $1 billion to settle with the federal government on loans to unqualified borrowers, and $11.8 billion contributed to a settlement of forclosure abuses by the big banks. Ken Lewis went ahead with the deal in January 2008, thinking that the housing market had hit bottom and things would start looking up. It is surprising how someone could become CEO of one of the largest banks in the United States and know so little about the housing and mortgage market. As of the end of 2012, total settlements were $29 billion. Bank of America paid $4.1 billion for Countrywide and incurred over $29 billion in losses—a new definition of synergy.

As if the Countrywide losses were not enough, in 2012, Bank of America agreed to pay $2.43 billion to settle a shareholder class action lawsuit brought by disgruntled shareholders who found out that Bank of America executives withheld information on the magnitude of Merrill Lynch's subprime crisis losses. Bank of America acquired Merrill Lynch in 2008 for $50 billion. However, Merrill Lynch was losing billions on mortgage-related losses, and when Bank of America's management started to get a sense of the size of the losses, they went ahead with the deal anyway.

The deal was not part of anything even close to a well-thought-out M&A strategy. Rather, it was a shotgun wedding between a financially troubled Merrill Lynch and an ever-acquisition-minded Bank of America. Bank of America was built through a seemingly unending series of M&A by the serial acquirer NationsBank, which ultimately acquired the larger Bank of America and assumed its better-known name. Hugh McCall led NationsBank through its prodigious M&A growth path to become one of the very largest banks in the United States. His successor, Ken Lewis, however, led Bank of America into two huge and almost disastrous deals.

The hurried nature of the Countrywide and Merrill Lynch acquisitions made careful planning difficult to do. In small deals, the risks are usually smaller. However, these were mega-deals. Such deals should not be done without careful planning. It is very difficult to do careful planning in the very short time window that was presented to Bank of America by the U.S. government.

While Bank of America's merger planning for its shotgun weddings with Countrywide and Merrill Lynch was an embarrassment for its management and a major cost for its shareholders, the opposite was the case with the highly successful and well-thought-out merger between Exxon and Mobil.

CASE STUDY: HORIZONTAL INTEGRATION— MOBIL MERGER WITH EXXON

In December 1998, Exxon announced that it was merging with the Mobil Oil Company. The $82 billion merger created the world's largest oil company. Both companies were vertically integrated with substantial oil reserves and a broad retail network. In spite of their substantial size, the companies were able to convince regulators that the new oil behemoth would not stifle competition. In part, this was due to the fact that while the combined company would be very large, the oil market was a global one and the combined Exxon-Mobil would have to compete with other companies of comparable size in a world where oil supplies have become increasingly hard to find, while oil demand continues to rise.

One of the difficulties in a merger between companies of the size of these two firms is the post-merger integration. To achieve the synergistic gains that they predicted to the media at the time of the deal, the companies had to be able to successfully integrate the varied resources of the two companies. At the time of the deal, the companies stated that they predicted merger savings on the order of $3.8 billion. In what was a little unusual for such mega-mergers, less than two years later the combined Exxon–Mobil announced that merger savings would be approximately 20 percent higher—$4.6 billion. It is all too common that the opposite occurs. The companies often have to explain why the merger failed to generate the gains the stated would occur.

The success of this deal, along with concerns that they would be left at a competitive disadvantage, led several of their competitors to do their own deals. One of the measures of economic power in the oil industry is the ownership of reserves. The pursuit of such reserves led British Petroleum (BP) to buy the Atlantic Richfield Company (ARCO) in 1999 for $26.8 billion. In the next year, Chevron bought Texaco for $36 billion, and in 2002, Conoco acquired (merged with) Phillips Petroleum for $15 billion. In 2001, Conoco had acquired one of the largest U.S. refiners, Tosco, for $15 billion as well as Calgary-based Gulf Canada Resources for $4.3 billion.

Even with these combinations, Exxon–Mobil still led the industry by a wide margin. The success of this deal was underscored when in 2006, Exxon–Mobil announced the highest annual profits of any corporation in history. The company's 2005 annual profits were $36 billion on sales of $371 billion and a market capitalization of

(continued)

(continued)

$377 billion, making it the largest company in the world using a variety of measures! Exxon–Mobil would surpass this in 2006, when it reported profits of $39.5 billion. In that year, it had the largest market capitalization of any public company—$503 billion!

It would be an error to attribute all of the gains Exxon (having now dropped the Mobil name) realized from the merger. Obviously, a prime factor was the price of oil. When the price of oil rises, petroleum companies are better situated to earn more profits. If you are significantly larger, as Exxon was as a result of this merger, you will be situated to generate even more profits. The opposite, of course, also applies. However, with a product where global demand, especially with the demand from nations like China, is growing faster than supply, coupled with the upward pressure put on oil prices by speculative demand, Exxon was able to gain substantially from oil price increases. When two close competitors, each of which is quite successful—such as Exxon and Mobil—merge, there should be no excuse if they are unable to quickly realize certain synergies. Both companies were giants in an industry that they knew well. Both maintained a large administrative structure that created many redundancies when the two became one. While we saw that the post-merger synergistic gains were very large, it would have been a major disappointment if they were not realized. When there are synergies to be gained, they will naturally be bigger if we are dealing with companies on a scale of Exxon and Mobil. In pre-merger planning, it is easy to delineate which facilities can be closed, generally which groups of employees can be laid off, as well as many other synergies. In a sense, while the synergistic gains were huge, they were actually easier to obtain in this deal than for many others where the synergies were not as clear a priori.

The challenge for Exxon has been what to do next. Pulling off a major M&A that would have the impact of the Mobil deal is not in the cards. The company was able to live off the great gains realized from the 1998 deal for many years. It also markets a product that is a commodity, and when oil prices rise sharply, as they did in 2008, it can really boost profitability for reasons that have little to do with managerial acumen. The company has been aggressively pursuing new sources of oil and natural gas. It expanded it's supplies of natural gas but was hurt by a glut of gas on the market. Oil and natural gas have been in great demand as countries like China help support prices with

(continued)

their rising demand. This led the United States to become a major natural gas exporter in 2011—something unusual for the United States, which has been a net importer of oil for many years. In fact, the development of a large natural gas business in the United States has moved the country greatly toward being much more energy independent. The International Energy Agency has projected that by the year 2030, the United States could be the world's largest oil producer. When one considers the troubled history the United States has had with oil, including events such as the mid-1970s recession following the OPEC oil price increases, this would be a truly amazing outcome.[a]

Some of the other companies that followed in Exxon's steps and pursued mega-deals did not fare as well. Chevron's $38 billion acquisition of Texaco in 2000 contained many disappointments for Chevron. While Chevron was also able to realize synergies such as the layoffs of redundant employees, some of the reserves it anticipated on acquiring turned out not to materialize. For example, it had to take a $1 billion write-down for the disappointing value of one California oil field. Another in Nigeria did not generate oil until five years after it was planned. In addition, the company also inherited significant environmental liabilities related to Texaco's activities in Ecuador. These potential liabilities reached an alarming level when an Ecuadorian court entered a judgment in the amount of $8 billion against Chevron, Texaco's acquirer. This is another example of hard to predict M&A liabilities.

---

[a] World Energy Outlook 2012, International Energy Agency November 2012, www.worldenergyoutlook.org.

NET BENEFITS OF HORIZONTAL DEALS = SYNERGISTIC GAINS − (EASY TO MEASURE COSTS + HARD TO MEASURE COSTS)

Proponents of deals will greatly emphasize the benefits of the M&A including various synergies—some real, some imaginary—and then they will often minimize the costs of the deal. They may be aided in this effort by highly paid investment bankers who want the deal to go through so as to receive their sizeable fees. In an acquisition, the easy to measure costs are the monies paid to target shareholders inclusive of the premium. Other easy-to-measure costs include various fees for professionals, financing, and so on. However, the hard-to-measure costs can often mean the death of a deal. These vary depending on the circumstances but include loss of market share from being distracted while dealing with integration issues. The bigger the target, the greater potential for troublesome integration costs.

HORIZONTAL MERGER SUCCESS, TARGET'S SIZE, AND POST-M&A INTEGRATION COSTS

M&A deals are all different, which is why doing research in M&A can be challenging. However, as a general rule, for which there have to be exceptions, the larger the target relative to the bidder, the greater the integration challenges. Some companies have handled merging two huge corporate entities into one seamless enterprise quite well. As we have noted, the merger of Exxon and Mobil is a great example.

When the target is small relative to the bidder, the bidder is better able to position the target within it without major disruptions. The sheer differences in size will likely make any bumps on the integration road less of a challenge. The many successful M&As that Cisco orchestrated prior to 2010 provide many examples of this. In fact, Cisco's very successful M&A program helped make it one of the largest market capitalization companies in the world in 2000 with a market cap of $431 billion! That value has long come back to Earth, and by the beginning of 2013, it was approximately a quarter of that amount.

When the target is much smaller than the bidder and when integration proves to be problematic, the problem is usually a smaller one. However, when the target is large, the acquirer now has a large problem. Daimler's acquisition of Chrysler is a great example of this, although there are many others. AT&T's 1991 acquisition of NCR is another example of a very large company acquiring another large, albeit comparatively smaller company, where the major cultural differences greatly elevated AT&T's true acquisition costs. Six years later, this resulted in one of AT&T's multiple reorganizations, which split the company into three parts: a smaller version of AT&T, Lucent Technologies (the old Bell Labs), and a computer company that retained the NCR name.

Integration costs are tough to estimate and quantify—particularly in advance of the deal. Naturally, this makes the incorporation of such costs into valuation models difficult. Difficult, however, does not mean impossible. Nor does it mean "we will put $0 on that one as we can't get a handle on it." One alternative would be to recognize the risks and add a risk premium to the discount rate. Often, this will be difficult to do for political and not analytical reasons. The valuation analysts can make a crude approximation of these costs and use an *integration-risk-adjusted discount rate*, which will lower the value of the target or the deal in general. Politically, however, discussion of such risks by deal proponents, such as the CEO and the investment bankers he or she has hired, may make the deal a harder sell to the board of directors who have to approve the deal. For such reasons, risks in general, and these risks in particular, are often dismissed and not even discussed. Rather, deal proponents emphasize the great benefits that the deal will confer. If the deal proves to be problematic years later, odds are that the CEO will be on his or her way to retirement or the next CEO position. If not, the CEO can state that the business or the industry has changed since the deal was completed or that now a restructuring or selloff of the target will present great gains for shareholders. It is rare that a CEO will admit that an expensive acquisition was a big mistake that cost the company a lot of money.

One great example of this occurred when Citigroup sold off the insurance units that Sandy Weill, Citigroup's empire-building CEO, squandered billions to acquire and then spent other large sums to unsuccessfully try to integrate. As we have noted earlier, he tried to build a financial supermarket or one-stop shop that the consumer did not want. The fact that the units were never really integrated made them easier to sell off. What is truly unfortunate is that management and the board did not have the courage to admit to the market and its shareholders that the deals were the product of a very poor strategy and that management and the board failed in their obligations to shareholders. In today's litigious world such admissions, while honest, could easily result in a spate of lawsuits. While that may excuse management and the board from being candid, it does not excuse the financial media for letting the company off so easily.

It is also difficult for managers reporting to the CEO to tell the CEO that the proposed merger is poorly conceived and will not be successful. Too often in corporate America, we have the managerial ranks filled with yes men (and women) whose main concern is the next promotion, pay raise, and bonus. These are often best achieved by telling the CEO what he or she wants to hear. When managers do the opposite, they are often shown the door. This was the case when Jamie Dimon provided some resistance to King Weill as he was building his empire and extracting huge financial gains for himself at shareholders' expense. Dimon was forced out and left to run the smaller Bank One.[5] As William Cohan puts it using a sports analogy, this will go down as "the worst trade" in banking history. When Bank One was taken over by JPMorgan Chase, the acquirer recognized that one of the major assets of Bank One was Dimon. If Weill or his ill-equipped successor Charles Prince had been forced out of Citigroup by a board who challenged his ill-conceived dream of building the one-stop financial shop, would Citigroup have fallen as far as it did? Would Dimon have questioned the taking on of additional risks and the bank's large investments into mortgage-backed securities that cost it dearly? When we consider the billions in losses that JPMorgan Chase incurred in the recent London Whale fiasco, Dimon starts to lose some of his luster. The fact that he initially insisted that the problem was of a much lower scale also raises questions of whether even a good manager can truly manage such a large, too-big-to-fail financial institution. It is also underscores how horizontal mergers can fail to yield meaningful gains when companies get too large to effectively manage.

MERGERS OF EQUALS

When a merger creates one of the larger companies in an industry, it does not necessarily convey competitive advantages. The combination of two very large and similarly sized companies may not result in gains for the shareholders. Take, for example, the case of the 2006 merger between Alcatel and Lucent. On the surface, this combination of two prominent competitors seemed to provide great opportunities for synergies and cost economies. In reality, it combined two companies with multiple problems to create a much larger behemoth that also was beset with larger versions of the same problems. In fact, the company reported steady losses after the deal and took a huge write-down on its goodwill. The merger did nothing to make the problems go away.

When the deal was announced, there was talk of cost economies and other efficiencies that would yield great synergistic benefits. The reality was far different. The combined entity marketed network gear that utilizes code division multiple access (CDMA) technology, which faces a declining demand in North America—its biggest market.

At the time of their merger, the two companies stated that they would pursue the merger to lower their per-unit costs and realize economies of scale. However, they failed to anticipate the expansion of lower-cost global competitors such as Chinese telecom manufacturers. As with the steel industry, which we will discuss laer in this chapter, Chinese companies greatly added to global output but did so with lower costs than their Western competitors.

In every field, it is always nice to develop rules that can be followed so as to allow for optimal performance. Unfortunately, while such rule development may work in mathematics or the physical sciences, it often does not work as well in economics or in the subfield of finance that is M&A. Each deal is different. In addition, M&A in different industries have different effects. What may look like an obvious rule that worked in certain deals could be irrelevant for others.

MERGERS OF EQUALS AND CHALLENGES OF INTEGRATION

Integrating a relatively smaller company into a larger one is a much easier task than integrating two large companies. The integration job can be even easier if the larger company has grown through many prior M&A and has the integration process down cold. We have discussed how Cisco arguably had, for many years, the best track record of success in doing this. Smaller deals are not only easier to do; they are also less risky. Not as many resources are put on the line in such deals, and if one does not work out, the costs are lower. In addition, when a smaller deal does not work out, it is easier for management to sweep it under the rug and deflect attention from the screwup. However, when two giants merge, the resulting mega-giant may be even more in the public and the media's eye than the two precursor companies.

A huge merger that requires great efforts at integration can create competitive advantages *for rivals* who are not beset with such challenges. They can take advantage of a company that is struggling with integration to try to gain market shares. There are numerous examples of companies that have achieved such success while the merged companies struggle with dealing with the unique challenges that mergers of equals bring. One leading example of this is the merger of Daimler and Chrysler.

CASE STUDY: DAIMLER–CHRYSLER MERGER OF EQUALS

The 1998 Daimler–Chrysler merger was touted as a *merger of equals*, much to the chagrin of some shareholders who clearly saw it as a takeover of Chrysler by Daimler. One of those disgruntled shareholders, Kirk Kerkorian, sued and partly based his suit on the remarks of the ego-filled Daimler CEO, Jurgen Schremp, who was quoted in the media as saying the deal, ostensibly referred to as a merger of equals, was really a takeover but that Daimler merely *said* it was a merger of equals. Kerkorian wanted his takeover premium, but the courts were not sympathetic to his position.

While Daimler may have prevailed in its lawsuit with Kerkorian, it struggled for years with Chrysler, an automaker beset with multiple
(continued)

(continued)

problems. Under Schremp, Daimler was to expand into an international automaker that sold a wide variety of cars throughout the world. Stated alternatively, he wanted to build an empire that would be a monument to his ego. He was not satisfied with running the premier luxury auto brand in the world. To fulfill his dream, he settled on Chrysler after overtures to Ford and GM, which were rebuffed.[a] Chrysler, however, had enjoyed gains from selling many SUVs and trucks, which were higher-profit-margin vehicles. Unfortunately, Daimler misjudged the tastes of U.S. consumers and demand for these gas-guzzling vehicles declined sharply not long after the acquisition. This left Daimler owning a company with flagging sales and a very high-cost labor force represented by a union that sought to extract every dollar it could from the U.S. automakers—even if it meant pushing the companies into bankruptcy. The union believed (somewhat correctly) that its political influence would enable it to procure tax dollars to rescue the company after it pushed the firm to the point of bankruptcy.

The problems of Chrysler became a major distraction for Daimler. The deal was a huge one and when Chrysler began to bleed millions and millions of dollars in red ink, fixing Chrysler became Daimler's primary occupation. The deal proved to not only be a major money loser, it distracted Daimler from its core Mercedes-Benz business. This manifested itself in rising quality problems for a brand that was known for luxury and high quality. From a rival's perspective, in this case companies such as BMW, one of the best competitive edges a company can have is for a rival do a poorly thought out and big money-losing deal. This creates an opportunity for competitors to focus on the core business and take market share from the acquisitive rival. The acquisition of Chrysler by Daimler was a great gift Daimler gave to rivals such as BMW.

When rivals pursue large mergers-of-equals deals, competitors should be poised to take advantage if the deal proves to be problematic, as many of them do. Companies considering doing a merger of equals should be extra wary as the costs of such large deals can be high. As a rule of thumb, the larger the deal, the more potential for integration problems.

---

[a] Bill Vlasic and Bradley A. Stretz, *Taken for a Ride: How Daimler Benz Drove Off with Chrysler* (New York: Harper Collins, 2000).

MERGERS-OF-EQUALS RESEARCH: ACQUIRERS VERSUS TARGET GAINS

We discussed the disastrous Daimler-Chrysler merger of equals. Could this be an anomaly? Perhaps most mergers of equals turn out well? Not really. Julie Wulf analyzed a large sample of 17,730 mergers, of which 1,457 were stock swaps and 273 were tender offers, over the period 1991 to 1999.[6] The results of her analysis of this sample proved to be very different from some of the M&A research discussed later in this book. On the surface, she found that the combined bidder and target returns for her sample were not that different from non–merger-of-equals deals. However, her results showed that bidders captured more of the gains, while target shareholders received lower returns. Bidders gained at the expense of target shareholders. It seems that the extensive negotiation process enabled bidders to extract more gains from target shareholders than what would occur in a more traditional combination of firms where a larger company buys a smaller target. It is worth considering why we get such a result. The answer may be very basic—managers of target companies may be pursuing their own self-interest at the expense of their fiduciary duties.

Research has showed that target management and directors seem to trade off higher returns for their shareholders in exchange for positions in the new company. This raises significant corporate governance concerns, as we would assume that managers and directors are fiduciaries for shareholders and should only be concerned about target shareholder gains and not their employment status. In addition, it seems that when the bidder can offer target management and directors opportunities in the combined entity, they may be able to get away with paying lower premiums and save their shareholders' money. Given that these target directors and managers can often be removed at a later date, these gains may be coming at a modest price.

COMPETITIVE ADVANTAGES OF HORIZONTAL DEALS: CASE STUDY—InBev AND ANHEUSER-BUSCH

In reality, horizontal acquirers may be able to gain competitive advantages beyond market power. These advantages can come from other sources than merely the ability to set price above marginal costs. That is, they can come from more than just raising price to a higher level and holding it there for an extended period. Bidders may be able to achieve competitive advantages from increasing their buying power as an industry consolidates and they become one, possibly the largest, buyer in the industry. This was apparent in the immediate cost efficiencies and procurement advantages that Inbev/Anheuser-Busch enjoyed following their 2009 merger. These were additional benefits on top of rising revenues received from price increases on lower shipments, which, in turn, means lower costs.

The story of the InBev takeover of Anheuser-Busch began with the 1999 merger between Brazilian brewers Brahma and Antarctica to form Brazil's largest beer company—Ambev. It went on to acquire other brewers in nations such as Uruguay. It then entered into a contract to distribute PepsiCo soft drink brands in South America.

From that vantage point, the Brazilian bankers/brewers orchestrated the 2004 merger with Belgium's Interbrew, which boasted the global brands Becks and Stella Artois. Interbrew was aptly named, as it was the product of over 30 acquisitions in Europe and Asia.[7] The combined company, InBev, gave the Brazilians global brands and allowed them to be truly global.

Anheuser-Busch (AB) was late to the game in going global. Senior management at this St. Louis-based company had a very insular perspective. It was led by four generations of Busch family children. Augie Busch III was reported to have actually not even traveled that much globally—never mind being prepared to effectively transform the U.S.-centric company into a global brewing powerhouse. Toward that end, Carlos Brito, the shrewd Brazilian CEO of Interbrew, negotiated a joint venture with Anheuser, which was eventually run by the young Augie Busch IV. Augie the Fourth, perhaps better known for his party lifestyle and troubling incidents of women dying in his car and at his home, completed the deal, which allowed penny-pinching Brito and his staff to get an inside look at the wasteful management of the iconic U.S. beer company. Brito could see how easily he could raise profitability by cutting the abundant waste at AB, including its corporate jets and company cars, while also getting higher prices for the leading American beer brand. Brito is a low-profile highly professional manager, while AB was run as though it were a kingdom.[8] At the time it was acquired by Inbev, Anheuser-Busch was a public company where the founding Busch family owned a relatively small percentage of the company's shares and thus had little real voting power and control. Brito and Inbev's management did not have difficulty convincing Anheuser's shareholders it could do a better job of managing the company than the Busch family.

After InBev completed its hostile takeover of AB, Brito and his managers set about lowering costs every way it could. They laid off 1,400 workers, which comprised 6 percent of its workforce.[9] This is a simple costs-economies attempt at cost synergies. However, Brito looked at every opportunity to lower costs. For example, his managers told suppliers that they could expect payments as late as 120 days and implied that they should be happy to be able to sell to the new giant in the industry. For companies whose contracts called for payment in 30 days and who usually got paid in 60 days, this was an unpleasant side effect of the deal. For InBev/Anheuser-Busch, it meant that they were able to enhance the working capital position of the combined company, which, of course, came at the expense of their suppliers who, in effect, had to provide some financing for their large buyer or pass on the large volume of business. For companies of the size of InBev/Anheuser, extending payables an extra 30-plus days can have a very significant effect on profitability. Some have estimated this to be equal to several hundred million euros. These are just a few examples of how Brito used his sharp pen, in place of the Busch king's dull paintbrush, to extract profits from AB.

Sometimes, a company can be hurt by aggressive costs cutters who sacrifice elements that are key to product quality and marketing leadership. Brito has been accused of lowering the quality of the beer by doing things such as buying cheaper hops and other components. Critics point out that Becks, for example, sold in the United States, is no longer made in Germany but made in the United States.[10] Naturally, Inbev/AB wants to avoid the high international transportation costs and have the product made with the original recipes but in the United States. The same critics cite a decline in quality; however, at least initially, those claims seem unsupported. Critics have cited that shipments have declined but perhaps these critics did not take Microeconomics 101 and are not aware of the inverse relationship between prices and quantity. In the case of AB, it worked this relationship to its benefit as it raised prices, which in this case happened to more than offset declines in quantity demanded, which is why revenues, but more importantly, profits, have risen. It was receiving higher per-unit prices but selling somewhat less as it moved up the demand curve. Somewhat lower quantity meant lower cost but the product elasticity was such that revenues rose, thereby boosting profits. The market has been impressed by the company's strong financial performance.

REGULATORY CONCERNS ON MERGER INTEGRATION

Horizontal deals can give rise to antitrust concerns. *Antitrust* is a term that is a holdover from the late 1800s when trusts—basically a holding company structure that acquired control of various companies—began to form. This led to the passage of the law that remains today the cornerstone of U.S. competition policy—the Sherman Antitrust Act. Elsewhere in the world, the more common terms are *competition policy* and *competition laws*.

It is ironic that at one time in U.S. antitrust history, enforcement was so intense, if not bizarre, that vertical deals, and eventually even conglomerate mergers, were the target of intense antitrust enforcement. This was the conglomerate era of the 1960s. In the United States during the 1950s and 1960s, antitrust enforcement was so intense that when the economy expanded, and companies wanted to expand through M&A, the only deals that brought with them a higher likelihood of passing through the antitrust regulatory barriers were conglomerate deals. We discussed the track record of the conglomerates in Chapter 3. Rather than say that such deals often made little strategic sense and that they should be passed on, expansion-minded CEOs chose to assemble huge and cumbersome corporate structures. Eventually, beginning in the 1970s and then by the 1980s, U.S. antitrust enforcement became more "normal," and deals that did not raise significant competitive concerns could have a good expectation of making it through the enforcement process. The enforcement relaxation process has continued since then in the United States, where antitrust enforcement is now somewhat modest.

Nonetheless, horizontal deals bring with them risks that the deal in its proposed form may not be acceptable to antitrust authorities. When that is the case, the bidder has to decide to change the deal, such as by agreeing to sell off some of the combined company, abandon the deal, or try to fight it out with regulators. The latter adds costs and uncertainties that make it a difficult and unpredictable outcome. This may help explain why AT&T simply decided to walk away from its proposed merger with T-Mobile, even though it meant paying a breakup fee of $4 billion in cash and airwave licenses. What is surprising is why AT&T and its high-paid advisors could not have anticipated this outcome given the very concentrated structure of the industry.

As we moved into the fifth merger wave of the 1990s and M&A became a truly global phenomenon, the competition policy review process became more complex. At one time, the main concern for U.S. dealmakers was dealing with either the Justice Department or the Federal Trade Commission. When the combined entity has a significant presence in markets outside the United States, non-U.S. competition policy regulators have to also bestow their approval. One of the most active of these is the European Commission (EU) regulators. At one time, the two had very similar views on deals so that if the Justice Department, for example, saw the merger of two large, international, U.S.-centered companies as legally acceptable, odds were that EU would also find the deal acceptable. That changed in the 2001 when the Justice Department took a favorable stance toward the proposed $43 billion acquisition of Honeywell by GE, only to be surprised that the EU found the deal objectionable. The EU's proposed solution would have made the deal quite unappealing for GE and it backed out. The EU's position on this deal, one that it has taken in other proposed high-profile deals, makes the landscape for global horizontal M&A a little less predictable and thus more risky. More risky really means the potential cost of the deal is higher.

Deals involving companies that have a broad global presence require more regulatory due diligence. In fact, mergers between truly global companies may involve filings with as many as 80 regulatory authorities from many nations.

One trend we have seen in global antitrust enforcement is competition agencies in certain countries using such enforcement not to promote competition but to protect local companies from large global competitors. This has been the case at times even in the EU. This is really not antitrust policy but nothing more than protectionism. However, M&A participants need to be realistic and understand the new rules of the game. Certain deals may actually promote competition in some national markets but be opposed by regulators on antitrust grounds.

HORIZONTAL M&A AND MARKET POWER: AN ECONOMIC PERSPECTIVE

Economists often look at the pursuit of horizontal combinations as the pursuit of market power. In microeconomics, market power is the ability to raise price above marginal costs. In a competitive market structure, the forces of many competitors, each supplying a homogeneous product or service, prevent any of the companies from raising price above marginal cost. Thus, they are each price takers where in the long run, price equals marginal cost. Suppliers then receive what is referred to in microeconomics as a *normal return*, which compensates them for their opportunity costs of being in the industry but fails to afford them any *economic rent*. This is one of the incentives of moving to a more concentrated market structure in that it allows the suppliers to sell above marginal costs and increase overall profitability as measured on a per-unit basis as the difference between price and average costs (see Figure 5.4). Sometimes the relationship between price and marginal costs is depicted through the Lerner Index:

$$L = (P - MC)/P$$

where the higher L is the greater market power

When an industry becomes so consolidated that it has just one supplier, then that firm has its maximum ability to raise price above marginal costs. This does not, however, assure that the supplier will be profitable. It just means that if it is able to produce at the point where its marginal costs equals its marginal revenues, its potential profitability will be as great as it is going to be. It still could be the case that its average costs are so high at that *profit-maximizing point* (Xm) that it still does not make any money (see Figure 5.5).

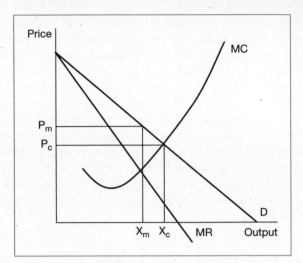

FIGURE 5.4 Consumers Benefit More from a Competitive Market. They Buy More Output (X_c) than in a Monopolized Market (X_m) and Pay Less ($P_c < P_m$).

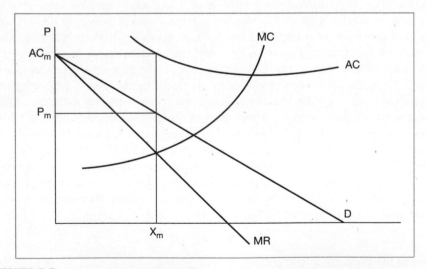

FIGURE 5.5 Money-Losing Monopolist

Microeconomics has reasonable models for dealing with the extreme, polar opposite industry structures of pure competition and monopoly. When we get away from the extremes, such as when we move away from monopoly and are dealing with an oligopoly, a *few* sellers (i.e., 3 to 12 but varies depending on the context), then the market power that a supplier possesses can be open to interpretation. This has become the case over the past 10 to 20 years when markets have become more globalized. Market shares in one's home country, even when it is the largest market in the world, the United States, may not be very relevant when U.S. suppliers are facing competition across the globe, where the degree of competition is increasing over time as emerging market participants enter the industry. Even when a supplier is able to produce above its marginal costs, and when it seems that the current degree of competition is modest, it may have to still consider the actions of potential entrants. Such a market may be considered a *contestable* market. The more attractive the market, and the greater the ability of the supplier to sell above marginal costs, the greater the prize for new entrants to try to snatch. Thus, in this rapidly changing, globalized world, market power can be fleeting. The world of the 2000s is not static but can change rapidly. Market power can be seemingly potent but its potency can be fleeting. Each industry is different and will dictate its own constraints upon market power.

EMPIRICAL EVIDENCE ON WHETHER FIRMS PURSUE M&A TO ACHIEVE MARKET POWER

There is little empirical evidence that firms combine to increase their monopoly power. In fact, this issue has been a focus of research in financial economics for the past quarter of a century. The findings of this research have been quite consistent.

Two studies emerged in 1983—each an outgrowth of a doctoral thesis. One was a small sample study by Robert S. Stillman of the University of Chicago. His study showed that competitors' stock prices failed to react when other firms in the same industry announced a combination.[11] The analysis considered the value of the stock of firms in the affected industry when events took place that increased the probability of mergers in that industry. It also considered the fact that product prices might rise after horizontal mergers, benefiting other companies in the industry. With higher product prices, resulting from a more concentrated industry, the equity values of the firms in the industry should also rise. The study examined a small sample of 11 mergers that were challenged on antitrust grounds under Section 7 of the Clayton Act. No statistically significant abnormal returns for 9 of the 11 mergers were found. Of the other two, one showed positive abnormal returns, and the other showed ambiguous results. These results fail to support the view that firms merge in an effort to seek monopoly power.

A similar study, also based on a doctoral thesis, was conducted by B. Epsen Eckbo on a larger sample of 126 horizontal and vertical mergers in the manufacturing and mining industries. Approximately half of Eckbo's sample were horizontal mergers. An average of 15 rival firms existed in each industry category. If the market power hypothesis delineated previously were valid, negative abnormal returns would be observed for firms in industries that had announced mergers that were challenged on antitrust grounds. The reasoning is that the merger is less likely when there is an antitrust challenge. When challenges take place, negative abnormal returns should be associated with the announcement of the challenge.

Eckbo found statistically insignificant abnormal returns. The study also showed that firms initially showed positive and statistically significant abnormal returns when the mergers were first announced but failed to show a negative response after the complaint was filed. Like Stillman's results, Eckbo's research does not support the belief that firms merge to enjoy increases in market power. Curiously, Eckbo's results reveal that "stockholders of bidder and target firms in challenged (horizontal) mergers earn larger abnormal returns than do the corresponding firms in unchallenged mergers."[12] Eckbo concludes that the gains found in mergers are not related to increases in market power but rather are motivated by factors such as efficiency gains.

Eckbo conducted another study of the market power hypothesis, in which he examined the level of competition in Canada, a country that, until 1985, had more relaxed antitrust enforcement policies. He refuted the hypothesis that the probability of a merger being anticompetitive was greater in Canada than in the United States. One conclusion that could be drawn from this research is that the more rigid antitrust enforcement that has sometimes been pursued in the United States, and that was pursued in Europe in recent years, is unnecessary. However, this is a complex issue that cannot be decided based a few studies. Although the Stillman and Eckbo studies of the early 1980s provide little support for the pursuit of market power as a motive for M&A, other recent research implies that market power may be a motive for some deals. Specifically, Kim and Singal found that mergers in the airline industry during the late 1980s resulted in higher prices on routes served by merging firms compared with a control group of routes that were not involved in control transactions.[13]

More recent research implies that horizontal mergers increase buying power of the merging companies in instances where the suppliers are concentrated. This was theoretically demonstrated by Snyder as well as by Stole and Zwiebel, who theorized that merged buyers could lower their cost of inputs that they purchase from concentrated supplier industries.[14] This was supported by other empirical work. Fee and Thomas analyzed a sample of 554 horizontal transactions over the period 1980 to 1997.[15] They found no significant stock market reactions by corporate customers (as opposed to competitors), which implies that the market perceived no change in market power as a result of the deals. However, they noticed negative stock market reactions by suppliers, which implies that the merged companies gain some buying power relative to their suppliers. The AB–Inbev merger is a good example of the merged company gaining at the expense of suppliers.

In the years after the initial Stillman and Eckbo studies, antitrust regulators in the United States pursued a more relaxed antitrust enforcement policy. Some have wondered: Could the *collusion* hypothesis have become more relevant in recent years as companies are less impeded by antitrust enforcement?

Research by Husayn Shahrur failed to find support for this view. He analyzed a sample of 463 horizontal mergers and tender offers over the period 1987 to 1999.[16] He found that efficiency considerations were the main factor driving the horizontal deals as opposed to the achievement of market power. His results lend support to the original Stillman and Eckbo findings some two decades earlier. He also found evidence that when competitors combine, they may enjoy gains relative to their suppliers. We discuss this issue later in this chapter in the context of the Arcelor–Mittal merger. Such merged companies may realize an increase in their buying power relative to suppliers. When this is the case, the merged firms may gain at the expense of suppliers. If that effect is significant enough, it may give rise to consolidation in the supplier industry. The result may be significantly more concentrated buyer and supplier industries. This was the case in recent years with the mining and steel industries.

COUNTERVAILING POWER, INDUSTRY CONCENTRATION, AND M&A

While analysis of a monopoly industry structure and monopoly power is a major component of textbooks on microeconomics, models of bilateral monopoly, where two firms that do business with each other both enjoy a monopoly position, are also discussed but generally receive less attention. However, from an M&A perspective, given that regulatory authorities across the world, especially in the United States and the European Union (EU), are reluctant to let companies use M&A to achieve a monopoly—or even come close to a monopoly—position, these discussions are less relevant. What is more relevant are industries that have a buy-sell relationship and that have consolidated through M&A to both become relatively concentrated oligopolies. In such cases, if one industry becomes more concentrated while the other is still fragmented, then the concentrated industry may enjoy certain benefits not available to the more fragmented and competitive industry. This was the case in the steel industry where mining certain companies, which were sellers of iron ore, merged and became more powerful while the steel industry remained more fragmented. This created an incentive for the steel industry to use M&A to become more concentrated as well as to vertically integrate. In doing so, buyers—steel companies—would increase their *countervailing power*, a concept popularized by John Kenneth Galbraith in the 1950s.[17]

The concept of countervailing power asserts that the power of one group, such as large corporations in an industry, needs to be balanced by other groups such as large unions. This reasoning may have been more relevant prior to the world economy becoming more globalized. When companies in a given country have to deal with a heavily unionized labor force, but have to compete even in their local markets with competitors that are not unionized, the concept of counterveiling power becomes misplaced. The U.S. auto industry is a good example. At one time, before the U.S. auto market featured many non-U.S. competitors, the United Auto Workers was a counterveiling power to the Big Four U.S. automakers (and then later Big Three when Chrysler acquired American Motors). Then, when major international competitors entered the U.S. auto market on a larger scale, and even opened plants in the United States with nonunionized workforces, the unions became a force that made the companies noncompetitive. What was once a counterveiling force can become a stranglehold as times changed.

In the context of our discussion, the power of one group of companies, such as sellers, may need to be balanced by the power of their counterparties— buyers (or vice versa). If this is not done, the sellers may be in a position to extract gains at the expense of the buyers. As buyers become more powerful, they may be able to enhance their negotiating position. This may be the case even if only one or two of the buyers become more powerful. Indeed, some have theorized that "buyer mergers may increase profit for all buyers," as their negotiating efforts may help set market prices.[18]

The case study that follows on the relationship between the iron ore mining industry and steel manufacturers is a good example of buyers—steel manufacturers—led by Arcelor–Mittal, improving their market position and acquiring more countervailing power.

CASE STUDY: STEEL AND MINING INDUSTRIES

In recent years, we have seen significant consolidation in both the steel and the mining industries. These industries have a buyer-supplier relationship with each other as output from mining companies, such as from companies that mine coal, is used as an input for steel production.

(continued)

The mining and steel industries are in many ways closely related—beyond just their buyer-seller relationship. Both industries benefit greatly from expanding scale, and both are very capital intensive. In addition, each faces high transportation costs, which makes having facilities in local markets important to gaining market share in those markets.

We have seen great consolidation in the steel industry through many mega-mergers. The biggest of them all was the 2006 mega-merger between Mittal and Arcelor, which resulted in Arcelor–Mittal becoming the largest steel company in the world. Arcelor, which was Europe's largest steel company, was itself a combination of three steel companies—Arbed, Aceralia, and Usinor. Mittal also was the product of mergers. In particular, in 2004, Mittal acquired the International Steel Group (ISG). ISG, in turn, was formed by Wilber Ross through the acquisition of two bankrupt steel companies—Acme Steel and the steel assets of LTV in 2002. LTV, once the great conglomerate of the 1960s, had owned the famous U.S. steel company—Jones and Laughlin Steel. In 2003, ISG acquired Bethlehem Steel and the plate steel business of U.S. Steel, and in 2004 it acquired Wierton Steel. Together, these companies comprised much of what was left of the once-storied U.S. steel business.

Mittal had been built by a variety of other M&A. Initially, the Mittal group focused on steel acquisitions outside of India, as the country leaned in a more socialist direction and was not a business-friendly environment.[a] Therefore, Lakshmi Mittal built the Mittal Group through steel M&A over a broad geographical area from Trinidad to Indonesia to Eastern Europe, such as in Poland. He excelled at finding inefficient, troubled steel mills and quickly acquiring and instituting more efficient practices and making them profitable. The story of Mittal's global success is truly an impressive one.

These steel mergers are just a few of several other mega-deals that occurred throughout the globe. They included the 2007 acquisition of the British steel company Corus by Tata Steel. Corus was the product of a 1999 merger between British Steel and Koninklijke Hoogoven. The combination had boosted Corus to the number-six-ranked steel company in the world prior to its merger with Tata.

One of several factors responsible for the consolidation we have seen in the steel industry is the market power the fragmented steel companies faced from the more concentrated iron ore mining companies. In the global market for iron ore, three companies account for the vast majority of the world's shipments. These are Brazil's Vale, the

(continued)

(continued)

world's largest; Rio Tinto, a British company that has operations in Australia and Canada; and BHP Billiton, which has operations in Australia and Brazil. These three are by far the largest, and the next largest is India's SAIL/NMDC, which is a fraction of the size of the others (see Figure 5.6).

The iron ore suppliers tend to dictate prices and the fragmented buyers have been basically price takers. In traditional economic terms, this allows the suppliers of iron ore to extract some of the economic rents that steel sellers seek to receive from their sale to their buyers— many of whom are also large. The buyers of steel include some of the large automakers.

For many years, the steel industry was in the middle—between relatively concentrated sellers of iron ore and the also relatively concentrated buyers of steel such as the large auto companies. When a fragmented industry faces such concentration on both sides, from both its sellers and buyers, its ability to enjoy higher rates of return is limited.

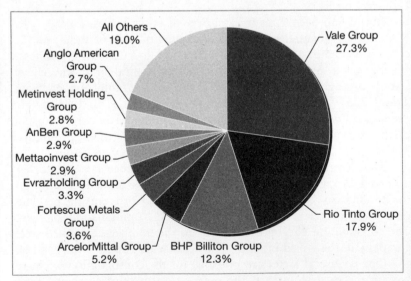

FIGURE 5.6 World's Largest Iron Ore Suppliers, 2011
Source: www.steelonthenet.com.

(continued)

Lakshimi Mittal, CEO of Arcelor Mittal, was well aware of the position of the industry. He decided to use M&A to take some bold steps to offset some of the advantages that the iron ore suppliers enjoyed. To try to grow internally would be a long, drawn-out process and other steel companies would seize on the opportunity presented by M&A to improve their position. Mittal was just the boldest and most prescient of the steel company CEOs. With his merger with Arcelor, the combined company became much larger than the world's other large steel companies. In fact, in 2011 Arcelor–Mittal was still three times larger than its nearest rival—Nippon Steel (see Figure 5.7).

In spite of the increased strength it enjoyed relative to the iron ore suppliers, the merger with Arcelor did not solve ArcelorMittal's purchasing price problems. Lakshimi Mittal pursued a multipronged strategy to address this problem by also using M&A to vertically integrate. As we will discuss in Chapter 6, vertical integration has a questionable track record. However, when a buyer faces a concentrated supplier industry that may extract many of the buyer's *economic*

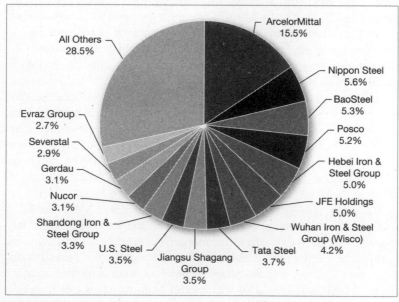

FIGURE 5.7 Top 15 Largest Steel Producer Companies, 2010–2011
Source: World Steel Association.

(*continued*)

(*continued*)

rents, becoming the industry's largest firm—and therefore, a more powerful buyer—is one key step to offsetting the advantages the iron ore suppliers enjoyed. Another one was to also become a significant supplier of iron ore itself. Through M&A, ArcelorMittal acquired iron ore mining facilities, which allowed it to become the sixth-largest iron ore supplier in the world, even though it is still much smaller than the Big Three.

As we will discuss in Chapter 6, many vertical M&A deals do not turn out well. However, ArcelorMittal's horizontal and vertical M&A strategy works, as it allows the company to buy iron ore on better terms (where geographic restrictions allow) while also giving the company more dependable sources of supply, which are located near the production facilities so as to minimize transportation costs. Mittal appears to have used a well-conceived M&A program to create a very successful steel giant. M&A cannot solve all the company's problems. It cannot eliminate the fact that the company faces a highly cyclical demand for its products, of which it was reminded when much of the West went into a recession following the subprime crisis. For example, in 2009, ArcelorMittal's revenues dropped to almost half of the 2008 level and profits all but totally disappeared (see Figure 5.8 b). However, the much larger steel manufacturer, which now commands many of its own sources of supply, was better equipped to deal with that downturn. In addition, as much of the world recovered following the global recession of 2008 to 2009, Arcelor–Mittal was much better positioned to increase its profits through being larger and being able to have dependable access to key inputs. Still, while its revenues rose steadily after 2009, the company's margins have been under pressure as evidenced by the fact that it showed only $2.2 billion of profits in 2011 on almost $94 billion of sales, compared to $10.3 billion of profits in 2007 on $105 billion in sales (see Figure 5.8).

Ironically, while the merger between Arcelor and Mittal initially increased the combined company's global market share, this fell somewhat in the years after the merger. There are several reasons for this. The merger with Arcelor expanded the company's production capacity in Europe, which collapsed not that long after the merger. Arcelor-Mittal was forced to idle several blast furnaces due to weak demand. At the end of 2013, European demand was down 30 percent from its 2007 level and the company had to take a $4.3 billion charge on its troubled European division. However, even more important was

(*continued*)

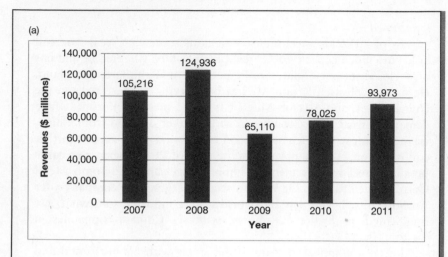

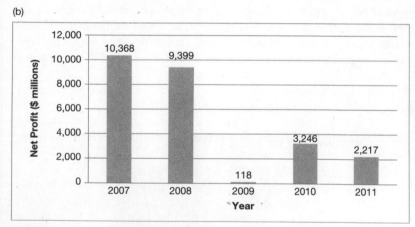

FIGURE 5.8   (a) ArcelorMittal Revenues and (b) ArcelorMittal Net Profits
Source: Value Line, June 15, 2012.

the rapid growth of Chinese steel production, which as of the end of 2012 accounted for just under one-half of world steel output. Normally, Mittal would have expanded aggressively into the rapidly growing Chinese market, but the Beijing government has, as they have in other industries, refused to allow foreign steelmakers to take majority ownership positions in major Chinese companies. In addition, being from India, Mittal was confident of being able to enjoy good revenue growth from the other huge and rapidly growing Asian market. This never happened either.

(*continued*)

(*continued*)

As of 2012, the steel industry remains somewhat weak and still holds too much capacity. RG Steel LLC has filed Chapter 11 and has now closed its huge Sparrows Point plant in Baltimore, Maryland. Germany's Thyssen Krupp AG has been trying to close mills in the United States, and Arcelor–Mittal has closed plants in Europe, where demand is weak. This, combined with weaker demand from China, leaves an industry, which used M&A to consolidate, in need of further consolidation. This happened at the end of 2012, when two large Japanese steel makers merged. Nippon Steel and Sumitomo Metal Corp. merged to form the world's second-largest steel company after Arcelor–Mittal. This left the world's steel industry somewhat less fragmented, as Figure 5.9 shows, with six Chinese companies in the top 10.

Mittal accomplished many of his goals with his horizontal and vertical M&A strategy. However, like many who failed to achieve all their goals with a major M&A strategy, he failed to forecast how the world would change and did not understand that the world evolves more now in the world of rapid globalization than it did in the past. As

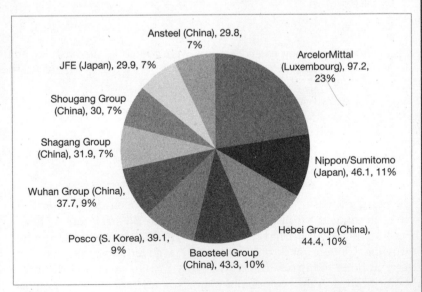

FIGURE 5.9 Global Steel Manufacturers' Market Shares After Nippon/Sumitomo Merger

(*continued*)

he moved to try to consolidate a fragmented industry, the industry continued to expand. As of 2013 the top five steel companies account for less than 20 percent of total global output. This compares with just over 50 percent for the five largest auto companies. In response to rising world capacity and continued weak demand, Arcelor Mittal announced in 2013 that it was selling a stake in its Canadian mining operations, partially reversing its vertical integration strategy in the face of weaker demand.

One of the lessons of Arcelor Mittal's struggles with its M&A strategy is that if one of the better CEOs in the world can find great challenges with large-scale M&A, all others need to tread lightly.

---

[a] Shirisha Regani, "The Mittal/ISG Merger—Creating a Steel Behemoth (Part A)," IBS Center for Management Research, BSTR/147, 2005.

HORIZONTAL INTEGRATION, CONSOLIDATION, AND ROLL-UP ACQUISITION PROGRAMS

We have discussed the fact that so many horizontal deals are based on efficiency considerations as opposed to other factors such as the pursuit of market power. Efficiency considerations were touted as the basis for many of the roll-ups we had in the 1990s. Many of these deals involved larger companies buying smaller rivals in a series of acquisitions. The acquired companies are then combined into an ever-growing larger company. Such deals are sometimes referred to as *roll-up acquisitions*.

The stock market of the 1990s liked roll-ups, although not as much as they were enamored with Internet companies. The typical market that was attractive to consolidators was one that featured many relatively smaller competitors in an industry that was fragmented and unconcentrated. Many of the targets in these industries, such as those in the bus transportation or the funeral home business, were closely held. The owners lacked liquidity, and being acquired by a large public company enabled them to convert their illiquid, closely held shares into a more liquid asset. Consolidators were able to convince the market that the large-scale acquisitions of these smaller targets would enable the combined company to realize scale economies, while also enhancing sales through a greater ability to service national clients. The scale economies were supposed to have many sources including increased buying power, which a national company would have compared to a small regional company. A whole host of roll-up companies were formed in the

United States during the fifth wave with names such as Coach USA, Metals USA, and Floral USA.

For many of the privately held sellers, the dream of liquidity combined with an attractive premium proved to be a nightmare. This was the case in the funeral home industry, where big consolidators like Service Corp and Leowen encountered financial problems and Leowen eventually had to file for Chapter 11 bankruptcy protection. Many consolidators were only good at one thing—doing deals. They were not good managers and, amazingly, it took the market a long time to come to this realization.

Rollups of the 1990s were sometimes referred to as *poof companies*. The name came from the fact that the dealmakers would combine many small companies and instantly create a large firm. Such combinations can carry with them many opportunities for synergies if it is the case that smaller companies are operating less efficiently. For example, the smaller companies could be buying in low volumes from relatively larger sellers and thus be unable to obtain the most beneficial prices.[19] This is how it might seem on paper. Dealmakers will tout the benefits while closing their eyes to the negatives such as the inefficiencies of having a larger bureaucratic structure—one that the managers may not have proven they can manage. The larger company may also have significant leverage if debt was used to fund cash buyouts of the smaller rolled up companies. These kinds of negatives were pervasive with roll-ups, and many simply went bankrupt. In the 2000s, the market has become less keen on roll-ups. This does not mean that they are permanently gone. In fact, since finance practitioners and the market have short memories, we should not be surprised if claims of such efficiencies bring about more rollups in what few fragmented industries may exist.

NOTES

1. Edward Paulson, *Inside Cisco: The Real Story of Sustained M&A Growth* (New York: John Wiley & Sons, 2001), 28.
2. Defense Industry: Consolidation and Options for Preserving Competition, General Accounting Office, Washington DC, April 1998.
3. Hensel Nayantara, "An Empirical Analysis of the Patterns in Defense Industry Consolidation and their Subsequent Impact," *Calhoun Institutional Archive of the Naval Postgraduate School*, 2007.
4. Hensel Nayantara, "Can Industry Consolidation Lead to Greater Efficiencies? Evidence from the U.S. Defense Industry," *Business Economics* 45, no. 3 (2010): 187–203.
5. William Cohan and Bethany McLean, "Jamie Dimon On the Line," *Vanity Fair*, November 2012.

6. Julie Wulf, "Do CEOs in Mergers Trade Power for Premium: Evidence from Mergers of Equals," University of Pennsylvania Working Paper, June 2001.

7. K. Preshanth, "The Interbrew-AmBev Merger Story," *IBS Center for Management Research Case Study*, 2004.

8. Julie Macintosh, *Dethroning the King: The Hostile Takeover of Anheuser Busch, an American Icon* (Hoboken, NJ: John Wiley & Sons, 2011).

9. Devin Leonard, "The Plot to Destroy America's Beer," *BusinessWeek*, October 29–November 4, 2012.

10. Ibid.

11. Robert S. Stillman, "Examining Antitrust Policy Towards Mergers," Ph.D. dissertation, University of California at Los Angeles, 1983. This dissertation was later published in the *Journal of Financial Economics* 11, no. 1 (April 1983): 225–240.

12. B. Epsen Eckbo, "Horizontal Mergers, Collusion and Stockholder Wealth," *Journal of Financial Economics* 11, no. 1 (April 1983): 241–273.

13. E. Han Kim and Vijay Singal, "Mergers and Market Power: Evidence from the Airline Industry," *American Economic Review* 83, no. 3 (June 1993): 549–569.

14. L. A. Stole and J. Zweibel, "Organizational Design and Technology Choice Under Intrafirm Bargaining," *American Economic Review* 42 (1996): 943–963.

15. C. E. Fee and S. Thomas, "Sources of Gains in Horizontal Takeovers: Evidence from Customer, Supplier, and Rival Firms," *Journal of Financial Economics* 74 (2004): 423–460.

16. Husayn Shahrur, "Industry Structure and Horizontal Takeovers: Analysis of Wealth Effects on Rivals, Suppliers and Corporate Customers," *Journal of Financial Economics* 76 (2005): 61–98.

17. John Kenneth Galbraith, *American Capitalism, The Concept of Countervailing Power* (Boston: Houghton Mifflin, 1952).

18. Christopher M. Snyder, "A Dynamic Theory of Countervailing Power," *RAND Journal of Economics* 27, no. 4 (Winter 1996): 747–769.

19. C. M. Snyder, "Why Do Large Buyers Pay Lower Prices? Intense Supplier Competition," *Economic Letters* 58 (1998): 205–209.

CHAPTER 6

Vertical Integration

While *horizontal integration* refers to combinations between competitors, vertical deals involve companies that have a buy-sell or upstream-downstream relationship. While they may not be as common as horizontal deals, there are still countless examples of vertical integration merger and acquisitions (M&A). The key question is what is the track record of such vertical deals? Unfortunately, too often it is questionable. In some instances and situations, it makes good sense for the companies involved. In these cases, vertical integration may be the best solution to a problem such as having a dependable source of supply. In other instances, it may fail to yield real benefits and result in a waste of corporate resources that could be better applied elsewhere.

BENEFITS OF VERTICAL INTEGRATION

The benefits of vertical integration vary depending on the industry. When the deals involve, for example, a manufacturer buying a retailer, the deal may allow the manufacturer to gain better access to the ultimate consumers of their products. Similarly, in the petroleum industry, many of the larger companies have been vertically integrated for many years. It is common to see oil companies be involved, in exploration, transportation, and pipelines and refining, while also owning a large network of gas stations. When they are involved in all these areas, we say they are fully vertically integrated. Whether that is good or not is a debatable issue.

RISK AND VERTICAL INTEGRATION

One of the benefits of being vertically integrated is that it can lower some of the risks a company faces in the marketplace. Buying a supplier can allow a company to have greater certainty in access to supplies. It may also allow these supplies to be more dependably available at more predictable prices.

When getting access to key supplies is a major risk factor, companies may be able to lower this risk through vertical integration. By acquiring a supplier, they may be able to get a dependable source of inputs while possibly being able to gain a competitive advantage by preventing these supplies from being available to the competition. This competitive advantage may carry with it antitrust ramifications, but as markets have become increasingly globalized, most deals, especially vertical ones, tend to move through the antitrust approval process without a great deal of opposition.

VERTICAL INTEGRATION AS A PATH TO GLOBAL GROWTH

When a company manufactures a product, it obviously has to get that product to its ultimate consumers. Even if a company has superior products, if competitors have the distribution channels locked up, the company may be at an insurmountable disadvantage. Sometimes, M&A can be the solution to this dilemma.

Many industries have different layers or stages with some being more competitive than others. For example, the petroleum industry has multiple stages from exploration and extraction to transportation and refining to the retail stage. Some stages are more profitable than others. We discuss later in this chapter how U.S. companies reacted to the changing profitability in the refining business to become less vertically integrated and to sell off their refining businesses. However, for other industries, being vertically integrated is a way of making sure that your products have a clear path to the consumer and that you will not be adversely affected by the actions of competitors. Companies may want to try to control as many outlets for their products as possible to ensure that they can maintain prices that allow them to extract maximum economic rents for their products. Often, such efforts are thwarted by regulators. One prominent example of how this was done in the United States, but also in the global, market without attracting resistance from antitrust regulators was that of eyeglass manufacturer and marketer Luxottica. We discuss this company's very successful use of a vertical integration strategy in the case study that follows.

CASE STUDY: LUXOTTICA—USING VERTICAL AND HORIZONTAL INTEGRATION TO ENSURE GROWTH

Luxottica Group S.p.A. was established in Milan, Italy, in 1961 as an eyeglass manufacturer. By the end of that decade, it had branched out into

(continued)

making its own frames and brands. Like many European companies, it is controlled by one individual or family. In this case, two-thirds of the shares are owned by Leonardo Del Vecchio.

The company has used M&A very successfully to geographically diversify outside of Europe, so when the sovereign debt crisis took told of the continent, Luxottica only had 20 percent of its sales come from that region.

Eyeglasses and sunglasses are not complex products to manufacture. Manufacturers have entered into agreements with designers to create brand names, which basically put a well-known name, such as Burberry, Polo Ralph Lauren, Versace, or Donna Karan, on a simple product and hope to enjoy the high profits that can come from the difference of the marginal costs and marginal revenues from selling brand name eyeglasses at prices they hope can be held at relatively high levels and free from competitive pressures. This is an application of what we discussed in Chapter 3 on synergy from information-based assets.

To effectively use brand names to create and maintain an elevated price that well exceeds marginal cost, a company needs to have its retailers not discount the product or pressure you, the supplier, for price concessions. In other words, to effectively prosecute this strategy to its maximum effectiveness, it helps to control your distribution chain. To do this on a global basis, you have to have such control in all the important markets from which you seek to extract these impressive profits. You are then basically utilizing market power to achieve extra-normal profits. However, to do so for an extended time period, special conditions need to apply. Luxottica has used M&A to make sure that they do.

In the United States, Luxottica did this through a series of acquisitions of some of the leading brands and retailers. For example, it acquired U.S. Shoe Corp., which owned the LensCrafters chain in 1995.[a] In 1999, it acquired Ray-Ban and the Sunglass Hut, which sells many Ray-Ban sunglasses as well as other leading U.S. sunglass brands. It then acquired the Pearl Vision Centers chain in 1995. Last but not least, it acquired an initially resistant target, Oakley, in 2007. When Oakley would not accept Luxottica's offer to be acquired, Luxottica stopped carrying the Oakley brands in its Sunglass Hut stores. This could not happen to Luxottica the manufacturer, as its distribution was controlled by Luxottica the retailer. Oakley did not have this power, and it eventually succumbed to Luxottica's pressure.

(continued)

(*continued*)

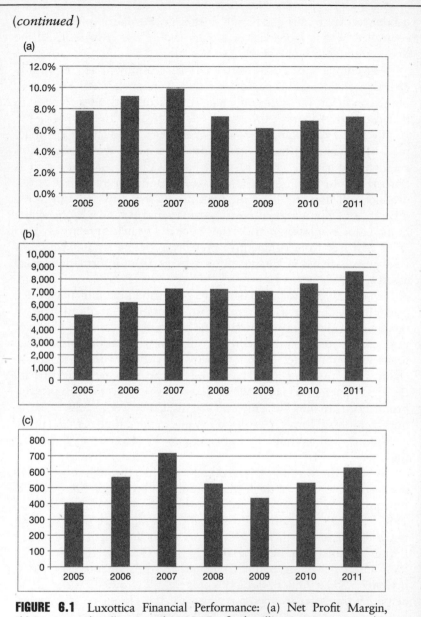

FIGURE 6.1 Luxottica Financial Performance: (a) Net Profit Margin, (b) Revenues ($ millions), and (c) Net Profit ($ millions)
Source: Value Line, November 2, 2012.

(*continued*)

Luxottica enjoys a leadership position in every aspect of the eyeware and eye care business in the U.S. market. It even owns EyeMed Vision Care, which is the leading U.S. vision benefits company.

The end result is that Luxottica, the initially small Milan manufacturer, through a comprehensive global program of successful M&A, has become the leader in the U.S. eyeglass industry and many other markets throughout the world. For example, not only has it acquired companies in markets such as Brazil, it has expanded its Sunglass Hut chain to many other emerging markets. It controls its distribution by being vertically integrated and in doing so insulates itself from price competition, which could kill its margins. While it is a little surprising that the company has been able to so aggressively pursue its preemptive vertical M&A program without catching the ire of antitrust regulators, one thing that probably saves them is that the company's net margins are good but not excessive. In fact, its net margin was as high as 9.9 percent in 2007, but when the world economy softened it fell as low as 6.2 percent in 2009, and then rose to 7.3 percent in 2011 (see Figure 6.1).[b]

---

[a] Yes, you read that correctly. The Cincinnati-based U.S. Shoe Corp., one of the largest importers and marketers of shoes in the United States, acquired the eyeglass retailer LensCrafters in 1984. Obviously, there are many synergies between marketing shoes and eyeglasses. For example, you have to be able to see the shoes to be able to buy them. Therefore, helping people see better should enhance shoes sales—right?

[b] Value Line, August 3, 2012.

HOW OWNING YOUR OWN SUPPLIER CAN BE A COMPETITIVE *DISADVANTAGE*

It seems obvious that owning your own supplier should provide benefits—how much may be a matter of degree but it seems that this would be a positive—not a negative. Amazingly, this is not always the case. Sometimes owning your own supplier can be a disadvantage—not an advantage!

CASE STUDY: OWNING YOUR OWN SUPPLIER IN THE AUTO INDUSTRY

For many years, the major U.S. automakers have been vertically integrated. This goes back to the days of Henry Ford, who established

(continued)

(continued)

his own suppliers and also had great influence over the distribution of cars through Ford's dealer network. In fact, he was able to enhance his cash flow by getting his dealer network to pay for auto shipments prior to delivery. Being the dominant automaker in the industry gave him that leverage over his dealers.

Initially, being backward integrated may have provided benefits to Ford and its chief rival, General Motors, but it eventually became a millstone around the automaker's necks. There are several reasons for this.

As the auto industry became unionized, the United Auto Workers (UAW) became a powerful union that was able to command relatively high wages and benefits for their union members. These high labor costs extended to not just the auto manufacturing business but also to the parts business. For years, the four U.S. automakers (American Motors was acquired by Chrysler in 1987 for $1.5 billion), all of whom were unionized, were able to pass many of these high labor costs to the consumer through higher car prices. This ability to pass on such costs changed when foreign automakers, such as Toyota, were able to capture a higher share of the U.S. market. These foreign automakers were not hamstrung by the high costs of UAW labor. When companies such as Honda and Toyota opened plants in regions such as the southern United States, they were often able to avoid unionization and enjoy labor costs that were a fraction of the U.S. automakers. The position of the American auto companies was further compounded by the fact that for a number of years, the quality of some foreign brands exceeded that of U.S. auto manufacturers. In recent years, U.S. automakers have finally addressed the quality problems and now make products that are now quite competitive from a quality and price perspective.

Ironically, while there were only four and then, later, three U.S. automakers, there were many auto suppliers. U.S. automakers would have liked to play the field and seek out the best prices for their products. The problem was that Ford and GM had their own suppliers, which were dependent on their parent companies to purchase from them. Unfortunately, these were high-cost suppliers with the same problems in labor costs that the auto manufacturers had. Both Ford and GM sought to improve their situations by spinning off their suppliers. In 1999, GM spun-off Delphi, and in 2000 Ford spun-off Visteon. Both were high-cost suppliers in a competitive and highly cyclical industry. Not a good position to be in. To make matters worse,

(continued)

the United Auto Workers reminded the manufacturers that if the high-cost suppliers, Visteon and Delphi, failed (and Delphi eventually did), Ford and GM still bore responsibilities to the workers who were operating pursuant to the UAW contract. Caught between a rock and a hard place, Ford took back Visteon in 2005, while GM kept Delphi independent and eventually both would fall into bankruptcy. The union relied upon its political power and its ability to get a new administration, which it would help get elected, use taxpayer money to bail out the companies that it helped drive into bankruptcy.

The lessons of the auto manufacturers owning their own auto parts suppliers are instructive. When the suppliers' market is quite competitive, it makes little sense to own your own supplier. To do so may hamstring you and prevent you from playing one supplier against another. If, however, there are major quality issues that require a company to own their own supplier, then maybe it is a consideration. However, if the market is competitive, and if the buyers provide large orders to suppliers, why would manufacturers believe that quality will improve if they own the supplier as opposed to suppliers being independent? Again, these issues need to be carefully considered before proceeding with a vertical acquisition.

In fairness to the U.S. automakers, as the market changed and became more globalized, they were aware of the advantages of being able to purchase inputs in a competitive market. Unfortunately, the autoworkers union limited the manufacturers' options and the result was that they became even less competitive and lacked the flexibility to do anything about it. We also do not mean to place the woes of the U.S. auto industry solely at the feet of the UAW. Management bears a great deal of the blame by not being able to make higher quality cars and letting the leading position U.S. companies such as GM and Ford be so easily taken away by foreign rivals. Fortunately, this has changed. Detroit is once again making high-quality cars that it sells at attractive prices. Excellent managers, such as Alan Mulally, were placed in control of companies such as Ford and have done a great job.

VERTICAL INTEGRATION AS A NATURAL OUTGROWTH OF A BUSINESS

In many industries, effective distribution can play a key role in corporate growth. This was the case in the U.S. soft drink market. The source of the profits is the margin associated with the brands and the goodwill that has been built up through years of successful marketing. For some companies product development yields a successful product that consumers want. Future sales are not so much a function of additional product development but of successful marketing in an industry that invests significant sums in marketing.

Pepsi was one manufacturer that knew that the main source of profits was in manufacturing and marketing the product—not in distributing it. It seemed logical for Pepsi to spin off its suppliers, or so they thought. One would think the management would have known its industry and therefore given serious consideration to the ramifications of not having control of its own supplier network. In just a few years, this decision would prove to be quite questionable.

CASE STUDY: PEPSI: SELL OFF THEIR BOTTLERS; NO, BUY THEM BACK AGAIN—WELL, WHICH IS IT?

Bottling and distribution were not major sources of profitability at Pepsi in the 1990s. In addition, the company was under pressure from investors to increase its rate of return, and one possible solution was to get rid of the lower-margin parts of the business. Management seized upon the fact that equity markets were strong, so it seemed to be a good time to release the bottling businesses through a public offering. They also used some of the proceeds of the sale to pay down debt, which seemed to be the prudent thing to do. However, just a few years later, this decision would come back to haunt Pepsi.

Pepsi sold off its bottling business in 1999. These bottling businesses became public companies and traded under the names of the Pepsi Bottling Group and Pepsi Americas. Both were substantial businesses (see Figure 6.2). They were still linked to Pepsi following the spin-off, as these two companies represented Pepsi's soft drink distribution system. The problem was that they were separate, individual companies with their own shareholders, their own boards of directors, and separate management. Each had its own strategy, and the bottlers' goal was no longer maximizing Pepsi's profits. Rather, their goal was to maximize their own earnings.

Pepsi marketed more than just soft drinks such as the well-known Pepsi Cola product. Over the years, as consumers became more health conscious, they shifted away from soft drinks, which had a higher sugar content and calories, to more healthy choices such as water and

(continued)

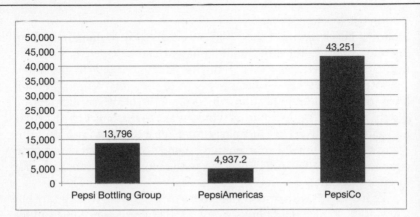

FIGURE 6.2 Comparative Revenues: Pepsi and Bottlers

healthy drinks. Toward that end, Pepsi added Aquafina water, Lipton teas, and Tropicana juices as well as Gatorade. Pepsi acquired Gatorade from Quaker Oats in 2000 for $13.4 billion.

Soft drinks are actually made at the local bottlers using the formula of the manufacturer. They are then distributed to retailers. The bottlers were attracted by the Gatorade brand and wanted to be able to sell this product as well. Pepsi, however, knew that Gatorade was manufactured using a different process and were concerned about giving this responsibility to the local bottlers. The company wanted to maintain quality control and the bottlers wanted to add to their product offerings and thereby enhance their revenues and profits.

When Pepsi would not agree to the demands of the bottlers, which, of course, they no longer controlled as they were not independent companies, the bottlers pursued other options. They then reached out to Pepsi's competitor Dr. Pepper/Snapple and began to distribute Snapple, Dr. Pepper, and Crush soda. Now, Pepsi had a problem. Its own distribution system was distributing the products of competitors. The distribution system that Pepsi developed and controlled was now working against Pepsi to take market share away from it. The situation became untenable and eventually, Pepsi made an offer to reacquire its bottlers.

In 2009, roughly a decade after it decided to get rid of the bottlers, Pepsi paid $7.8 billion to reacquire the businesses. The question is how could management know so little about its own business, and the ramifications of selling off the bottlers, that it could have made such a

(continued)

(continued)

blunder? This is akin to a chess player being unable to think more than one move ahead. For a beginning amateur chess player, this may be normal. However, Pepsi had a highly paid management team and supposedly a very knowledgeable board of directors. Could they not have foreseen the ramifications of losing control of the distribution system and that the distributors would want to maximize their profits and gain access to all not just part of the Pepsi product line? Was this really such a surprise? Unfortunately, such M&A blunders are all too common. Again, the fault clearly lies with managerial errors and poor director oversight.

Pepsi's errors with respect to its vertical integration strategy are but a few of its managerial failings. Some have criticized the company for failing to invest sufficient monies to support its five major brands: Pepsi-Cola, Mountain Dew, Gatorade, Tropicana, and Lipton. By 2012, the company announced that profits would fall 5 percent that year and that it would cut its dividends by 4 percent and repurchase shares to support the stock price, while also laying off 8,700 employees.[a]

---

[a] Matt Esterl and Paul Ziobro, "PepsiCo Overhauls Strategy," *Wall Street Journal*, February 10, 2012, B3.

VERTICAL INTEGRATION: A GROWTH STRATEGY?

Companies in mature markets, or markets where they face intense competition, often look elsewhere to find growth opportunities. Sometimes this involves diversifying outside their industry. We discussed diversification as a strategy in Chapter 4. However, we can merely note now that there is abundant evidence to indicate that the benefits of diversification strategy are often questionable.

Acquiring a supplier of a downstream business involves expanding into a different aspect of the same general business market. This can be an advantage over expansion outside the industry as, presumably, the acquirer knows the overall industry and may have done business with the company that is being acquired. Thus they may know the strengths and weaknesses of the target better than companies outside the industry. All other factors being constant, this gives vertical deals a possible advantage over other deals. Unfortunately, this is not that significant an advantage and can be outweighed by many other factors.

For managers of companies that are struggling to grow, acquiring another company gives the *appearance* of growth. Revenues are added and with them additional profits (ideally). A quick look at the company's revenue and profit history would imply growth. Of course, this would be a very superficial analysis, as the acquirer would have paid the target's shareholders in advance for these additional profits. In addition, to give the target an incentive to sell, the buyer usually has to pay a premium. This places the burden on the bidder to generate a return even greater than what the seller expected to realize. This payment could appear on the balance sheet in the form of a loss of cash and/or an increase in debt, which carries with it future interest and principal payments, or the issuance of equity, which brings with it dilution issues. So the key is that there have to be synergies where the combination of the companies will yield greater revenues and/or profit beyond what the acquirer paid for the target. This is true for all acquisitions. In the context of vertical deals, there has to be a reasonable basis for believing that such gains will manifest themselves. Too often, however, this is not the case. This is illustrated in the Home Depot case study that follows.

CASE STUDY: HOME DEPOT—ACQUIRING A SUPPLIER

Home Depot is the very successful home improvement chain founded in 1978 by Arthur Blank (maybe better known now for being the owner of the Atlanta Falcons football team) and Bernie Marcus. They were succeeded in 2000 by Robert Nardelli, the former protégée of GM's Jack Welch. Prior to that, the two founders, Marcus until 1997 and Blank until 2000, ran the company. Ironically, Jamie Dimon, who would lead JPMorgan Chase to become the biggest bank in the United States, briefly considered accepting the position of running Home Depot.[a]

Nardelli was one of three competitors who fought to be the successor of Jack Welch at GE. Welch basically set up a contest to be his successor with the agreement that the two "losers" would have to leave the company. James McNerney left to become CEO of 3M and eventually Boeing. Nardelli came to Home Depot.

Nardelli made numerous changes when he took the reins of the company. He slowed the rate of expansion of new stores so that the company did not cannibalize its own market.[b] He also expanded

(continued)

(continued)

globally by opening operations in South America, but they were not successful, and the company eventually retired from these markets.

Nardelli struggled to increase Home Depot's market share and profitability. In the early 2000s, Lowes was an aggressive competitor and had made significant inroads in Home Depot's markets. Home Depot was running out of good locations to open new stores while Lowes was eating into its market share on some of Home Depot's more profitable markets. Lowe's also worked on making its stores generally more appealing and also tried to market to women to pick up extra market share. As Home Depot slowed the rate of its new store openings, Lowes increased its rate thereby picking up more of the market.

Nardelli came up with the brainstorm to try to enhance profitability by acquiring a supplier and then expanding that business. On a very superficial basis, this might seem to make sense. However, as one thinks about it more carefully, if the seller demands that the buyer pay it a value tied to the present value of its profits, plus a premium, then the only real gains that can result from the deal have to be tied to profit gains that are beyond what the target itself could realize. As we have noted, in order for this to occur, the buyer needs to realize significant gains above what the seller expected to realize. This usually means that there have to be synergies between the acquirer and that the target can make the target, after it is owned by the acquirer, more valuable than it was on its own.

In 2006, Nardelli and Home Depot paid $3.47 billion for Hughes Supply. This was a 21 percent premium. Hughes Supply itself was a product of several acquisitions such as Las Vegas-based Standard Wholesale (electrical and plumbing supplier) and California and Las Vegas–based Todd Pipe and Supply (plumbing). These regions would be hard hit by the collapse in the real estate market, which was particularly pronounced shortly after the acquisition.

While Home Depot was able to purchase some products, such as wood, from its own supplier, the company it had acquired, Hughes Supply, was more oriented toward the commercial supply market while Home Depot was focused on the retail consumer. Therefore, acquiring such a supplier was not as much help with Home Depot's core retail market.

Nardelli did the deal when the economy and the market were very strong. This is a great time to sell a business—especially a cyclical one

(continued)

like Hughes Supply. It was not necessarily a great time to buy a cyclical business. The seller was obviously very aware of this as well.

Hughes Supply was one of the largest suppliers of construction and building materials in the industry. So the acquisition made Home Depot an instant player in this segment of the market. However, the real question was how would Home Depot realize gains from this vertical deal sufficient to more than offset the price plus the premium it paid?

Home Depot was hoping the acquisition of suppliers would provide it with better pricing. On a very simplistic basis, if you own the supplier, you can mandate better pricing than what you were paying. While this is true, the target's former pricing was part of the profits that the buyer paid for when it bought the vertical target (or any target for that matter). Lowering the supplier's prices lowers its profits, while possibly raising the buyer's profits. It is a zero sum game.

Home Depot never realized gains from this acquisition. The highly paid Nardelli was a troubled CEO and was terrible at relating to shareholders, who chafed under his imperious manner, which was not backed up by good returns. Understandably, Nardelli's successor, Frank Blake, reversed this strategy and immediately sold off what it then called Home Depot Supply in 2007. The company announced that the new strategy would be to focus on its core retail business. When Blake took the reins of Home Depot, he saw that the supply division was a good business but was not the core business, which was the *retail* business. He also noticed that while Home Depot worked to integrate the supply business into the overall business model, it was continuing to lose ground in the retail business. Surveys showed that consumer satisfaction had declined at Home Depot as consumers found sales personnel harder to find and less knowledgeable. Blake decided to sell off the supply business and invest more in what made Home Depot the market leader. Acquiring Hughes Supply did not in any way help solve Home Depot's problems with its core business. In fact, it delayed its efforts to successfully fix its real problems in that business. A major acquisition can have that effect. Large M&A can be a big distraction and this is another M&A cost that is very hard to measure and factor into deal calculus. In addition, it can be an opportunity for rivals, such as, in this case, Lowes.

Unfortunately, Home Depot pursued the sale of the expensive supplier it acquired just as the subprime crisis was taking hold. The

(continued)

(*continued*)

private equity buyers, Clayton Dublier & Rice, Carlyle Group, and Bain Capital, were able to negotiate the price down in such an atmosphere by $2 billion! This is not an unusual event. A new CEO comes in and undoes the prior CEO's erroneous acquisitions, incurs a loss for the company but can blame the result on the prior CEO.

As is too often the case in the field of M&A, it is hard to make this stuff up. Home Depot made a poorly thought-out acquisition when it paid a premium consistent with a strong market and then shortly afterward sold it off in a weak market. Nardelli's strategy was a bust. Equally important, the board of directors who approved these deals let shareholders down when they did not question the logic of this strategy. Obviously, they did not question how Home Depot could reasonably expect to make sufficient gains in the supply business that would be in excess of the premium-inclusive price it was paying. They also did not question how an acquisition of a supply company that operated mainly in the commercial segment of the business was going to help solve its problems in the core retail business. Clearly, it would not. The fault has to lay as much with the board as with Nardelli. However, the board handled the failure of someone it hired and paid handsomely but who screwed up, the way U.S. corporate boards in general do. They paid him $210 million as a going away present. Presumably, their defense is that such payouts were influenced by the agreement they entered into when they hired Nardelli. However, this is a poor explanation. In effect, such a defense is that they hired a CEO who they believed was a star. They did not make the huge compensation contingent on star performance. In fact, the agreement allowed the CEO to profit handsomely from poor performance. Such absurd payouts for failure are all too common in the United States but are much less common outside the United States. As we discuss in Chapter 9, there are many reasons why corporate governance is often poor in the United States and why CEO compensation is often out of control. Unfortunately, none of them are good reasons.

One would think that after such a disastrous experience at Home Depot that Bob Nardelli would have a tough time finding a job. Nothing could be further from the case. When the private equity firm Cerberus Capital invested in the ailing Chrysler, the car company that Daimler could not fix, they could not wait to scoop up the highly skilled Nardelli to run the automaker. He readily assumed leadership of the third-largest U.S. automaker and sought to learn something about the auto industry while attempting to be a faster learner than he was at Home Depot. Unfortunately this worked out even worse and Cerberus saw its entire foolish equity investment wiped out. As we have said elsewhere in this book, you can't make this stuff up.

---

[a] William Cohan and Bethany, "Jamie Dimon On the Line," *Vanity Fair*, November, 2012.

[b] Shirisha Regani, "Home Depot's Strategy Under Bob Nardelli," IBS Center, BSTR/141, 2004.

CONTINUALLY REEVALUATING A VERTICAL INTEGRATION STRATEGY

Companies that are vertically integrated need to regularly reevaluate their structure and examine the returns that come from the different parts of the vertical chain. The question that needs to regularly asked is: Is the overall company better off with the different vertical units within the same corporate structure, or would shareholders be better off if the units were separated? It is not enough to just accept that if a company has had a vertical structure for many years that this is the essence of the company and it is how it should remain. The reason is that market conditions evolve over time. For example, a corporate structure that worked when markets were more stable may not work in volatile markets. The opposite can also be the case.

A good example of an industry that responded to more volatile markets by undoing its vertical structures is the U.S. petroleum industry. This industry had long been vertically integrated and that seemed to be the natural way. However, as the case study below illustrates, that changed in the 2000s.

CASE STUDY: U.S. OIL COMPANIES GETTING OUT OF THE REFINERY BUSINESS

For many years, many of the larger oil companies were vertically integrated. In the oil industry, the structure goes from oil exploration and production to refining to pipelines or transportation to retail. Pipelines are actually involved in different stages of the process, and the product moves from the ground to gas tanks of consumers. Refiners

(continued)

(*continued*)

(a)

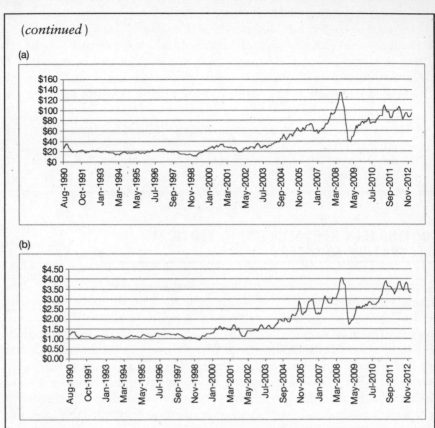

(b)

FIGURE 6.3   Prices of (a) Oil ($ per Barrel) and (b) Gasoline ($ per Gallon)
Source: EIA.

buy oil at market prices and then sell the refined product. There is competition on the purchase side and on the sell side. Refiners make their money by being able to buy crude oil at one price and sell the refined product at a sufficiently higher price to allow then to earn a reasonable return. Figure 6.3 shows the trend in the price of gasoline and the price of oil.

The more volatile the market for crude oil, the more difficult it can be to earn a profit in this business. In 2010 and 2011, U.S. oil companies began to consider the meager returns their refining

(*continued*)

businesses were earning to be a drain on the overall profitability of the business. This is why a number of them decided to part ways with their refining units.

In June 2011, Marathon Oil decided to spin off its refining business. With such a spinoff, the company could then concentrate on crude oil production and exploration. The new structure, Marathon Petroleum Corp, would house the oil production business while the spunoff entity would include a refining business but also its retail network and its pipeline business.

The move by Marathon marked the first of a series of refinery selloffs by U.S. companies. Earlier in 2011, the troubled BP had announced it was going to sell off its refining business. In March 2011, Chevron decided to sell its U.K. refinery to Valero Energy Corp for $730 million.

Within two weeks of the Marathon spinoff announcement, Conoco Phillips, the third-largest U.S. oil company, announced a one-two spinoff of its refining business. Like Marathon, Conoco's oil production business generated the bulk of the company's profits thus keeping the less profitable refining business lowered the overall return to shareholders.

In the copycat world of corporate management, it is common to see one company initiate an action and then have its rivals follow in its footsteps. This was the case in 1998, when many of the larger oil companies, such as Exxon and Mobil, but also Conoco and Phillips as well as BP and Amoco, merged in mega-deals. It was, therefore, not surprising that in September 2011, the Philadelphia-based Sunoco announced it would sell off two of its refineries in Pennsylvania. In the case of Sunoco, however, it would then concentrate on its large retail network as well as its pipelines.

In each of these instances, the companies who have long been vertically integrated reacted to the changing market conditions and realized one segment of the vertical structure was the major contributor of its profits and another contributed to a much lesser extent. Management then decided to downsize and separate the refining businesses, which had come to be a drain on overall shareholder return. Given that investors often evaluate companies within the context of a category and their peers, when one company undertakes an initiative as a response to changing market conditions that have dragged down shareholder returns, it is common to see competitors take similar actions to the first mover.

REGULATION OF VERTICAL INTEGRATION

While horizontal M&A may in certain circumstances attract the ire of antitrust regulators, vertical deals usually go unopposed. This is partly due to the changed regulatory view of vertical deals over the past three decades. Prior to the 1980s, vertical deals were seen by some as possibly anticompetitive in situations where they could result in the foreclosure of sources of supply to competitors. The thinking was that the acquired supplier could now choose to not provide products or services to competitors of the acquirer. These views were challenged by economists who were often associated with the Chicago School. The term *Chicago School* refers to views espoused by certain economists, including a number of Nobel-prize-winning economists, such as George Stigler and Milton Freidman, as well as Ronald Coase and Gary Becker, who were professors at the University of Chicago.[1] Their path-breaking accomplishments have given rise to a long list of followers, many of whom are on the faculty of the University of Chicago as well as many other universities.

Among other ideas, these Chicago School views often emphasize the benefits of free markets and lower regulation. The School's adherents often argued that vertical deals could bring with them enhanced efficiencies and were often competitively neutral. Courts began to adopt this view and for a while did not oppose vertical deals. This changed somewhat as courts began to consider a post-Chicago view, which adopted a game-theoretic approach that considered how a vertically integrated company might be able to engage in certain maneuvers so as to gain advantages over competitors.

While it is certainly possible that proposed vertical deals may be opposed on competitive grounds, vertical transactions usually experience much smoother sailing compared to horizontal M&A. This makes vertical deals less uncertain and costly from a regulatory perspective. While this is a clear advantage over horizontal M&A, these advantages may be greatly outweighed by strategic considerations.

CASE STUDY: ANTITRUST APPROVAL FOR LIVE NATION—TICKETMASTER MERGER

In 2009 Live Nation, the largest concert promoter in the United States and Ticketmaster, the number one ticket seller, announced their merger and drew close antitrust scrutiny. Live Nation annually puts on about 20,000 shows globally for about 2,000 artists. It is by far the industry leader.

Ticketmaster held itself out as the "world's leading live entertainment ticketing" company. It also owned Tickets Now, which was a

(continued)

secondary-market ticket seller. In addition, Ticketmaster pursued some vertical integration through its operation of an artist management business called the Front Line Management Group.

Some were surprised when the Justice Department allowed the merger between these two leaders in their respective vertical segments. The Justice Department did so only after the companies agreed to terms, which included Ticketmaster agreeing to license its ticketing software to competitors and also to sell off one of its ticket selling units. Christine Varney, then head of the Justice Department's antitrust division, stated that she believed that the merger would result in a decline in ticket prices.

The changing economic conditions of the industry help explain why the deal received antitrust approval with such weak conditions imposed on the merger partners. In the years leading up to the merger, artists had seen their revenues from record and CD sales decline as digital music downloading began to replace the more traditional album sales. Consumers would simply download a particular song on iTunes and often pay just $0.99 whereas in the past they may have paid prices such as $10 to $15 for the whole album.

In years gone by, artists used concerts to promote album sales, and concert tickets were somewhat underpriced to reflect those promotion efforts. With the decline in music sales, artists then had to look to concert tours to recoup these lost revenues, and prices began to rise.

The Justice Department believed the claims of the merger partners that the combination of the two companies would lead to greater efficiencies, which, in turn, would work to the consumer's benefit through lower prices. This result remains to be seen.

COPYCAT VERTICAL INTEGRATION

When one major company in an industry becomes vertically integrated, its competitors may think it has gained competitive advantages over them, and they may pursue their own vertical integration strategy. Sometimes these responses are nothing more than knee-jerk reactions and not the product of a well-thought-out strategy. Let us think back to the failed merger between Merck and Medco, which we discussed in Chapter 3. The original deal between Merck and Medco was poorly thought out, and Merck did not anticipate the backlash regarding the potential market power that Merck could acquire in possibly giving their drugs preference over the products of competitors, which certain physicians might prefer. Eventually the deal had to be undone, and Medco was spunoff in 2003. Nonetheless, the series of deals in the pharmaceutical industry is instructive in that it shows how competitors, in this case Roche and Eli Lilly, reacted to another company's M&A program.

Interestingly, in 2012, with the folly of Merck's failed vertical integration strategy long behind it, Medco, which had 2011 revenues of $66 billion, was acquired in a horizontal deal by a somewhat smaller competitor Express Scripts, which had 2011 revenues of $45 billion. In the years following its spinoff, Medco had diversified into fields like genetic testing and clinical research, and had also expanded into Europe. However, Express Scripts stayed focused on its core business.

The combination of Medco and Express Scripts resulted in the largest company in the pharmacy-benefit business. This merger then put pressure on the two largest rivals—CVS Caremark and United Health Group's Optum Rx. The deal exemplifies how the prior vertical strategy did not work in this industry, but the companies decided there were benefits in a horizontal combination.

Sometimes copycat M&A is merely a response to changing market conditions. This was the case in the selloffs by petroleum companies of their less-profitable refiners, which we have just discussed. The major causal factor in these sales was the impact that changing market conditions had on the profitability of the refining segment of the vertically integrated business. Various oil companies reacted similarly, as they sought to divest these segments of their business so that they did not lower the profitability of the overall business.

NOTE

1. While George Stigler and Milton Friedman have passed away, Gary Becker continues to be an active member of the economics department at the University of Chicago.

CHAPTER 7

Growth through Emerging Market M&A

In this chapter, we will discuss both the merger and acquisition (M&A) opportunities that exist in emerging markets for companies in the developed markets as well as the rise of the emerging market acquirer. We will first focus on M&A in emerging markets by companies in more developed economies that are seeking faster growth. Then we will shift to focusing on the emerging market acquirers. The emerging market acquirers are a relatively new breed of acquirer from emerging markets, which have targeted companies in the developed world for a variety of reasons.

A comprehensive discussion of the M&A opportunities in all the major emerging markets throughout the world is well beyond the bounds of this chapter. Instead, we focus on the opportunities, but also the pitfalls, of doing M&A in some of the major emerging markets. As with the rest of this book, we demonstrate many of our points through discussing actual M&As—some that have worked out well and some that have not. In doing so, we hope to raise many of the issues that dealmakers and would-be acquirers have to be cognizant of prior to doing deals.

Companies can benefit from doing M&A in emerging markets by realizing an expanded demand for their products or services. They can also secure better sources of supply in emerging markets. Such deals are not new but have been going on for a long time. Our initial discussion focuses on companies in developed nations pursuing growth and greater demand for their products or services. Part of the reason why companies in developed markets are looking to emerging markets for growth is the weakness in the economies of the major so-called developed nations.

ECONOMIC CONDITION OF MAJOR ECONOMIES IN THE POSTSUBPRIME WORLD

In recent years, the leading developed markets have been growing slowly or not growing at all. Figure 7.1 shows the anemic growth of the United States, European Union, and Japanese economies. The United States was rocked by the subprime crisis and the Great Recession that followed. The 18-month recession in the United States was followed by a weak recovery. It was only by the start of 2012 that the United States began to shows signs of steady growth, even though this growth was relatively modest and hovered around 2 percent per year. Economic history tells us that recoveries from recessions that are preceded by financial crises tend to take longer. Reinhart and Rogoff have shown that, on average, such financial crisis-related recession aftereffects last longer than recessions that were not associated with a financial crisis and feature unemployment that rises an average of 7 percentage points over the phase of the cycle.[1]

The subprime crisis that gripped the United States and Europe was followed by the 2011 to 2012 sovereign debt crisis, which further dampened the European economy. The combined effects of these events has resulted in minimal growth in Europe with Southern Europe being economically worse off then Northern Europe, which itself has not been all that strong (see Figure 7.1). The impact of this is that many companies seeking growth have to look to high-growth markets as opposed to trying to wring out some growth from mature markets, or even worse, stagnant markets like Europe. In fact, this was already the case prior to the Great Recession and the European Sovereign Debt Crisis, but the need became even greater afterwards.

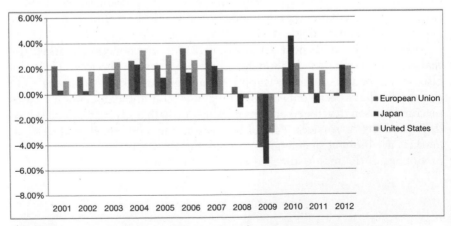

FIGURE 7.1 U.S., European Union, and Japanese Annual GDP Growth
Source: IMF, World Economic Outlook Database, October 2012.

In Japan, the outlook has also not been very positive for some time. Even through the Japanese economy remains weak, foreign currency markets, at times, chose to increase the value of the Japanese yen relative to currencies such as the dollar. The different binges of quantitative easing that the U.S. Federal Reserve implemented to try to jump-start the U.S. economy did not do much to uplift the value of the yen. Being more of an export-oriented economy, Japanese companies, like their U.S. and European counterparts, have had to look increasingly outside their own borders for rapid growth M&A opportunities. While U.S. outbound M&A volume was quite stable over the two-year period from 2010 to 2011, Japan's outbound M&A volume was up sharply in 2011, reflecting this pursuit for growth outside of the stagnant Japanese economy. The obvious question then is what markets provide the greatest growth opportunities?

LOW-GROWTH MARKETS' DIMINISHING RETURNS

A company seeking to achieve growth in a mature or low-growth market will find that growth gains are difficult and very expensive to achieve. Rather than being the result of an expansion in the underlying economy and market, they often have to be achieved at the expense of competitors. In mature markets where there are often several formidable competitors, these gains can require large amounts of expensive inputs such as marketing and advertising. Consider the beer market in the United States. Companies with established brands, such as Anheuser-Busch, which markets the well-known Budweiser brand, had achieved a stable market share but continually had to invest considerable sums to maintain this share. Miller Brewing invested very substantial amounts in colorful advertising but was never able to supplant Budweiser's and Budweiser Light's dominant position. This was the case even though for a number of years Miller was owned by Philip Morris/Atria, which enjoyed sizeable and steady cash flows from tobacco sales. As we have discussed, while Anheuser-Busch reveled in its dominant position in the U.S. beer market, the industry became increasingly globalized, and other companies began to become more powerful.

One of these rapidly growing beer companies was InBev. This company became a major global marketer of beer through a series of well-conceived *global* acquisitions. Anheuser-Busch, however, with its insular Midwestern U.S. management, moved *too late and too little* into the global market, which made it vulnerable to a takeover. Had it been better managed, instead of having been a company run as though it were a kingdom where the throne was passed to four Busch heirs in a row, it might have seized upon globalization and remained independent.[2] Instead, it became a valuable target acquired by the more globally oriented management of InBev. Anheuser had the opportunity to aggressively take its leading brand to the world market, but its feeble and belated attempts to do so cost the company its independence. However, from the perspective of shareholders, this is not necessarily a bad thing. In the end, the firm's assets were transferred to a company with a management team that had an impressive record. We discussed the takeover of Anheuser-Busch by Inbev in Chapter 5.

Emerging markets can present great opportunities for established companies from developed markets. It is often the case that companies with established brands that have achieved significant success in their home markets can take advantage of the considerable investment that went into developing their products and market positions. Such companies may have significant advantages over newer companies in the emerging markets in that they have highly developed products and brands, which may be world renowned. The quality of the products and their brand names may be quite attractive to emerging market consumers. It is difficult for emerging market companies to match such advantages. There are numerous examples of this, but a particularly interesting one is the British distiller Diageo, which we will discuss later in this chapter. At this point, it is useful to identify the high-growth geographical regions and countries.

ROLE OF DEMOGRAPHICS

When we consider the markets that will be high-growth markets worthy of a concerted M&A strategy, we have to identify the crucial factors that will influence such a decision. One of these key factors has to be demographics. Markets with very large populations have to be ones that warrant the closest focus. This type of reasoning certainly proved right in the case of China. In general, for the BRICS, a term coined by Jim O'Neill of Goldman Sachs, which refers to Brazil, Russia, India, and China, this has generally proved correct.[3] To varying extents, all four countries have emerged as major growth markets. However, demographics alone cannot be the deciding factor. While all four of these nations have exhibited growth, Russia and India have been held down by major limitations in governmental and regulatory systems. Therefore, the choice of growth markets needs to be driven by a collection of factors, of which demographics has to be key.

One of the great merger growth challenges is to identify the next growth markets after the BRICS. Will, for example, Indonesia with its 242 million people or Bangladesh with its 150 million people be the next India if not China (see Table 7.1)? Indonesia is an interesting economy that boasts steady economic growth and controlled inflation—a good combination. Currently, it is the fourth-most-populous nation in the world. It has a young population and shows a lot of promise. However, it has great limitations in government and infrastructure.

TABLE 7.1   Top 15 Countries by Population and Their per Capita GDPs[4]

Country	Population (in Millions)	Per Capita GDP (in current US $)
China	1,344.1	5,444.8
India	1,241.5	1,488.5
United States	311.6	48,441.6
Indonesia	242.3	3,494.6
Brazil	196.7	12,593.9
Pakistan	176.7	1,194.3
Nigeria	162.5	1,452.1
Bangladesh	150.5	735.0
Russia	141.9	13,089.3
Japan	127.8	45,902.7
Mexico	114.8	10,064.3
Philippines	94.9	2,369.5
Vietnam	87.8	1,411.2
Ethiopia	84.7	374.2
Egypt	82.5	2,780.9

Source: World Bank: http://databank.worldbank.org/ddp/home.do.

THE NEXT 11

Researchers at Goldman Sachs and Jim O'Neill have identified what he termed the Next 11 (N-11), which refers to the following countries:

1. Bangladesh
2. Egypt
3. Indonesia
4. Iran
5. Korea
6. Mexico
7. Nigeria
8. Pakistan
9. Philippines
10. Turkey
11. Vietnam

O'Neill concedes that although given the size disparities, the N-11 "may not have the scale to have a 'BRIC-like' impact, they could rival the G7."[5] The G7, originally formed in 1975 as the G6, included France, Germany, Italy, Japan, United Kingdom, and the United States. Canada was added the next year. Of the N-11 countries, four—Mexico, Indonesia, South Korea, and Turkey—make up approximately three-quarters of the GDP of the total overall N-11.

M&A strategies of many companies are driven by the time focus of the CEO and upper management. When we consider that the average CEO may be in office for approximately seven to eight years, then he or she may not be interested in projects that will bear fruit long after he or she has left office. Whether this is in shareholders' interests or not is a different issue. What we are focusing on now is reality as opposed to how the corporate world should be run. The U.S. corporate world has become so myopic that much of the focus is on the next quarterly earnings report—never mind performance over the next 5 to 10 years. With that in mind, which markets will pay returns from an M&A strategy with a time horizon that may span 5 to 10 years? If this is the time horizon, then demographics alone will clearly not be the driving factor. It has to be demographics combined with infrastructure and governmental systems that can all be in place in the foreseeable future. This then narrows the field.

M&A IS NOT ALWAYS THE BEST WAY OF ACCESSING HIGH-GROWTH MARKETS

Prior to getting into a detailed discussion of which countries would warrant an M&A strategy, it is important to determine if there are other ways in which a company's goals can be achieved. Often these ways, such as joint ventures and strategic alliances, are less expensive alternatives. We discuss this in greater detail in Chapter 8. However, at this time, let us consider the recent case of Citigroup, which in March 2012 sold its remaining stake in Shanghai Pudong Development Bank. This was part of an overall trend by Western banks to shed some of their overseas investment positions, as regulators were requiring banks to hold more capital associated with such investments. These greater capital requirements, known as Basel III, caused not just Citigroup, but also Morgan Stanley, which sold its roughly one-third investment in China International Capital Group and Bank of America and virtually unloaded its entire stake in China Construction Bank, to change the way they approached the Chinese market.

When the U.S. banks acquired equity positions in these Chinese banks, they assumed such stock acquisitions would be necessary in order to do business in China. This has been a requirement by the Chinese government in other industries such as automobiles. However, in recent years the Chinese government has given U.S. banks the green light to offer lucrative banking services, such as credit cards, in China. Citigroup was the first bank to acquire such a capability. Credit cards are a very profitable business for U.S. banks, which are more retail-oriented than banks of other large nations such as Japan. The ability to offer some of the more lucrative banking services in a huge market like China without having to establish an equity position with a Chinese partner, which also would bring with it higher capital requirements, is akin to having one's cake and eating it, too. Here, the U.S. banks were able to access the high-growth Chinese market without an M&A strategy. This could prove beneficial in the long run.

HIGH-GROWTH REGIONS AND COUNTRIES

The fast-growing markets we focus on in this section each present their unique growth opportunities but also challenges. Our discussion starts with Asia, as it is there that the two fastest-growth mega-economies are located: China and India.

Asia

Obviously, Japan and Korea are two huge Asian nations, and by virtue of their sheer size they account for a high level of M&A. In 2011, Japan recorded $57.2 billion of M&A while Korea notched $24.9 billion of deals (see Figure 7.2). However, both of these nations are mature and not growing rapidly, In fact, Japan, which was recently supplanted by China as the world's second-largest economy, has been stagnant for the past 15 years. It was mired in a decade-long recession during the 1990s and has never fully recovered. It appeared on its way to some modest recovery when the global subprime crisis derailed its and most of the developed world's recovery. However, while both markets are large and feature consumers with impressive buying power, they are each slow-growth economies. Their markets, while big, are mature, slow growing, and already filled with competitors.

The outlook for the Korean economy is somewhat more optimistic than for the Japanese economy. The Korean economy has stabilized and resumed growth following the global recession. In addition, Korea does not have the same demographic problems that Japan does. Nonetheless, it is a mature economy and cannot be considered a major growth market.

Japan We have discussed Japan in the context of being the epitome of economic stagnation in major economies. However, we have to recognize that Japan is still one of the largest economies in the world and can boast of having leading corporations such as Toyota, Mitsubishi, and Sony.

Given the difference in growth between very-slow-growth Japan and many of the other nearby high-growth markets, one wonders why so many Japanese acquisitions in recent years have been in somewhat more

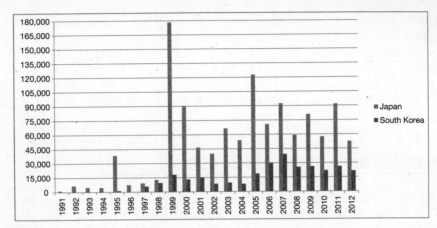

FIGURE 7.2 Japanese and Korean M&A, 1991–2012
Source: Thomson Financial Securities Data.

developed markets. In the years 2010 to 2012, for example, many Japanese companies, like U.S. firms, were flush with cash. However, it seems Japanese firms were more eager to use their cash to fund M&A programs than their comparably liquid U.S. counterparts. The answer is the poor long-run growth prospects of the Japanese market compared to alternatives elsewhere across the globe.

The deals that were done in 2011 to 2012 were not the trophy deals of prior Japanese M&A forays. In fact, the track record of some Japanese M&A from years gone by has been abysmal. When we consider M&A failures, we immediately think back to the huge Japanese acquisition flops like the Rockefeller Center acquisition and the Universal Studio deals of the 1980s and early 1990s. However, the Japanese deals of recent years are not being done to acquire trophies but rather to find sustainable growth in the face of stagnation in the home market.

We see that Japanese dealmakers are very cognizant of the fact that the Japanese market is stagnant and that achieving growth is a challenge there. For this reason, they have looked abroad for their growth opportunities. An example is Softbank's 2012 bid to acquire of a large stake in Sprint Nextel.

The two biggest growth markets in Asia, if not the world, are China and India. The prospects for growth differ sharply from Japan and Korea. However, both China and India bring with them unique challenges for companies in large mature markets seeking to exploit the growth that is occurring in these markets.

China: Economics and Demographics   As Figure 7.3 shows, China has grown impressively following the opening of its economy. The notion of a free market is relatively new in the Middle Kingdom. Starting in the late 1970s,

(a)

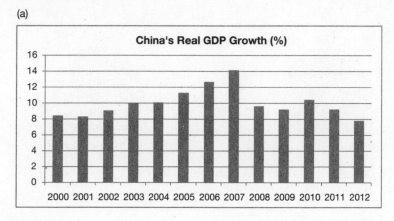

(b)

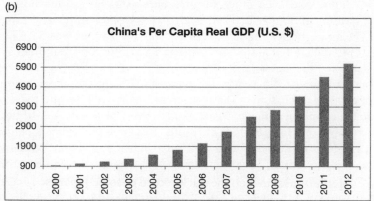

FIGURE 7.3 China's Growth in (a) Real GDP and (b) per Capita GDP
Source: International Monetary Fund (IMF), World Economic Outlook Database, October 2012.

China began to decollectivize agriculture. The country also created various incentives for agricultural workers to switch to higher-value-added activities such as industrial production.[6] Then in the late 1980s, the nation began to privatize much of the state-owned industry. Frankly, the privatization process is ongoing with the government still maintaining too much control of the nation's industry.

China's government is relatively stable by international standards. Essentially, the government changes every 10 years with a new leader having been selected at the end of 2012. The trend in Chinese leadership has been one of increasing openness to economic and financial reform.

With its huge population of 1.3 billion people, China presents great potential buying power. However, *potential* is the key word as per capita

(a)

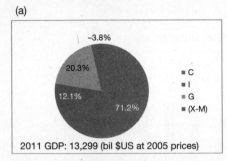

(b)

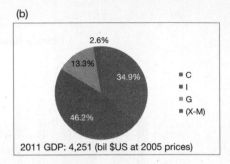

FIGURE 7.4   Breakdown of (a) U.S. and (b) China's GDP
Source: The Economist (Economist Intelligence Unit).

GDP in China, and even more so in India, is still far below those of the leading nations in mature markets such as the United States and Japan. As of 2011, China's per capita GDP was $8,466 and India's was $3,652. This compares to the United States' $48,400 and $34,394 for Japan (using Wold Bank data) for the same year.

There are major differences between the U.S. and Chinese economies. While a detailed discussion of these differences goes well beyond the scope of this book, a couple of comments can go a long way. A few of these differences are readily apparent from looking at Figure 7.4. China's investment percentage of GDP is significantly higher than the United States' percentage. Moreover, in most market economies, investment tends to be the most volatile of the four major components, and this can lead to a more cyclical economy. Also, the higher investment by China has paid great dividends by accelerating the rate of economic growth. The opposite is the case for the U.S. economy.

Consumption is over 70 percent of U.S. GDP but only a little over one-third of China's total output. In addition, exports are 44 percent of China's GDP but only 13 percent of U.S. GDP. No numbers more than these summarize the great differences between the two economies. Herein lies the great challenge for China in its next stage of economic development. China needs to rely less on the simple export-oriented model of economic growth that has worked so well in transforming China into the second-largest economy in the world. However, part of this export growth was fueled by a managed, as opposed to free market, currency. China needs to continue to increase the wealth of its citizens, and with their higher incomes and wealth they need to be able to purchase more of China's output and the output of other nations as opposed to relying on one-sided international trade. In addition, the Chinese government needs to reduce its role in the economy and become less of a driving force. The government played a very important and largely beneficial role in guiding China to its impressive position in the world economy. It is now time for the government to start to step back and let the free market allow Chinese companies and people to take more of the reins of the economy. When this happens, growth may accelerate even more.

A simple comparison between China's per capita income, such as that shown in Figure 7.3, with that of the United States and Japan, can be very deceptive and may not fully indicate the potential buying power of Chinese consumers. China has yet to make a meaningful transformation from an export economy to a more consumer-driven economy. In addition, while consumers in America may make purchases from current income and debt (future income), Chinese consumers have high average savings rates and make many big ticket purchases in cash using savings. Any visitors to major Chinese cities, such as Beijing and Shanghai, can verify China's buying power through sights such as the large number of luxury cars on the roads. However, this buying power diminishes somewhat as one departs from the major cities. In fact, the pattern of economic development in China has raised many concerns about income inequality—however, this is not a unique issue for China but seems to be a byproduct of economic development in most, but certainly not all (consider the Scandinavian countries) major economies.

If our goal is to seek growth from high-growth markets, then our gaze should shift from the large and established nations of Japan and Korea, not only huge markets like China and India but also to the other high-growth economies of Asia. When we do so, we look to nations such as Indonesia, Thailand, Malaysia, and the Philippines. These nations are far smaller than China and India and thus bring with them much smaller M&A opportunities. Nonetheless, some of them, such as Indonesia, present interesting growth prospects—particularly when we consider the size of that economy with its quarter of a billion people. The nation is growing impressively and with it a burgeoning middle class is on the rise.

Doing M&A in the Chinese Market   The Chinese government has imposed barriers on foreign companies entering their markets. They have sought to limit the ability of foreign companies to buy a controlling position in Chinese companies. In addition, they have pressured foreign companies seeking to establish operations in China to work with Chinese "partners" and to limit their stake in such entities to just under control (51 percent). For example, this was the case for U.S. and European companies who entered the Chinese automobile market. General Motors was partnered with the Shanghai Automotive Industry Corporation, who together formed Shanghai General Motors. While GM had to give up a lot to enter the Chinese market, the venture proved to be highly successful and for a while was one of the few areas of growth for the troubled American automobile giant (see case study "GM Open for Business in China" later in this chapter).

Entrants into the Chinese market find that M&A dealmaking in China follows a new set of rules and mores. Being a somewhat controlled economy, the government plays a major role in the business sector. By government, we mean the central but also the local government. The central government has made no secret of the fact that it wants Chinese companies to ultimately be major players in global markets, making their own high-quality products and offering Chinese brands. The success that Lenovo has enjoyed after its acquisition of the personal computer business of IBM is a case in point.

For other companies, such as automobile and aircraft manufacturers, this can be a stumbling block. China has basically told entrants that if they want access to the huge and rapidly growing Chinese market, they will have to sacrifice their technology and possibly their intellectual property. Entering China is very different from entering emerging markets of years gone by. In China we have highly educated and sophisticated government and corporate officials who know well the value that the Chinese market presents to non-Chinese companies.

The situation is even more limiting in the Chinese banking sector. Here, the market is dominated by the five large, state-owned banks led by the International and Commercial Bank of China. The way banks can expand in China, or any other market, is to open branches and attract deposits. However, the Chinese government has imposed limits on how many branches foreign banks can open. As of 2012, this was under 400, whereas the big five Chinese state-run banks had over 65,000 branches. According to the IMF, the average deposits accounted for by foreign-country banks is approximately half of the market. Even in the United States, it is almost 20 percent. Clearly, the Chinese government has intervened in all of the major Chinese markets to steer the economy in a way that it believes will better the nation (or at least its political leaders and their families). It does not take into account foreign companies' M&A plans.

Regulatory Changes in Recent Years China has conflicting goals when it comes to foreign investment and M&A by outside companies. It wants to protect state-owned and local companies against competition from large outside competitors. However, it also wants to derive the benefits that the technology and other capabilities of these companies could bring to the Chinese market. Often, these goals are inconsistent with each other.

In 2003, Chinese laws were changed to allow easier acquisition of Chinese companies for foreign firms. This law was updated in 2006 and 2009. The rules address the capital that is invested and the fairness of the price paid, and they set forth a myriad of restrictions. The government is ever present in the process and the Ministry of Finance is particularly keen on making sure that "key industries" are protected, "national economic security" in not endangered, and that China's "time honored brands" are not lost to foreign control.[7] Suffice it to say, no deals of any significance can get done if the government does not want them to go through. So when Chinese companies or the Chinese government complains that they are not allowed unrestricted access to engage in M&A

in other nations, they have a point up until we consider the tremendous restrictions the Chinese government imposes on foreign entrants to its market. Then their complaints fail to hold water. In fact, developed markets are incredibly open to Chinese M&A compared to how Chinese markets are to developed countries and their corporations.

Technology Transfer and M&A   In some cases, the technology transfer is clear and upfront where the foreign companies are told in advance that this is a requirement of being able to pursue M&A. China thus has the ability to play one foreign company against an other as it did with GM and Ford. In other areas, there are contentious disputes brought by U.S. and European companies, who claim that their technology has been stolen and their intellectual property rights have not been protected by Chinese courts. For example, U.S. companies allege the Chinese telecom giant Huawei has blatantly stolen U.S. technology. In 2012, this has come to haunt the Chinese firm as it encountered resistance when it tried to expand into the lucrative U.S. telecom market. Some in the United States would say that this was a small price they had to pay in light of the technological gains they enjoyed without having to pay for them.

Foreign companies have to weigh the loss of technology, which may have been the product of a substantial long-term investment, against the gains that come from rapid growth in sales in China. Much of this growth could be realized in the future as China transforms from an export-oriented economy to one based more upon consumer expenditures. The concern for non-Chinese companies is whether those future gains will be realized by them or by local companies using the technology developed and paid for by foreign companies.

Realizing the Potential of the Chinese Market   While China is a huge market with tremendous potential, realizing that potential can be a great challenge. The requirements imposed by the Chinese government for 50:50 joint ventures add significant challenges for new entrants to be successful. New market entrants find that establishing a business in China takes much longer than it would elsewhere. In addition, managing becomes a major coordination process with two totally different entities, the United States and the Chinese corporate partners, which have to be integrated into one entity. This can slow growth greatly compared to how it would be if foreign companies were allowed to enter the market as a single entity or through an acquisition where the target were actively integrated into the acquirer.

GE's experience in China is a classic example of the frustrations a very successful global company can have when trying to extract growth from the Chinese market. Ironically, the company generated comparable annual revenues from Australia with its 23 million people compared to 1.3 billion in China. While we emphasize the power of demographic forces, population is one key, but far from the only, determinant of growth. GE's experiences in China and Australia serve as an amazing contrast. Buoyed by rising commodity prices, Australia, along with nations such as Canada and Brazil, have become excellent markets for large industrial companies such as GE. Beyond the dramatic population differences between Australia and China, Australia is a highly developed free market whose growth has been partly fueled by China's growth. Market entrants find a receptive economy with minimal regulation compared to the highly regulated Chinese economy. While China has done so many things right in its march to economic development, the overreaching hand of the government and regulators has at times stifled progress. A good argument can be made that China would never have enjoyed the growth and success that it had in such a relatively short period of time without the guiding and supportive hand of the central government. However, the transition to a more open and free economy with a larger consumer sector has been somewhat slow. It is difficult for the government to find the perfect path and timeline for this transition, and whichever path it chooses will inevitably draw criticism. The overreaching hand of the government has also limited the opportunities for foreign companies to conduct M&A in China.

In the following section, we see that somewhat comparable yet different impediments are present in India—the next-most-populous economy.

India

India, the second-largest nation by population with over 1.2 million people, has also grown impressively at annual rates that have ranged between 7 and 10 percent in recent years (See Figure 7.5). While so much of the world's economic focus has been on China more than any other nation, and for good reason, India also presents attractive opportunities but brings with it its own impediments. We have already pointed out the huge importance of demographics. However, if one adopts a long-term focus, India will be the world's most-populous country in the not too distant future. In fact, current estimates by the United Nations of population growth project India surpassing China by approximately the year 2030. This is due to the fact that India's population growth has continued unabated, while the one child policy has slowed the growth of the gigantic Chinese population. Thus, *some* corporations with a long-term focus may find even greater long-term opportunities in India than in China. However, India comes with its own set of problems.

India has been hampered by a government that has not made the same commitment to infrastructure development as China. It also has a political system that has impeded economic growth by not cracking down enough on bribery and other illegal activities. One can get a sense of the differences between the two economies when we compare the great public relations

(a)

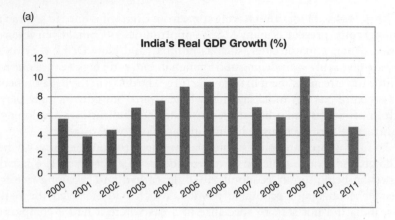

(b)

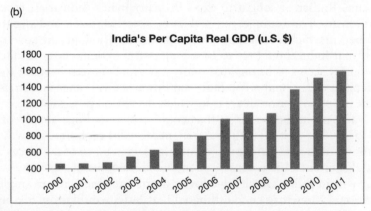

FIGURE 7.5 India's (a) Real GDP Growth and (b) per Capita Real GDP
Source: International Monetary Fund, World Economic Outlook Database, October 2012.

success China enjoyed with the 2008 Olympics and the embarrassment India endured with the Commonwealth Games just two years later.

On the surface, India is a much more open economy. It is a democracy whereas China is not. Unfortunately, India is plagued with corruption, which results in an economic system that does not reward the most efficient and innovative companies, but rather those who are willing to compensate non-market parties. In addition, while China made a decision years ago to invest great sums in developing its infrastructure, India took a long time before making a similar commitment. For example, over the past 20 years, China created many miles of new highways and impressive modern airports that make highways and airports in the United States look ancient (and in some cases, they are).

If one looks at India after having come from China, it is hard to see that this economy could present as many M&A opportunities as China. Even when one considers India's major cities, such as Bombay and New Delhi, they do not compare favorably with Beijing and Shanghai. India still lags behind due to its too little too late investment in infrastructure. The delay in the development of infrastructure has left India lagging behind China but convincingly playing catch up. It seems India has started to take the challenge of developing its infrastructure more seriously, but it still has a long way to go.

To fully appreciate India's potential, we need to consider how far India has come. India only achieved its independence as a nation in 1947. It then focused on being totally economically independent and breaking free from dependence on major economic powers, which had enslaved the nation. Thus, India did not seek to specialize in areas where it had a comparative advantage. Rather, it sought to excel in many major industries, especially heavy industry. For example, rather than be a steel *importer* and an exporter of products in which it could enjoy a comparative advantage, the government decided that India should try to be a major steel *manufacturer*. In fact, the steel industry seems to be one that many governments seem to have focused on as a point of national pride. India did this in several other industries, and this lack of specialization in areas in which the nation possessed a comparative advantage, including many that could utilize its huge supply of low-priced labor, has cost the nation dearly in terms of economic growth. This substitution of the pride of governmental leaders in place of the forces of the free market stunted the country's economic development.

Growth in India has clearly slowed in recent years. For example, the International Monetary Fund estimated that India would grow 6.9 percent in 2012. This is good growth, but it is still below the rates of some prior years where the rates approached double digits. However, it came at a time when the world economy was growing slowly—especially Europe.

When evaluating the M&A prospects of the Indian market we need to remind ourselves that in 2011, per capita income in India was $3,627 (behind Nicaragua and the Congo), whereas in China it was $8,400 (behind Ecuador and Tunisia). Clearly, there is greater buying power in the Chinese market. There is also a greater volume of M&A activity in China than there is in India (see Figure 7.6). However, the impediments to entry are different in India from what they are in China. It is not that there are no impediments—they are simply different. In India, foreign entrants may not face the same kind of governmentally imposed barriers as they do in China. The Indian government had not created a development plan that places great limits on the ability of foreign companies to enter the market as they have in China. However, the fact that this was not formally done does not mean somewhat similar impediments don't exist.

While from an M&A perspective, India brings with it many opportunities, it also has a troubling sense of unpredictability. This was underscored by the recent

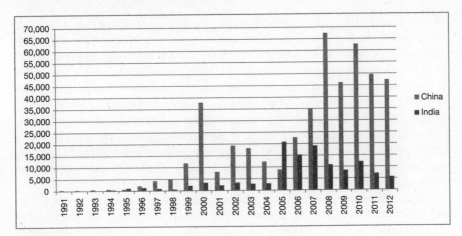

FIGURE 7.6 Chinese and Indian M&A (in $ millions)
Source: Thomson Financial Securities Data.

Vodafone tax debacle. Vodafone acquired 67 percent of Hutchinson Essar Ltd's telecom business but was shocked to find that India's tax authorities wanted Vodafone, the acquirer, to compensate the sellers for their capital gains taxes on the gains they, the sellers, made! Eventually, Vodafone avoided such a payment through a favorable ruling by the Indian Supreme Court. The Indian income tax department still pursued Vodafone by trying to change the law after the fact.

The unpredictability of the laws and the regulatory process affects much of the Indian economy. Unlike developed countries where illness and death rates have declined and life expectancy has risen, the ranks of the poor, and therefore many of the ill, remain troublingly high. India faces a dilemma of being a nation that could benefit greatly from the successes of the U.S. and European pharmaceutical industries, which have developed so many successful treatments for illnesses that plague less developed nations but that are relatively under control in the United States and Europe. The problem is that India is a poor country and so many of the ill who could benefit from these miracle drugs can't pay for them. Microeconomics and development economics tell us that having a healthier population can be a public good, making workers more productive and having fewer people to transmit contagious illnesses. Unfortunately, the "solution" of the Indian government is to deny some Western pharmaceutical companies patent rights for drugs that were very costly to develop. For example, in 2012, India's patent office ordered Germany's Bayer AG to issue a license to a local Indian pharmaceutical company to enable it to copy Bayer's cancer drug Nexavar. In effect, India is expecting private foreign companies to subsidize Indian health care. This is a job for the Indian government. The government needs to be aware that drug prices have to reflect the huge costs of drug development and it needs to understand that drugs that are successful have to pay for the many failed development efforts that are part of the drug development process. The relevance of these discussions for M&A is that the Indian government is unpredictable, thus making India a less stable environment for long-term foreign investment. In finance, unpredictability lowers the ex-ante expected return of any capital investment, including M&A. The greater the unpredictability, the greater the risk premium that needs to be embedded into the discount rate that is used to compute the present value of a deal's projected cash flows. The greater the predictability, the higher the present value of the M&A's investment returns. Higher investment returns will usually, all other things constant, lead to more M&A investment.

India is a growing nation, and growing nations need capital. Rates of return in the West have been at all-time lows, where they have remained for an extended time period. India needs to be more accommodating to foreign investment and to provide a stable environment so that foreign investors have an expectation that their projected cash flows will be stable. Securing foreign investment will be good for facilitating Indian growth, but foreign investors need to have an assurance that they will enjoy a good return. Like China, India is uncomfortable with foreign investment in its economy. Both nations, but more so India, are paying a price for their inability to adapt to free market solutions to growth.

The Indian government is well aware of this issue. In 2012, the New Delhi government announced various reforms aimed at allowing more foreign invest-ment and cutting inefficient subsidies on products such as diesel fuel. These were the most significant set of economic reforms the country has made since 1991. They were long overdue. However, whether they will be effective remains to be seen. The reforms have been strongly opposed by some who feared that small businesses, especially those in the retail sector, will be adversely affected by larger foreign rivals such as Walmart. It seems likely, though, that such opposition will only delay, not halt, India's path to realizing the great potential of this nation.

Southeast Asian Markets   When we move our focus away from China and India, we can still find large markets that are growing well. They are relatively smaller than China and India but carry with them much promise for the future. The nations of this region include Indonesia, the Philippines, Malaysia, Singapore, Vietnam, Thailand, Myanmar, Lao PDR, Cambodia, and Brunai.[8] It is important to note that the whole Southeast Asian economy has been growing steadily for several years now and together is larger than India. A comprehensive discussion of the various rising economies in this region is beyond the focus of this book. Rather, we will comment on a couple of the leading nations as examples of the potential in the region.

Indonesia and the Philippines, for example, feature two large populations, and each brings with it unique opportunities. Indonesia is a resource-rich country, and it is likely that the extent of its true resources is still unknown. Its

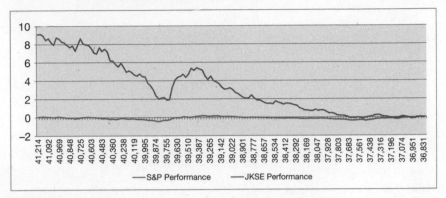

FIGURE 7.7 Indonesia Stock Market (JKSE) versus S&P 500
Source: Yahoo! Finance.

population of a quarter of a billion people continues to grow, making it an even more important market in the future.

The Indonesian economy grew 6 percent in 2011 and 2012. The nation is investing large sums in infrastructure projects such as modern highways, airports, seaports, and railways. Companies such as GE are already enjoying the fruits of this infrastructure investment (see Figure 7.7). The Philippines is also a very interesting market for potential M&A. It has a population of just under 100 million people. Its people are more educated than many other emerging market countries. Moreover, and this is very important for M&A, its legal system is comparable to Western legal systems. This is especially true for issues such as property rights. Its people are easy to work with and eager for economic development. The Philippines economy has been growing nicely over the past decade and investors seem to be quite sanguine about its prospects, as shown by the performance of its stock market relative to the S&P 500 (see Figure 7.8).

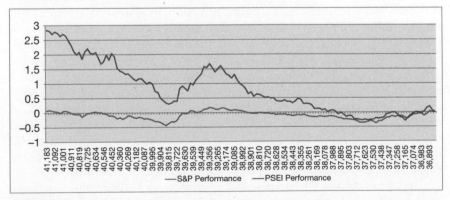

FIGURE 7.8 Philippine Stock Market (PSEI) versus S&P 500
Source: Yahoo! Finance.

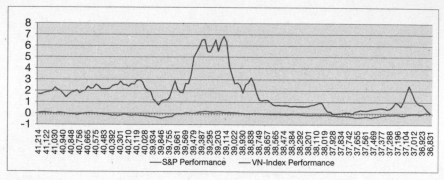

FIGURE 7.9   Vietnamese Stock Market (VN-Index) versus S&P 500
Source: Yahoo! Finance.

Vietnam is also a market that offers much potential. It has just under 90 million people and, despite its communist past, the government has worked to promote foreign investment. Indeed, these efforts have been somewhat successful in enabling Vietnam to attract business away from its larger neighbor—China. Vietnam certainly does not offer the scale that China does, but it does present some interesting M&A possibilities. Unfortunately, like many developing markets, it has its share of corruption, which hopefully will abate as development continues. (See Figure 7.9.)

Australia

We have already discussed some of the positive attributes of the Australian economy. It is only the fiftieth-most-populous country in the world with 23 million people. So it does not have anywhere near the same scale as some of the large Asian nations we have discussed. However, 89 percent of the population lives in urban areas making it one of most urbanized countries in the world. In addition, the economy has greatly benefited from exports of commodities, in which the relatively small economy is rich. A large percentage of these exports have been to China, which has a seemingly inexhaustible demand for many commodities. Some have described the Australian economy as one that "digs things out of the ground and sells them to China." While this may be humorous (and partially truthful), it overlooks the many positive attributes of the Australian economy. The country features a highly developed free market economy, which makes it very attractive to new entrants. Australia has an 82.5 economic freedom ranking, making it third in the world behind Hong Kong and Singapore and just ahead of its neighbor New Zealand.

As we have noted, GE had invested much money and time trying to achieve meaningful growth in the huge Chinese market. By 2012, the company came to realize that demographics alone is not enough to ensure a good return on investment. Ironically, Australia with its great commodity-related demand for machinery and equipment provided GE with a comparable but hassle-free return compared to its frustrating experience with China. GE is definitely not leaving China but it has realistic expectations about this huge market and sees the company's total market to be the entire globe, including even many smaller but growing nations in parts of the world, such as Africa, that in the past would not have received as much attention from the U.S. conglomerate.

Central and South America

By far the two biggest economies in this region are Brazil and Mexico (see Table 7.2). Brazil has been one of the leading growth markets in the world. Its bountiful supply of natural resources has left it well positioned to take advantage of the demand for such resources from high-growth markets all over the world such as China. It is by far the leading national economy in the region. The question is: What other countries may present growth M&A opportunities for foreign firms?

M&A activity is different in Mexico from what it is in Brazil. In Brazil, we see foreign companies roughly equal in dealmaking activity as local companies. In Mexico, M&A activity is much more dominated by local companies. There is a big falloff after we move our focus from Brazil and Mexico. The next-largest M&A market is Chile, followed by Colombia and Argentina.

Brazil Economic growth provides many M&A opportunities for both domestic and foreign companies (except in countries that deliberately inhibit such opportunities like China). Brazil is no exception. However, in order to properly assess the M&A prospects of a nation, one has to analyze the source of the growth and make a determination if it will continue or if it is short lived. While Brazil has been the fastest-growing major nation in South and Central America, that string was broken in 2011. In 2011 and 2012, Mexico grew faster than Brazil.

TABLE 7.2 Largest Latin American Economies (in billions of 2005 dollars)

Rank	Country	2012 Real GDP
1	Brazil	1,159
2	Mexico	1,000
3	Argentina	284
4	Colombia	203
5	Venezuela	186

Source: World Bank World Development Indicators, International Financial Statistics of the IMF, and IHS Global Insight.

Much of Brazil's growth can be traced to commodity markets and the derived demand for such products from fast-growing nations such as China. When China's growth slowed, so did Brazil's. Not a nation to take this lying down, Brazil has engaged in active fiscal and monetary policies to try to regain lost momentum. Not unlike China, Brazil's government has played a very active role in trying to foster growth. However, the pervasive government involvement in the economy has brought with it its share of economic burdens. These have come in the form of high taxes and inefficiency that is endemic to governments world-wide, as well as inefficiency in protected industries, which renders them less competitive in the global marketplace.

When the Brazilian economy began to feel the effects of the global slow-down that was exacerbated by the European debt crisis, the government enacted stimulus programs to try to offset the decline in global demand. However, students of economic history will remember that Brazil pursued similar policies in the late 1960s and early 1970s, and their effects were short lived.

In 1964, Brazil's civilian government was toppled by right-wing generals. In an effort to placate a population that was now under military rule, the government pursued large infrastructure investment projects and made loans readily available. These policies are not unlike those the nation has followed in its recent slump. Hopefully, it will not have the same result as the economic boom in Brazil of the late 1960s and early 1970s, which collapsed in 1973 following the rapid jump in oil prices. The expansion was short lived as many artificially induced expansions prove to be. The nation was left with a stagnant economy and high inflation—something any student of monetary economics would have expected.

Brazil's M&A market, and its overall economy, are influenced by its National Bank for Social and Economic Development. This Rio de Janeiro–based bank's lending far exceeds that of the global lending of the World Bank. It finances large infrastructure projects but also minority equity stakes in many large, privately held companies such as JBS—the world's largest meat packer. Fueled with equity infusions by the National Bank, Brazilian companies have used such capital to become global powerhouses. In addition, pension funds of some of the large, state-owned companies also provide investment capital to Brazilian companies. These policies were strongly supported by former president Luiz Inacio Lula Da Silva (Lula) and his successor, Dilma Rousseff. This lending has given Brazilian companies the financial wherewithal to out-pay global rivals, which may lack such government support. However, such policies did not prevent the slowdown in the economy and it remains to be seen if it can offset the large forces of the global economy.

There are several reasons to believe that the demise of Brazil's "second economic miracle" will be short lived. Under its past civilian governments,

Henrique Cardoso (1995–2002), Luiz Inacio da Silva (Lula, 2003–2010), and Dilma Rousseff (2011–), the government has done a better job of sharing the rising wealth of the nation with transfer programs. In addition, the nation enjoys a rising middle class and with that presents an attractive market for domestic and foreign entrants.

Mexico   For companies located in North America, Mexico is a very interesting economy. The manufacturing sector of Mexico has greatly spurred the growth of this country. Mexico's growth was not as artificially inflated by commodity-based growth or demand from China. When that is taken into account, the prospects for Mexico are quite interesting. We say *interesting* as opposed to automatically *optimistic*, as Mexico is still weighed down by its troublesome crime problem—particularly drug-related killings that have captured headlines in the United States. Other Latin American economies have done a better job of controlling this problem—or at least keeping the lid on the adverse publicity such crime creates. We do not mean to imply that the problem is all Mexico's doing, as the demand for the illegal drugs comes mainly from Mexico's northern neighbor—the United States.

China's huge manufacturing sector has benefited from its large workforce, which, in the past, was willing to work for relatively low wages enabling China to export to Europe and the United States and still easily overcome the high transportation costs. For example, in 1978, the average Chinese wage was 3 percent of the wages of the average U.S. manufacturing worker. However, in recent years, Chinese wages have been growing rapidly.[9]

As we know from Economics 101, as the expectations of the lower and middle class rise, wage demands go up with them. In addition, overall inflation in the Chinese economy, including housing prices, has driven up wage demands. These problems in China's export-oriented economy have created an opportunity for countries such as Mexico.

By 2012, the wage gap between China and Mexico had closed to the point where Chinese wages were 85 percent of that of Mexican workers. In addition, Chinese wages have been rising at around 6 percent per year, while in Mexico they have been flat if not decreasing. When we consider that for exports to the United States and Canada as well as South America, Mexico has a significant transportation cost and delivery time advantage, the outlook appears promising. In addition, Mexico also benefits from participation in the North American Free Trade Agreement (NAFTA), which conveys a further advantage on Mexico.

We are already seeing great growth in Mexican manufacturing and exports in certain industries such as automobiles. A half a decade ago Mexico was barely one of the top 10 exporters of cars. As of 2012, it was number four after the big two—Japan and Germany, followed by South Korea! Manufacturers such as

TABLE 7.3   Comparative Annual Percent Change in Real GDP

			Largest Latin American Economies			
Year	Brazil	Mexico	Argentina	USA	China	Eurozone
2000	4.3	6.0	−0.8	4.1	8.4	3.751
2001	1.3	−0.9	−4.4	1.1	8.3	1.973
2002	2.7	0.1	−10.9	1.8	9.1	0.917
2003	1.1	1.4	9.0	2.5	10.0	0.723
2004	5.7	4.0	8.9	3.5	10.1	2.207
2005	3.2	3.2	9.2	3.1	11.3	1.698
2006	4.0	5.1	8.5	2.7	12.7	3.249
2007	6.1	3.2	8.7	1.9	14.2	2.981
2008	5.2	1.2	6.8	−0.3	9.6	0.366
2009	−0.3	−6.0	0.9	−3.1	9.2	−4.424
2010	7.5	5.6	9.2	2.4	10.4	2.032
2011	2.7	3.9	8.9	1.8	9.2	1.431
2012	1.5	3.8	2.6	2.2	7.8	−0.413

Source: International Monetary Fund, World Economic Outlook Database, October 2012.

Volkswagen, Nissan, and Honda have established significant manufacturing operations in Mexico. In fact, Mexico enjoys such a cost advantage over their South American rivals that some, such as Argentina (never a country to enjoy any free trade) and Brazil imposed caps on automobile imports from Mexico. This is unfortunate, as those who are vaguely familiar with what they learned in Economics 101 know that such free trade would be a win-win for both workers in Mexico as well as for consumers in Brazil and Argentina.

In spite of all its promising attributes, Mexico has not been very successful in attracting foreign investment. Figure 7.10 shows how not only the amount of foreign investment in China is much greater (as expected given the size differences) than Mexico but the trend for China is sharply upward, while for Mexico it is flat and at times declining. This needs to change if Mexico, and its M&A market, is to achieve meaningful growth.

Argentina   Argentina is a fascinating economic story. The country had been mired in economic stagnation for many years. It has a governmental system that has hampered the country's growth. This is indeed unfortunate, as years ago Argentina was one of the great growth economies—not unlike Brazil is today. The country has amazing potential that continually goes unrealized. Probably the biggest contributor to this failure has been the government's inept interference in the economy.

Since 1980, Argentina has defaulted on its debt three times! The story of the Argentinean economy is fascinating when one considers the country's current

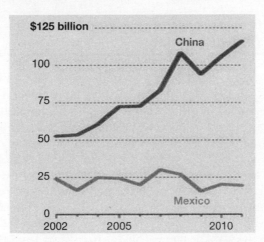

FIGURE 7.10 China and Mexico's Foreign Direct Investment
Source: INEGI (Mexico FDI); Ministry of Commerce (China FDI); Wall Street Journal, September 17, 2012. Reprinted by permission of The Wall Street Journal. Copyright © 2012 Dow Jones & company, Inc. All Rights Reserved Worldwide. License number 3041501494032.

position in light of the European economic crisis. Between 1998 and 2002, the IMF strongly pressured the country to enact fiscal austerity and to cut government expenditures, which it did. The economy contracted sharply. Finally the country, under the leadership of Christina and Nestor Kirchner switched course and raised export and import taxes, rarely a good economic idea, and used the proceeds to fund infrastructure investment and social programs. This occurred when the country happened, by luck, to get the benefit of a commodity boom. The result was higher economic growth and lower unemployment but, unfortunately, higher government expenditures as a percent of GDP.

The Argentinean economy has been held back by the socialist policies of the Kirshners. Nonetheless, Christina Kirchner was reelected to a new four-year term in 2011. It is difficult to believe any of the official economic numbers, but it appears that economic growth is once again stagnant and inflation is rising. For a while, rising commodity prices for products, which, in part, were fueled by the Federal Reserve's quantitative easing, helped the economy. However, if commodity prices weaken significantly, this could easily change. Nonetheless, the overreaching arm of the Argentinean government makes this country a somewhat risky nation in which to use M&A to pursue growth. This was underscored by the adverse position the country has taken toward foreign investment. The takeover of Respol's affiliate YPF is a case in point. This situation is highlighted in the case study that follows.

CASE STUDY: EMERGING MARKET RISKS—ARGENTINA VERSUS RESPOL

In 2012, Argentina seized control of YPF—the affiliate of the Spanish company Respol, YPF. Up until April 2012, Respol owned 57 percent of YPF. That was until Christina Kirchner announced that her government would seize 51 percent of the company. The seizure came shortly after the company announced that its costly exploration efforts proved successful and it has discovered up to 23 billion barrels of oil in Patagonia. The seizure underscores the risks of dealing with a government that has a reputation for not being pro-business. It the case of YPF, relations seemed friendly but turned sharply in the opposite direction when it appeared that YPF's investment would bear fruit. This put Respol in the awkward position of having to engage in an uphill fight for fair compensation. It also underscores the risk of emerging market investments, which can bring with them a higher degree of uncertainty. In finance, that translates into a higher discount rate, which, in turn, means a lower expected value of return on investment.

Central and Eastern Europe

When we think of economic growth opportunities in Central and Eastern Europe, the logical first country that comes to mind is Russia. Being one of the four original BRICS, this is a logical response. However, there are a number of other nations in the region that may also provide interesting growth opportunities. We will just touch on some of the opportunities in the region.

Russia   By far, the dominant country in this region is Russia. The GDP of the Russian Federation and its M&A volume dwarfs anything else in the area. However, as with many other economies, Russia brings with it its own unique set of challenges. The economy is very influenced by commodity costs such as the price of oil. Higher oil prices mean greater wealth and greater demand for M&A. When oil prices are low, the economy is much weaker and thus M&A volume is lower. In addition, the content of Russian oil is such that it needs a higher price than oil from other nations to be profitable to refine.

As for M&A, there have been a number of instances of foreign companies entering the Russian market only to lose their investment due to corruption and other illegal activity. The continuing direct and indirect control of the nation by Vladimir Putin, a former lieutenant colonel in the KGB, has also hampered economic development. Foreign companies can be attracted by the market and the potential of Russian consumers, but often are afraid to invest in this market due to the unique risks that it presents. This was underscored recently with investors' reaction to Rosneft, Russia's huge government-controlled oil company, and its 2012 acquisition of BP's Russian joint venture TNK-BP. BP's better management made TNK more efficient than the less-efficient and Kremlin-controlled Rosneft. Rosneft pursued the acquisition of TNK, which was Russia's third-largest oil company, in part to benefit from TNK's better management. The concern is whether Rosneft's inefficiencies, caused in part by its government ties, contaminate the managerial practices put in place by BP. To its credit, when so much of Europe was in the economic doldrums dealing with the sovereign debt crisis, the Russian economy was somewhat insulated from these troubles. This can be seen from the relatively low unemployment rate the nation had during this time period (see Figure 7.11). This nation would show much more promise for foreign investment and M&A if it could provide more political and regulatory certainty to outsiders. This would also pay great dividends for the nation by making it less dependent on oil—a depletable resource in the long run.

Turkey Turkey has been this region's great growth story. The Turkish market is much smaller than Russia's but it is faster growing and not as dependent on volatile factors such as commodity prices. Indeed, this has resulted in Turkey being the target of some of the hot money that has floated around the world market. These hot money flows can be partly attributed to the quantitative easing policies pursued by central banks such as the U.S. Federal Reserve. It is interesting that both Brazil, and to a lesser extent Turkey, have

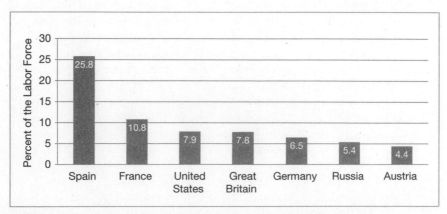

FIGURE 7.11 Comparative Unemployment Rates, November 2012
Source: U.S. BLS, Eurostat, U.K. Office for National Statistics, OECD.org.

taken measures to limit the influx of such funds so as to try to avoid the inflationary pressures that the rapid rise in such funds can cause. These inflationary pressures are caused by the fact that the output of the economy cannot respond as quickly to the relatively sudden inflows of monies into the country, which can lead to a demand-pull inflation. As of the end of 2011, Turkey's economy, like so many others throughout the world, slowed and it ran the risk of falling into a recession partly due to the steps the nation took to slow the economy. This is a more of a major issue for Turkey, as it does not have the depth of commodity-based export demand that Brazil has. Nonetheless, Turkey presents some very interesting opportunities for foreign investment, and M&A in particular.

CASE STUDY: DIAGEO FOCUSES ON EMERGING MARKETS

Diageo's brands are much more well-known than the name of the company itself. The British distiller markets Smirnoff and Ciroc vodka, Guinness, and Johnnie Walker scotch whiskey. Recognizing the growth potential in Asia and Latin America, the company shifted resources from mature markets, such as Europe, to Asia. This shift in emphasis has paid off for Diageo. When the debt-laden economies in Europe failed to rebound strongly from the Great Recession, the company was able to realize good growth in revenues and profits from Asia and Latin America.

In 2010, the company had no growth in its operating profit on $5.3 billion in sales in North America and a 1 percent decline in operating profit in Europe on $4.4 billion in revenues. However, the company enjoyed 6 percent growth in operating profits in the Asia-Pacific region on $1.6 billion in revenues. The growth picture was even more impressive in other emerging markets such as Latin America, the Middle East, and Africa. Together, these regions showed 25 percent growth in operating profits on revenues of $4.2 billion.

Diageo was able to realize the impressive growth in emerging markets partly through its M&A program. In China, it acquired control of the liquor company Shui Jing Fang through a reported $1 billion purchase of the holding company Sichuan Swellfun. In Vietnam, it acquired 24 percent of that country's largest distiller—Halico. In other emerging markets, the M&A strategy was equally active. In Guatemala, Diageo acquired a controlling interest in rum-maker Zacapa for a reported $100 million. In Turkey, it paid $2.1 billion to acquire Mey Icki.

(continued)

Indeed, the use of M&A is a process that is very natural to Diageo. The company formed in 1997 through a merger between Guinness and Grand Metropolitan. Partly through M&A, it has become the world's largest producers of spirits and is one of the world's largest producers of beer and wine. It has achieved this success by a global yet industry-focused strategy. It owned Pillsbury, which Grand Metropolitan had acquired in 1989, but sold it off to General Mills in 2000. It also owned Burger King but exited the fast food business when it sold off this division in 2002 to private equity buyers Texas Pacific. The resulting company is a truly global company selling leading brands in 180 countries.

Diageo's pattern of highly successful emerging market M&A was capped off in 2012, when it acquired a controlling interest in the Bangalore-based United Spirits for $2 billion. This is India's largest liquor company. The company's goal is to have 50 percent of its revenues come from emerging markets by the year 2015. As of 2012, it is about 10 percent short of that goal, but the Untied Spirits' acquisition in the world's second-most-populous nation should accelerate its path to that target.

AFRICA

While a full discussion of the potential of the African market is beyond the scope of this book, we would be remiss if we did not at least make some brief comments on the potential of the African market—especially Sub-Saharan Africa. This area includes most of Africa after excluding North Africa, which is often grouped with the Arab world.

This large region consists of a number of nations with large populations—some of which appear on the cusp of pursuing economic growth in a more meaningful way than they have in the past. For many years, these nations struggled in poverty and were governed by corrupt and inept leaders. There are signs this is changing. Several African nations are rich in untapped resources. As world demand grows, the pressure to start to develop such respources will naturally follow. This, in turn, will create a natural pressure for the resource-rich African nations to effectively address their huge infrastructure and political corruption problems. Progress on these problems is being made, albeit, slowly.[10]

Growth of the Sub-Saharan African economies has been roughly in the 5 percent range in the past few years. Many of the trends we have been seeing with other growing emerging markets, a rising middle class and greatly increased urbanization, have also been occurring in this region.[11]

The potential of Africa was underscored when several large private equity firms, such as the Carlyle Group established investment funds that focus on the region. However, from an M&A perspective, it is premature to focus on the region as first we have to have more rapid economic growth and then there is more to discuss regarding M&A. It would be surprising, however, if larger M&A opportunities do not appear in the not too distant future.

RISKS OF EMERGING MARKETS

For many established companies from developed markets, companies that have very well developed brands and consumer awareness, it makes great sense to take advantage of emerging markets that are growing rapidly to keep up the growth of the company. Frankly, as we have noted, the name *emerging markets* should not apply to many of the key markets for which term continually gets applied. Markets such as China, and to a lesser extent, India and Brazil, would really be better termed *rapidly growing markets* than emerging markets. They have emerged, and did so some time ago, but continue to grow rapidly while their earlier developed counterparts have seen their own growth slow significantly.

While emerging markets can present very attractive growth possibilities and can help stagnant companies in developed countries to try to jump-start their growth, this growth comes with a unique set of risks that are not as present in their home markets. For example, consider the number of Chinese companies that have gone public in the United States through reverse mergers. Many of these investments turned bad when it was discovered that their records of good performance were falsified and their accounting standards were at times nonexistent or simply false. In Russia, some investors have seen illegal activity destroy the value of their investments. We have already discussed Vodafone's acquisition of 67 percent of Hutchinson Essar Ltd's telecom business where Vodafone was requested to pay the sellers for their capital gains taxes.

One of the risks that companies in developed countries incur when they put too much focus on emerging market expansion is that they can take their eye off the ball in their main home-country market. To expand aggressively in multiple emerging markets at the same time often requires a major managerial effort. Sometimes companies can take their strong position on their home market for granted. This can open the door for foreign rivals. In recent years, this is exactly what happened with the British grocery company Tesco. The company faced a stagnant British market in a country (mistakingly) pursuing fiscal austerity during a very weak economy. It saw the path to growth as expansion in high-growth markets such as China and Central Europe and Turkey. Indeed, this was exactly what Tesco's main rivals, such as Walmart and Carrefour, were doing. Tesco worked hard to achieve growth in these other markets while some of these same competitors, such as Walmart and also J. Sainsbury, began to take away sales from Tesco in the United Kingdom (see Figure 7.12). By the end of 2012, the company decided to cut back expansion in China, leave the Japanese market and U.S. markets.[12] In 2012, it also announced it was spending $1.6 billion to revive its U.K. business.[13]

Emerging markets can present great opportunities for companies that are stuck in a home market that is stagnant. However, when such firms pursue emerging market expansion it is very important that they not do so while losing focus on their home markets, which may represent the bulk of the company's business.

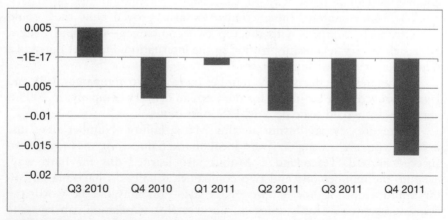

FIGURE 7.12 Tesco U.K. Same-Store Sales
Source: Adapted from Paul Sonne, "Tesco Loses Its Appetite for Growth," *Wall Street Journal*, November 10, 2012, B3.

ENTERING LARGE SLOW-GROWTH MARKETS
INSTEAD OF FAST-GROWTH EMERGING MARKETS

The struggles of Tesco, which we discussed in the prior section, in trying to derive gains from the large but mature U.S. market highlight the challenges of entering a mature market that already has major competitors in it. T Mobile faced a similar challenge when it entered the U.S. mobile market and could not compete against AT&T and Verizon. Consider also the example of the German delivery company Deutsche Post AG, which sought to expand into the United States, the world's largest economy and largest package delivery market. On the surface that seems to make a lot of sense. If you are going to find growth opportunities there should be more such opportunities in the largest market in the world—right? Not necessarily.

In 1998 Deutsche Post acquired an ownership position in DHL Worldwide Express. Then in 2003 DHL acquired Airborne Express for $1.05 billion. These were major names in the U.S. delivery market. However, Deutsche Post was never able to make a success of its U.S. business. In part, its failure underscores the advantages of being in the number one or two position. United Parcel Service and Federal Express account for approximately 70 percent of the U.S. market. Companies like Airborne did a great job trying to succeed but never could move up into the top two positions. However, both DHL and Airborne were major players in the U.S. market and it seemed logical that acquiring proven companies would be a way to successfully expand in the large U.S. market. Unfortunately, these companies also proved that they could not effectively compete with the top two companies—UPS and FedEx. DHL held a very successful position in the international market but was a minor player in the United States.

The aggressive efforts of the number one and two companies, UPS and FedEx, proved to be too much for the German delivery company. In 2008 it announced it would scale back its U.S. operations.

There are several lessons in this M&A failure. Number one, just because you are strong in your local market does not mean you can succeed abroad. Tesco and T Mobile also learned this the hard way. Second, the number one and two companies usually do have big advantages and acquiring one or two of the also-rans may not be worth the acquisition prices. Third, doing an unsuccessful acquisition can be quite costly, with costs often being well in excess of the purchase price. Management of the acquirer never wants to admit that a major strategic effort and M&A was a big failure. This is why such companies will often pour more money into a failure hoping it will turn around. Daimler's acquisition of Chrysler and all of the costs this failed M&A imposed on Daimler is still another example.

REDUCING COUNTRY M&A RISK: INVESTING IN LOCAL COMPANIES THAT ENGAGE IN SUBSTANTIAL EMERGING MARKET M&A

Investors who want the benefit of the shareholder gains and the diversification benefits that come from faster-growing emerging markets may be able to achieve some of these gains without all of the risk of outright M&A. One way to try to have your cake and eat it, too, is for investors to invest in major companies in developed markets that aggressively pursue emerging market M&A. This can lower risk significantly. Major companies in developed markets such as the United States have to adhere to more strict accounting standards and close scrutiny from a large number of investors and analysts. Lesser-known companies in emerging markets do not have to adhere to such scrutiny and, therefore, are, *ceteris paribus*, more risky. Therefore, when major companies in developed markets pursue emerging market M&A, they may be able to accelerate growth and thereby advance shareholder's interests but they may also be able to help their stockholders realize lower-risk international portfolio diversification. An example of a company that has been quite successful in doing that is Caterpillar.

CASE STUDY: EMERGING MARKET M&A BY MAJOR DEVELOPED COUNTRY COMPANIES— LOWERING COUNTRY RISK

As the U.S. economy fell into the 18-month Great Recession and experienced a very slow recovery, companies with very cyclical products normally would show weak performance. While this might have been expected by companies such as Caterpillar, which makes heavy equipment used in agriculture and mining, the company used M&A to position itself in some respects to be more of an international company than a U.S.-centric firm. This can be seen by looking at Figure 7.13, which shows that in 2006, 54 percent of its sales were derived from outside the United States. By 2011, this percentage rose to 70 percent!

(continued)

(continued)

(a)

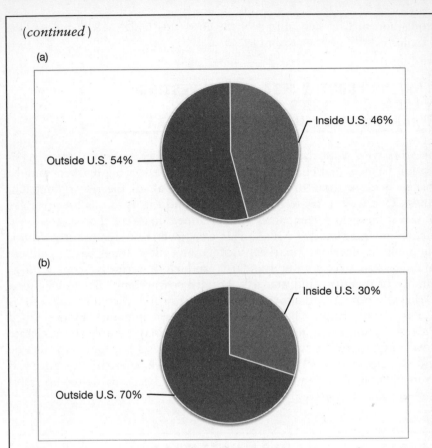

(b)

FIGURE 7.13   Caterpillar Sales (a) 2006 and (b) 2011
Source: Caterpillar Year in Review (a) 2006 and (b) 2011.

While Caterpillar enjoyed great benefits from its emerging market expansion it also was rudely awoken to the fact that such investments are fraught with risk. In 2013 Caterpillar's CEO Doug Oberhelman announced that it paid hundreds of millions of dollars too much for Chinese firm Siwei due to "deliberate, multi-year coordinated accounting misconduct" by the target's management. Caterpillar acquired ERA Mining Machinery Ltd and its subsidiary Siwei in June 2012 for $653 million. These entities were the fourth-largest makers of hydraulic roof supports in China. However, the fraud was so extensive that Caterpillar basically had to write off most of the whole purchase. This is yet another example of the risks of emerging market M&A. Such
(continued)

risks are hard to identify and quantify but some risk factor has to be built into the risk-adjusted discount rate that is used to evaluate deals in these markets. Failing to make such as adjustment due to its difficulty to measure, in effect, by default quantifies it at zero, which is not accurate as Caterpillar will attest to.

FINDING GROWTH IN HIGH-GROWTH MARKETS

As we have discussed, when a business has tapped out the growth potential in a given market, and when many competitors are aggressively competing for the same market, achieving real growth can be a challenge. Often it takes increasing expenditures on marketing just to achieve some growth or even just to maintain a company's current condition. This was the case in the 1990s and 2000s for many U.S. and European as well as Japanese companies. In the case of the U.S. auto industry, the situation was even worse. The major U.S. automakers struggled with quality problems and a competitive disadvantage caused by having to assume the burden of high labor costs imposed by an inflexible union—the United Auto Workers (UAW). The following case study of GM features a sick company that found success and growth in the fastest-growing market in the world—China.

CASE STUDY: GM OPEN FOR BUSINESS IN CHINA

For many years, GM was a well-run company that built on the management principles developed by the legendary Alfred Sloan. Applying these principles enabled it to become the biggest automaker in the world. However, it slowly but steadily began to slide into long-term decline. There are a whole host of reasons for this decline but paramount among them was bad management along with the stifling effect of a very burdensome agreement with the UAW. GM also had its share of bad M&A, which included the acquisition of EDS in 1984 for $2.55 billion ($6 billion in 2013 dollars). The popular CEO of EDS at that time, Ross Perot, was an outspoken critic of GM. He is quoted as having said that GM spends so much money per year on R&D that a new GM model should have the ability to fly to the moon. Instead, the huge bureaucratic structure turned out cars that were boring with few differences from year to year other than the introduction of additional quality problems. He

(continued)

(*continued*)

also said GM took so long to design a new car that the United States won World War II in less time. Amazingly, its management was arrogant and reluctant to engage in major meaningful changes.

Just when things were looking the most bleak, GM made one major move that would provide it a glimpse of greener pastures to offset the continual gloom of Detroit and the U.S. auto industry's never-ending problems. In 1992, GM and the Shanghai Automotive Industry Corporation (SAIC) entered into an agreement that would ultimately result in the creation of a joint venture in 1997. The entity, Shanghai General Motors, was 50 percent owned by SAIC and GM.

GM was definitely not the first foreign automaker to enter the Chinese market. In fact, companies like Volkswagen were there in a big way. Visitors to Shanghai cannot miss the large number of Santana sedans that flow through the city's streets. Volkswagen had entered into its own joint venture with SAIC in 1985 and considered itself to be the leading foreign auto company in the Chinese market. GM was late to the game and it brought with it its own set of problems including not just quality concerns but also an unproven ability to make the smaller, "underpowered" but highly fuel-efficient cars, which were demanded by Chinese buyers but would never sell in the U.S. market. To sell in China, GM had to be able to market a very different type of car from what it was used to marketing.

When a foreign company wants to manufacture and sell cars in the huge and growing Chinese market, it must enter into an agreement with the government. This includes a local government as well as the central government. China's policy has been that this can only happen if a joint venture is formed with a Chinese company, and the foreign company cannot own more than 50 percent of the joint venture. So if you want access to the Chinese market, and with it the huge potential for sales or profits, this is the deal—take it or leave it. In fact, the Chinese government has perfected the art of playing one foreign company against another. Indeed, it played Ford against GM for an extended beauty contest that ultimately culminated in the somewhat unlikely winner, GM, getting business.

The Chinese auto market is huge. Figure 7.14 shows that by 2011, the size of this market had reached the size of the United States. Even more promising is the fact that while the U.S. auto market is mature and has been weighed down for a number of years by weak consumer demand, the Chinese economy has been growing at rates of between

(*continued*)

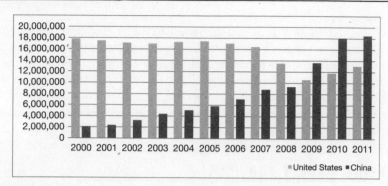

FIGURE 7.14   U.S. versus China Vehicle Sales: 2000–2011
Source: Wards Auto Group.

9 percent and 10 percent, and the Chinese demand for cars seemed insatiable. While the subprime crisis and the impact of de-leveraging consumers hurt U.S. car sales, the vast majority of Chinese car buyers saved up for their cars and purchased them for cash.

One of the very interesting aspects of the GM-China success story was the fact that an acquisition that drew little attention was GM's acquisition of Korean carmaker Daewoo in 2002. A number of the Korean carmakers were in financial trouble in the early 2000s. Hyundai was pressured by the Korean government to absorb Kia. However, the government was unwilling to bail out Daewoo, which went bankrupt in 2000. GM had an association with Daewoo in the past but it never amounted to anything. When Daewoo ran out of options, it agreed to be acquired by GM for $400 million—a price that turned out to be a steal for GM. Frankly, this was a rare GM success in the field of M&A.

The acquisition of Daewoo helped facilitate GM's development of smaller, low-powered cars for the Chinese market. Daewoo had valuable technology that helped GM become successful in China. GM has great expertise making larger and more powerful cars, which, unfortunately, use a lot of gas. However, Chinese consumers wanted the look of an upscale car and preferred the more gas-efficient and—from a U.S. consumer standpoint—underpowered cars. GM was not good at making small, gas-efficient cars. However, Daewoo was.

GM still faces many global challenges, and Volkswagen, the world's second-largest automaker behind GM, continues to expand in China, which is its largest sales region. In addition to selling automobiles such as

(continued)

(*continued*)

VWs and Audis, VW acquired the Swedish truck brand Scania AB and MAN to form a major European truck company. In doing so, VW has a full line of cars and trucks to help lead it to its goal of being the world's largest automaker before 2020. The great and still untapped potential of the Chinese market may help it to achieve that goal.

EMERGING MARKET ACQUIRER

The rise of the emerging market acquirer is a relatively new phenomenon in that it was not until the past 10 to 15 years that we have seen large acquisitions of companies in the developed world by emerging market companies. However, this type of M&A has become much more commonplace. For example, we have seen many large acquisitions by certain major Indian companies such as Tata Group and Mittal. The Tata Group's $10.7 billion 2007 acquisition of British steelmaker Corus is an example. Those of Indian descent may enjoy the irony of a major Indian company acquiring a major British firm when roughly half a century earlier, India was under the control of Britain and the imperialist policies it pursued prior to the collapse of the British Empire following the end of World War II. It was a case of the colony acquiring the colonists.

The Tata Group is a global conglomerate that was, until recently, run by Ratan Tata. A man who commands a reputation for integrity, he oversaw a program of international acquisition that built the Tata Group into an international corporate empire. Table 7.4 shows some of the major acquisitions of the Tata Group. A review of these deals clearly shows their diverse nature.

In Chapter 4, we discussed diversification strategies and we raised questions about the effectiveness of the conglomerate corporate structure. One has to wonder if there really are any synergies between selling tea (Tetley brand) and manufacturing and marketing of steel and autos. It certainly seems a stretch to have these many diverse businesses within the same corporate umbrella. While companies such as the Tata Group and Mittal stand out as a great symbol of Indian pride and the giant conglomerates match up very favorably with the leading companies in the world, at least in the case of the conglomerate structure of the Tata group, one has to wonder if the diverse M&A program makes sense.

The Tata Group's conglomerate structure contrasts sharply with the more streamlined and strategic focus of Mittal, which as we discussed in Chapter 5, is now Arcelor–Mittal. Mittal is a steel company and its expansion it has done through M&A within the company's main areas of focus. The company has gone outside of horizontal expansion to engage in some vertical

TABLE 7.4 Largest Acquisitions by the Tata Group

Company Name	Stake	Year of Acquisition	Deal Value (in billions)
1. Corus Group	100%	January 2007	$12
2. Jaguar Cars and Land Rover	100%	March 2008	$2.3
3. PT Kaltim Prima Coal and PT Arutmin Indonesia	30%	June 2007	$1.1
4. General Chemical Industrial Products	100%	March 2008	$1.005
5. Citigroup Global Services	100%	December 2008	$0.50
6. Tetley Tea Company	100%	February 2000	$0.45
7. Olam International, Republic of Gabon	25.1%	April 2011	$0.29
8. NatSteel Asia Pte	100%	February 2005	$0.28
9. Teleglobe International	100%	July 2005	$0.23
10. Eight O'Clock Coffee Company	100%	June 2006	$0.22

Source: Tata Group: www.tata.com/htm/Group_MnA_YearWise.htm.

deals, which would give it more dependable quantities and pricing of these inputs. However, Arcelor-Mittal is a quite focused company whereas the Tata Group is a broad-based conglomerate.

Both Tata and Mittal are very impressive emerging market acquirers that were originally from India but have taken very different strategic paths. Only time will tell if the conglomerate structure of the Tata Group will last. One thing that stands out in its favor is that the company is much more insulated from the pressures of equity markets and of aggressive outside shareholders who could pressure the company to maintain returns or split the company up.

The reigns of the Tata Group have been turned over to Cyrus Mistry from Ratan Tata. He is related to the Tata family by marriage, and he worked for his family's construction business and his father in the largest shareholder in Tata Sons. Ratan Tata, along with steel mogul Lakshimi Mittal, had enjoyed unique reputations for high integrity, which is sometimes missing in the high-flying world of M&A. It remains to be seen if Mistry will be able to effectively navigate the Tata Group of more than 100 companies as India's economy grows rapidly and the world economy becomes more globalized.

We would also be remiss if we did not comment again on the inability of Arcelor-Mittal to grow in the Chinese, but especially the Indian market. Lakshimi Mittal failed to anticipate how much and how rapidly steel capacity in China would grow. As he used M&A to consolidate steel capacity and gain market share and, with it, buying power, the business changed and China became a huge steel producer. With the growth in steel production, the market share gained that Arcelor-Mittal enjoyed became less relevant. In addition, he was never able to achoieve any real growth in India—his native country. When one considers that he is one of the world's leading CEOs, we can appreciate the challenges of achieving growth in profitability through M&A in a rapidly changing global ecnoomy.

CHINA AND ITS EMERGING MARKET ACQUIRERS

Chinese companies have been making acquisitions all across the globe. Many of these companies are state owned or state controlled. Therefore, the reactions to their acquisitions are likely different than they would be if they had been done by private companies with shareholders from all over the world. To some it seems like a nefarious Chinese plot to use the country's export earnings to take over the world. There are varying degrees of resistance to China's form of state capitalism and the nation's rising role in global M&A. The reactions are similar whether they come from the nation's sovereign wealth fund, the China Investment Corporation (CIC), or from the various state-controlled corporations that never got fully privatized. Those who automatically criticize the acquisitions by China's sovereign wealth fund have obviously not spent much time studying the nature of their acquisitions. Up to this point, they have been purely for diverse investment purposes and have displayed no interest in control. This is exactly in line with their stated intentions. Moreover, their investments have been quite transparent and public. In fact, one could easily argue that they have purposely avoided any deals that could attract negative attention or controversy.

Chinese companies have begun their global expansion for various reasons. One is to gain access to natural resources. China's economic growth, while slowing, is still outstripping the ability of the country to internally source resources needed to fuel its growth engine. For example, the China Petroleum and Chemical Corporation, also known as Sinpec, acquired Conoco Phillips' stake in Canada's Syncrude project. Sinopec had already acquired Total's 50 percent stake in the Northern Lights project, and Petro-China, another of China's huge oil companies, acquired Athabasca Oil Sands Corp. Yanzhou Coal Mining acquired Australian mining company Felix Resources. These are just a few examples of Chinese companies traveling the world to use M&A to acquire more resources. These resource-oriented deals were typical of what can be called the first wave of outbound Chinese M&A. However, while such deals continue as China's resources needs are great, the second round of Chinese outbound M&A featured more broad-based M&A—not just resource-oriented transactions.

Examples of second round Chinese M&A deals include some of those done by the conglomerate Fosun. This company was founded by four graduates of

Shanghai's Fudan University. Its initial deals were within China and included buying stakes in formerly state-owned steel and mining companies but then later branched out into a variety of businesses such as publishing and shopping centers. Today, it is one of China's largest privately owned companies. However, it has also branched out past the Chinese border and has been acquiring companies in other nations. For example, it acquired a 10 percent stake in French travel company Club Med or a stake in Greek jewelry and fashion company Folli Follie. Fosun's approach is not to seek control. Rather it is to acquire stakes in targets for investment purposes. Given that the positions are often not controlling ones, they usually do not encounter the local government resistance that other deals do, such as those pursued by Huawei Technologies.

As the Chinese economy grows and incomes and consumption spending rise, the demand for more income-elastic goods also will rise. Chinese consumers are often very brand conscious and demand high-end European and U.S. products. This has led some cash-rich companies to pursue what we may call third round Chinese M&A. These are companies that make products for which there may be a great demand in the future in China. An example is state-owned Shandong Heavy Industry Group, which acquired the Italian luxury yacht builder Ferretti Yachts in 2012. This is an example of a win-win, as it enabled Shandong to offer luxury yachts from a high-quality manufacturer to increasingly rich Chinese consumers. It also allows the Italian sellers to sell their company at a time when economic demand, and M&A demand in particular, was very weak in Europe.

Chinese companies are also seeking to do what Western economies have been trying to do in China—find new markets for their products. An example was Lenovo, which acquired IBM's PC business. The company then was able to use its natural cost advantage to compete with the hulking high costs of U.S. PC companies such as HP. It also expanded globally through M&A. For example, in 2011, it acquired German electronics maker Medion for just under $1 billion.

Certain Chinese companies have experienced more resistance in their U.S. expansion efforts than others. One company in particular, Huawei Technologies, has attracted more negative attention than any other Chinese company due in part to its alleged ties to the Chinese military and the Chinese government. As an example, its 2011 acquisition of 3 Leaf Systems was not favorably received by the Committee on Foreign Investment in the United States (CFIUS). Huawei has also suffered from a backlash for alleged stealing of technologies, which many have said were much more extreme than other Chinese companies. This has hurt efforts of the company to sell telecommunications equipment in the large U.S. market.

The case of Huawei, however, is something of an exception. When we consider the slow economic growth in the U.S. economy, combined with a less than desirable rate of investment in the United States, foreign investment should be more welcome than it is. In part, this is a public relations problem, which potential Chinese acquirers can do a better job of handling. In fact, given the weak employment markets in the United States and Europe, the employment generating potential of Chinese investment in these slow-growth, but large, markets has not been well explained by Chinese acquirers. In fact, this obvious benefit to the economies of the selling companies has been ignored by Chinese dealmakers. One would think this might change in the future.

Chinese M&A has been motivated by finding resources but also new markets for Chinese products—especially those products that enable Chinese companies to take advantage of the relatively lower labor costs. The fact that the consumer sector is a much smaller part of GDP than in most developed countries, such as the United States, has left Chinese companies having to pursue consumer demand outside of its home market. However, as inflationary pressures rise in China and workers demand higher wages, it becomes more difficult for China to enjoy a comparative advantage over Western companies. We say more difficult, but this is still very much achievable.

NOTES

1. Carmen M. Reinhart and Kenneth Rogoff, *This Time Is Different: Eight Centuries of Financial Folly* (Princeton, NJ: Princeton University Press, 2009).
2. Julie Macintosh, *Dethroning the King: The Hostile Takeover of Anheuser Busch, an American Icon* (Hoboken, NJ: John Wiley & Sons, 2011).
3. Jim O'Neill, *The Growth Map: The Economic Opportunity in the BRICs and Beyond* (New York: Portfolio Penguin, 2011).
4. All data is for the year 2011. Data for 2012 is available only for a few countries, while others are just estimates by the United Nations. To make it uniform, I chose to go with the 2011 data.
5. Dominic Wilson and Anna Stupnytska, "The N-11: More Than an Acronym" (Goldman Sachs Global Economics Paper No. 153, March 28, 2007), 1.
6. Yasheng Huang, "How Did China Take Off?" *Journal of Economic Perspectives* 26, no. 4 (Fall 2012): 147–170.
7. Dezan Shira & Associates, *Mergers & Acquisitions in China*, 2nd ed. (Heidelburg: Springer Verlag, 2011), 11.
8. Association of Southeast Asian Nations, www.asean.org.
9. Hongbin Li, Lei Li, Binshen Wu, and Yanyan Xiong, "The End of Cheap Chinese Labor," *Journal of Economic Perspectives* 26, no. 4 (Fall 2012): 57–74.
10. "Deal Drivers in Africa: A Comprehensive Review of African M&A," 2012, Mergermarket, New York.
11. "Despite Global Slowdown, African Economies Growing Strongly—New Oil, Gas, and Mineral Wealth as Opportunity for Inclusive Development," The World Bank, Press Release, October 4, 2012.
12. Paul Sonne, "Tesco Loses Its Appetite for Growth," *Wall Street Journal*, November 10–11, 2012, B3.
13. Julia Werdigier, "Tesco to Sepnd $1.6 Billion to Revive U.K. Business," *New York Times*, April 18, 2012.

CHAPTER 8

Joint Ventures and Strategic Alliances as M&A Alternatives

The focus of this book has been on how companies can achieve growth through strategic mergers and acquisitions (M&A). When we analyze the benefits a company may derive from an M&A, one has to also consider whether there are lower-cost alternatives that could achieve the same goals. As we will see, joint ventures and strategic alliances are often much less expensive alternatives to M&A. However, they have significant limitations. In some instances, such as in the pharmaceutical industry, they can possibly work even better than M&A. In other instances, their limitations are too great to allow for the desired benefits to be realized. Therefore, it is useful to go over a brief discussion of these M&A alternatives.

In a joint venture, two or more companies combine certain assets and work together to achieve a particular business objective. Unlike M&A, where the time horizon is indefinite, in a joint venture the time period is usually defined and limited in duration. In some cases, however, such as in acquisition by private equity firms, the bidder has in mind a desired time period within which to exit the deal and flip the target.

The companies involved in a joint venture maintain their own separate business operations and continue to exist apart as they did before the joint venture. This venture is then formally created as a business entity such as a separate corporation or partnership. A formal agreement among the venture participants sets forth the extent to which they each will exercise control over the venture's activities and will participate in the entity's profits or losses. Presumably, this will be a road map that each can follow to assess the venture's progress toward achieving its goals.

Just like with any new business that is formed, a joint venture should have its own strategic plan and goals. This plan and set of goals may differ significantly from each venture partner's goals as the venture usually has a more focused purpose and complements the venture partner's overall business strategy.

There are many examples of successful joint ventures. One long-lasting example is Dow Corning, which is a venture that is equally owned by the Corning Corporation and Dow Chemical. Dow Corning is headquartered in Michigan and was created to specialize in silicon and silicon-based products. This entity has developed thousands of products since it was formed in 1943.

Another more recent, high-profile joint venture is Miller Coors. This venture was formed at the end of 2007 by SAB Miller and the Molson Coors Brewing Company. At the time the venture was founded, these two companies were the second- and third-largest U.S. brewers behind Anheuser-Busch. The venture was formed to jointly market the two companies' well-known beer brands. These include Miller, Miller Lite, Coors, Coors Light, Molson, and Blue Moon, as well as others. Both SAB Miller and Coors remain independent companies but benefit from the joint marketing of these various beer brands in the United States.

CONTRACTS VERSUS JOINT VENTURES

Rather than establishing a formal entity, companies considering joint ventures need to determine if their goals can be achieved by an even simpler arrangement. One such alternative is simply a contract agreement. For example, rather than form a joint venture to develop and then supply a particular product to one of the venture participants, one could contract with the other to purchase the product following its successful development. However, while this seems simpler, it may not get done. The developer may not have the financial wherewithal to undertake such development. If the other party agrees to fund the development, it may want to retain an ownership interest in the product and its future marketing. It may also not want to lose the competitive advantage the product bestows and may not want it sold to its rivals. When we have a set of issues such as these, a joint venture, while it is a more time-consuming and work-intensive process compared to a simple contract, may better accomplish the ultimate goals.

POTENTIAL PROBLEMS WITH JOINT VENTURES AND STRATEGIC ALLIANCES

Many potential problems can arise with joint ventures and strategic alliances. They are certainly not a cure for the ills of M&A, nor will they come close to achieving the goals of many M&A. This is obvious from the fact that we continue to do so many M&A, and if joint ventures and strategic alliances were the solution, we would see more of them instead of M&A.

The potential problems with joint ventures are as varied as the types of ventures. They may fail because the venture partners do not work well together. There may be disagreements between the participants, which may get in the way of accomplishing the venture's goals. The venture may require participants to share intellectual property or other proprietary knowledge, and they may be reluctant to do so, or one venture partner may be using such information in a way that was not intended by the other venture participant. The participants may not see themselves as fully committed as they might if the activities of the venture were part of the overall business. This lack of full commitment may prevent the venture from achieving its goals. Other problems may be that the venture simply does not accomplish what it set out to achieve. We will see that many of these same problems can also occur with strategic alliances.

CASE STUDY: AMYLIN AND ELI LILLY—ALLIANCE GONE BAD

An example of problems that can occur in joint ventures and strategic alliances is the alliance between Eli Lilly and Amylin, intended to develop and market a diabetes drug—exenatide. Amylin was a small company with no marketed products when it formed the alliance with Lilly, which is a leader in diabetes pharmaceutical treatments. Lilly made an upfront cash payment to Amylin and purchased shares in Amylin.

The marriage broke up when Amylin accused Eli Lilly of "cheating" on Amylin in favor of another drug developer. This was somewhat surprising as the two companies had worked together as alliance partners for 10 years before falling out.

The San Diego–based Amylin alleged that Eli Lilly engaged in improper behavior when it announced plans to implement an alliance with Boehringer Ingelheim GmbH to commercialize Boehringer Ingelheim's linagliptin product. This other diabetes drug would compete directly with Amylin's exenatide product. Amylin initially sought to have Lilly prevented from proceeding with plans to use the same sales force to sell both products.

After a hot legal battle, the two parted ways. Amylin, burned by its former suitor, Eli Lilly, agreed to sell the company to Bristol Myers Squibb in 2012 for $5.1 billion. Ironically, Eli Lilly's deal with Amylin provided that it would also get paid if Amylin was sold, so Lilly received a payment of $1.26 billion. Not too shabby for an alliance gone bad.

SHAREHOLDER WEALTH EFFECTS OF JOINT VENTURES

In spite of the problems that can occur with joint ventures, the market response to their formation is usually positive. Let us now explore the average shareholder wealth effects of joint ventures.

The research literature shows that the shareholder wealth effect on bidders doing M&A leaves a lot to be desired. So often the market responds negatively when a company announces that it is making an acquisition. As we will see in Chapter 10, however, that when companies announce selloffs, the market response is often positive. This is often also the case for joint ventures. Such deals tend to be well received by the market. Research studies on the shareholder wealth effects of joint ventures paint these deals in a positive light.

McConnell and Nantell did a study of 136 joint ventures involving 210 U.S. companies over the period 1972 to 1979.[1] The joint ventures they studied were drawn from a variety of industries. The most represented were real estate development (13 percent) and television and motion pictures (10 percent). Their methodology was the typical short-term event study approach that looked at the market-adjusted response to the announcement of the joint venture. The event study period focused on a three-day window around the announcement. Like comparable studies of M&A, this study sought to capture the market's assessment of the long-term impact on shareholders of the joint ventures.

The results of the McConnell and Nantell study indicated that shareholders in companies entering into joint ventures enjoyed positive announcement period returns equal to 0.73 percent. The results were similar when some of the over-represented industries, such as real estate, were eliminated from the sample. This is important, as the authors wanted to determine if the results were really being driven by just one dominant industry and therefore were not a reflection of the effects of joint ventures in general. Indeed, they found that the shareholder wealth effects were fairly evenly distributed across venture participants. When the authors tried to convert that seemingly small percentage return to a dollar amount, they found it corresponded to an average value of $4.8 million, which does not sound large by public company standards, but one has to remember that this result applied to ventures from the 1970s. In 2013 dollar terms, that amount translates to over $21 million.

The McConnell and Nantell study indicates that the market tends to like joint ventures. When we combine these results with the M&A research we have viewed, we wonder if the negative response of some acquirers' stock prices would have been positive if the companies had done a joint venture instead of an M&A. We have reason to believe that the answer is—maybe not.

The McConnell and Nantell study is not the only one showing positive shareholder wealth effects of joint ventures. Woolridge and Snow analyzed a sample of 767 announcements of strategic investment decisions involving 248 companies operating in 102 industries.[2] These strategic investment decisions included joint ventures as well as R&D projects and major capital investments. Their methodology featured an examination of the stock market reaction to the announcement of these decisions. In general, they found positive stock market responses to these various announcements. When the sample was divided into subsamples for the different types of announcements, they were able to determine that the shareholder wealth effects were positive for joint venture announcements. These results are consistent with the McConnell and Nantell findings.

SHAREHOLDER WEALTH EFFECTS BY TYPE OF VENTURE

We have differentiated between horizontal deals, which we discussed in Chapter 5, and vertical M&A, which we covered in Chapter 6. The McConnell and Nantell study did not differentiate between the two types of joint ventures. This raises the question: Do vertical ventures yield comparable shareholder wealth effects as horizontal ventures? We saw that for M&A, they often do not.

Johnson and Houston analyzed a sample of 191 joint ventures over the period 1991 to 1995.[3] They divided their sample into vertical joint ventures (55 percent) and horizontal joint ventures (45 percent). *Vertical joint ventures* involve transactions between buyers and suppliers. In the pharmaceutical industry, if a biotech drug researcher formed a venture with a pharmaceutical manufacturer and marketer, this would be considered a vertical transaction. *Horizontal joint ventures* are those involving companies in the same general line of business. For example, each could use products from the venture to sell to their own customers or to create an output that can be sold to the same group. In the steel industry, if two steel manufacturers formed a venture to mine iron ore, which they would jointly share in the output of the mining operation, this would be considered a vertical venture.

The results of the Johnson and Houston study showed average positive gains from joint ventures equal to 1.67 percent. For horizontal joint ventures, it appears that the gains are shared by the venture participants. The average returns for vertical joint ventures were somewhat higher—2.67 percent. However, what was particularly interesting when they looked at the vertical sample was that the gains did not accrue to both parties. Suppliers gained an average of 5 percent, with 70 percent of the returns being positive, while buyers received an average return of only 0.32 percent, which was not statistically significant and of which only 53 percent of the returns were even positive. For vertical joint ventures, the biggest winners were suppliers, who were able to capture the bulk of the gains, while the market did not see major benefits for buyers.

We have already discussed that an alternative to a joint venture is not just an M&A but also a simple contractual arrangement. Johnson and Houston tried to shed some light on the shareholder wealth effects of contracts compared to joint ventures. They analyzed a sample of announcements of contracts and found positive shareholder wealth effects with such announcements. However, they found that companies enter into joint ventures, as opposed to contracts, when transaction costs are high. They referred to these transaction costs as *hold-up hazards*. This could occur, for example, if a supplier had to make substantial buyer-specific investments, such as investments in certain machinery and capital goods needed to produce the buyer-specific products. While a contract may provide some temporary protection to the supplier over the contract period, as there would be an assurance of revenues to offset the capital purchase costs, the supplier may be vulnerable unless this capital equipment could be redeployed to another buyer. In the pharmaceutical industry, a drug company may want to assist a biotech firm to develop a new drug and may provide assistance. However, once the drug is developed, it would be vulnerable if it could then be easily sold to rivals. In such a situation, a formal joint venture may work well while a simple contract may not.

RELATEDNESS AND SIZE

When we analyzed M&A, we noticed that diversifying deals often tended to lose shareholder value. In addition, the more related the two companies were, the somewhat greater likelihood that the shareholder wealth effects would be positive. Therefore, it is a natural extension of the joint venture research to see if relatedness also plays an important role in joint ventures.

Consistent with the research on M&A, which showed deals involving related companies yield better returns than deals with companies that were not related, Koh and Venkatraman found that the positive shareholder wealth effects from joint venture announcements were greater for deals involving companies that were more related to each other.[4] In addition, they found that the smaller joint venture partner benefited more than the larger one. This is an intuitive conclusion, as the venture is probably much more significant for the smaller partner in relation to its overall business. Given the size differences, even if the venture is successful, it may not be that significant to the larger partner, which may have a much broader range and volume of business.

MARKET'S ASSESSMENT OF RISK OF JOINT VENTURES

Johnson and Houston have suggested that one source of the positive shareholder wealth effects could be risk-sharing benefits. However, Denning, Hurlburt, and Ferris found that 96 percent of their sample of 271 joint ventures over the period 1989 to 1997 experienced a change in risk.[5] While companies may believe that joint ventures lower their risks, this is often not how the market sees it. In their study, the authors did find that the market often rewarded risk increases when the joint venture partner was a foreign company and when the venture gave the company options to expand the venture in the future if there were increased perceived benefits. They found that the greater the size of the venture relative to the parent company's size and the more profitable the venturing firm was prior to pursuing the venture, the greater the shareholder wealth effects.

STRATEGIC ALLIANCES

Strategic alliances differ from joint ventures in that they typically reflect a less formal association between companies compared with joint ventures. In a joint venture, we usually have a new entity created but this often is not the case with strategic alliances.

Strategic alliances are collaborative efforts by two or more companies in which each company maintains its own independence. They are really contractual agreements between two legally separate entities that provide for sharing of costs and benefits of some mutually beneficial business activity.[6] When such alliances are formed to facilitate the achievement of the company's strategic goals, they are considered strategic alliances.

Strategic alliances are more common in some industries than others. For example, we often see them in the airline, computer, and pharmaceutical industries. Airlines that want to offer a larger geographical network of flights than what their supply of aircraft can handle often choose to join airline alliances. The airlines can preserve their independence while sharing routes, thereby allowing each airline to attract passengers seeking to travel beyond the limit of the alliance partners. The airlines then appear to passengers to be bigger than they really are.

Under airline alliance agreements, the alliance partners remain separate airlines but share routes. This enables them to keep a customer who wants to fly beyond the range of a given airline's routes. Each airline alliance partner can market the entire route, and the same flights may be marketed under different flight numbers for each partner. This is referred to as *code sharing*. With such alliances, the various partners may be able to provide customers with a global network. In addition, as various companies in an industry form such alliances, this puts pressure on competitors to follow suit so they are not at a disadvantage because of a smaller network.

One leading example of an airline alliance is the Star Alliance. It was formed in 1997 and is headquartered in Frankfurt, Germany. It was established with five founding airlines—Air Canada, Lufthansa, Scandinavian Airlines, Thai Airways International, and United Airlines. As of 2012, the alliance includes 28 member airlines and features over 21,000 daily departures. The alliance covers over 1,000 airports in almost 200 countries.

Often, a strategic alliance is an intermediate step toward a more formal association. For example, both United and Continental were members of the Star Alliance, but that membership only conveyed some of the benefits they were seeking to achieve. It allowed them to broaden their networks but not realize the cost benefits of a merger. For example, the alliance really did not offer the potential for the same kind of economies of scale that a merger would. Controlling costs is a key to profitability in the airline industry. For this reason, while many airlines use strategic alliances, the trend has been toward consolidation through M&A, which allows airlines to try to cut costs. From United and Continental's perspective, they were both alliance members and after their 2011 merger they still maintained the international route extension benefits of the alliance while using the merger to try to achieve some economies of scale.

We would be remiss if we did not note that after they merged, United and Continental came to a much clearer understanding of the true costs of merging the two huge airlines. The company experienced a number of problems with the reservation system and integration brought with it some challenges that they eventually overcame.

STRATEGIC ALLIANCE PROCESS

The process of developing a strategic alliance first starts off with an alliance partner conducting a strategic analysis of the goals it wants to achieve. If, as a result of that process, it is determined that these goals may best be achieved through a strategic alliance, then the company will begin a search for an alliance partner. Once a partner or partners are identified, initial communications followed by negotiations ensue. This process may require an investment of legal resources to work out all terms and to establish remedies should there be disputes. For example, the partners may agree to general terms for how disputes could be arbitrated so as to avoid more costly and time-consuming litigation. Most alliances terminate at some point. Thus, this would be the final step in the life of a given alliance.

SHAREHOLDER WEALTH EFFECTS OF STRATEGIC ALLIANCES

The research on the shareholder wealth effects of strategic alliances paints a very favorable picture. Chan, Kensinger, Keown, and Martin looked at the shareholder wealth effects of 345 strategic alliances over the period 1983 to 1992.[7] Almost one-half of their sample involved alliances for marketing and distribution purposes. For the overall group, they found positive abnormal returns equal to 0.64 percent. This is somewhat comparable to what was seen with the research of McConnell and Nantell for joint ventures. The Chan, Kensinger, Keown, and Martin study also found no evidence of significant transfers of wealth between alliance partners. This implies that there was no evidence that one partner was gaining at the expense of another. This result supports the use of strategic alliances as an alternative to M&A—*in the limited circumstances where it is appropriate.*

SHAREHOLDER WEALTH EFFECTS BY TYPE OF ALLIANCE

Chan, Kensinger, Keown, and Martin looked at how the shareholder wealth effects varied by type of alliance. They separated their sample into horizontal and nonhorizontal alliances. They defined horizontal alliances as those involving partners with the same three-digit SIC code. They found that horizontal alliances that involved the transfer of technology provided the highest cumulative abnormal return—3.54 percent. This may help explain why strategic alliances occur so often between technologically oriented companies. Nonhorizontal alliances that were done to enter a new market provided a positive but lower return—1.45 percent. Other nonhorizontal alliances failed to show significant returns. This result reminds us of the dubious benefits companies seek to realize when they use M&A to move outside their core business.

Another study conducted by Das, Sen, and Sengupta also looked at the types of alliances that might be successful, as reflected by their initial announcement shareholder wealth effects.[8] They were able to show how the announcement effects varied by type of alliance as well as by firm profitability and relative size of the alliance participants. They discovered that technological alliances were associated with greater announcement returns than marketing alliances. These are two of the more common types of alliances. In his research of 4,192 alliances, Hagedoorn has previously shown that, as expected, technological alliances were more common in high-growth sectors, whereas marketing alliances were more common in mature industries.[9] Das, Sen, and Sengupta also showed that the abnormal returns were negatively correlated with both the size of the alliance partners and their profitability. We see that the market is concluding that larger and more profitable partners will capture fewer of the gains from the alliance. Stated alternatively, the market sees greater benefits for smaller and less profitable businesses to partner with larger and more profitable companies. The smaller and less profitable companies seem to have more to gain from strategic alliances. This does not imply that the partnerships are not also good for larger companies. Given that they are bigger and their profits are greater, it would be reasonable to expect that when such companies partner with smaller firms, they have less to gain because the impact of that alliance will have a smaller impact on the overall business of the larger company. That larger company may enter into several such alliances, and the aggregate effect of all of these alliances may make the difference less.

NOTES

1. John J. McConnell and Timothy J. Nantell, "Corporate Combinations and Common Stock Returns: The Case of Joint Ventures," *Journal of Finance* 40, no. 2 (June 1985): 519–536.
2. J. Randall Woolridge and Charles C. Snow, "Stock Market Reaction to Strategic Investment Decisions," *Strategic Management Journal* 11, no. 5 (September 1990): 353–363.
3. Shane Johnson and Mark Houston, "A Reexamination of the Motives and Gains in Joint Ventures," *Journal of Financial and Quantitative Analysis* 35, no. 1 (March 2000): 67–85.
4. Jeongsuk Koh and N. Venkatraman, "Joint Venture Formations and Stock Market Reactions: An Assessment of the Information Technology Sector," *Academy of Management Journal* 34, no. 4 (1991): 869–892.
5. Karen C. Denning, Heather Hurlburt, and Stephen P. Ferris, "Risk and Wealth Effects of U.S. Firm Joint Ventures Activity," *Review of Financial Economics* 15 (2006): 271–285.
6. David T. Robinson, "Strategic Alliances and the Boundaries of the Firm," *Review of Financial Studies* 21, no. 2 (2008): 649–681.

7. Su Han Chan, John W. Kensinger, Arthur Keown, and John D. Martin, "Do Strategic Alliances Create Value?" *Journal of Financial Economics* 46, no. 2 (November 1997): 199–221.
8. Somnath Das, Pradyot K. Sen, and Sanjit Sengupta, "Impact of Strategic Alliances on Firm Valuation," *Academy of Management Journal* 41, no. 1 (February 1988): 27–41.
9. John Hagedoorn, "Understanding the Rationale of Strategic Technology Partnering: Interorganizational Modes of Cooperation and Sectoral Differences," *Strategic Management Journal* 14 (1993): 371–385.

CHAPTER 9

Role of Corporate Governance in M&A

One of the real challenges in mergers and acquisitions (M&A) is doing good deals and avoiding bad ones. We have discussed how the volume of bad deals is troublingly high. Admittedly, armed with hindsight, the amount of poorly conceived M&A that turned out to be major failures is hard to explain. For major deals, that is, those that are significant in terms of asset size compared to the size of the bidder, the deals generally have the recommendation of senior management and most importantly, the CEO, and then are approved by the board of directors. Thus, for major deals, these two parties, the office of the CEO and the board, bear the responsibility for a deal's success or failure. Therefore, we will discuss the role each plays in corporate governance in general, but also specifically related to M&A.

AGENCY COST PROBLEM

Shareholders are the ultimate owners of the company. However, for large corporations, the term *owner* conveys a different meaning from what it does for small businesses. In a small business, the owners pick the managers, and they also may play a major role in management themselves. With large companies, however, most shareholders hold a relatively small percentage of the total shares outstanding. This is often true for large institutions and even aggressive hedge funds. For institutions, their stockholdings in a given company are one of many investments they may have. Thus, they do not have a big incentive to closely monitor the company. Even if they wanted to, such institutional investors have diverse portfolios and cannot micromanage particular companies in which they have investments. When they are dissatisfied with the performance of the company and its governance they typically "vote with their feet" and their shares rather than waste their time fighting it out with an entrenched management. This was the case when some institutional investors unloaded their shares in Chesapeake Energy Corp. rather than continue to suffer the "Aubrey Discount" caused by its CEO Aubrey McClendon. Certain activist hedge fund, however, take the opposite approach. This is not the case with certain activist hedge funds. As an example, William Ackman's Pershing Square Capital Management LP, a large hedge fund, took a $2 billion stock position in Procter & Gamble Co. (P&G) in 2012 and tried to use their equity position to bring about changes in the company. In the past, companies such as P&G thought they were immune to such threats given their huge market capitalization, which in the case of P&G is in the $175 billion range. Even after a $2 billion investment, Pershing's stake was less than 1 percent of P&G's equity, as the company has a market capitalization that has often hovered just under $200 billion!

Shareholders who are not activist investors must rely on managers to run the business in a manner that maximizes shareholder wealth. The problem is that managers may pursue their own personal goals and consequently may not run the company in a manner that will maximize shareholder wealth. For this reason, shareholders elect directors to oversee management. Typically, this is done through a voting process where for each share investors own, they get one vote for each director position. It is more common that directors come up for election every year, and it is less common that director positions are *staggered* and only a percentage, such as one-third, of the board are up for election each year.

Directors have a fiduciary responsibility to make sure management runs the company in a manner that maximizes the value of shareholder investments. They are paid fees to do this work. As part of that oversight process, they are expected to attend and participate in board of directors meetings, where they hear reports from management on the company's performance. The position of a director is not a full-time position, and directors often pursue other work including possibly serving on other boards. One survey of directors reported that on average, there were 5.6 board meetings per year and that they devoted an average of 19 hours per month to board issues.[1]

Since most (hopefully) directors are not full-time employees at the company, many boards include some members of management. These board members are referred to as inside board members. The remainder of the board, ideally the majority of the board, consists of outside directors. In fact, the New York Stock Exchange and NASDAQ require that a majority of the board members of companies listed on these exchanges be independent.

If management does pursue policies that shareholders oppose, their relatively small share holdings often do not allow them to take actions to effectively oppose management. Shareholders have to put their trust in the board of directors and hope that they will look after their collective interests when they monitor management. This is the essence of the board's fiduciary duties. When directors are insufficiently diligent and do not require managers to act in shareholders' interests, they violate their fiduciary duties.

Most shareholders are not activists. Even large institutional investors tend to vote with management and support the reelection of the board that is proposed to them. Only when the company's performance is very poor are there good opportunities for activists to pursue proxy fights to displace management.

One of the goals of the board is to minimize agency costs. It is not practical to try to get such costs to zero. Management always has something of their own agenda and the goal of the board is to minimize these costs. In fact, the practical way to think of it is to put it into a basic microeconomic framework where a company pursues these efforts until the marginal benefits equal marginal costs. The result will logically be a positive level of agency costs, which are simply a cost, albeit an efficiently controlled one (hopefully), of doing business as a public entity.

One concern for shareholders is if the CEO is running the company to maximize his or her own compensation and perks. Management may also want to maximize the psychic income that they may derive from running a very large company. Company expansion may make those at the top feel good about themselves but it may not be in the shareholders' interests to have such a large firm. Think back to Dennis Kozlowski's reign at Tyco (before he went to prison) when he grew the company in multiple directions at once and always at light speed. Certainly, all would agree that he did maximize his perks while the board was asleep at the wheel as he pursued his freewheeling growth strategy. It is important for the board to make sure that M&A is done to make the *company* more profitable and not to further the personal goals of management. The poor job analysts and the media did in critically reviewing the company's totally unsynergistic growth strategy enabled management to escape being pressured by the media to explain its pattern of highly disparate M&A.

CEO COMPENSATION AND AGENCY COSTS

In the United States, CEOs are paid quite handsomely. Their compensation seems particularly high when compared to their counterparts in Europe and Asia. The difference in these compensation levels can be readily seen in data compiled by the Hay Group in a study commissioned by the *Wall Street Journal*, which shows that in 2011, the average CEO compensation at the 300 largest U.S. companies was $11.8 million. Of the $11.8 million, $1.2 million was base salary and the rest included items such as incentives.[2] The large percentage of the total that is in the form of incentives can be a concern, as it is often not fully transparent. In fact, some argue that this lack of transparency may be by design in an effort to disguise upper management extracting unjustified gains or *rents* from shareholders.[3]

According to the Institute for Policy Studies, senior executives of European companies only earned about a third of what their U.S. counterparts earned.[4] Another survey by Towers Perrin (now Towers Watson) found that the average U.S. CEO earned about twice as much as his or her British counterparts.[5] Part of the reason for this is that corporate reforms were adopted in Britain, which required that shareholders vote annually on executive compensation. When we consider that institutional investors wield significant power at some British corporations, it is not hard to understand why executive compensation seems under better control in that nation. Frankly, the United Kingdom has done a much better job of protecting shareholders' rights than the United States or its European counterparts.

The differences in CEO compensation levels are particularly stark when you compare the compensation of CEOs of the leading U.S. banks with those of bank CEOs in the next largest economy—China. At times, bank CEOs, such as Sandy Weill, former CEO of Citigroup, have taken almost a quarter of a billion dollars in annual compensation. Presumably, the efforts he exerted to build the hugely dysfunctional financial conglomerate were responsible for such outsized compensation. When the very troubled financial conglomerate had to be dissembled after he left the bank, there were no calls by the board to retrieve some of the gross overcompensation Weill unabashedly took at shareholders' expense. Clearly, Citigroup had a very poorly performing board. However, it was quite amusing to hear Weill's 2012 testimony before Congress and his subsequent comments to the media where he recommended that something akin to Glass Steagall be brought back and the big diversified banks be broken up.[6] It was Weill, probably more than anyone else, who fought to have Glass Steagall *deactivated* so that he could build a financial supermarket that included accepting deposits and offering checking accounts along with merger advisory, proprietary trading, and insurance. This huge corporate structure allowed him to extract his outsized compensation. Then, when he retired with so much of shareholders' money in his pocket, he admitted that the structure did not work but never offered to give back some of the compensation he took for doing a bad job.

The Citigroup board of recent years has become more active in the critical monitoring of its CEO. This was underscored in the fall of 2012 when it asked Vikram Pandit to step down. Some have questioned his background; while he had considerable investment banking experience, he had no experience in commercial banking.[7] This made him an odd hire considering he had to take over one of the largest commercial banks in the world in a period of turmoil. While the board should get credit for replacing him with an internal hire who had considerable commercial banking experience, the board should not get a pass for appointing Pandit, given his total lack of a background in commercial banking. Perhaps they were patting themselves on the back for the Pandit hire, as he was an upgrade from the ill-equipped Charles Prince, who led the bank into disaster. Citigroup's board's continues to leave a lot to be desired.

In contrast to some of the large U.S. banks, if we look at the compensation of CEOs in China's leading banks, some of the largest banks in the world, we see that those CEOs earn a fraction of what their U.S. counterparts have made. For example, in 2008, the CEOs of the three largest banks in China each earned in the $250,000 range. The obvious question arises: Is it that much more work to run one of the larger U.S. banks than it is to run the huge Chinese banks? Perhaps the answer is that U.S. banks have many clever investment strategies to be monitored such as JPMorgan Chase's brilliant efforts to hedge some of their investments, which resulted in the "London whale" loss of over $7 billion. Perhaps if Jamie Dimon was paid more he would have been more on top of that situation. In fairness, though, Dimon is widely regarded as being the best CEO in the industry. What the London whale disaster shows us is that these institutions are too big for even the best managers to manage.

DO SHAREHOLDERS GET VALUE FOR THE HIGH COMPENSATION PAID TO U.S. CEOs?

We have established that U.S. CEOs are the highest paid in the world. The obvious question arises: Do shareholders get what they paid for? That is, do they generate outsized returns to compensate them for the outsized compensation they pay shareholders? If so, then the "investment" was worth it. Unfortunately, there is little research support for this assertion.

Cooper, Gulen, and Rau analyzed a large sample of the firms included in the S&P ExecuComp database covering the period 1994 to 2006. They found that companies in the highest decile ranking of executive compensation earned significant negative excess returns![8] In fact, their results showed that for each dollar that was paid to CEOs, their shareholders lost $100. They also found that these higher-paying firms generated stock returns that trailed their peers by over 12 percentage points.

Other research has come to a similar conclusion but approaches the problem differently. Bebchuk, Cremers, and Peyer looked at the CEO *slice*— the percentage of total compensation of the top five managers in companies that goes to the CEO.[9] In analyzing a sample of more than 2,000 companies, they found that the CEO pay slice, which was approximately 35 percent, was negatively related to firm value as reflected by industry-adjusted Tobin q values.

Another study looked at management perks. Management perks have clear direct costs that are measurable, but there is some evidence that indicates that such expenses may have costs well beyond these direct costs. A study by New York University (NYU) finance professor David Yermack looked at certain high-profile perks such as use of corporate aircraft and showed that companies that disclosed such managerial perks tended to *underperform* annual market benchmarks by 4 percent. His study analyzed 237 large corporations over the years 1993 to 2002. The magnitude of the aggregate dollar underperformance was significantly greater than the actual monetary costs of the specific perks. One explanation is that the market takes the revelation of the perks as an indication of corporate waste and management that may not be running the company in a manner that will maximize shareholder value.

A study by Jesse Edgerton found that companies controlled by private equity firms were 25 percent less likely to operate corporate jets compared to comparable public firms.[10] The data were adjusted for industry and size effects. The study also found that when private equity–controlled companies had corporate jet fleets they were 40 percent smaller than their public conterparts. This research underscores the agency problems of large public companies.

The research literature does not lend any support for the large compensation paid to U.S. CEOs. The explanation has to lie elsewhere. A good place to look is the close relationship U.S. CEOs tend to have with their boards of directors.

BOARD CHARACTERISTICS AND CEO COMPENSATION

We have established that the research literature fails to provide support for the notion that shareholders receive benefits for the relatively higher compensation that U.S. CEOs receive relative to the non-U.S. counterparts. Why then do boards approve such excess compensation? Research by Core, Holthausen, and Larker provides some insight into the relationship between CEO compensation and the makeup of boards.[11] Over a three-year study period, they examined 205 large corporations in 14 different industries. They related the levels of CEO compensation to different characteristics of boards.

Implicit in their analysis, Core, Holthausen, and Larker assumed that larger boards were less effective and more susceptible to CEO influence. This conclusion is intuitive, as at a larger board, each director constitutes a smaller percentage of the total board and commands a smaller percentage of the total votes needed to approve board decisions. Additionally, Core, Holthausen, and Larker also looked at the percentage of outside directors on boards as well as the number of *gray* directors. These were directors who receive other compensation or benefits beyond the director payment that directors receive for serving on the board. In addition, the study's authors also assumed that if the director was appointed to the board after the CEO was in place, then the CEO played a role in that decision. Their analysis further highlighted interlocked directors, as those directors may be weaker from a corporate governance perspective (interlocked boards will be discussed in greater detail later in this chapter). They also assigned a negative value to CEOs being older (over 70) and being on too many other boards.

Core, Holthausen, and Larker's findings are consistent with human nature. Their research showed an inverse relationship between CEO compensation and the percentage of outside directors on the board. When a board has more outsiders and fewer insiders, it is more likely that management and the CEO will have less influence on the board. They also found that CEO compensation was positively related to board size. When boards are larger, each individual board member has less influence, and the CEO may be able to pursue a divide and conquer strategy on his or her way to getting more compensation. We will return to these issues later in this chapter, where we focus on boards of directors.

CEO compensation was also greater for the directors who were gray, over age 69, or who served on three or more boards. There was also an inverse relationship between CEO compensation and the size of the share holdings of the CEO. In addition, they also found that CEO compensation was lower when there were external blockholders who owned 5 percent or more of the outstanding shares. These external blockholders had sufficient power to try to keep the CEO's pursuit of higher personal compensation in check. The lower the size of the holdings of the largest shareholders, the less likely they will have the power, or the incentive, to hold the CEO in check. Large blockholders, particularly, if they are willing to be activists, plan an invaluable role in preventing value-reducing deals.

BENCHMARKING AND HOW BOARDS DETERMINE CEO COMPENSATION

The compensation subcommittee of the board of directors sets CEO compensation. As a guidepost for doing this, they often select a peer group of CEOs of companies who in the committee's view are sufficiently comparable to be included in the comparison. This may be done in consultation with a compensation-consulting firm. Securities and Exchange Commission rules require that when peers groups are used, they be disclosed to shareholders.

Research by Bizjak, Lemmon, and Nguyen provides support for the contention that the peer group is often opportunistically selected to arrive at a higher compensation level for the CEO.[12] Their research shows that S&P 500 companies appear to select peers that are similar or smaller than their company in an apparent effort to justify the compensation of the CEO, where non-S&P 500 companies appear to select peers that are larger in an apparent effort to support higher compensation levels.

CEOs are selected by the board of directors. Board members like to think that they have picked the best CEO—perhaps the best in the industry. For this reason, it is reasonable to expect many boards to be willing to pay their CEO above-average compensation for the fact that they have picked an above average CEO.[13] In fact, if they determine their CEO deserves below-average compensation, then they must have picked a below average CEO, which implies they are a below-average board. That can't be. Therefore, the *solution* may be to pay their CEO above-average compensation even when he or she does not deserve it. If this is how the compensation of CEOs is determined, then we will have an ever-rising spiral of CEO compensation—which is exactly what we have had in the United States. Only the blunting impact of the subprime crisis and related Great Recession has temporarily slowed this down.

ARE THE HIGH PAID SUPERSTAR CEOs SIMPLY WORTH THE MONEY? NOT

Consistent with the above reasoning, boards like to think they have picked the best CEO. There is also a certain comfort level with picking a CEO who is clearly a superstar. Are these superstar CEOs worth the extra high pay they tend to receive?

Malmendier and Tate analyzed the performance of companies run by CEOs who were awarded this status in the form of relatively high compensation, awards, and press coverage.[14] They found that such companies underperformed relative to their prior performance as well as the performance of their peers. The compensation of the CEOs rose significantly on attainment of the superstar status, but their performance as CEOs thus declined. In fact, they showed that such CEOs spent a disproportionate amount of time doing other activities such as attending public and private events as well as writing books—work for which the company may derive little benefit. Their peers who may not have had as many of these opportunities presumably devoted more of their time to running the company, which may explain why they outperformed the superstars. One of the lessons of this research is that hiring a superstar and paying the high price tag associated with that status may not be in the company's best interest. The company may be better served by hiring an executive who will work efficiently and not require superstar pay.

ARE CEOs PAID FOR LUCK?

Companies, such as those in a commodity-oriented industry like the oil industry, have their performance greatly affected by variables that are generally outside of their control such as movements in the price of oil. If oil prices rise, as they did in 2007 to 2008, the profits at companies such as Exxon can simply rise along with them, without any meaningful change in managerial efforts. Should the CEO then be rewarded for such *performance*? An empirical study by Bertrand and Mullainathan found out that they were.[15] However, more efficiently governed firms pay their CEOs less for luck. For example, they found that adding a large shareholder to the board reduces pay for luck by 23 to 33 percent. This again underscores the positive role that large blockholders can (but definitely not always) play.

CEO COMPENSATION AND M&A PROGRAMS

Larger companies have higher revenues and greater assets and they also have higher costs. Part of these costs is management compensation and CEO compensation in particular. Therefore, one of the ways CEOs of companies can get paid more is to run larger companies. They can do that by finding a position managing a large company or by converting their current corporation into a larger one through M&A. It is this latter motive, and the link between CEO compensation and M&A programs, that we want to explore.

Hallock and Torok examined the compensation packages of more than 2,300 CEOs of publicly traded companies of various different sizes. They found out that for every 1 percent increase in company size, CEO compensation went up by one-third of 1 percent.[16] Another study of the largest 1,000 U.S. companies by Steven Hall & Partners showed that the median 2005 CEO compensation at the top 27 companies in their sample, $16.8 million, was five times greater than the $3.2 million median compensation of the CEOs at the smallest quintile.[17] Thus, CEOs have a great incentive to use M&A to make their companies bigger and their paycheck larger. It is up to the boards to make sure that CEOs are pursuing M&A programs for the financial gain of the shareholders' and not just for their own personal gain.

DO BOARDS PAY CEOs FOR DOING M&A?

There is evidence that boards give CEOs extra compensation as a reward for doing M&A. This makes sense for deals that do well, but as we now know, a great many deals do not do well. Grinstein and Hribar conducted a study of 327 large M&A that occurred during the fifth merger wave period, 1993 to 1999.[18] Their examination of corporate proxy statements relating to CEO compensation showed that boards specifically awarded CEOs compensation for being able to complete M&A. They indicated that in 39 percent of the cases they considered, part of the CEO compensation was due to the CEO being able to complete a deal. This is not necessarily bad if the deal was a good one. However, it is often the case that a board will not know how successful a deal really is until years after the transaction. In that sense, perhaps some of these rewards were premature.

Another study also found that companies that were active in M&A paid higher compensation to their managers. Schmidt and Fowler analyzed a sample of 127 companies, of which 41 were bidders that used tender offers to make acquisitions, 51 were nontender offer acquirers, and 35 were control firms.[19] They found that both bidders and acquirers showed higher managerial compensation than the control group.

These studies show that boards tend to pay greater compensation to managers of companies that are active in M&A. When one considers the questionable track record of many M&A, we have to conclude that boards need to rethink such M&A-based incentives.

DO BOARDS PUNISH CEOs FOR DOING BAD M&As? CASE OF RIO TINTO

Boards may punish CEOs for doing bad deals but there seems to be too many instances of boards failing to do their duty and allowing CEOs to pursue M&A programs that are not in shareholders' interests and that destroy equity values. One recent example of a board giving a CEO his "walking papers" was the ouster of CEO Tom Albanese from mining giant Rio Tinto. Rio Tinto is a British/Australian mining company that is one of the world's leaders in the production of commodities such as aluminum, iron ore, and copper. Albanese led Rio Tinto into a huge $38 billion investment in aluminum when it acquired Alcan in 2007. Alcan was originally the target of a friendly bid from Alcoa that turned hostile, causing Alcan to seek out white knights. Albanese, obviously, was not aware of the research that showed the negative shareholder wealth effects of white knight bids.[20]

Part of Albanese's strategy was to reduce the company's dependence on iron ore, which is cyclical and subject to the vicissitudes of the steel industry. Unfortunately this was an "out of the frying pan and into the fire strategy" as aluminum is also quite cyclical. Rio Tinto had to write off the majority the $38 billion acquisition cost! In addition, this was not the only flop Rio Tinto had on Albanese's watch. He made an ill-fated $3 billion investment in Riverside Mining, which had coking-coal assets in Africa. This also was a bust. Finally the board asked Albanese to step down.

CEOs in the mining industry are not known to have long tenures in their positions. This is intuitive given the volatile commodity-based nature of the business. If the relevant commodity prices are high, the CEO is a genius.

When they are down, he or she does not know what they are doing. In the case of Rio Tinto, the CEO led the company into new areas of the mining industry that greatly expanded its losses.

GOLDEN PARACHUTES AND M&A

Golden parachutes are payments made to members of management upon the occurrence of events such as the taking over of their company. The rationale behind such large payments is that they help retain senior managers when the company is under the threat of being taken over. However, they also have a dark and ominous side.

CEOs who are in the position of negotiating the sale of their own company are also in a position to trigger a deal that will give them their golden parachute. While they are negotiating the sale of the company, they may also be negotiating their own severance package or a pay package in exchange for staying on at the combined company and providing "consulting" or other management services. This can give rise to a conflict of interest.

Some CEOs have received huge payouts following the sale of their companies. For example, in 2013 William Johnson, CEO of H.J. Heinz Co., was reported to receive $200 million upon his exit following the sale of his company to Berkshire Hathaway, Inc. $56 million of this total was a golden parachute. In 2005, James Kilts, CEO of Gillette, received a reported $165 million following the sale of his company to Procter & Gamble Co. Another example was the $102 million that Bruce Hammonds was reported to have received in connection with MBNA's acquisition by Bank of America, and the $92 million that Pete Correll was reported to have received in connection with the 2005 sale of his company, Georgia Pacific, to Koch Industries. Even companies known for poor performance still have similar payouts for their CEOs when they are finally sold. For example, AT&T CEO David Dorman was reported to have received $55 million in connection with the sale of his company to SBC Communications. Given AT&T's long history of poor performance and horrendous deals, such a high compensation level is difficult to explain.

With such huge potential conflicts of interest at play, boards need to be extra vigilant—whether they actually are is a different issue.

CEO SEVERANCE PAYMENTS

Boards are not just generous with shareholder money when it comes to paying takeover premiums; they are just generally generous when it comes to paying CEOs with other people's—shareholders'—money. Goldman and Huang showed this in an empirical analysis of every CEO who left his or her position in an S&P 500 company over the years 1993 to 2007.[21] They measured the excess severance pay for departing CEOs and defined excess as the amount beyond what the company contractually agreed to pay as severance in the CEO employment contract. As shocking as it sounds, *excess* CEO pay was an average of $8 million, which was over 240 percent of the CEO's annual compensation. They found that for the CEO who left voluntarily, weak corporate governance was positively associated with the size of the excess severance pay. This is no surprise. For CEOs who were forced out, however, they believed the data showed that a desire to protect shareholders' interests and preserve an orderly transition were more important explanatory factors than weak governance. Another key factor has to be that the boards that approve such compensation are paying the CEOs with shareholder's money, not their own, and shareholders have very little ability to challenge the decision of these directors.

ARE CEOS EVALUATING M&A BY THINKING, "WHAT'S IN IT FOR ME?"

CEOs should be devoting their efforts to maximizing shareholder returns. This is what they are paid for. However, there is troubling research evidence that some may be simply evaluating M&A to determine, "What's in it for me?" Harzell, Ofek, and Yermack analyzed 239 acquisitions that occurred in the three-year period of 1995 to 1997.[22] They found that target CEOs enjoyed mean wealth increases between $8 million and $11 million. The bulk of these financial gains came from increases in stock and options as well as from golden parachute payments. Some CEOs even received last-minute increases in their golden parachute agreements—presumably in exchange for promoting the deal. They also found that about one-half of the CEOs became officers in the buying entity, although their departure rates over the three years following the merger were very high. Even for these exits, however, the former target CEO received enhanced compensation.

The Hartzell, Ofek, and Yermack study also showed that in deals where target CEOs enjoyed extraordinary personal treatment, shareholders received *lower* acquisition premiums. If the premiums were higher, one could possibly think that they earned their extra compensation. However, when the premiums are lower, one has to wonder if the CEOs are trading shareholder premiums for their own personal gains. More fundamentally, is that why the company is being sold?

CEO OVERCONFIDENCE AND M&A

Intuitively, one can theorize that an overconfident CEO is not a good thing and that such a CEO may pursue deals that are not in the company's interests.

Overconfident CEOs may superimpose their own valuation of a target on top of the market's valuation and assert that a target is undervalued and thus is worth a higher premium. This was obviously the case when Quaker Oats, and its CEO William Smithburg, acquired Snapple for $1.7 billion in 1994, only to sell it off for $300 million in 1997. Not surprisingly, 1997 was the year that Smithburg retired from Quaker Oats. It is a shame the board could not have persuaded him to stay on longer and continue to give shareholders the benefit of his great valuation expertise.

Malmendier and Tate analyzed the role of CEO overconfidence in the tendency for CEOs to engage in M&A.[23] They measured CEO overconfidence using factors such as the tendency for CEOs to hold options in their company's stock until expiration, thereby exhibiting bullishness about the company's prospects and their ability to create stock gains. Their study analyzed a sample of large companies covering the period 1980 to 1994. The results showed that overconfident CEOs were more likely to conduct acquisitions and, in particular, more likely to do *value-destroying* deals. As part of this value-destruction process, they found that overconfident CEOs were more likely to pursue *diversifying* deals. We have discussed in Chapter 4 some research that shows how such deals *may* destroy value. They also do not find that the relationship between overconfidence and acquisitiveness varies with CEO tenure, implying that for overconfident CEOs, it is a function of their position and their personal hubris, not how long they were with the company.

ARE OVERCONFIDENT CEOs GOOD FOR ANYTHING?

There is convincing research support for the notion that overconfidence can lead to value-destroying M&A. This gives rise to the question: Are overconfident CEOs good for anything? The answer may be *yes*. Hirshleifer, Low, and Teoh analyzed a large sample of 2,577 CEOs covering 9,807 firm years drawn from the time period 1993 to 2003.[24] They found that overconfident CEOs are more likely to pursue risky projects and, in general, are better innovators. They tend to invest more in research and development and their companies tend to apply for and receive more patents. In addition, the returns of their companies tend to be more volatile. So for investors willing to gamble, an overconfident CEO can be "just the ticket."

MANAGEMENT COMPENSATION AND POST-ACQUISITION PERFORMANCE

Is the compensation of senior management affected by the success or failure of acquisition programs? For companies that pursue large-volume acquisition programs with M&A being an integral part of their growth strategy, linking managerial compensation to the success of those deals makes good sense. Schmidt and Fowler analyzed a sample of 127 companies, of which 41 were bidders that used tender offers to make acquisitions, 51 were nontender offer acquirers, and 35 were control firms.[25] Consistent with research previously discussed, bidder companies, those that would more likely be involved in initiating hostile takeovers, showed a significant decrease in postacquisition shareholder returns. This was not the case for acquirers who did not use tender offers, as well as for the control group. Also interesting from a corporate governance perspective is that both bidders and acquirers showed higher managerial compensation than the control group. While takeovers pay "dividends" for management in the form of higher compensation, even though they may generate losses for shareholders of those companies that use tender offers and hostile takeovers to pursue the acquisition strategy. Takeovers may enhance the personal wealth of managers, they may not be in the interests of shareholders. It is for this reason that boards have to be extra diligent when overseeing managers who may be acquisition-minded. There is greater risk of shareholder losses and managers, in effect, gaining at shareholder expense. For this reason, the board needs to make extra sure the deals will truly maximize shareholder wealth and not just provide financial and psychic income for managers.

ROLE OF THE BOARD OF DIRECTORS

The board of directors has to provide clear oversight to make sure that all that can be done to avoid bad M&A and to pursue beneficial ones is done. Just like we have good CEOs and not so good ones, we have good and bad boards. There has been abundant and convincing research in the field of corporate governance regarding the characteristics of good boards and the characteristics that are likely to cause problems. If we want good M&A and we want to avoid bad deals, the board is the last step in the approval process and it is imperative that shareholders elect good directors. Unfortunately, while normal political democracy does not work well, corporate democracy is a process that is even less responsive to its constituents—shareholders. Shareholders have little power, and only when performance is significantly poor are shareholders in a position to change management and replace the board.

In this section, we discuss the following board characteristics that can be determinative of good corporate governance:

- Director independence
- Busy directors

- Interlocked boards
- Board size

Director Independence

Boards have two groups of directors: (1) inside board members and (2) outside board members. Inside board members are also management employees of the company. These board members may include the CEO as well as certain other senior members of management whose input may be useful in board deliberations. A 2009 survey conducted by *Corporate Board Member* found that the average number of inside directors is 1.41, down from 2.7 in its 2003 survey, while the average number of outside directors is 6.95, down from 7.2, giving an average size of a board of 8.36 directors.[26] This same survey found that 52.7 percent of the time the chairperson was an insider.

A 2011 survey of large U.S. corporations by Spencer Stuart found that 84 percent of board members were independent.[27] In fact, they found that the CEO was the only non-independent director at the S&P 500 companies. The ratio of independent to non-independent directors was 5.3 to 1 compared to a 2006 survey they conducted where it was 3.4 to 1.

The pressure for improved corporate governance as well as regulatory requirements has led companies to have a majority of their board members as outside directors.

There is support in the research literature for the belief that shareholder wealth will be higher with a board dominated by outside directors than one where insiders control the board. For example, Cooter, Shivdasni, and Zenner showed that shareholders in companies with more outside directors will realize greater gains if their companies are taken over.[28] They studied 169 tender offers over the period 1989 to 1992. They found that targets with independent boards received higher premiums and, in general, greater shareholder gains when their boards were independent. In addition, their research implied that some of these gains were at the expense of target shareholder returns. In other words, having an independent board enabled the target to negotiate a better deal than what shareholders would have received.

Another study by Rosenstein and Wyatt noted that stock prices of companies tend to increase when an outside director is added to a board.[29] These findings are quite intuitive, as directors who are more independent should be less influenced by personal agendas and more likely to pursue shareholders' interests.

When decisive action is needed and the performance of management needs to be critically reviewed, outside boards will be in a better position to implement such an objective review. However, we have to understand that there are good reasons why boards have certain managers on them. These management board members can provide useful insight on the performance of the company that other, outside directors may lack. However, we would not want a board composed solely of such directors. Indeed, much can be said for a mixed board composed not just of insider and outside directors but also of outside directors of diverse backgrounds who can bring a wide range of expertise and experience to the management-monitoring process. Outside directors can play a key role when action such as removal of an incumbent CEO is needed.

Additional research evidence supports the preference for outside rather than inside directors. A study by Weisbach showed that boards with a greater percentage of outside directors were more likely to discipline their CEO for poor corporate performance than those in which insiders played a more prominent role.[30]

While these studies provide convincing support for the preference for outside directors, outsider-dominated boards are not a panacea. There are still many factors that can cause outside directors to have conflicts or to perform their oversight role poorly. An independent director may have fewer obvious conflicts than a nonindependent director, but the "independent" director could still be personally aligned with the CEO and therefore not diligent in pursuing shareholders' interests.

Busy Directors

The term *busy directors* has a different meaning in the corporate governance research literature than what most would associate with it. In this context, *busy* refers to directors who sit on multiple boards at the same time. Board members who are asked to sit on multiple boards may have wide-ranging stature and abilities, which may be a good characteristic when pursuing their oversight role. However, overseeing many companies at the same time may leave them spread too thin. This is particularly the case when the director is the CEO of another company.

One example of a CEO who simultaneously sat on four boards is Nolan Archibald, CEO of Stanley Black and Decker. In addition to being on Stanley's board, he also was on the boards of Lockheed Martin Corp., Huntsman Corp, and Brunswick Corp. Some situations are obvious problems. Consider the former CEO of troubled Avon, Andrea Jung, who also sat on Apple's and GE's boards. Given the problems at Avon, did she really have the extra time to oversee these other two huge companies? Or how about Meg Whitman, CEO of Hewlett Packard, also being on the boards of ZipCar and Procter & Gamble. Does she really have the time to be on these other boards given the troubles of HP? Still another example is Charles Prince, former CEO of Citigroup, who helped lead that company back to disaster. Xerox and Johnson and Johnson seem to find his presence on their boards a benefit.

Perhaps he can help them understand how not to run a large bank in case they may want to diversify into that field (assuming, for the sake of humor, that regulators would allow this).

Fich and Shivdasani have shown that companies that have over half of the outside directors sitting on three or more boards have lower financial performance as reflected by lower market-to-book ratios, and they have weaker corporate governance in general.[31] However, not all research has reached this same conclusion.[32] In addition, research has shown that when CEOs receive excessive compensation, their boards are more likely to have busy outside directors.[33]

Corporations and their boards have come, albeit slowly, to recognize the obvious—it is difficult to diligently monitor many companies at the same time, especially if you have a full-time job, such as being a CEO of a another company. So, in recent years, corporations have placed limits on the number of boards their board members may sit on. This tightening up process coincides with the passage of Sarbanes Oxley in 2002. A survey by Korn Ferry showed that 62 percent of the 891 companies in the Fortune 1000 reported that they limited outside board service, compared to 23 percent in their 2001 survey.

In some countries, such as Great Britain, corporations often have limits on the number of boards their directors can sit on. Ironically, in Great Britain, a nation whose laws and corporate culture are known for their concern for shareholder rights, this issue seems to have become less important. The same Korn Ferry survey found that in 2007, 65 percent of the respondents had such limits, compared to 71 percent in 2006.[34] An analysis by Equilar showed that in 2006 there were four individuals who sat on five boards whereas that number was down to one in 2011. There were 15 who sat on four boards in 2006, but that is down to nine in 2011. However, there were 106 directors who sat on three or more boards in 2011, and that is barely down from 119 in 2006.

Interlocked Boards

Interlocked boards are ones where the directors sit on each other's boards. For example, the CEO of one firm may sit on the board of another company that has its CEO sitting on his or her board. The problem is that this can become a little too cozy.

Interlocked boards also raise some obvious questions. If we have CEOs who run other large companies sitting on the boards of one or more other large companies, you have to wonder where they have the time for such activities? Are they really working hard to monitor these companies in which they have these positions? Doesn't this take away from their main full-time jobs? Does the typical CEO of Fortune 500 company really have the extra time to sit on the boards of other companies and oversee their operations as well? If so, then is being the CEO of a Fortune 500 company really only a part-time job? If so, then why are such CEOs being paid as if it were an extremely demanding position?

Hallock analyzed a dataset of 9,804 director seats covering 7,519 individuals and 700 large U.S. companies and found that 20 percent of boards are interlocked.[35] He defined *interlocked* to be where any current or retired employee of one company sat on another company's board where the same situation was the case for the other company. He found that approximately 8 percent of CEOs are reciprocally interlocked with another CEO.

Hallock's study also showed that interlocked companies tend to be larger than noninterlocked firms. Interestingly, the compensation of CEOs who reported to interlocked boards tends to higher than that of those working with noninterlocked boards. This implies that CEOs stand to gain when their boards are interlocked.

Hallock's findings apply to boards of the 1990s, as opposed to boards of the post-Sarbanes-Oxley era. Boards of the 2000s are under more pressure to avoid such obvious conflicts.

Other research has shown that interlocked boards are less likely to occur when more of a CEO's compensation comes from stock options as opposed to salary.[36] They are also less likely when boards are more active and meet more frequently. Clearly, interlocked boards are not desirable.

CASE STUDY: A WELL-FUNCTIONING BOARD— COCA-COLA'S PROPOSED ACQUISITION OF QUAKER OATS

While it seems that many boards simply rubber-stamp the M&A proposed by their CEOs, some boards have the foresight and the courage to stand up to the CEO and question proposed deals. This was the case when a $15.75 billion offer for Quaker Oats was proposed by the Coca-Cola Company in November 2001. Quaker Oats had a certain appeal to Coca-Cola because it included its popular Gatorade line, which might fit in well with Coke's other soft drink products. Gatorade commands more than 80 percent of the sports drink market, whereas Coke's own Powerade brand accounted for just over 10 percent of that market. The whole sports drink business had grown significantly, and Powerade had a distant second position to the leader Gatorade, and Coke was having great difficulty gaining ground

(continued)

on the leader. Acquiring Gatorade through an acquisition of Quaker Oats could have been a quick solution to this problem. However, the acquisition also presented a problem because Coke most likely would have been forced by antitrust regulators to divest Powerade in order to have the deal approved.

Coke was not the first bidder for Quaker Oats. On November 1, 2000, Pepsi made an initial offer for Quaker following negotiations between Robert Enrico, Pepsi's CEO, and Robert Morrison, Quaker's CEO. However, after Quaker could not get Pepsi to agree on improved terms, including a stock collar provision, negotiations between Pepsi and Quaker broke down. Quaker was then in play, and other potential bidders, such as Coke and French food giant Group Danone, expressed interest in the U.S. food company. Both companies made competing bids, which featured improved terms over Pepsi's bid, yet Pepsi held fast and declined to exceed its prior offer. Coke's CEO assured Quaker Oats that he had been keeping his board app-rised of the bid's progress, and had asked and received agreement from Quaker to exclusively negotiate with Coke. Coke's CEO, Douglas Daft, however, did not count on the negative response of the market to the deal (see Figure 9.1).[a] The board, however, was mindful of the market, and after a long meeting on November 21, 2000, they forced Daft to go back to Quaker Oats and inform them that Coke was pulling out of the negotiations. The market loved this,

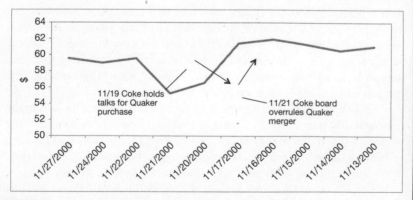

FIGURE 9.1 Coca-Cola Stock Price Response to Quaker Oats Bid
Source: Yahoo! Finance.

(continued)

(*continued*)

and the stock price immediately rose. Pepsi eventually acquired Quaker Oats in August 2001 for $13 billion.

There were some clear problems with the deal, to which Coke's board obviously paid attention. As already noted, the market did not like the proposed acquisition, and it voiced its displeasure by dropping its valuation of Coke's stock. In the years before the Coke bid, the company had experienced problems with other failed acquisitions, and the spotlight was on its merger strategy. Right at the start, management faced an uphill battle. Another problem with the deal was that the acquisition would require Coke to be able to effectively manage the components of Quaker Oats' business that were outside of Coke's soft and sports drink business lines. These were Quaker's food brands, which included Captain Crunch cereals, Rice-a-Roni, and Aunt Jemima pancakes, as well as other snack products such as rice cakes and granola bars. Some of Quaker's brands were impressive, but they were a little far afield from Coke's core business. Another problem with the deal was its defensive nature. Coke's bid was in response to Pepsi's original offer. Such defensive responses are not the best motive for a merger or acquisition.

One of the reasons why the Coke board stood up to this proposal lies in the nature of its board and their relationship with the CEO. Coke had a CEO, Roberto Goizueta, who was highly acclaimed. Unfortunately, after many successful years at the helm of the soft drink giant, Goizueta passed away in October 1997 at a relatively young age. He was succeeded by Douglas Ivester, who resigned at the end of 1999 and was replaced by Douglas Daft, who was well thought of but could not draw on the track record of success that Goizueta enjoyed. Perhaps if Goizueta had brought this deal to the board, they might have considered it more seriously. Nonetheless, there is little reason to believe that they would have ultimately approved it no matter who proposed the deal because they considered it generally flawed.

Coke's board featured some leading business figures, including the renowned Warren Buffett, who is considered by many to be one of the market's shrewdest investors, as well as a new CEO who was looking to make a name for himself. This board would have none of it. In 2006, Buffett announced he would step down from Coke's board.

The board of directors is one of the last lines of defense against poorly conceived merger strategies. In order for it to work with maximum effectiveness, the board needs to be knowledgeable and strong willed. However, it is not enough that a board be composed of

(*continued*)

individuals who are strong willed and capable of standing up to the management leaders of the company. Knowledge of the industry and the company's operations is also essential to being an effective director. Management, who run the company on a day-to-day basis, should have a distinct advantage over board members who are engaged full-time in other activities, such as running their own companies, and have not invested nearly as much time as management in studying the company. However, there is a certain minimum level of knowledge that the board must have in order for it to function properly. When considering the commitment of billions of dollars in merger costs, the board needs to get whatever resources it requires to effectively evaluate management's proposals. If this means retaining outside consultants to study the proposal in depth, then this should be done. This is sometimes difficult to do because the proposals may be time sensitive and require a quick response. Nonetheless, the board must apply all of the necessary resources to reach an enlightened and impartial decision. The bigger the deal, the more work and research the board needs to do. In the case of Coke's offer for Quaker Oats, the board's studied response was clear and strong. In properly exercising their fiduciary responsibilities, they saved shareholders from a potentially costly acquisition.

Source: Patrick A. Gaughan, *Mergers: What Can Go Wrong and How to Prevent It* (Hoboken, NJ: John Wiley & Sons, 2005), 237–239.

---

[a] Carliss Y. Baldwin and Leonid Soudakov, "PepsiCo's Bid for Quaker Oats (B)," Harvard Business School, 9-801-459, August 5, 2002.

Board Size

Over the years, boards have gotten smaller. In its 34th Annual Survey of Boards of Directors, the Korn Ferry Institute found that the average board consists of 10 directors compared to 1973, the first year of their board survey, when one-fifth of the boards had between 16 and 25 directors.[37] The 2011 Stuart Spencer survey had similar findings of shrinking boards. They found 83 percent of the S&P 500 boards had 12 or fewer directors versus 73 percent in their 2001 survey.[38]

While the trend in board size in North America has been toward smaller boards, there is still a lot of variability. For example, Stuart Spencer reports that the CME Group has 32 directors, which is absurd. However, Blackrock and Merck each have large boards with 18 directors. For these companies, the large boards are the result of mergers with board members of the combined entities staying on the post-merger larger board. Some boards are relatively small. For example, the Stuart Spencer survey showed Microchip Technology having only five board members and D. R. Horton, MetroPCS, and Paychex having only six.

Some countries that are known for poor corporate governance seem to feature large boards. In Japan, for example, it is not unusual to see corporate boards with as many as 30 directors. However, the pressure of years and years of weak economic performance seems to have gotten some Japanese companies to finally improve their corporate governance as a way of trying to improve corporate performance. We are starting to see more Japanese companies reduce the size of their boards and put more focus on shareholder returns than they did in the past.

The size of a board plays an important role in how effectively it may oversee management. In a larger board, each board member may wield less influence, and this may shift the balance of power to the CEO in a way that may reduce shareholder wealth. There is evidence to support this proposition, but the relationship between board size and firm value is not that simple.

NYU's David Yermack examined the relationship between the market valuation of companies and board size. He analyzed a sample of 452 large U.S. corporations over the period 1984 to 1991. In his sample, the average board size was 12 directors.[39] Yermack found that there was an inverse relationship between market value, as measured by Tobin's q, and the size of the board of directors. That is, smaller boards had higher market values and larger boards tended to receive lower valuations. The higher valuations often come from relatively smaller boards that have fewer than 10 members.

Yermack found that financial performance, as measured by profitability and operating efficiency, was inversely related to board size. He also found that smaller boards were more likely to fire the CEO if the company performed poorly.

There is evidence that the discipline imposed by takeover activity may serve to move companies to a more optimal board size. For example, Kini, Kracaw, and Mian found that board size tended to shrink after tender offers for firms that were not performing well.[40] There is abundant evidence that the threat of takeovers tends to force companies to be more efficient. Reducing the board size to one that is more efficient to monitor management may help bring about changes that are necessary if a company is going to avoid a hostile takeover. The Kini, Kracaw, and Mian study, and others, imply that, in general, large boards are inefficient and don't result in good corporate governance.

There is also evidence that suggests the conclusion that smaller is generally better may not apply to certain types of companies. We know that some larger boards persist even in the face of evidence that smaller boards are more optimal.

(a)

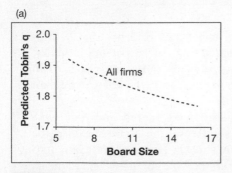

(b)

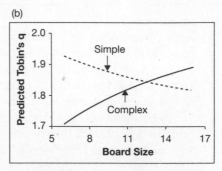

FIGURE 9.2   Board Size and Tobin's q: (a) All Firms and (b) Simple versus Complex Firms

Source: Reprinted from *Journal of Financial Economics*, Jeffrey L. Coles, Naveen D. Daniel and Lilitha Naveen, "Boards: Does One Size Fit All," 87, p. 342, Copyright 2008, with permission from Elsevier.

Could it be that this is a function of the efforts of CEOs to minimize the power of individual directors? Could it be that directors of such companies simply are unresponsive to the corporate governance needs of shareholders? While these explanations are probably true in some cases, it is too simplistic an answer to explain all the large boards that still exist.

Coles, Daniel, and Naveen found that complex firms, those that are diversified or larger or that have more leverage, tend to have larger boards.[41] They did this by looking at the relationship between companies' Tobin's q and the size of their boards. They found that the relationship was "U-shaped." High Tobin's q amounts were associated with both small and quite large companies. They concluded that the reason had to do with differences between small and large companies.

Coles, Naveen, and Naveen found that more focused firms tended to have smaller boards while larger and more diversified companies had larger boards. They also found some weak evidence that the more R&D-intensive firms tend to have more insiders on the board, which makes sense as boards may benefit from the specialized knowledge that such directors or managers could bring to board deliberations.

CASE STUDY: LEHMAN BROTHERS— A DYSFUNCTIONAL BOARD

Lehman Brothers was a century-old investment bank that bad and arrogant management and an incompetent board drove into the largest bankruptcy in U.S. history. Prior to the failure of Lehman Brothers, the

(continued)

(continued)

largest bankruptcy was Worldcom. It is no coincidence that World-com's bankruptcy can also be attributed to an incompetent board that did not come close to living up to its fiduciary duties, as well as to an arrogant CEO who would not listen to managers who knew more than he did about managing the company.

Nine members of Lehman's board were retired and four were over the age of 75.[a] Just before its collapse, the board included the 83-year-old actress Dina Merrill. I am sure she provided great insight to CEO Dick Fuld as he aggressively increased the company's investments in real estate at a time when market prices were at their peak. She was not the only representative from the theater community on the investment bank's board. Seventy-five-year-old theater producer Roger Berlind was also on the board, and we can be sure he provided much insight about the bank's rising investments in mortgage-backed securities. It is likely both had sage advice about the quality of some theater productions. Unfortunately, one can conclude that they had little valuable advice about Lehman's real estate and mortgage-backed securities investments.

The board also included former navy admiral Marsha Johnson Evans as well the former chairman and CEO of the Spanish language television network Telemundo. Only two of the board members had any experience in finance, so how could they possibly question what long-time investment banker Dick Fuld was doing? They couldn't even understand it. One of those who did have some experience in economics and finance was the aging economist Henry Kaufman. However, he last worked at an investment bank 20 years earlier—well before the mortgage-backed securities that Lehman Brothers invested so heavily in became so popular.[b]

The New Jersey Department of Investment filed a lawsuit in 2009 seeking compensation for losses incurred by the state's pension fund. Gillespie and Zweig feature the following excerpt from one of the legal findings in that lawsuit:

> *The supine Board that defendant Fuld handpicked provided no backstop to Lehman's executives' zealous approach to the company's risk profile, real estate portfolio, and their own compensation. The Director Defendants were considered inattentive, elderly, and woefully short on relevant structured finance background. The composition of the Board according to recent filing in the Lehman bankruptcy allowed defendant*
> *(continued)*

> *"Fuld to marginalize the Directors, who tolerated an absence of checks and balances at Lehman." Due to his long tenure and ubiquity at Lehman, defendant Fuld has been able to consolidate his power to a remarkable degree. Defendant Fuld was both the chairman of the Board and the CEO. . . . The Director Defendants acted as a rubber stamp for the actions of Lehman's senior management. There was little turnover on the Board. By the date of Lehman's collapse, more than half the Director Defendants had served for twelve or more years."[c]*
>
> ---
> [a] Lawrence G. McDonald and Patrick Robinson, *A Colossal Failure of Common Sense: The Inside Story of the Collapse of Lehman Brothers* (New York: Crown Business, 2009), 226.
> [b] John Gillespie and David Zweig, *Money for Nothing: How the Failure of Corporate Boards Is Ruining American Business and Costing Us Millions* (New York: Free Press, 2010), 14–15.
> [c] Ibid., 16.

CEO TENURE, BOARD COMPOSITION, AND THE DISCIPLINARY EFFECTS OF TAKEOVERS

The takeover process tends to eliminate some poorly performing boards. Kini, Kracaw, and Mian analyzed a sample of 244 tender offers and looked at the effects that these hostile bids had on CEO and director turnover.[42] They found an inverse relationship between posttakeover CEO turnover and pretakeover performance. Companies that generated poor results prior to a takeover were more likely to have their CEO replaced. CEO replacement at poorly performing companies was more likely at companies that had insider-dominated boards. It is unfortunate that the expensive takeover process has to be used to get CEOs and boards to do their jobs diligently.

ANTITAKEOVER MEASURES

Potential takeover targets often install antitakeover measures to make the takeover of their company on unfavorable terms more difficult. There has been a great debate in financial economics as to whether these measures are installed for the purposes of management entrenchment or for the advancement of shareholder interests.[43] Throughout this book, we have been focusing more on bidder companies and the potential gains and losses they may derive from M&A. However, it is also important to consider the target and its shareholders' interests.

There is a significant body of research that shows when certain antitakeover measures are enacted, shareholder wealth suffers, as the companies are less likely to be takeover targets and to ultimately receive a takeover premium. There is also concern that the threat of a takeover may keep management honest. However, if management becomes entrenched and insulated from the threat of a hostile takeover due to having installed a strong defense, such as poison pills, then shareholder wealth may suffer.

Antitakeover defenses, however, are not all bad. That would be too simplistic an assessment. Research has shown that for companies that are taken over, the ones with strong defenses, such as poison pills, tend to receive higher takeover premiums. Poison pills can be quickly and inexpensively deactivated if the board chooses to do so. So, in the hands of diligent directors whose only concern is shareholder interests, such defenses may promote shareholder wealth. On the other hand, in the hands of boards overly influenced by managers who are pursuing their own personal goals at the expense of shareholders, shareholder wealth may be decreased.

There is some evidence that poison pills can be used to entrench managers. Malatesta & Walking as well as Ryngaert found that the *adoption* of poison pills was associated with negative shareholder wealth effects.[44] On the other hand, for those companies that are eventually taken over research by Comment and Schwert found poison pills were associated with higher takeover premiums.[45] These results were consistent with two other studies conducted by Georgeson & Company, which showed that pill-protected companies received higher takeover premiums.

There is also other evidence that CEOs have an incentive to install poison pill and other antitakeover defenses. For example, Bertrand and Mullainathan found that antitakeover laws were associated with increases in CEO compensation.[46] Once again, this lends support to the management entrenchment hypothesis. It also implies that shareholders have to be concerned when antitakeover defenses are put in place.

In addition to the concerns about CEOs' installing antitakeover defense to further their own personal gains, there is also evidence that companies that the market views acquirers with more antitakeover defense in place differently from those who do not. Masulis, Wang, and Xie found that acquirers with more antitakeover defenses in place have significantly lower announcement period returns. This implies that the market is skeptical about the motives for deals by companies that have installed defenses to protect themselves against takeovers.[47]

CORPORATE GOVERNANCE AND
THE DIVESTITURE DECISION

In Chapter 10, we discuss the fact that selloff announcements are typically associated with positive shareholder gains. In cases where the unit is a prior acquisition, this may require managers to admit that the prior M&A was a mistake. When the M&A took place under a different CEO, this may be an easier decision. In this chapter, we have seen that better corporate governance enhances shareholder wealth and that the market tends to respond better to M&A by companies with better corporate governance. The same is the case for divestiture announcements. Owen, Shi, and Yawson analyzed a sample of 797 divestitures over the years 1997 to 2005.[48] They found that companies with more independent boards and/or who have large blockholders had greater positive shareholder wealth effects after an announcement of a selloff. Their results provide additional evidence to support the value of independent boards. They also show that companies may need the pressure of a large blockholder to get them to admit that a prior acquisition was a mistake and that it needs to be sold off. In recent years, this large blockholder pressure has sometimes come from activist hedge fund managers who seek out under-performing companies where some obvious solutions, such as asset sales, can be implemented to achieve a quick improvement in shareholder value.

NOTES

1. "What Do Directors Think?" Study: 2003, *Corporate Board Member* (July 2003).
2. The *Wall Street Journal*/Hay Group, 2008 CEO Compensation Study, April 2009.
3. Lucian Arye Bebchuk, Jesse M. Fried, and David Walker, "Managerial Power and Rent Extraction in the Design of Executive Compensation," *University of Chicago Law Review* 69 (2002): 751–846.
4. Executive Excess 2007: The Staggering Social Cost of U.S. Business Leadership, Institute for Policy Studies, August 29, 2007.
5. Joanna L. Ossinger, "Poorer Relations: When It Comes to CEO Pay, Why Are the British So Different?" *Wall Street Journal*, April 10, 2006, R6.
6. Michael J. DeLa Merced, "Weill Calls for Splitting Up Big Banks," *New York Times*, July 25, 2012.
7. Sheila Bair, *Bull by the Horns: Fighting to Save Main Street from Wall Street and Wall Street from Itself* (New York: Free Press, 2012).
8. Michael Cooper, Huseyin Gulen, and P. Raghavendra Rau, "Performance for Pay? The Relationship Between CEO Incentive Compensation and Future Stock Price Performance" (Working Paper, December 2009).

9. Lucian A. Bebchuk, Martijn Cremers, and Urs Peyer, "The CEO Pay Slice," *Project Syndicate*, January 2010.

10. Jesse Edgerton, "Agency Problems in Public Firms: Evidence from Corporate Jets in Leveraged Buyouts," paper presented at the American Finance Association Meetings, San Diego, California, 2013.

11. John E. Core, Robert W. Holtausen, and David Larker, *Journal of Financial Economics* 51 (1999): 371–406.

12. John Bizjak, Michael Lemmon, and Thanh Nguyen, "Are All CEOs above Average? An Empirical Analysis of Compensation Peer Groups and Pay Design," *Journal of Financial Economics* 100, no. 3 (2011): 538–555.

13. Rachel Hayes and Scott Schaefer, "CEO Pay and the Lake Wobegon Effect," *Journal of Financial Economics* 94, no. 2 (2009): 280–290.

14. Ulrike Malmendier and Geoffrey Tate, "Superstar CEOs," *Quarterly Journal of Economics* 12, no. 4 (November 2009): 1593–1638.

15. Marianne Bertrand and Sendhil Mullainathan, "Are CEOs Rewarded for Luck? The Ones Without Principals Are," *Quarterly Journal of Economics* (August 2001): 901–932.

16. Kevin F. Hallock, "The Relationship Between Company Size and CEO Pay," *Workspan*, February 2011.

17. "By the Numbers: Dramatic Differences in CEO Pay by Company Size, Steven Hall & Partners Survey Shows," *BusinessWire*, November 3, 2006.

18. Yaniv Grinstein and Paul Hribar, "CEO Compensation and Incentives: Evidence from M&A Bonuses," *Journal of Financial Economics* 73, no. 1 (2004): 119–143.

19. Dennis R. Schmidt and Karen L. Fowler, "Post-Acquisitions Financial Performance and Executive Compensation," *Strategic Management Journal* 11, no. 7 (November/December 1990): 559–569.

20. Ajeyo Banerjee and James E. Owers, "Wealth Reduction in White Knight Bids," *Financial Management*, 21 (3), Autumn 1992, 48–57.

21. Eitan Goldman and Peggy Huang, "Contractual Versus Actual Severance Pay Following CEO Departure" (Working Paper, March 2010).

22. Jay Hartzell, Eli Ofek, and David Yermack, "What's In It For Me? CEOs Whose Firms Are Acquired," *Review of Financial Studies* 17, no. 1 (2004): 37–61.

23. Ulrike Malmendier and Geoffrey Tate, "Who Makes Acquisitions? CEO Overconfidence and the Market's Reaction," *Journal of Financial Economics* 89 (2008): 2043. Note that prior research had shown that optimal investment decisions suggest that CEOs should sell their options prior to expiration, as failing to do so would result in their assuming too much company-specific risk.

24. David Hirshleifer, Angie Low, and Siew Hong Teoh, "Are Overconfident CEOs Better Innovators?" *Journal of Finance* 67, no. 4 (2012): 1457–1498.

25. Dennis R. Schmidt and Karen L. Fowler, "Post-Acquisitions Financial Performance and Executive Compensation," *Strategic Management Journal* 11, no. 7 (November/December 1990): 559–569.

26. "What Directors Think: Research Study," *Corporate Board Member/Pricewaterhouse Coopers Survey* (2009).

27. 2011 Spencer Stuart Board Index, Spencer Stuart.

28. James Cooter, Anil Shivdasni, and Marc. Zenner, "Do Independent Directors Enhance Target Shareholder Wealth During Tender Offers?" *Journal of Financial Economics* 43 (1997): 195–218.

29. Stuart Rosenstein and Jeffrey Wyatt, "Outside Directors, Board Independence, and Shareholder Wealth," *Journal of Financial Economics* 26 (1990): 175–192.

30. Michael Weisbach, "Outside Directors and CEO Turnover," *Journal of Financial Economics* 37 (1988): 159–188.

31. Eliezer M. Fich and Anil Shivdasani, "Are Busy Boards Effective Monitors?" *Journal of Finance* 61, no. 2 (2006): 689–724.

32. Stephen Ferris, Murali Jagannathan, and Adam Prichard, "Too Busy to Mind the Business? Monitoring by Directors with Multiple Board Appointments," *Journal of Finance* 58 (2003): 1087–1111.

33. John E. Core, Robert W. Holthausen, and David F. Larker, "Corporate Governance, Chief Executive Officer Compensation, and Firm Performance," *Journal of Financial Economics* 51 (1999): 371–406.

34. Ibid.

35. Kevin Hallock, "Reciprocally Interlocked Boards of Directors and Executive Compensation," *Journal of Financial and Quantitative Analysis* 32, no. 3 (September 1997): 331–344.

36. Eliezer Fich and Lawrence White, "Why Do CEOs Reciprocally Sit on Each Other's Boards?" *Journal of Corporate Finance* 11, no. 1–2 (March 2005): 175–195.

37. 34th Annual Board of Directors Survey, Korn Ferry Institute, p. 6.

38. 2011 Spencer Stuart Board Index, Spencer Stuart, p. 14.

39. David Yermack, "Higher Market Valuation of Companies with a Small Board of Directors," *Journal of Financial Economics* 40 (1996): 185–211.

40. Omesh Kini, William Kracaw, and Shehzad Mian, "Corporate Takeovers, Firm Performance and Board Composition," *Journal of Corporate Finance* 1 (1995): 383–412.

41. Jeffrey L. Coles, Naveen D. Daniel, and Lilitha Naveen, "Boards: Does One Size Fit All," *Journal of Financial Economics* 87 (2008): 329–256.

42. Omesh Kini, William Kracaw, and Shehzad Mian, "Corporate Takeovers, Firm Performance and Board Composition," *Journal of Corporate Finance* 1 (1995): 383–412.

43. See Chapter 5, Patrick A. Gaughan, *Mergers, Acquisitions, and Corporate Restructurings*, 5th ed. (Hoboken, NJ: John Wiley & Sons, 2010).

44. Paul H. Malatesa and Ralph Waking, "Poison Pill Securities and Shareholder Wealth, Profitability and Corporate Structure," *Journal of Financial Economics*, 20, no. 1/2 (January/March 1988): 347–376; and Michael Ryngaert, "The Effects of Poison Pill Securities on Shareholder Wealth," *Journal of Financial Economics*, 20, no. 1/2 (January/March 1988): 377-417.

45. Robert Comment and G. William Schwert, "Poison or Placebo? Evidence on the Deterrence and Wealth Effects of Modern Antitakeover Measures," *Journal of Financial Economics*, 39, 1995, 3-43.

46. M. Bertrand and S. Mullainathan, "Is There Discretion in Wage Setting? A Test Using Takeover Legislation," *Rand Journal of Economics*, 30, 1999: 535-554.
47. Ronald W. Masulis, Cong Wang, and Fei Xie, "Corporate Governance and Acquirer Returns," *Journal of Finance*, August 2007
48. Sian Owen, Liting Shi, and Alfred Yawson, "Divestitures, Wealth Effects and Corporate Governance," *Accounting and Finance* 50 (2010): 389–415.

CHAPTER 10

Downsizing: Reversing the Error

We have discussed that oftentimes, the market reacts negatively to mergers and acquisitions (M&A). It is the market's way of saying, "Oh no, not another merger or acquisition." We have also seen the performance of acquirers often leaves a lot to be desired. Many other times, the market and the media will give the acquirer a pass and see how the deal works out. However, in cases where it does not work out and the target is not performing up to expectations, then there may be pressure on management to make some changes. When the target is relatively small compared to the overall business, then there may not be much pressure as the deal is just not that significant. However, the bigger the poorly performing M&A, the more likely management may eventually be forced to make changes. These efforts can either be directed at fixing the acquired entity and making sure it fulfills the pre-deal expectations or getting rid of it. It is the latter option that is the subject of this chapter.

Selloffs and downsizing are sometimes referred to as *demergers*. They can come in many forms. The most basic, and actually the most common, is a divestiture. This is when the company sells off the one-time target to another buyer who, hopefully, will have better luck with the company. Divestiture deal volume tends to follow M&A deal volume, which makes sense as one company's divestiture is another's acquisition. This is clear in Figure 10.1, which shows the trend in U.S. M&A and divestitures over the period 1980 through 2011.

Divestiture deal volume in Europe is comparable to that of the United States (see Figures 10.2 and 10.3a). However, as with M&A deal volume, divestiture volume in Asia is smaller (see Figure 10.3 (a) and (b)).

A divestiture is often the preferred option and the deal tends to be quicker than other forms of downsizing. In addition, it usually generates cash for the seller. The sale may or may not bring significant tax liabilities; part of the uncertainty arises from the difference between the price the company paid for the business and what it sells for. For deals that have been failures, this

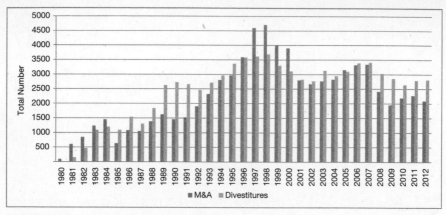

FIGURE 10.1 U.S. M&A versus Divestitures, 1980–2012
Source: Thomson Financial Securities Data.

difference can be significant. Too many classic examples exist but a good one
is one we already commented on, Snapple, which was acquired by Quaker
Oats in 1994 for $1.7 billion and was sold off by Quaker, and its brilliant
CEO William Smithburg, for $300 million three years later. Much to every-
one's surprise, as we noted in Chapter 9, Smithburg retired in that year.[1] The

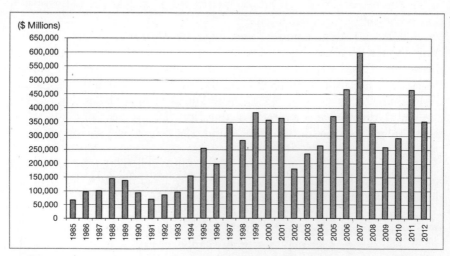

FIGURE 10.2 U.S. Divestitures
Source: Thomson Financial Securities Data.

(a)

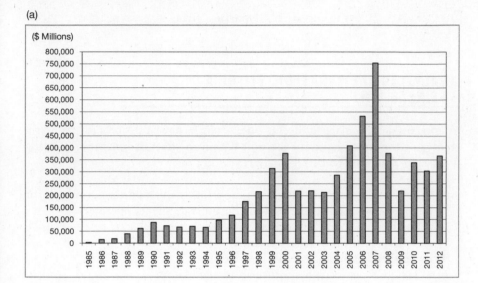

(b)

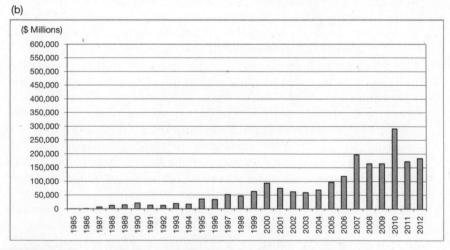

FIGURE 10.3 Divestitures, 1985–2012: (a) Europe and (b) Asia
Source: Thomson Financial Securities Data.

market was at a loss to explain his departure given his great success in M&A strategy.

ANALYZING THE STRATEGIC FIT OF A BUSINESS UNIT

A company, particularly a diverse one, needs to have a process for regularly analyzing the strategic fit of each unit within the overall company.[2] Among the issues that need to be regularly revisited are:

- What is the near-term, but more importantly the long-term, outlook for the markets in which the various business segments operate?
- What has been the performance of each unit relative to the overall company, and other business units?
- For poorly performing units:
  - Has this just been a short-term phenomenon?
  - Is there a good basis to believe that the performance will turn around in the near term?
  - Does the unit play some other synergistic role in the company that can be considered as a factor to offset the shortcomings in its performance?
  - Is the company maximizing the performance of the unit, or is there a reason to believe that it would do better if it was separated from the company and on its own or part of another firm?
- What is the market's assessment of the various business units and their strategic fit? This is important, as the market, an interaction of many investors who are critically evaluating the company, may be more, if not much more, objective than management and the board of directors.
- What are the company's cash flow needs? Are some units nonessential to the long-term vision and goals of the company? Could their sale be a meaningful source of cash, which could relieve cash flow pressures? Chrysler's sale of its valuable military tank manufacturing unit in 1982 to General Dynamics for $348.5 million ($871 million in 2013 dollars) and Ford's sale of Hertz in 2005 for $15 billion are good examples. Both units were valuable but not part of the core business. When the overall companies were in trouble, both firms had to part ways with these valuable units. This highlights some of the concerns with cash flow-induced asset sales. Buyers are often only interested in the more valuable assets, which may be the ones that the company wants to retain. The ones it wants to get rid of may not be desirable to potential buyers for the same reasons that the seller wants to divest them—they are losers.

MARKET CONDITIONS

If a company decides it makes sense to pursue a disposition of a business unit, it needs to analyze current market conditions. If the goal is to pursue an outright divestiture, is this the best time to sell the unit? For example, the post-subprime crisis U.S. economy, which featured the Great Recession and the anemic recovery that followed, were not good time periods to sell off assets. Values were at near-term lows and buyers were looking for bargains. However, more often than not, companies were not looking to incur debt or risk their increasingly scarce cash flows to expand. Thus, in such market conditions, even when a company has made a decision that it really wants to get rid of a unit, it may be best to wait out the market downturn until a better economic climate with higher valuations returns. Remember, with recessions that were caused by financial crises, this time period can be quite long.

REGULATORY CONCERNS

While a downsizing effort tends not to raise regulatory concerns from the seller's perspective, it may be an issue as it relates to the impact on the buyer. This is why divestitures that meet the filing threshold of Hart–Scott–Rodino require a filing in the United States, and for units that are global, a filing in other jurisdictions as well. Sellers need to evaluate the antitrust ramifications of the sale so that they do not go too far down the road pursuing a deal that may never come to fruition. Doing so may not only waste much time but may also cause the seller to miss out on other more qualified buyers. In addition, pursuing a deal that falls apart often has negative ramifications for the seller. It often puts the seller in a weaker negotiating position, thereby resulting in a lower price when the unit is eventually sold. From a negotiating perspective, it may be useful to engage potential buyers who the seller believes may have an antitrust conflict just to expand the potential group of suitors while the seller is really focusing on qualified buyers (although the seller may not disclose these assessments).

DIVESTITURE LIKELIHOOD AND PRIOR ACQUISITIONS

Kaplan and Weisbach conducted an empirical study of 271 large acquisitions over the period 1971 through 1982, which they followed through the fourth merger wave until 1989. They found that a total of 43.9 percent of the deals were divested by 1989. While this percentage seems high, it is actually lower than what other researchers, such as Michael Porter, have found.[3] Porter found that companies divested over half of their acquisitions that were made in entirely new fields.

Kaplan and Weishbach also found that the acquirer returns, as well as total acquirer and target returns, were lower for M&A that were later determined to be unsuccessful. This provides further evidence, beyond the large body of other research on announcement period returns, that the market's initial reactions to deals generally tends (with many exceptions) to be reasonably accurate.

Kaplan and Weisbach also found that diversifying M&A were four times more likely to be subsequently divested than non-diversifying deals. We mentioned this study in Chapter 4. The authors found that 13 percent of related M&A were unsuccessful, compared to 38 percent for diversifying deals. It was one of several studies that raised questions about the benefits of a diversification strategy.

ANOTHER OPTION: EQUITY CARVE OUT

Another option other than an outright divestiture is an equity carve out. This is when the company does a public offering of shares in the business unit it is seeking to sell off. A benefit of an equity carve out is that, like divestitures, the company receives cash for the shares it sells. It may be able to sell the entire business at one time, or it may retain some percentage of the business. Usually, if the goal is to get rid of the business, it may prefer to sell all the shares unless market conditions are not strong enough to absorb that much equity.

A divestiture is usually a simpler and quicker option than an equity carve out. In a divestiture, the seller, usually working with an investment banker, finds a buyer and the two companies work out the terms of the deal. In an equity carve out, the seller has to go through the whole time-consuming public offering process and arrange to have the shares sold to many buyers in the public market. Depending on the circumstances, however, the equity carve out option may be more attractive, particularly if the only buyers are shrewd private equity firms who are in the business of buying as low as possible and selling as high as they can while extracting as many benefits from the target as they can during the period of time they own the business.

Sometimes a company may pursue a partial equity carve out even when it seeks to do mainly a spinoff. In this situation, it may do a public offering of a percent of shares so as to not only get a cash infusion but also to establish a price that can be used later to determine an exchange ratio in a *split-off*, which we will discuss a little later in this chapter. Another benefit a partial equity carve out may provide is to generate a shareholder base, which may create interest among the parent company's current shareholders in extending that shareholder relationship with the split-off entity.

ANOTHER OPTION: SPINOFF

Sometimes the parent company may prefer doing a divestiture or an equity carve out, but the demand is just not there. If the company is determined to part ways with the business, it may simply do a spinoff. This is when the parent company gives shares in the business it is getting rid of to shareholders in accordance with their ownership interest in the parent company. Usually, this starts with identifying the *core* business as well as the non-core part, which is what will be spun off.

The spunoff entity then becomes a separate business that is independent of the parent company. Shareholders of the parent are also shareholders of the spunoff business, but the two companies usually operate independently. There is a pro-rata distribution to the parent company's shareholders, which is usually done through a dividend. Because the spinoff is done through the payment of a dividend, the courts usually regard dividend payments as part of the normal responsibilities of the board of directors; thus shareholder approval is usually not required unless the amount of assets being spun off is substantially the bulk of the company's assets.

In a spinoff, the shareholders involved in the transaction may stay the same as the original company, whereas with an equity carve out, a new set of shareholders is established. However, there are other variations that can be pursued such as a sponsored spinoff. In a *sponsored spinoff*, an outside party acquires an interest in a spunoff entity. Often, this is done by giving the sponsor an incentive in the form of a discount on the price of the shares.

The debt of the overall company is allocated between the remaining parent company and the spunoff entity. Usually, this is done in relation to the respective post-transaction sizes of the respective businesses.

Spinoffs are usually easier to implement and also less expensive compared to equity carve outs. For example, one study found that the direct costs of carve outs (investment banking and exchange fees) were 3 times greater than spinoffs.[4] Spinoffs are also much less time consuming to implement than equity carve outs.

If the business that is being spun off is well integrated into the parent company, then it will usually require much more work to create a distinct and separate business to spin off. If, however, the business was a prior acquisition that was not well integrated into the parent company, then the job may be easier.

Spinoff volume follows patterns similar to M&A and divestitures (see Figure 10.4 (a), (b), and (c)). That is, divestitures and spinoffs follow M&A deal volume, which, in turn, is greatly influenced by the overall level of economic activity in the relevant economy. This is logical as companies first decide to part ways with a business unit and after this decision has been made they then choose which alternative—divestiture, carve out, or spinoff—is most appropriate.

SPINOFF OR EQUITY CARVE OUT: WHICH OPTION IS BETTER?

In many circumstances, an equity carve out is the preferable option. As we have noted, in an equity carve out, the seller receives cash for the shares that are sold. The process can take longer than an outright sale to a single buyer but it at least results in a cash infusion, which a spinoff does not. Carve outs also require the seller to engage in a lot more disclosure than spinoffs. Such heightened disclosure can have costs, ranging from giving away information to competitors to enlightening the market about the potentially poor performance of a business—which may have been a prior acquisition—that the company would like to sweep under the rug.

Under both circumstances, the parent company accomplishes its goal of parting ways with the business unit. While both accomplish the general goal, the carve out route provides cash flow benefits that spinoffs do not. That being the case, the logical question is: Why do firms do spinoffs at all (as opposed to equity carve outs)?

Research by Michaely and Shaw has shed some light on the choice between equity carve outs and spinoffs.[5] In their study of 91 master limited partnerships, they found that the companies that chose to go the spinoff route tended to be more debt-laden and less profitable than *carve out firms*. Those with fewer negative characteristics more often were the ones that went the carve out route. Michaely and Shaw found that carved out firms were generally less risky and better performers compared to spinoff companies. In other words, they were more saleable and were not fixer-uppers.

The Michaely and Shaw findings were supported in another study by Johnson, Klein, and Thibodeaux.[6] In their study of 126 spinoffs, they found that the companies doing the spinoffs were more highly leveraged and had lower asset growth than their industry peers. They also helped shed light on the reasons for the positive stock market responses to spinoffs. They found that following the spinoffs, there were gains in the cash flow margin on sales and asset growth for both the parent company and the spunoff firm.

(a)

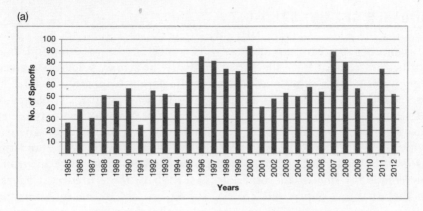

(b)

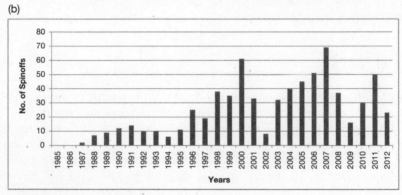

(c)

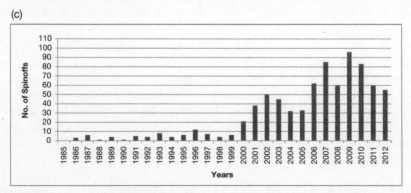

FIGURE 10.4 International Spinoff Volume, 1985–2012: (a) United States, (b) Europe, and (c) Asia

Source: Thomson Financial Securities Data.

*We use the number of spinoffs as opposed to value due to the fact that a large, and annually quite variable, percent of spinoffs do not have announced values.

ANOTHER OPTION: SPLIT-OFF

Still another restructuring alternative is a split-off. In this situation, two entities are created from the parent company and shareholders are given the option to pick either one—shares in the parent company or shares in the new entity. This can be advantageous if, for example, the company has a value business and a growth business. Some shareholders may prefer one type over the other. Here, shareholders are given a choice, whereas with a spinoff they still remain shareholders in both the value and the growth business, even though some shareholders may have a strong preference for one or the other. In cases where there are *extra shares* in the separated entity that are not subscribed for by parent company shareholders, the company may then handle these extra shares via a second-step spinoff transaction.

TAX EFFECTS

In these different transactions, the tax effects of the parent company and the different shareholder groups are often key to determining whether a deal ultimately gets done. Spinoff and split-offs are usually tax efficient in that they may be structured in a way that will not result in tax liabilities for shareholders.[7] However, when there are two distinct businesses, such as very different growth and value businesses, shareholders in a spinoff may then choose to sell their shares in the business they do not prefer and this may then create tax liabilities for them. Thus, in this particular situation, split-offs may be tax preferable.

For divestitures, the likelihood of a tax liability may be significantly greater, especially in situations where the unit being sold was acquired many years ago at a much lower price. However, even in a divestiture, there may be things that sellers can do to reduce or possibly avoid adverse tax effects. This is why M&A taxation is such an important legal field and why not just deal lawyers, but also tax lawyers, play a key role on the legal M&A teams.

SHAREHOLDER WEALTH EFFECTS OF SELLOFFS

While it seems intuitive that undoing poorly performing M&A is a good thing, it is important to determine if there is empirical evidence to support or contradict this belief. Fortunately, there is considerable empirical support from about a quarter of a century of research, which lends great

TABLE 10.1 Shareholder Wealth Effects of Voluntary Selloffs

Study	Days	Average Abnormal Returns	Period Sampled	Sample Size
Alexander, Benson, and Kampmeyer (1984)	−1 through 0	.17	1964–1973	53
Hite and Owens (1984)	−1 through 0	1.50	1963–1979	56
Hite, Owens, and Rogers (1987)	−50 through −5	.69	1963–1981	55
Jain (1985)	−5 through −1	.70	1976–1978	1,107
Klein (1983)	−1 through 0	1.12	1970–1979	202
Linn and Rozeff (1984)	−1 through 0	1.45	1977–1982	77
Loh, Bezjak, and Toms (1995)	−1 through 0	1.50	1982–1987	59
Rosenfeld (1984)	−1 through 0	2.33	1963–1981	62

Source: Patrick A. Gaughan, *Mergers, Acquisitions, and Corporate Restructurings*, 5th ed. (Hoboken, NJ: John Wiley & Sons, Inc., 2011).

credence to the idea that selloffs in general, regardless of the specific mechanism used to implement them, usually benefit shareholders.

Table 10.1 summarizes the findings of a few of the many academic studies on the shareholder wealth effects of selloffs. The research is clear in showing that when a company announces it is selling off a business unit, the market responds positively. Other corporate research that looks at equity carve outs and spinoffs also shows very favorable results. For example, J.P. Morgan conducted a few studies in the mid-1990s on the benefits of equity carve outs and spinoffs. Not surprisingly, their findings were that both the parent company and the subsidiary that is sold or spun off both do well over the first year and a half, which was their study period.

The market's positive reaction to selloff announcements is basically the market saying, "Thank God you finally woke up and are selling off that dog of a business." This is a bit of a humorous exaggeration (and is also very unfair to canines), but it is likely the case in many instances. In general, it is reasonable to conclude that the sold-off business units are not making a valuable contribution to the overall company. If they were, you would think that the parent company would not be getting rid of them. The unit could be more valuable on its own, or as part of another corporation with which there are better synergies.

ROUND TRIP WEALTH EFFECTS

When a company announces an acquisition, in many cases the market response is negative. The research we have just reviewed indicates that when a company announces a selloff, perhaps a prior acquisition, the market response is often positive. This raises the question: What is the net, round trip effect? Marquette and Williams analyzed 79 acquisitions and 69 spinoffs over the period 1980 to 1988.[9] They examined the shareholder wealth effects of both the acquisition and subsequent spinoffs of the acquired entity. They tried to determine if paired acquisitions and selloffs, what they called flips, drawing on real estate terminology, generate—on average—positive or negative values. If the value was positive, then we might conclude that M&A has a positive impact even if the acquired entity is subsequently sold off. However, their results did not indicate positive or negative effect—rather, they showed mainly a neutral response. While they did find negative effects for acquisitions and positive ones for selloffs, the combined effects were not statistically significant. There was, however, an interesting exception. When the target was a research and development (R&D)-intensive business, and where there is evidence that the parent may have supplied capital to fuel the target's R&D needs, the net effect was positive. Hypothetically, we could imagine this type of effect when a huge capital-filled conglomerate, such as GE, acquires a growing R&D-intensive business. Here, the parent can accelerate the target's growth. If the target does not fit into the parent's long-term plans, then it could possibly be sold off at a higher value, in part based upon the parent's capital contributions during its ownership of the target. Here, we can make a more convincing argument for the benefits of financial synergy.

SPINOFFS AS A MEANS OF INCREASING FOCUS

When a company does a spinoff, just as when it does a divestiture or an equity carve out, the result is that it usually becomes a more defined or focused entity. How much more depends on the size of the unit that is separated from the parent as well as whether or not the unit was in a different business from the parent company. When it is a different business, we can refer to such spinoffs as *cross-industry spinoffs*. When it is in the same industry, these are referred to as *own-industry spinoffs*. The obvious question is which type of spinoff has the greatest positive shareholder wealth effects?

Daley, Mehrotan, and Sivakumar analyzed 151 spinoffs, which they followed over a five-year window that included two years before and two years after the spinoff.[10] Their research found significant value creation around the spinoff announcement. They traced the source of this value creation to cross-industry spinoffs. In fact, they found no value creation in cases of own-industry spinoffs. For example, they found a 3 percent performance improvement in the return on assets going from the year before cross-industry spinoffs to the year after. However, there was no change in the return on assets for own-industry spinoffs. Moreover, the performance improvements occurred mainly at the parent or continuing entity—not at the spinoff unit. They reach the intuitive conclusion that the gains are the result of management being able to run a more focused entity and not having to stretch their managerial efforts across more diverse business units.

DIFFERENCES IN TYPES OF FOCUS INCREASES

The Dasilas and Leventi study discussed earlier also shed light on which types of focus-increasing spinoffs had the greatest positive shareholder wealth effects. They compared spinoffs that increased industrial focus to those that increased geographical focus. They found spinoffs that increased industrial focus generated positive shareholder wealth effects, while those that increased geographical focus do not. In addition, the positive market response to increases in industrial focus was greater for U.S. spinoffs than it was for European deals.

CASE STUDY: PEPSI'S REFOCUSING STRATEGY

In the late 1990s, most consumers associated the name Pepsi with the very successful soft drinks the company markets; however, many were unaware Pepsi was also one of the largest packaged food companies in the world. While its core business was the Pepsi soft drinks, other major brands marketed by Pepsi included snack foods, marketed by the Frito-Lay business unit. Frito Lay is a market leader. Over time, this diverse, soft drinks and packaged food business found that its revenues were rising but its profit margins were weakening. To understand this we need to explore how the company found itself in such a situation.

(continued)

(*continued*)

PepsiCo was created through M&A with the merger of Pepsi Cola and Frito Lay. Both brands had long histories of success. Pepsi was invented in 1898 and Frito Lay was formed in 1932. From the start, the merging of these two businesses led to the combined entity seeking synergies through related diversification. Not satisfied with operating in leadership positions of being the number-two brand in soft drinks behind Coca Cola and the number-one business in snack foods, Pepsi could not resist spreading its wings further into even less related businesses.

Pepsi marketed not just its successful Pepsi and Diet Pepsi soft drinks but also Mountain Dew and Lipton Tea beverages. Frito Lay also marketed more than just Frito Lay chips. It sold Doritos, Ruffles, and Tostitos, as well as the associated dips and salsa. The combination of these *food* products would not win any nutrition awards, but they would bring in billions from non-health-conscious consumers.

Pepsi used M&A to make a major entry into the fast food segment of the restaurant business. It acquired Pizza Hut in 1977, Taco Bell in 1978, and the Kentucky Fried Chicken chain in 1986. The combined effect of these M&A was to make PepsiCo a major player in yet another business—the highly competitive fast food industry. The M&A also made the company a huge corporation—moving it up the Fortune 500 ranking to number 25.[a] The deals made PepsiCo bigger, but they didn't make it a company with good profit margins (see Figure 10.5). In addition, the company continued to lose ground in the beverage business to Coca Cola.

After significant impatience registered by the market about the company's pursuit of size instead of profits, PepsiCo decide to exit the fast food business. In 1997, it spun off the restaurant business into an entity it created called Tricon. Shareholders received one share of Tricon for every 10 shares of PepsiCo; thus, they continued to benefit from both businesses—each of which was more focused than it had been prior to the spinoff. PepsiCo also exited the food distribution business it had previously entered.

The remaining PepsiCo business still had a dual focus of being in beverages and snack foods. However, PepsiCo was not finished with slimming down the company by getting rid of less profitable operations. In Chapter 6, we discussed how PepsiCo misjudged the need to be vertically integrated in order to control its distribution. And in the

(*continued*)

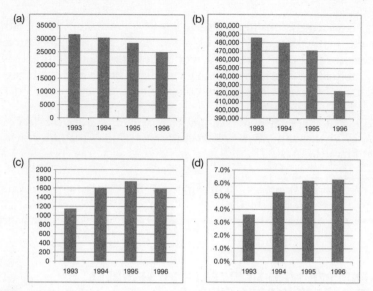

FIGURE 10.5 Pepsi's Growth in Size and Decline in Profitability: (a) Pepsi Revenues ($millions), (b) Pepsi Employees, (c) Pepsi Net Income ($millions), and (d) Pepsi Net Profit Margin

late 1990s, PepsiCo's management could not see the adverse ramifications of losing control of its distribution system. It only could shortsightedly compare the relative profit margins of these two segments and naively conclude that if they got rid of the lower-margin bottler business, the average profit margin would be higher. This was true following the 1998 spinoff of that unit, but the adverse competitor and revenue ramifications would come to roost years later when PepsiCo had to engage in an expensive reacquisition of these businesses it once controlled.

With freed-up cash and higher margins, PepsiCo set about expanding in its core businesses. In 2000, it acquired Quaker Oats in a stock-financed transaction for $13.4 billion. While the name Quaker Oats is more associated with the popular cereal, the company had earlier acquired the successful Gatorade sports drink. In that same year, PepsiCo had acquired the South Beach Beverage Company (SoBe) line of *new age* drinks.

(*continued*)

(*continued*)

These acquisitions did not solve PepsiCo's problems. It still faced the the market-leading Coca Cola company, an incredibly strong competitor that owns one of the world's leading brand names. However, at least the company is more focused and better equipped than it may have been in prior years to compete head-on with Coca Cola.

Source: This case study draws on some facts derived from the excellent case study by Vivek Gupta, "PepsiCo's 'Focus' Strategy," IBS Center for Management Research, BSTR/118, 2004.

---

[a] Vivek Gupta, "PepsiCo's 'Focus' Strategy," IBS Center for Management Research, BSTR/118, 2004, p. 2.

SHAREHOLDER WEALTH EFFECTS OF SPINOFFS: UNITED STATES VERSUS EUROPE

Much of the research literature of the shareholder wealth effects of selloffs, and spinoffs in particular, focuses on U.S. companies and markets. Boreiko and Murgia, however, analyzed 97 European spinoffs. They found that in Europe, spinoffs were often triggered by what they called "governance earthquakes," such as the appointment of a new CEO or a threat of a takeover.[11] Indeed, Shimizu and Hitt analyzed a sample of U.S. divestitures and similarly found that the appointment of a new CEO increased the probability of a unit being divested.[12]

Another study by Dasilas and Leventi compared the shareholder wealth effects of 239 U.S. and European spinoffs from 2000 to 2009. They found that there was a stronger positive stock market response to U.S. spinoffs than there was for European spinoffs. Statistically, there was a 4.21 percent average positive stock market reaction to U.S. spinoffs, whereas it was only 1.36 percent for European parent companies. The positive reaction by the market to U.S. spinoffs is not necessarily supported by better performance than their European counterparts. U.S. parent companies showed lower operating performance than the European parents, while European parent companies also invested more in capital expenditures in the years after the spinoff.

Corporate spinoffs have been more common in England than in continental Europe, although they are becoming more frequent in Continental Europe. The typical ownership structure in Europe is more concentrated than it is in England or the United States.[13] This puts Continental European shareholders, other than those large, controlling equity holders who are often family-related, in a less influential position than their British counterparts.

Like much of the research on U.S. spinoffs, Boreiko and Murgia's European sample showed positive shareholder wealth effects for spinoff announcements. Also consistent with U.S. findings, they found higher (5.7 percent) effects for focus-enhancing spinoffs than for non-focus-enhancing deals (3.3 percent). They did not find operating performance improvements at parent companies after the spinoff, but they did find such effects for the spunoff entity. The spunoff firms that had the greatest improvements were typically the internally grown units, as opposed to the ones that enabled the parent company to be more focused. This contrasts with research on U.S. spinoffs, which tend to show performance improvements only for focus-enhancing deals.

CORPORATE GOVERNANCE AND SELLOFFS

Managers may be reluctant to sell off a unit—especially if they played a role in its acquisition. The selloff ends up being an admission of a mistake, which is something that many managers are reluctant to do. Owen, Shi, and Yawson analyzed a sample of 797 divestitures over the years 1997 to 2005.[14] Consistent with other related research, they found that divestitures created wealth. However, their most significant contribution to the research literature was to determine the role that corporate governance played in the divestiture decision and the magnitude of the positive wealth effect.

They found that companies with more independent boards and large blockholders had greater positive shareholder wealth effects. Their research implies that the decision to divest requires more impetus than the obvious recognition of poor performance on a unit or a poor fit of that unit within the overall company. It seems that management often needs some pressure from independent directors and large equity holders to be sufficiently motivated to do the right thing. In the United States this pressure has often been coming from hedge funds that acquire significant blocks of stock in undervalued companies, with their goal being to force value-increasing corporate restructuring. However, in many Continental European companies, controlling shareholders may be less responsive to the concerns of smaller shareholders who oppose the acquisition strategies the companies have pursued and who therefore would want to pursue selloffs, which could release value to the shareholders. This need may be even greater in Japan, where managers of some of the hulking and inefficient corporate structures have been slow to respond to the realities of the world economy.

MANAGERIAL OWNERSHIP AND SELLOFF GAINS

Many companies have used various incentives to try to deal with the agency problems and align the interests of management and shareholders. One of the main compensation tools are stock options, which makes managers also owners. This does not eliminate the agency problems, as managers may still get the bulk of their compensation from non-equity-based sources such as salary and perks. Hansen and Song analyzed a sample of 152 divestitures.[15] They found that not only did sellers enjoy positive shareholder wealth effects—these effects were positively related to the equity ownership of managers and directors. This is an intuitive result, as it shows that when managers and directors are playing with their own money, they are less likely to hang on to losers.

ACTIVISTS AND SELLOFFS

One trend that has been relatively prominent in recent years has been the aggressiveness of activists. These are typically hedge funds, which monitor and analyze companies, especially diverse companies, with a mind toward seeing if structural changes could improve shareholder return. For example, in 2011, William Ackman and his Pershing Square fund acquired an 11 percent stake in the conglomerate Fortune Brands. Fortune Brands was an odd mix of businesses that included the fourth-largest liquor company in the world, the Titleist line of golf products, as well as a home and security business that included well-known brands such as Moen, MasterLocks, Simonton Windows, ThermaTru Doors, and other brands. The combination of liquor, golf products, and home products is hard to explain. As a result of Ackman's pressure, Fortune sold off the Titleist and FootJoy businesses to a group of foreign investors.

Activists analyze the public filings of diverse companies and will try to ascertain if some of the divisions show low margins. If that is the case, then the overall margin of the company can be improved by a sale of the lower-margin businesses. From an activist perspective, it may also be convenient if the overall company's performance is less than spectacular. Other disgruntled investors may then be very receptive to the quick solution of a selloff of a lower margin business—a "solution" that, if they don't pursue it, management may have a hard time explaining without external pressure.

MARKET LIQUIDITY AND THE DECISION TO SELL A UNIT

Various factors can motivate a company to sell a unit. One of the most obvious is poor performance of that business. One would think that this would be the most fundamental and obvious factor. Surprisingly, research by Schlingemann,

Stulz, and Walking, however, shows that market liquidity is actually more important.[16] In an analysis of 168 divesting companies over the years 1979 to 1994, they found that companies in industries that were more liquid were more likely to be divested. In a liquid market, sellers have a better opportunity to receive the full value, if not an even higher value, for their asset than in markets that are less liquid. Schlingemann, Stulz, and Walking measured liquidity by the volume of assets that were being sold in a given time period. So when firms want to divest an unrelated segment as part of a focus-enhancement program, those who can sell in liquid markets will be more likely to do so whereas those that face a less liquid market may hold on to the unit until market liquidity improves.

INVOLUNTARY SELLOFFS

While the markets tend to like selloffs, the reaction is not the same with involuntary selloffs. Involuntary selloffs, such as those required by regulatory processes, tend to be regarded as bad news by the market, and these kinds of deals do not share the same positive shareholder wealth effects that voluntary selloffs enjoy.

Involuntary selloffs are typically the product of some unwelcome regulatory process such as an antitrust action. Antitrust regulators could require a company to dispose of certain business units, such as those acquired in M&A. In the global business environment in which we live, there may be several competition policy bodies, such as the U.S. Justice Department or Federal Trade Commission as well as the European Commission, which have to lend their approval. When gaining the approval of these entities means that a unit that was expected to be a valuable part of the combined business has to be disposed of following an M&A, the market usually does not respond well. Research shows that involuntary selloffs fail to enjoy positive shareholder wealth effects and often have negative effects.[17] Research on antitrust-related selloffs clearly shows negative shareholder wealth effects. Ellert's review of 205 defendants in antitrust merger lawsuits showed a 21.86 percent decline in the value of the equity of these firms during the month the complaint was filed.[18]

VOLUNTARY/INVOLUNTARY SELLOFFS

As we have noted, companies complete deals even when they know that the combination of the two firms will be problematic from an antitrust or other regulatory perspective. When they do this, they typically have a strategy for how they will handle the troubling aspects of the deal. When these issues are generally well known to the market, it should not receive a negative response unlike in the case of an unexpected regulatory challenge to a deal. For example, in March 2012, Kinder Morgan Energy Partners LP agreed in August 2012 to sell its Rocky Mountain Natural Gas processing and pipeline business to Tallgrass Energy Partners for roughly $1.8 billion in order to receive approval for its $21 billion acquisition of El Paso Corp, which closed in May 2012. Kinder Morgan agreed to make this sale in order to secure approval from the Federal Trade Commission. Tallgrass is owned by various entities including Energy & Minerals Group, Kelso and Co, and management.

It is common for companies to announce a general solution, or at least a willingness to arrive at a mutually agreeable solution, at or near the time they announce a deal. Usually they, the market, and the media have a sense if there will be a problem. To avoid an adverse reaction by the market, it is wise to give the market a heads-up to acknowledge the problem and to give a sense of what a general or specific solution is and why it is likely to prevent a regulatory holdup. If the solution is credible and reflects the likely industry effects and shows respect for the power of the regulators, it will likely be favorably received. For this reason, such voluntary/involuntary sales do not often bring about an adverse market reaction.

Nowadays it is not as common to have a company complete a deal and to find out that there is an antitrust problem. In fact, this was the purpose of the Hart-Scott-Rodino AntiTrust Improvements Act passed in 1978. Typically, companies work out in advance an asset sale plan that is acceptable to regulators. If that can't be worked out, the deal is usually cancelled. The alternative is to do the deal and then have a long and distracting battle with regulators after the fact. Usually the bidder loses this regulatory battle. The exception is in the financial services industry where the lobbying power of financial institutions can be so significant that they can do deals that are illegal and get the law changed after the fact! This is what happened when Citicorp acquired Travelers in a deal that was illegal according to the Glass Steagall Act. The deal was pushed and/or supported by the now retired (but rich with shareholders' money) Sandy Weill and the all-knowing *Committee to Save the World*—Robert Rubin, Laurence Summers, and Alan Greenspan. In retrospect, they were far from all knowing but at least Sandy Weill and Robert Rubin are richer in part because of such deals. Shareholders suffered a very different outcome. Once again, shareholders should never expect an apology for a job badly done—only excuses if not outright lies.

VOLUNTARY DEFENSIVE SELLOFFS

There is a wide array of defensive actions that a company can engage in to prevent it from being taken over in a hostile bid. Elsewhere, we have categorized them into preventative and active measures.[19] Preventative measures are those actions, such as implementing a poison pill plan or enacting certain antitake-over charter amendments, that are done in advance of a specific hostile threat. Research shows that when selloffs are used as an antitakeover device, they may not yield the same positive shareholder wealth effects as selloffs that have other fundamental strategic goals.

In a sample of 59 firms from 1980 to 1987, 13 of which featured takeover speculation, Loh, Bezjak, and Toms found cumulative average abnormal return equal to 1.5 percent over a one-day period up to the selloff date.[20] However, when they divided their sample into two sub-samples—those with and without takeover speculation—the 13 firms that were the targets of takeover speculation failed to show any significant changes in shareholder wealth. These results suggest that when firms engage in selloffs to prevent themselves from being taken over, the market treats the transactions differently and does not consider it to be a positive change.

Sometimes these changes involve selling off valuable assets so that the seller/target will now be less appealing to the bidder. This may lead to an adverse response by the market, as it may also result in a restructured company that is less valuable to shareholders. Additionally, such changes may be viewed by the market as a sign of management entrenchment, where managers are taking steps to maintain their positions and the compensation and perks that come with them rather than to improve the company as a whole.

TRACKING STOCKS

A company can create a new class of shares that do not have ownership rights, but which pay dividends that are a function of earnings of a specific subunit within the overall company. For example, the Loews Corporation created a tracking stock called the Carolina Group, which tracked the performance of the Lorrilard tobacco company, a unit that was within the Loews company umbrella. U.S. tobacco companies generate steady cash flows but come with litigation-related liabilities that can drag down their equity values. When a parent company owns a tobacco subsidiary, this unit can drag down the value of the overall company's stock. Creation of a tracking stock was one attempt to release value of the tobacco unit to shareholders while also trying to insulate parent company shareholders from the negative aspects of this unit. AT&T created such a class of stock so that it could release some of the value of its wireless unit.

Companies may issue tracking stocks when they determine that the value of the unit within the overall company is not reflected in the market capitalization of the parent company. For example, a large diversified, but slow growth, company may create tracking stocks to allow the market to gain from the growth that may be going on in one of their divisions.

Initial research on tracking stocks painted a favorable picture of such shares. For example, D'Souza and Jacob found a statistically significant 3.61 percent stock price reaction within a three-day window of an announcement of proposed tracking stock issues.[21] They tried to determine whether the creation of tracking stocks achieves some of the same benefits that a company would receive if it were a totally independent entity. To explore this, they examined the correlation between the returns of the tracking stock and the overall firm, as well as the correlation between the returns of the tracking stock and similar firms in the tracking stock's industry. They found a greater correlation between parent firms and tracking stock returns than the returns between the tracking stocks and their industry counterparts. That is, they found that the *firm effect* was greater than the *industry effect*. They postulate that the firm effect exists because of the shared resources and liabilities between the division and the parent company.

While the D'Souza and Jacob study found positive shareholder wealth effects of tracking stocks, later research was not as favorable. Billett and Vijh examined 29 completed tracking stock restructurings over the period 1984 to 1999.[22] They found that shareholders of tracking stocks experienced significant post-issue wealth *losses*. Shareholders of the parent company experienced insignificant returns, although they incurred negative returns for the year prior to the tracking stock restructuring announcement. These negative preannouncement returns are not surprising, as the issuance of a tracking stock is usually an attempted partial solution to poor performance of the parent. While the creation of a tracking stock seems to have stopped the negative returns, the event did not show the positive stock price response that earlier tracking stock wealth effects research showed or the positive shareholder wealth effects of selloffs.

Looking back, it seems that companies attempted using tracking stocks as a less drastic solution to the problem of having a business unit, perhaps a prior acquisition that did not fit well within the overall company. Initially, the market reacted positively to such attempted solutions. Then the market came to view these steps as ways to try to merely sweep the problem under the rug. Thus, the market lost its taste for tracking stocks.

Creating a tracking stock does not fix the problem of poor corporate fit. The solution is to sell off the unit and use the resources more productively.

MORE DRASTIC SOLUTIONS: VOLUNTARY BUST-UPS

Certain large corporations, perhaps ones that include many diverse businesses, may (with many exceptions) destroy shareholder value. When this is the case, a drastic solution can be to simply liquidate the company. In this scenario, all business units are sold, liabilities are satisfied, and the net proceeds are used to pay a liquidating dividend to shareholders. Like other forms of restructuring, we look to research to provide guidance on whether such moves are in shareholders' interests. Like less drastic forms of restructuring, such as sales of specific units, the market looks favorably on the sale of all units and the liquidation of the company. When this is done, the monies are returned to shareholders who can each put them to their own best use rather than relying on corporate managers to release the minimal amount needed to keep shareholders off their backs.

One early study of voluntary bust-ups was done by Skantz and Marchesini, who analyzed liquidation announcements made by 37 firms from 1970 to 1982 and found that they generated an average excess return of 21.4 percent during the month of the announcement.[23] Hite, Owers, and Rogers found similarly positive shareholder wealth effects during the month of the announcement of voluntary liquidations made by the 49 firms in their sample, which covered the years 1966 to 1975.[24] They showed a positive abnormal return in the announcement month equal to 13.62 percent. Almost half the firms in their sample were the object of a bid for control within two years of the announcement of the liquidation plan. These bids included a wide range of actions, such as leveraged buyouts (LBOs), tender offers, and proxy contests. Additionally, more than 80 percent of the firms in their sample showed positive abnormal returns. This suggests that the stock market agreed that continued operation of the firm under its prior operating policy would reduce shareholder wealth.

The positive stock market reaction was affirmed by two other studies. Kim and Schatzberg found a 14 percent positive return for 73 liquidating firms during a three-day period associated with the liquidation announcement.[25] They revealed that a 3 percent return was added when shareholders confirmed the transaction. Kim and Schatzberg failed to detect any significant wealth effect, either positive or negative, for the shareholders of the acquiring firms. In a study of 61 publicly traded firms that completed voluntary liquidations between 1970 and 1991, Erwin and McConnell found that voluntary liquidations were associated with an even higher average excess stock return of 20 percent.[26] They also confirmed the intuitive expectation that firms that decide to voluntarily liquidate face limited growth prospects. The liquidation decision is the rational one because it releases financial resources to be applied to higher-yielding alternatives. As suggested previously, these research studies imply that the stock market often agrees that the continued operation of the firm under its prior operating policy will reduce shareholder wealth. This is not surprising because most firms that are considering liquidation usually are suffering serious problems. Liquidation then releases the firm's assets to other companies that might be able to realize a higher return on them.

While the research on total breakups is quite positive, there are always notable exceptions. For example, in 1996, when Hansen, a United Kingdom conglomerate, announced that it was spinning off almost all of its business and would retain only a small building materials business, the market reacted negatively. The general explanation for this is that the market preferred the company's strategy of acquiring diverse businesses and trying to improve them, and with the radical spinoff of virtually all of its units, it was essentially out of the fixer-upper business.[27]

RECENT MAJOR EXCEPTIONS TO POSITIVE SHAREHOLDER WEALTH EFFECTS OF SELLOFFS

While the research on the positive stock market reactions to selloffs is generally quite positive, there are many exceptions. In addition, the market did not react positively to some major relatively recent selloffs. Examples include the CBS–Viacom breakup as well as the Sara Lee initial breakup announcement.

In 1999, CBS and Viacom merged in a deal that was clearly a big flop. At the time, the deal combined the motion picture and cable production assets as well as the television and cable networks of Viacom with the TV and radio stations of CBS. The merger created the second-largest media company behind Time Warner. Time Warner would later merge with AOL in what can be considered the worst merger in history. The AOL–Time Warner deal destroyed a large part of the value of Time Warner shareholder investments, while AOL shareholders ending up getting shares in a valuable company, Time Warner, for their temporarily inflated AOL shares.

While the CBS–Viacom deal was a huge flop, it was still a smaller flop than the AOL–Time Warner deal. Both prove that so many of the very highly paid media and entertainment senior executives have no idea what they are doing when it comes to M&A. For some, their main skill is getting as much compensation for themselves, at shareholders' expense, as they can. When a weak stock price put so much pressure on Viacom and its CEO, Sumner Redstone, to spinoff CBS, the market failed to reward the company with the typical positive stock price effects. The

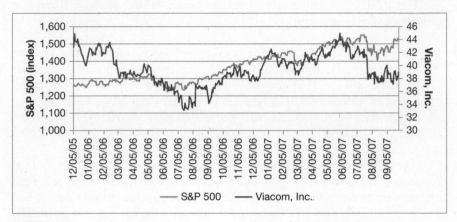

FIGURE 10.6 Viacom's Stock Performance Compared to the Market
Source: Yahoo! Finance.

reason may be that if the market thinks the problems that were weighing down the stock price still persist, they will not change their assessment of the stock (see Figure 10.6). Post–CBS spinoff Viacom was still a company run by Sumner Redstone, its controlling shareholder. Thus, the market assigned what is termed the *mogul discount*. This is a discount that is sometimes applied by the market to companies that do not exhibit normal corporate governance and sensitivity to the interests of all shareholders, but that are instead run in a very autocratic manner. So the spinoff, while a major deal in terms of size, did not fix the fundamental problem of the company.

It is instructive to review what the CEO of Viacom said at the time of the $80 billion merger of these two media giants and what they said when they announced the breakup.

At the time of the merger in 1999, Sumner Redstone, CEO of Viacom, said:

> *This exciting merger creates the industry-leading media company for today and a dynamic growth vehicle that will benefit shareholders well into the future. Our union will be king [emphasis added]—not just in content, but in its distribution, marketing, and packaging. We will be global leaders in every facet of the media and entertainment industry, financially strong from day one, with an enviable stable of global brands.*[28]

Then, less than six years later, the same CEO, Sumner Redstone, announced the following:

> We believe that a separation of our businesses into distinct and strong operating entities would allow us to optimize our capital structure and create unique investments that are more appealing to investors with different objectives. . . . Separately, these new publicly traded entities could each pursue strategic paths that would maximize their long-term potential.[29]

It is no wonder that the market failed to react positively to this spinoff. The same management that put together the failed merger strategy less than six years prior was still running the show. How can the market get excited and provide the positive shareholder wealth effects that are normally accorded to such breakups?

Sumner Redstone has a very high regard for himself and given his rise from running a regional theater chain to being CEO of a huge media conglomerate, one certainly has to concede that he has enjoyed much success in his long corporate career. However, one thing about such moguls is that it seems that they think they can do no wrong. He engineered the merger with CBS in a deal in which Viacom did not have to pay a premium (as it was a *merger* and not an acquisition) and he did not lose voting control of his company as Viacom, a company he maintained voting control over, issued nonvoting shares. He was able to get control over an ever-larger media empire. Unfortunately, there were some major strategic flaws in Redstone's takeover of CBS. CBS was very vulnerable to variations in advertising expenditures. Advertising is quite pro-cyclical, so in good times, companies such as CBS, which generates such a high percentage of its revenue from advertising, will do well. However, if we have a deep recession, as there was in 2008 to 2009, with a stagnant recovery afterward, businesses like CBS will weigh down companies such as Viacom. So in retrospect, it looks as though this media merger, like so many others, was simply a big flop.[30]

The case of Sara Lee is similar to CBS–Viacom in that the spinoff did not prove to be a panacea, but it was different in that Sara Lee's problems did not stem from having an ego-fueled mogul making costly M&A decisions. The announcement in 2005 that the company planned to dispose of 40 percent of its assets and the subsequent spinoff of Hanesbrands and the European meats division in 2006 were partial fixes to a dysfunctional combination of very diverse assets that had no synergistic benefits. Prior to 2006, the company was a big conglomerate mess, and after 2006 it was just a somewhat smaller but equally dysfunctional mess. Thus, the inherent problems of the company still existed after the initial, piecemeal attempts at restructuring—just on a smaller scale. Accordingly, the market chose not to assign a significant stock market increase in response to these partial fixes.

These examples and others, including Tyco, Sara Lee, and Dun and Bradstreet, show that not all selloffs will have positive stock responses. If you are a fundamentally flawed company or you are run by management that is doing a questionable job before and after a selloff, don't expect to be rewarded for a selloff that probably should have occurred long before and does not address the core problems of the company. On the other hand, if you are generally a reasonably well-managed firm and you decide a unit, perhaps a prior failed acquisition, does not fit and you want to increase your focus, odds are the market will receive such a strategic move well.

NOTES

1. Paul B. Carroll and Chunka Mui, *Billion Dollar Lessons* (New York: Portfolio Publishers, 2008), 27–28.
2. For a good discussion of the decision-making process underlying divestitures, see William J. Gole and Paul J. Hilger, *Corporate Divestitures: A Mergers and Acquisitions Best Practices Guide* (Hoboken, NJ: John Wiley & Sons, 2008).
3. Michael E. Porter, "From Competitive Advantage to Corporate Strategy," *Harvard Business Review*, 1987, 43–59.
4. Roni Michaely and Wayne H. Shaw, "The Choice of Going Public: Spinoffs vs. Carve Outs," *Financial Management* 24, no. 3 (Autumn 1995): 5–21.
5. Ibid., 1.
6. Shane Johnson, Daniel Klein, and Verne Thibodeaux, "The Effects of Spinoffs on Corporate Investment and Performances," *Journal of Financial Research* 19 (Summer 1996): 293–307.
7. See Patrick Gaughan, *Mergers Acquisitions and Corporate Restructurings*, 5th ed. (Hoboken, NJ: John Wiley & Sons, 2011): 607–622.
8. Apostolos Dasilas and Stergios Leventi, "Wealth Effects and Operating Performance of Spin-Offs: International Evidence" (Working Paper, International Hellinic University, Greece, 2010).
9. Christopher J. Marquette and Thomas Williams, "Takeover-Divestiture Combinations and Shareholder Wealth," *Applied Financial Economics* 17 (2007): 577–586.
10. Lane Daley, Vikas Mehrotra, and Ranjini Sivakumar, "Corporate Focus and Value Creation: Evidence from Spinoffs," *Journal of Financial Economics* 45 (1997): 257–281.
11. Dmitri Boreiko and Maurizio Murgia, "Which Spinoffs Generate Value and Performance Improvements?" (Working Paper, unpublished).
12. Katsuhiko Shimizu and Michael A. Hitt, "What Constrains or Facilitates Divestitures of Formerly Acquired Firms? The Effects of Organizational Inertia," *Journal of Management* 31, no. 1 (2005): 50–72.

13. M. Faccio and L. Lang, "The Ultimate Ownership of Western European Corporations," *Journal of Financial Economics* 65 (2002): 365–395.

14. Sian Owen, Liting Shi, and Alfred Yawson, "Divestitures, Wealth Effects, and Corporate Governance," *Accounting and Finance* 50 (2010): 389–415.

15. Robert Hansen and Moon H. Song, "Managerial Ownership, Board Structure, and the Division of Gains in Divestitures," *Journal of Corporate Finance* 6, no.1 (March 2000): 55–70.

16. Frederik P. Schlingemann, Rene M. Stulz, and Ralph A. Walking, "Divestitures and the Liquidity of the Market for Corporate Assets," *Journal of Financial Economics* 64 (2002): 117–144.

17. Ronald Kudla and Thomas McInish, "The Microeconomic Consequences of an Involuntary Corporate Spin-Off," *Sloan Management Review* 22, no. 4 (1981): 41–46.

18. James C. Ellert, "Mergers, Antitrust Law Enforcement and the Behavior of Stock Prices," *Journal of Finance* 31 (1976): 715–732.

19. Patrick A. Gaughan, *Mergers, Acquisitions, and Corporate Restructurings*, 5th ed. (Hoboken, NJ: John Wiley & Sons, 2011).

20. Charmen Loh, Jennifer Russell Bezjak, and Harrison Toms, "Voluntary Corporate Divestitures as Antitakeover Mechanisms," *The Financial Review* 30, no. 1 (February 1995): 41–60.

21. Julia D'Souza and John Jacob, "Why Firms Issue Targeted Stock," *Journal of Financial Economics* 56, no. 3 (June 2000): 459–483.

22. Matthew T. Billet and Anand M. Vijh, "The Wealth Effects of Tracking Stock Restructurings," *Journal of Financial Research* 27, no. 4 (2004): 559–583.

23. Terrence Skantz and Roberto Marchesini, "The Effect of Voluntary Corporate Liquidation on Shareholder Wealth," *Journal of Financial Research* 10 (Spring 1987): 65–75.

24. Gailen Hite, James Owers, and Ronald Rogers, "The Market for Interfirm Asset Sales: Partial Selloffs and Total Liquidations," *Journal of Financial Economics* 18 (June 1987): 229–252.

25. E. Han Kim and John Schatzberg, "Voluntary Corporate Liquidations," *Journal of Financial Economics* 19, no. 2 (December 1987): 311–328.

26. Gayle R. Erwin and John J. McConnell, "To Live or Die? An Empirical Analysis of Piecemeal Voluntary Liquidations," *Journal of Corporate Finance* 3, no. 4 (December 1997): 325–354.

27. Michael Pearson, "Wall Street Loves Spinoff Announcements, But Do Spinoffs Actually Increase Shareholder Value?" *Journal of Business Strategy* 19, no. 4 (July/August 1998): 31–35.

28. Viacom Company Press Release, September 7, 1999.

29. Viacom Press Release, March 16, 2005.

30. Jonathan A. Knee, Bruce C. Greenwald, and Ava Seave, *The Curse of the Mogul: What's Wrong With the World's Leading Media Companies* (New York: Portfolio Publishers, 2009), 223–226.

CHAPTER 11

Valuation and Merger Strategy

A correct valuation analysis that accurately determines a target's price can be a key factor in determining if a deal will be a good one or a bad one. Certainly there are many companies that would not be a good acquisition at any price. A poor acquisition, such as Daimler's failed mega-deal with Chrysler, can absorb many corporate resources, which can have multiple adverse effects through the acquirer's organization. Firstly, the deal must be a good strategic fit. Obviously, we are not considering deals such as what private equity firms or firms such as Berkshire Hathaway would do, which have a very different purpose. Once the acquirer is confident that this is the case, then determining the correct price is the next step. It is important that the process not work the other way around. For example, consider cases where white knights acquire targets that they did not seek out. Often the acquisitions are presented with favorable financial terms but the targets may not be good strategic fits. This is why the research on the success of white knight acquisitions shows poor results.[1]

For many companies, however, there is a price that will enable a buyer to gain from the deal. When buyers pay more than that *true value*, they will lose unless they take some extraordinary steps to overcome paying too much for the target. In this chapter, we discuss some of the main valuation issues that affect merger strategy. The goal of this chapter is not to provide a mini-primer on valuation. Rather, it is to tie the strategic issues that we have discussed to the valuation process. In doing so, we hope to highlight how certain elements of the valuation process are linked to the success or failure of M&A. We will try to focus on what in the valuation process can cause M&A to go from success to a failure. That is, what converts a good deal into a bad one?

FINANCIAL VERSUS NONFINANCIAL BUYERS

The valuation process is somewhat different for financial buyers, such as private equity firms, who sometimes are simply flipping business. Even though they may sometimes talk about combining certain companies they

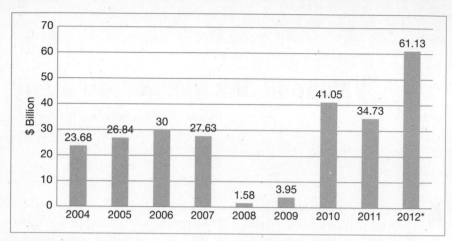

FIGURE 11.1   Volume of Debt Sold for Private-Equity Dividends
*Annualized using October 19, 2012, data.
Source: Standard & Poor's Capital IQ LCD, *Wall Street Journal*, 10/19/12

have bought and achieving synergistic gains, this is usually a pie in the sky. Private equity buyers typically try to acquire an undervalued target, and, during their holding period, they try to take steps to make it more profitable. This often includes cost-cutting measures and short-term changes that will enable them to sell the target at a higher price in the not too distant future. Unfortunately, this often also involves them loading the acquired companies up with debt where they extract the borrowing proceeds for themselves, instead of investing the money for the betterment of the company. It is amazing that lenders are so eager to fund these so-called *dividend recapitalizations* (see Figure 11.1) and it is equally amazing that future buyers of the debt-laden entity are willing to pay so much more for the then more risky company than what the private equity buyers paid. One thing is clear: From a valuation perspective, nonfinancial buyers and sellers need to be very wary of dealing with private equity firms, as so often the private equity firms seem to end up getting the better side of the deal. Part of the problem seems to be unrealistic and naive valuation analysis by the nonfinancial parties.

Before we discuss nonfinancial buyers, we would be unfair to the private equity industry if we left the impression that all they do is extract gains for themselves and generate little value in exchange. This definitely occurs all too frequently. However, they also do the opposite. One excellent example of this was the investment that a private equity group led by Cerberus Capital made when they acquired a number of the Albertson stores in 2006 while another supermarket chain, Supervalu, acquired other Albertson stores. This is an excellent experiment in which type of buyer should generate the greatest value. On the surface, we would expect the management of Supervalu, who had been operating in the industry for many years, to outperform the private equity "beginners." However, the private equity buyers hired an experienced managerial team who were given capital to invest as needed. They were able to make the business profitable while Supervalu could not make its group of stores generate profits. In addition, the private-equity-based group was aggressive in shedding poorly performing stores and cutting labor costs. The Supervalu group seemed to apply their traditional managerial ways and did not approach the business with the aggressive and open-minded approach of the private equity team. In 2013 the Cerberus-led group bought out the stores held by Supervalu. This is a great story for Cerberus to tell potential investors, especially those with short memories who may not recall the really bad investment it made in Chrysler where it saw all of its equity wiped out.

Nonfinancial buyers, however, usually have a more long-term focus and often want to try to realize longer-term gains. For these buyers, the factors we discussed in Chapter 3, which might result in synergistic gains, can be quite important. For financial sellers, these factors are more often just things to talk about in a sales pitch to nonfinancial buyers. Nonfinancial buyers need to have a clear strategic focus. The target has to fit a need or provide a long-term opportunity for the nonfinancial buyer. Therefore, the time horizon for the nonfinancial buyer is necessarily longer than for the financial buyer who is looking for the optimal time, which is usually the shortest time, to flip the target.

TARGET AND BIDDER VALUATION EFFECTS

Prior to doing deals, dealmakers need to be aware of the valuation effects of M&A and how they are different for bidder and targets. The good news is that there is a large body of research on these effects. The bad news is that most dealmakers and the management and boards of the companies involved are unaware of this research. Thus, it is not surprising that we have a seemingly endless supply of bad deals and poorly priced transactions.

Numerous studies have considered the valuation effects of mergers and acquisitions. Many utilize an event study approach that analyzes the short-term market responses to announcements of deals.

A good number of the often-cited valuation effect studies were done in the early 1980s. Their results, however, also apply to later time periods. Some more recent research, such as studies that consider the magnitude of returns over longer time periods, as well as studies that look at the impact of the medium of exchange on returns, are also discussed later in this chapter.[2]

The studies on the valuation effects of mergers and acquisitions have five general conclusions:

1. *Target shareholders earn positive returns from merger agreements.* Several studies have shown that for friendly, negotiated bids, target common stockholders earn statistically significant positive abnormal returns.[3] The source of this return can be traced to the premiums that target shareholders receive. So this result is quite intuitive, if not obvious.

2. *Target shareholders may earn even higher significant positive returns from tender offers.* Target common shareholders of hostile bids that are tender offers also receive statistically significant positive returns.[4] The hostile bidding process may create a competitive environment, which may increase the acquiring firm's bid and cause target shareholder returns to be even higher than what would have occurred in a friendly transaction. Once again, this is an intuitive result. It is also the underlying reason why U.S. courts have encouraged boards of companies that are for sale to promote the auction process and it is also why they have punished those who have taken steps to foreclose the auction process and have not fulfilled what is termed under Delaware state law as *Revlon Duties*.

3. *Target bondholders and preferred stockholders gain from takeovers.* Both target preferred stockholders and preferred bondholders gain from being acquired.[5] Given that bidders tend to be larger than targets, the addition of the bidder and its assets as another source of protection should lower the risk of preferred stocks and bonds, thus making them more valuable. Like the target common stockholder effects, this is an intuitive conclusion.

4. *Acquiring firm shareholders tend to earn zero or negative returns from mergers.* Acquiring firm stockholders often do not do well when their companies engage in acquisitions. These effects are either statistically insignificant or somewhat negative. Presumably, this reflects the fact that markets are skeptical that the bidder can enjoy synergistic gains that more than offset the fact that the bidder is paying a premium for the target. The fact that the bidder's stock response is small compared with that of the target is partly due to the fact that bidders tend to be larger than targets.

   Later in this chapter we will examine the shareholder wealth impact on acquirers as a function of their size and the size of their targets. We will see that larger deals tend not perform as well. We will also compare how private acquirers fare relative to public company bidders. We will see that private acquirers tend not to overpay and to do better. We will also see that when the acquirers' share distribution features some large blockholders, or when the board is dominated by outsiders, the acquirer shareholder wealth effects may be less negative. Such companies are much less likely to overpay.

5. *Acquiring firm shareholders tend to earn little or no returns from tender offers.* Returns to acquiring firm shareholders following hostile bids are not impressive at all. There is some evidence that there may be a response that ranges from mildly positive to zero. Once again, these findings are not a surprise, although, frankly, the fact that they are not more clearly negative is maybe a little surprising. This is due to the fact that there is often more pressure on bidders to pay a higher premium in hostile bids so as to overcome the resistance of the target. Also, aggressive bidders in auctions are more likely to come away with the winner's curse.

WHAT TYPES OF ACQUIRING FIRMS TEND TO PERFORM THE POOREST?

Given that acquiring firms often perform poorly in M&A, the question arises as to the types of firms that do the worst and the ones that do better when pursuing M&A. Rau and Vermaelen analyzed a sample of 3,169 mergers and 348 tender offers between 1980 and 1991.[6] They compared *glamour firms*, companies with low book-to-market ratios and high past earnings and cash flow growth, with *value firms*, companies with higher book-to-market ratios and poorer prior performance. The results of their research showed that glamour firms underperformed value companies. As reflected by their low book-to-market ratios, the market is more enthralled with glamour firms, which can boast about their relatively higher earnings and cash flow growth. Value firms, on the other hand, are not as highly valued by the market, as reflected by their higher book-to-market ratios, which may be a function of their relatively poorer financial performance.

Rau and Vermaelen attribute the relatively poorer M&A performance of glamour firms to factors such as hubris. They also noted that glamour firms tend to more frequently pay with stock. This is understandable because their stock is more highly valued than that of so-called value firms. Because they are glamour firms, the market has valued their equity highly—perhaps more highly than a systematic valuation would indicate. Therefore, these companies have an incentive to use this more highly valued equity to finance a bid, as it enables them to acquire targets at a "discount."

PREMIUMS

When a bidder is considering making an offer for a target, one key issue is what premium to pay for the target. Premiums vary by industry and by market conditions. Figure 11.2 shows a time series of premiums paid by U.S. companies over the period 1980 to 2011.

HISTORICAL TRENDS IN MERGER PREMIUMS

Merger premiums vary over time. When we look back at the two most recent merger waves, we see that during the initial and middle part of the waves, merger premiums were actually below average. It is interesting to note that, when we consider the research of Moeller, Schlingemann, and Stulz, which showed that toward the end of the fifth merger wave, acquirers incurred huge shareholder losses, the two phenomena can be linked.[7] As we discuss in the following section, premiums in the latter part of both the fourth and fifth merger waves rose (see Figure 11.2). While these premiums declined when the fourth wave came to an end and the economy entered a recession, merger premiums rose sharply even after the fifth wave came to an end. In fact, 2002

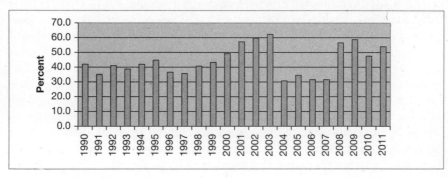

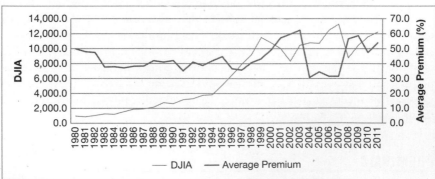

FIGURE 11.2 Premium Paid over Market Price: 1980–2011
Source: Mergerstat Review and Econstats.com.

and 2003 featured premiums of 59.7 and 62.3 percent, respectively, even though the merger wave was only beginning to rise again after a hiatus following the end of the fifth wave.

STOCK MARKET ACTIVITY AND MERGER PREMIUMS

The normal ups and downs of the stock market cause stock prices to rise and fall more than may be explained by variations in their earnings or dividends.[8] This can cause some stocks to be overpriced at times and underpriced at other times. Managers know that in a bear market, their stock price may be below the long-term value of the firm. Believing that their stock price is only temporarily undervalued, managers are inclined to resist selling in bear markets unless a higher than average premium is forthcoming. Thus, sellers want to adopt a long-term focus while bidders want to opportunistically focus on the short-term movements of the target's stock price. Similarly, in bull markets, such as in the period 1994 to 1997, bidders are less inclined to pay the same average premium, knowing that the market has already over-valued equities. During this period, the average takeover premiums declined, which is what we would expect (see Figure 11.2). However, as the market continued to rise in the latter part of the 1990s, premiums began to rise with it. That is, target stock prices continued to rise sharply, even though the earning power of these same companies would reasonably not rise propor-tionately. Instead of tempering the premiums they offered, as bidders did in 1994 to 1997, bidders began to offer even higher premiums on top of the overly inflated stock prices! It is not surprising that Moeller, Schlingemann, and Stulz's research shows that during the period 1998 to 2001, acquiring firm shareholders lost a total of $240 billion!

When a merger wave takes hold, especially in the economically rich environments that merger waves feed on, managers may start out being more rational but the rapidly rising equity values can quickly go to their heads. Hubris can quickly invade their thinking. Managers of potential bidders soon start to think that the rising value of their firm's stock is due to some great managerial efforts they exerted. More often than not, however, it was the uplifting effects of an irrational market if not an outright bubble. It is tough for a board to tell a CEO that his or her next great M&A idea is poorly thought out when that CEO can point to the great performance of the company's equity during his or her reign. Unfortunately, they and their boards start to believe the CEO's press clippings. Part of the problem is that the media also believes this nonsense and this perception then permeates throughout the business community.

STOCK MARKET–DRIVEN ACQUISITIONS

It seems logical that when the market rises, the value of the "currency" that a bidder uses to acquire a target in a stock-for-stock deal rises. However, in such a stock deal, isn't the target also highly valued when the market is up? Do the effects offset each other? The answer: It depends.

Shleifer and Vishny have presented a basic model, which, to some extent, helps explain the decision-making process that determines whether a bidder will make a stock or cash bid.[9] One key factor is the *relative valuations* of the two companies. That is, if the bidder's stock price is more overvalued than the target's, there is a greater incentive for the bidder to make a stock-financed bid. So we will see more stock-financed valuations not just when the market is up, but also when there is greater variation in valuations so that some companies are more overvalued than others. In addition, the greater synergistic gains that the bidder perceives, rightly or wrongly, the more likely the bidder will pay a premium. Moreover, the more prevalent these conditions, high market valuations with a high degree of heterogeneity in these valuations, the more fertile conditions for merger waves.

DETERMINANTS OF ACQUISITION PREMIUMS

The magnitude of acquisition premiums is often attributed to a combination of the bidder's estimate of the acquisition gains and the strength of the target's bargaining position. The acquisition gains may come from a variety of sources, including anticipated synergistic benefits derived from combining the bidder and the target, or the target being underpriced or poorly managed. The bidder's bargaining position may also be affected by several factors, including the presence of other bidders and the strength of the target's antitakeover defenses. Varaiya analyzed the role of these various factors in determining acquisition premiums in 77 deals between 1975 and 1980.[10] He found significant support for the role of competitive forces in the auction process and the presence of antitakeover measures in determining premiums but mixed results for the role of anticipated benefits. This is a disappointing result because one would be think in a well-thought-out and rational world, anticipated benefits would be the key determinant of the magnitude of the premium offered.

PREMIUMS FROM STRATEGIC MERGERS

Roach investigated whether the size of the control premium is greater for strategic mergers versus those transactions that lack such a strategic focus.[11]

Nonstrategic acquisitions have been criticized as deals that add little value to the acquiring firm. In theory, if strategic deals are more valuable, the seller should be in a better position to demand higher premiums. In a study of 1,446 transactions between 1992 and 1997, Roach failed to find any difference in the control premiums for those deals in which the merging companies have the same or different SIC codes. This implies that strategic focus is not a determinant of merger premiums.

On its surface, the Roach finding seems counterintuitive—especially in light of the discussions we had on synergies and how at least the hope for synergies could lead to higher profits for the combined entity. However, when we see the Roach results together with the Varaiya findings, they paint a troubling picture. Synergistic benefits are, amazingly, not on the top of the list when managers are determining how high a premium to pay for a target—especially in competitive auction contests. Sometimes the more important item on their agenda seems to be fighting it out with other bidders and overcoming the target's resistance. Somewhere in this misplaced reasoning are oversized egos and hubris.

HUBRIS AND MERGER PREMIUMS

Many years ago, Richard Roll proposed an interesting hypothesis regarding the reasons managers sometimes seek to take over other companies.[12] He focused on the role that hubris, or the pride of the managers in the acquiring firm, may play in explaining takeovers. The hubris hypothesis implies that managers seek to acquire firms for their own personal motives and that the pure economic gains to be gained by the acquiring firm are not the sole motivation or even the primary motivation in the acquisition.

Roll and others have researched this hypothesis to see if there is evidence that can help explain why managers might pay a premium for a company that the market has already possibly correctly valued. Managers, they claim, have superimposed their own valuation over that of an objectively determined market valuation.[13] Their position is that the pride of management allows them to believe that their valuation is superior to that of the market. Implicit in this theory is an underlying conviction that the market is efficient and can provide the best indicator of the value of a firm.

A large body of research covering a quarter of a century has lent support to the hubris hypothesis as an explanation for many takeovers and the premiums that bidders pay. Early research sought to see if the announcement of deals caused the target's price to rise and the acquirer's to fall, the combination of the two thereby resulting in a net negative effect. Various studies lend support for some or all of these effects.

EARLY RESEARCH

A number of studies show that the acquiring firm's announcement of the takeover results in a decline in the value of the acquirer's stock. Dodd found statistically significant negative returns to the acquirer following the announcement of the planned takeover.[14] Other studies have demonstrated similar findings.[15] Not all of the early studies support this conclusion, however. Paul Asquith failed to find a consistent pattern of declining stock prices following the announcement of a takeover.[16]

There is more widespread agreement on the positive price effects for target stockholders who have been found to experience wealth gains following takeovers. Bradley, Desai, and Kim showed that tender offers result in gains for target firm stockholders.[17] Admittedly, the hostile nature of tender offers should produce greater changes in the stock price than in friendly takeover offers. Most studies, however, show that target stockholders gain following both friendly and hostile takeover bids. In addition, as we have already discussed, Varaiya showed that bidders tend to overpay.[18]

In a study that examined the relationship between the bid premium and the combined market values of the bidder and the target, it was found that the premium paid by bidders was too high relative to the value of the target to the acquirer. The research on the combined effect of the upward movement of the target's stock and the downward movement of the acquirer's stock does not seem to provide strong support for the hubris hypothesis. Malatesta examined the combined effects and found, "The evidence indicates that the long-run sequence of events culminating in merger has no net impact on combined shareholder wealth."[19] It could be countered, however, that Malatesta's failure to find positive combined returns does support the hubris hypothesis.

LATER RESEARCH

Somewhat more recent research lends support to the hubris hypothesis by approaching the problem differently.[20] Using a sample of 106 large acquisitions, Hayward and Hambrick found CEO hubris positively associated with the size of premiums paid. Hubris was measured by the variables such as the company's recent performance and the CEO's sense of self-importance (as reflected by media praise and compensation relative to the second-highest-paid executive in the company). The study also considered independent variables such as CEO inexperience, as measured by years in that position, along with board vigilance, as measured by the number of inside directors versus outside directors.

Other studies provide support for the hubris hypothesis involving take-overs of U.S. firms by foreign corporations. Using shareholder wealth effect responses similar to those theorized by Roll, in a sample of 100 cross-border deals over the period 1981 to 1990, Seth, Song, and Pettit found that hubris played an important role in these deals.[21] Other factors, such as synergy and *managerialism*, also played a role. Managerialism is somewhat similar to hubris in that both may involve overpaying for a target. In managerialism, however, the bidder's management knowingly overpays so as to pursue their own gains, even though it comes at the expense of their shareholders—to whom they have a fiduciary obligation.

Malmendier and Tate investigated the role that overconfidence played in deals done by 394 large companies.[22] They measured overconfidence by the tendency of CEOs to overinvest in the stock of their own companies and who are overconfident based upon their statements in the media. They found that the likelihood of doing acquisitions was 65 percent higher for the overconfident group of CEOs in their sample. They also determined that overconfident CEOs were more likely to make lower quality, *value-destroying* acquisitions. Billet and Qian further researched the role of over-confidence by examining the acquisition history of 2,487 CEOs and 3,795 deals over the years 1980 to 2002.[23] CEOs who had a positive experience with acquisitions were more likely to pursue other acquisitions. These CEOs' net purchases of their company's own stock was greater prior to the subse-quent deals than it was prior to the first deals. They interpret this result as these CEOs being overconfident and attributing the success of the original deal to their own managerial abilities and superior insight.

Atkas, de Bodt, and Roll showed that overconfident and hubris-filled CEOs tend to do deals more rapidly and there is less time between their deals.[24] They also noted there is a *learning effect*, where CEOs who have done more deals in the past tend to act faster and have less time between their deals. This learning effect has been supported in other research by these same authors.[25] Clearly, companies such as Cisco and Oracle have demonstrated a successful M&A learning process.

WINNER'S CURSE HYPOTHESIS OF TAKEOVERS

The winner's curse of takeovers is the ironic hypothesis that states that bidders who overestimate the value of a target will be the ones most likely win a bidding contest. This is due to the fact that they will be more inclined to overpay and outbid rivals who more accurately value the target. This result is not specific to takeovers but is the natural result of the bidding contest in general.[26] One of the more public forums where this regularly occurs is in the free agent markets of professional sports such as baseball and basketball.[27] In fact, in professional sports there are all too many examples of this. A famous one was the bidding contest for shortstop (later third baseman) Alex Rodriguez. The Texas Rangers outbid other teams, such as the New York Mets, by overpaying for the infielder. In doing so, they limited their ability to secure other free agents. Rodriguez was never able to help Texas win a championship and when the Rangers fell on hard times, they unloaded the remainder of the burdensome contract to the New York Yankees, with their bulging payroll. While in New York, Rodriguez was combined with many other good players and the whole team won a championship. In later years, however, they were also stuck with his high contract, as he had to be taken out of the lineup in the playoffs for hitting so incredibly badly. Texas (and later, indirectly, the New York Yankees) won the bidding contest but overall they lost on the deal by overpaying. In doing so, they acquired the winner's curse.[28]

There are many parallels between the sports free agent bidding process and some M&A auctions. Bidders who get involved in bidding contests often find it difficult to walk away when the price gets too high. A classic example of this was the bidding contest for Federated Stores by Canadian real estate magnate Robert Campeau. Campeau had already taken over the very large department store chain Allied Stores. We discuss this bidding contest in detail in the case study that follows.

CAMPEAU'S MEGA-BUST

Robert Campeau was a Canadian real estate magnate who, while he enjoyed very good success in the Canadian real estate market, decided that this gave him the requisite expertise to venture into the U.S. department store market. In 1986, he acquired the sixth-largest department store chain in the United States—Allied stores. The deal was highly leveraged and brought with it the need to service debt through cost cutting and asset sales. Allied was a major player in the market, owning chains such as Ann Taylor, Brooks Brothers, Jordan Marsh, and Sterns. The linkage between department store retailing and real estate is a stretch but one that does have some common elements. These large retail chains can be anchor stores for large malls, which are real estate investments. Campeau knew real estate but his track record shows he did not know retail.

Not satisfied with trying to improve and get the most out of Allied, Campeau wanted to become the largest department store CEO in the world. In 1988, Campeau made a hostile bid to acquire Cincinnati-based Federated Stores. Federated boasted huge department store brand names such as Abraham & Straus, Bloomingdales, Bullocks, Burdines, Filenes, I. Magnin, and the ill-fitting Ralphs Grocery, which was a California supermarket chain.

While Allied may have needed improvement, Federated was relatively well run by seasoned retail executives who knew this industry far better than Campeau, who was a novice at retailing.

In January 1988, Campeau bid $47 per share, which was roughly a 42 percent premium. Federated did not want to fall into the clutches of this intruder in the industry and sought out white knights. May Department Stores and Macy's entered the fray and a bidding contest ensued. If one were to guess which of the three bidders, seasoned retailers May or Macy's, or nouveau-retailer Campeau, would be most likely to overpay, we would have to pick Campeau. Robert Campeau was assisted by investment bankers, such as the late Bruce Wasserstein of First Boston and his own firm Wasserstein Perella. However, the track record of M&A provides all too many instances where bankers who should have, and likely did, know better supported a highly leveraged and overpriced bid in exchange for rich fees.

May Department Stores was the first to drop out when the price got too high. Macy's hung in there but also decided to drop its offer—however, not before it was able to get Campeau to agree to sell I. Magnin and Bollock's for $1.1 billion while also paying Macy's $60 million to cover its fees and expenses.[29] Macy's and its CEO Edward Finkelstein knew something about the financial pressures of highly leveraged deals. In 1986, Macy's had done its own $3.74 billion leveraged buyout. The company would eventually succumb to the pressures of the LBO leverage in 1992 after it had trouble servicing that debt when the cash flows weakened during the 1990 to 1991 recession. It was one of several companies, the ranks of which included Greyhound and Southland Corp (7–11), which could not handle LBO debt. Many of these companies had one thing in common: They had thin margins in cyclical businesses—bad candidates for high leverage.[30]

Campeau did not seem to care about the additional expenses. The money was coming from an ever-mounting volume of debt that would be used to finance a bid that commanded a 120 percent premium! Investment bankers and other real estate magnates, such as Edward DeBartolo and the Reichmann's of Olympia and York, also provided expensive financing. Investment bankers provided bridge loans, which had to be refinanced in the about-to-collapse junk bond market. Campeau ended up paying a blended interest rate in the 16 to 17 percent range![31]

As with many of the failed highly leveraged deals of this era, high premiums were paid and burdensome interest agreements were entered into based upon overly optimistic assumptions built into valuation models. One has to assume that the investment bankers, such as Wasserstein, realized these valuation and debt service requirements were unrealistic but forged ahead anyway so as to receive high fees for their advice and debt commitments. In fact, this would not be the first time that Wasserstein would be associated with a highly leveraged bankruptcy where the valuation models and their assumptions were called into question. A somewhat similar situation occurred in the leveraged takeover of Interco.

Retailers are cyclical businesses. They do not make good candidates for LBOs, as often their margins are thin and their cash flows are somewhat volatile. Campeau, who was used to highly leveraged deals from his real estate background, was not used to the volatility of this industry and could not anticipate the changes that would occur in the debt market, nor could his well-paid investment bankers who should have known better.

Campeau could not service the debt and having paid a very high price for the overall company and the divisions it contained, he could not get buyers to pay him comparable multiples for chains he sought to sell off. However, he needed to sell off divisions to come up with money to pay down the debt and lower the debt service pressures. The walls closed in and in January 1990, Campeau filed for bankruptcy. The bankruptcy was quite complex with many levels of debt providers, many of whom lost a great deal of money.

When the time bomb waiting to happen finally blew up, Campeau Corp, but also Robert Campeau himself, had to file for bankruptcy. While Campeau won the bidding contest for Federated Stores, he really acquired the winner's curse, and the rest is history.

RESEARCH ON WINNER'S CURSE OF TAKEOVER CONTESTS

In a study of 800 acquisitions from 1974 to 1983, Varaiya showed that, on average, the winning bid in takeover contests significantly overstated the capital market's estimate of any takeover gains by as much as 67 percent.[32] He measured overpayment as the difference between the winning bid premium and the highest bid possible before the market responded negatively to the offer. This study provides support for the existence of the winner's curse, which, in turn, also supports the hubris hypothesis.

MARKET PERFORMANCE, VALUATION, AND TAKEOVER PROBABILITY

Companies that have valuable assets, but choose to trade on the market at a discount to the values of those assets and the cash flows they should generate, create a buying opportunity for bidders. Managers who fail to realize the values the market believes are achievable will face the disciplinary effect of takeovers. Theoretically, the lower the market value of the company relative to the potential value, the more likely the company is to become a takeover target. Edmans, Goldstein, and Jiang analyzed a large sample of 6,555 deals over the period 1980 to 2007.[33] They pointed out that while higher discounts will increase takeover probability, the market builds such a takeover likelihood into the market valuation. These two effects offset each other to some extent, thus partially counteracting the expected disciplinary effect of takeovers. Badly managed companies with the potential to be much more profitable will go on the radar of potential bidders and hedge funds, but, ironically, the poor management may at times uplift the market value of the company as investors start placing bets on the likelihood that the poorly managed corporation will be taken over. Without this market reaction, the discount to potential value would be even greater.

DEAL SIZE AND SHAREHOLDER WEALTH

For some time, researchers have contended that shareholders do worse with large deals than they do with smaller transactions. Loderer and Martin contend that this is due to bidders paying more for larger targets.[34] Others postulate that this is due to overconfidence on the part of the managers of the bidding companies.[35]

Some have theorized that the effects could work the other way. For example, large bidders can afford to hire more prominent advisors who, presumably, could give them better advice and avoid overpaying. However, when we look at the track record of some of the big mega-flops, of which there are so many that it makes little sense to provide even a sample listing, we see that all of them featured high-paid advisors whose advice has to be considered questionable and tainted by conflicts. Indeed, there is considerable support for the notion that larger advisors will encourage bidders to enter into bigger deals, which will provide them with bigger fees—even if it is not in the bidder's interest.

Moeller, Schlingemann, and Stulz analyzed a sample of 12,023 acquisitions over the period 1980 to 2001. They found, "Large firms make large acquisitions that result in large dollar losses."[36] On the other hand, they found that smaller firms made smaller acquisitions and registered positive gains. Specifically, they found, "The abnormal return associated with acquisitions announcements for small firms exceeds the abnormal return associated with acquisition announcements for large firms by 2.24 percentage points."[37] The combined impact of the two is that acquisitions in general, small and large, often result in negative shareholder wealth as the negative impact of the large deals more than offsets the positive impact of smaller transactions. Moeller and colleagues point to the propensity of large bidders to pay outsized premiums as the source of the negative returns in large deals. However, more recent research provides evidence that points in another direction.

Alexandridis, Fuller, Terhaar, and Travlos analyzed a sample of 3,691 U.S. acquisitions of public companies over the period 1990 to 2007.[38] They found that bidders paid lower premiums for acquisitions of large targets. The medium premium was 38 percent for the highest tercile, compared to 54 percent for the lowest. Their results on takeover premiums seem to imply that larger deals will generate greater gains for shareholders. However, this is not the case. They found that acquirers of larger targets generated negative long-run returns for their shareholders, whereas smaller deals had positive shareholder wealth effects.

These seemingly conflicting results do have a reasonable explanation. The lower premium is evidence that bidders in large deals are not necessarily overpaying for their targets. Therefore, the source of the differences in returns is not based upon the price paid for the target but rather the *choice of the target*. It seems bidders in acquisitions of large companies, which typically are other large companies, do not engage in sufficient strategic analysis and perhaps their decision-making process is clouded by psychological factors such as hubris. When it comes to M&A, the whole strategic acquisition process leaves a great deal to be desired.

VALUATION ANALYSIS AND SOURCE OF THE FLAWS IN BAD DEALS

The valuation process seems complex, and indeed it can incorporate many interacting and hard to forecast aspects, but the models themselves are not that complicated. Two main models are typically used: (1) discounted free cash flows or DCF and (2) comparable multiples. For deals involving companies that have clear asset values, a more asset-oriented approach, such as adjusted net worth, is also used. A look at DCF valuation is shown in equation (11.1):

$$\text{Business Value} = \begin{matrix} \text{Present Value of Operating} \\ \text{Cash Flows during the} \\ \text{Specific Period} \end{matrix} + \begin{matrix} \text{Present Value of Operating} \\ \text{Cash Flows Thereafter} \\ \text{(Terminal Value)} \end{matrix}$$

$$BV = \frac{FCF_1}{(1+r)} + \frac{FCF_2}{(1+r)^2} + \ldots + \frac{FCF_5}{(1+r)^5} + \frac{\left[\frac{FCF_6}{(r-g)}\right]}{(1+r)^5} \qquad (11.1)$$

where: BV = value of the business
FCF_1 = free cash flows in the period i
g = the growth rate in future cash flows after the fifth year
r = risk-adjusted discount rate

Equation 11.1 includes three main components or parameters: (1) free cash flows, (2) the growth rate of free cash flows, g, and (3) the risk-adjusted discount rate. The equation seems simple, yet embedded in these three explanatory variables are assumptions about a number of other important variables that we do not see in this equation. For example, the forecasted values of the free cash flows, which are a function of the starting value, FCF_0, and the growth rate, g, include assumptions about revenues and costs as well as the potential revenue-enhancing and cost-reducing synergies. We have seen in Chapter 3 that these gains are much easier to theorize about than to realize. It can also be seen that the resulting value for the business can be quite sensitive to key subjective inputs such as the growth rate.

In many of the failed highly leveraged deals, dealmakers used models like these to value the companies. When the target would not accept the offer price, and where more debt would be needed to finance a higher price, they would simply change the growth rate and instantly the company would become *more valuable*. This was the case in so many deals we have discussed, including the Campeau case study and the celebrated Interco failed highly leveraged transaction (HLT) being another of many.

One of the problems with the process is that investment bankers often do not have accountability for their analysis. If a deal fails, they may blame the management for the M&A not achieving the synergies they expected. However, if investment bankers are charging millions for their advice, and then many more millions for the financing, of what value is this advice if it results in the failure of the business? We have to recognize that, in some instances, the value of the advice accrues to the investment banker advisor who gains at the expense of the shareholders of the company who counted on the bankers to provide value for the fees they received.

It is often easy to analyze the financial track record of a company and its industry and get a pretty reliable sense of what the future cash flows will be. Sometimes this can be more difficult, such as when there is great volatility. But usually such great volatility only affects short-term periods. If, on the other hand, the contention is that the business and industry are so volatile that no reliable forecasting can be done, then that by itself raises question about the desirability of the target. Sometimes the best advice an investment banker can give a client is to not do the deal. If the client insists, the banker can walk away. This was the case in the Campeau buyout where Eric Gleacher, then head of M&A for Morgan Stanley, simply declined the assignment when it made little sense to him. He knew at the time that he would be missing out on high fees. However, he also had the self-confidence that he would continue to succeed without that deal, which was a disaster waiting to happen. Gleacher went on to enjoy great success in M&A and eventually left Morgan Stanley to form Gleacher & Co.

When situations such as the Campeau failure occur, there can be two parties at fault—the CEO, and the well-paid "advisors" who should have known better. In too many cases, these advisors, seeking short-term fees and year-end bonuses, have lost sight of the sage advice of Goldman Sachs founder Sidney Weinberg who supported being "long-term greedy." In the words of actor Michael Douglas in the M&A movie *Wall Street*, "Greed is good." Weinberg would say long-term greed is good, as that is where the investment bank helps the client become financially successful and, in doing so, also enjoys great *long-term* financial gains. Such a situation is a win-win. However, it is difficult to be long-term greedy if the client incurs a major loss on the deal or, as in the case of Campeau, goes bankrupt. Probably greater blame lies with the incompetent managers of the bidder who, in the case of many M&A failures, are clearly terrible at valuation analysis. Managers who can do good valuation analysis need to be employed by the acquirer. What is even more important is that senior management, and possibly even an ego-filled CEO, need to listen to their (hopefully) objective analysis.

COMMENTS OF THE RESIDUAL VALUE

We can see from equation (11.1) that a large percentage of the value of the company comes from the capitalized value of the cash flows that are projected to occur in years six and thereafter. Most DCF models only feature specific forecasts for an initial period such as five years. The thinking is that it is difficult to put forward specific forecasts for after five years. Knowing that the remaining years have value—in fact, substantial value—they are valued using capitalization. Let us first comment on the operating cash flow forecast, and then discuss the determination of the discount and capitalizations rates and how each of these factors can cause a misevaluation, which can lead to a failed deal.

FREE CASH FLOWS

The value an acquirer derives from a business comes from the free cash flows the entity generates. Free cash flows are defined as:

$$FCF = EBITDA - CE - CWC - CTP \qquad (11.2)$$

where: FCF = free cash flows
$EBITDA$ = earnings before interest and taxes
CE = capital expenditures
CWC = changes in working capital
CTP = cash taxes paid

Much could be said about the details of measuring the elements of equation (11.2). However, let us make a few basic comments on issues that can greatly affect a valuation or a misevaluation. The free cash flow projection starts with a base, which is derived from historical values, and in the case of a growing business, may even be based upon the last full year's value. However, to the extent that the future is expected to be quite different from the past, the values that actually occur in the future may differ. In addition, the annual investment in capital expenditures is often judged by the amount that was paid in the past. Often, evaluators take historical capital expenditures for a period, such as the past five years, average them, and then use this as the annual amount for the five-year forecast period. This seems reasonable, except when there are specific reasons why the amount of capital expenditures should differ in the future. A classic example of this occurred in the 1986 hostile takeover battle between the late TV personality Merv Griffin and the more recent TV personality and casino mogul Donald Trump, who were each battling for control of the Resorts Casino. The battle was hard fought and Merv Griffin even won control but clearly came away with the winner's curse. Merv and his team of advisors did not accurately analyze the very significant capital expenditures that would be needed to refurbish the older Resorts Casino to make it competitive with the new modern casinos that were at the time being built in Atlantic City.[39] Resorts had not been investing in necessary capital improvements leaving a new buyer, in this case, Merv Griffin, to have to invest significant sums after the deal to catch up with the competition and their glitzy modern casinos. In this case, using the historical capital expenditures did not reflect what the future free cash flows would be.

COST CUTTING AND HISTORICAL FREE CASH FLOWS

The lesson from the Resorts takeover battle is that a buyer needs to carefully research the target before it automatically assumes that historical values will apply to the future. For companies that were taken over by cost cutters who try to squeeze out higher profits by mortgaging the future, the buyer needs to factor in the extra costs of repairing damage from insufficient prior maintenance. This can be the case in many industries, including those that are not very capital intensive. Companies in marketing-intensive businesses that cut advertising can survive for a period of time based upon the half-life of prior marketing. This can cause profits to rise temporarily, but a buyer may end up paying the price in the form of lost market share and may have to invest extra-normal marketing expenditures to repair the brand awareness in the marketplace.

We would be remiss if we did not comment further on being wary of managerial cost cutters. Examples include Al Dunlop of the 1980s (ex-Sunbeam CEO) and Eddie Lampert in more recent years (Sears and Kmart). Dunlop was called "Chainsaw Al" and "Rambo in Pinstripes." He was well known for very aggressively cost cutting and critics would say he did not have a clue as to how to create value. He became CEO of Sunbeam in 1996 and cut costs so aggressively that the company reported record earnings of almost $190 million in 1997. When he could not find a buyer for the newly very profitable company, as buyers were not fooled by how the profits were achieved, he then proceeded with an M&A program, which was not what he was hired for. He acquired a controlling interest in camping equipment makers Coleman, coffee company Signature Brands (Mr. Coffee), and smoke detector company First Alert. However, the combined company quickly fell into bankruptcy and an investigation revealed all kinds of accounting irregularities.

The point of this discussion is that the buyer needs to be very wary of targets being run by short-term cost cutters who can boost earnings as they prop the company up for sale, while possibly destroying the long-term competitiveness of the business.

GROWTH RATE FOR PROJECTION

An assumed growth rate is applied to a historical free cash flow base to project future cash flows over a specific forecast period, which usually is five years. It does not have to be five years, but that is the number most commonly used.

One source of the growth rate can be the historical growth of the target's free cash flows. In very stable industries where not a lot has changed in recent years, and where similar stability is expected in the future, this can be a reasonable assumption. In more volatile industries, the past may be an imperfect guide and more industry and firm-specific information may have to be utilized to get a better handle on what the growth rate should be. We need to be careful to make sure that higher growth is not coming from overly optimistic assumptions about synergies.

The valuation process depicted in equation (11.1) is highly sensitive to the choice of growth rate. Even varying g by 1 percent can have a very significant impact on the business value. Therefore, much care needs to go into the selection of this parameter.

CAPITALIZATION RATES AND THE EXIT MULTIPLE

Another way of viewing the capitalization process that appears at the end of the forecast period in DCF is to focus on the value as measured by an *exit multiple*, which is applied to the cash flows in year 6. This multiple should reflect the risk-adjusted present value of the cash flows in year 6 and thereafter. It also should be consistent with the market value of the target as of year 6. However, much can happen (and possibly won't happen—such as in the case of synergistic gains) between year 0 and year 6, so these values are often very different from what was believed when the initial acquisition analysis was done. Remember, the projected free cash flow value for year 6 is computed by applying a growth rate to the value in the prior year. Each year before that is computed using the same kind of compounding process. Gains that are wrongfully assumed to incur in early years result in an overestimate of succeeding years, which has multiple effects on the capitalized residual value for year 6. If we value this residual using an exit multiple, we would be applying a multiple to too high of a base.

One has to take a hard look at the capitalization rate and exit multiple and make sure they are realistic. Growth that is built into the capitalization rate is reflected in the difference between the discount rate and an assumed growth rate $(k - g)$. The higher the growth rate, the lower the capitalization rate, and the higher the value. Therefore, synergies that are assumed and that make the growth rate higher really need to be closely scrutinized. For all the reasons we have discussed in Chapter 3, we need to be quite confident the synergies really will occur and all the factors that could cause them to fail to materialize will not apply with the given acquisition. If the questionable track record of synergies gives any pause, then the evaluator needs to backtrack on the growth rate or add an additional risk premium to the discount rate.

DISCOUNT RATE

The risks of a deal are incorporated into the discount rate. Using a method such as the build-up method, one starts off with a risk-free rate, and adds a premium for various factors such as an equity risk premium, a size premium, and various other target-specific premiums. For example, if an industry is undergoing significant changes, this may warrant an additional premium. One has to wonder if Hewlett Packard (HP) fully appreciated the highly competitive nature of the PC industry and incorporated an accurate risk premium into their valuation analysis when the company acquired Compaq. Clearly, the track record of that deal implies they did not. In addition, given the great internal debate at HP about the advisability of the acquisition that occurred at the time of the deal, it is likely that the deal proponents, such as CEO Carly Fiorina, would not want to include such a realistic risk premium. However, if they had chosen to include it, maybe the company would have less of a footprint today in the low margin, highly competitive PC industry.

Managers at companies change over time so one might think it would be difficult to generalize about certain companies being bad at M&A. However, if that is the case, how can we explain the miserable M&A track record of AT&T and HP? Both companies have undergone many managerial trans-formations, especially AT&T, but both seem to be terrible at M&A. This was underscored by the recent huge billion-dollar write-off taken by HP as a result of the disastrous Autonomy acquisition. It raises the question: If you have had a terrible track record doing M&A, should an extra "incompetence" pre-mium be built into the discount rate?

The greater the risk premium, the higher the discount rate. The higher the discount rate, the lower the present value of the cash flows and the target. Given the poor M&A performance of so many companies, it is clear that growth assumptions and risk premiums were flawed in many of the deals that are now considered failures.

In business valuation for M&A, a common source for the discount rate to be used to convert future free cash flows to present value terms is the weighted average cost of capital (WACC). We define WACC as:

$$\text{WACC} = (\text{E/TC}) \times r_e + (\text{D/TC}) \times (1 - t_d) \times r_d \qquad (11.3)$$

where:
$\quad$ D $=$ the value of debt

$\quad$ E $=$ the value of equity—usually measured by the market value of equity or total capitalization

$\quad$ TC $=$ the total value of Debt and Equity Capital $=$ E $+$ D

$\quad$ D/TC $=$ the proportion of Debt in Total Capital

$\quad$ E/TC $=$ the proportion of Equity in Total Capital

$\quad t_d =$ the firm tax rate

$\quad r_d =$ the cost of debt capital

$\quad r_e =$ the costs of equity capital. When the Capital Asset Pricing Model is used to value the costs of equity, this can be expressed by the following relationship:

$$r_e = r_f + \beta(r_M - r_f) \qquad (11.4)$$

where:
$\quad r_f =$ the risk-free rate of the return. This is usually measured using the long-term Treasury rate. It is free of default risk although not totally risk-free as it still has an interest rate, which its short-term counterpart, T Bills, do not.

$\quad \beta =$ Beta that measures systematic risk

$\quad r_M =$ the return on the market, which is usually measured using the return on the S&P 500, which, in turn, is available from sources such as Morningstar (formerly Ibbotson Associates)

$\quad (r_M - r_f) =$ the equity risk premium or risk premium of the market

WHOSE CAPITAL COSTS ARE WE MEASURING?

When a buyer performs the above WACC calculations, it may use it as a *hurdle rate* to assess the return it may get from an acquisition. One problem that can arise is when the buyer is much less risky than the target. Using the buyer's WACC, the resulting discount rate may then over-estimate the value of the acquisition. On the other hand, if being part of a larger and more secure acquirer, the buyer (which can provide needed capital to the target) lowers the target's risk profile, then this may be a reasonable approach.

Consider a case where the bidder is diversifying and moving into a business that is very different from its own. It adds the risk that a large body of research shows is inherent in such diversifying acquisitions. It can be even more risky if the target is not only in a very different business, but it is also in one that is known to be much more risky. In this case, being in a different field, in which the acquirer may not have expertise, is a risk element and if this new field is known to be risky, this should be held as a separate and additional risk factor. Shouldn't these factors form the basis for using a higher risk premium for determining the discount rates?

The issue can be further clouded when the target is in a foreign country. Does this cause one to lean further toward using the target's WACC? Once again, this is an issue to be considered, although more often than not bidders still continue to use their own WACC.[40]

USING THE BUILD-UP METHOD

An alternative to WACC is the build-up method. The method does not rely on the capital asset pricing model. It starts off with a risk-free rate, such as the long-term Treasury rate, and then adds various risk premiums to make the resulting discount rate one that generally reflects the risks of the company being valued. Such a calculation could be as follows:

$$r = r_f + r_{ep} + r_{ip} + r_{sp} \qquad (11.5)$$

where: r_f = risk-free rate
 r_{ep} = equity risk premium
 r_{ip} = industry risk premium
 r_{sp} = size premium

Other risk premiums can also be added to reflect unique risks not fully captured by the above general list of risk premiums. There is abundant research literature on the size of the equity risk premium. In fact, this topic has been the subject of an active debate for many years in finance.[41]

Data are readily available on these various premiums.[42] However, as with much of business valuation, there is a fair amount of *subjectivity* that goes into the selection process. The various formulas that are used for the calculations give the impression the process is very scientific and exact. It is exact in the sense that a specific number is ultimately derived. The process, however, contains many key subjective judgments, which can lead to an erroneous value if not arrived at in an enlightened manner. Obviously, we would have to conclude that this was the case in so many of the merger failures we have discussed.

CASE STUDY: OVERVALUATION AND TERRIBLE PRE-DEAL DUE DILIGENCE: HP

When we want to find examples of bad pre-deal M&A analysis, we can always look to AT&T and, more recently, HP for great cases. In the case of HP, their most recent flop was the $11.5 billion acquisition of Autonomy in October 2011. In November 2012, HP announced that it was taking an $8.8 billion charge largely related to this acquisition and alleged fraud and financial performance misstatements.

To put this in perspective, one has to think back to the fact that HP forced out Mark Hurd, who most regarded as a very good manager— something that has been rare at HP. Larry Ellison at Oracle could not believe this and quickly snapped up Hurd. In November 2010 HP's dysfunctional board then hired Leo Apotheker, reportedly, without even interviewing him. In August 2011, he announced that HP was going to spin off its PC business. Then two months later, the company said, essentially, "Sorry, we were just kidding; we will keep the PC business." It is hard to make this stuff up. Instead of downsizing, which we have seen often creates value through more focused businesses, Apotheker announced further M&A expansion through the disastrous Autonomy deal.

It is useful to think back to HP's 2008 acquisition of EDS for $13.9 billion. While at the time of the acquisition CEO Mark Hurd called it a historical day, it also proved to be disastrous. In August 2012, HP announced an $8 billion write-down in connection with the EDS acquisition. Given that this was a related acquisition of a business HP should have known a lot about, the fact that it proved to be such a large failure is amazing.

(continued)

Fast forward to the Autonomy deal. Given the terrible managerial and M&A track record of HP, shouldn't the board have required that a special *M&A* and *overall managerial incompetence* premium be built into any valuation analysis HP intends to do? This may sound absurd, but when you consider the track record of the company and how good its management has been at destroying value, such a premium fits the facts very closely. What due diligence did HP engage in going into the Autonomy acquisition? It is curious that Meg Whitman continues to run the company when she was on the board at the time of the Autonomy acquisition and obviously approved it. When a CEO is fired, the remaining managers often seek to blame all the problems they can on the prior manager while taking little, if any, responsibility for their own failings. However, after the huge Autonomy M&A charge was announced, HP's stock price fell to a 10-year low (see Figure 11.3). Management, and the current CEO Meg Whitman, have to accept some significant responsibility for this huge loss of shareholder value of this iconic company, which was caused by a long series of bad managers and members of the board of directors.

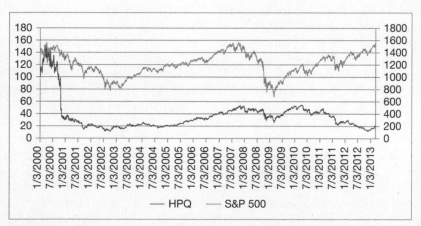

FIGURE 11.3 HP's Stock Price Compared to the S&P 500

SHORT-TERM INTEREST RATE TRENDS

The recent subprime crisis and worldwide economic downturn that ensued left central banks scrambling to do what they could (which often was very little when they were working in a liquidity trap and dealing with a zero bound problem of near zero interest rates) to provide some monetary stimulus to their respective economies. This resulted in highly unusual interest rates, which were held at low levels for an extended time period. These low levels first appeared in short-term rates but as the Federal Reserve went from basic quantitative easing to Operation Twist, both short- and long-term rates were pushed down. This created an interesting issue when doing M&A valuations. Should the temporarily low interest rates be used as a measure of the long-term rate when they are not expected to last for a long time and certainly not for the life of the acquisition? Moreover, if the low interest rates and weak economic environment have resulted in *yield repression*, which also has brought down the equity risk premium, should these rates be used if they are not expected to last for the long term? If evaluators want to avoid M&A errors and lean on the conservative side, they will adopt a more long-term perspective and not necessarily use the current rates on the day of the valuation.

USING COMPARABLES

The analytical challenges of valuation are also present when analysts use the comparables, such as EBITDA/FCF or P/E multiples from prior transactions in the industry. Here, we can also have much subjectivity. In the initial search for comparable multiples, we may come across many possible comparable transactions and have to make a subjective determination of which ones to discard. Our likely rationale is that these companies are not truly comparable or that the market was at a different level at the time of some of these past deals. We have to make sure, however, that we are not conducting the selection process with rose-colored glasses. If we do not throw out so many of the potential comparables, do we get a very different value when we apply the resulting average multiple to the target? If we do, then we have to go back and revisit the process and determine if we are really being objective. It is common that many potential comparables get rejected based upon further analysis. However, we have to recognize that there is a significant element of subjectivity inherent in the process.

PUBLIC VERSUS PRIVATE ACQUIRERS

Many acquisitions of public and private companies are done by private bidders. Sometimes these bidders are private equity firms and private operating companies. The usual research methods of event studies, which examine the stock market reaction around a relatively short window, cannot be applied to

TABLE 11.1 Median P/E* Offered: Public versus Private, 1990–2012

Year	Public P/E	Private P/E
1990	17.1	13.2
1991	15.9	8.5
1992	18.1	17.6
1993	19.7	22.0
1994	19.8	22.0
1995	19.4	15.5
1996	21.7	17.7
1997	25.0	17.0
1998	24.0	16.0
1999	21.7	18.4
2000	18.0	16.0
2001	16.7	15.3
2002	19.7	16.6
2003	21.2	19.4
2004	22.6	19.0
2005	24.4	16.9
2006	23.7	21.4
2007	24.9	21.6
2008	22.1	10.6
2009	18.1	18.4
2010	20.9	9.3
2011	21.3	14.9
2012	21.1	18.5
Average 1990–1999	20.2	16.8
Average 2000–2009	21.1	17.5

*Excludes negative P/E multiples and P/E multiples larger than 100.
Source: Mergerstat Review.

private buyers, as their shares do not trade in the marketplace. Bargeron, Schlingemann, Zutter, and Stulz analyzed a sample of 453 acquisitions by private buyers and 1,214 by public companies over the period 1980 to 2005.[43] They found that the average takeover premium paid by public buyers was 46.5 percent, while private operating company buyers paid 40.9 percent. However, the average premium paid by private equity firms was only 28.5 percent! Similar trends are apparent in data from Mergerstat, shown in Table 11.1, for the average P/E paid by public and private buyers.

Clearly, private equity bidders are shrewd buyers. It is also clear that sellers need to be very mindful of this when they sell to private equity firms. Wouldn't Ford have gotten more for Hertz if the company had taken more time and methodically conducted an auction for Hertz while holding out for a better price? We will never know, but the private equity buyers were able to quickly flip Hertz in the market for a handsome profit.

Another interesting finding of the Bargaron and colleagues research has to do with bargaining behavior. Private buyers are much more willing to simply walk away when the terms of the proposed deal are not to their liking. They found that private buyers withdraw offers 37.4 percent of the time, while public companies did so only 16.9 percent of the time. With private buyers, there is usually a closer linkage between the performance of a deal and the eventual gains of the dealmakers themselves. However, with large public companies, the managers of the bidders are playing with shareholders' money. It is not surprising that they are less careful with this money than private buyers. Once again, human nature can, a priori, tell us the direction of the research results.

PUBLIC VERSUS PRIVATE SELLERS

We see there is evidence that private buyers do better than public buyers. How do private sellers do? Fuller, Netter, and Stegemoller analyzed a sample of takeover bids over the period 1990 to 2000.[44] They found the companies that did many acquisitions showed higher returns when they acquired private companies than when they acquired public targets. Their explanation for this result was that it was due to the market for private companies being less liquid then the market for public firms. Since the equity of private companies is not traded in a public market, it is less liquid, and Fuller, Netter, and Stegemoller believe that an illiquidity discount inures to the benefit of the serial acquirers. These researchers also found that the larger the public target, the more negative the acquirer returns would end up being. They conclude that this is caused by overpaying on behalf of the bidder. They noticed that this overpayment was greater when stock, as opposed to cash, was used to buy the target.

The results of Fuller, Netter, and Stegemoller are consistent with earlier research by Saeyoung Chang.[45] He analyzed a sample of 281 private acquisitions over the period 1981 to 1992 and 255 acquisitions of public companies over the period 1981 to 1988. He found positive bidder returns when the targets were private companies and negative returns when they were public firms. Of the acquisitions of private companies, the positive returns were driven by deals using stock. Those that used cash showed zero abnormal returns.

As if the Fuller, Netter, and Stegemoller and Chang results were not enough evidence, still another study arrived at a similar conclusion. Faccio, McConnell, and Stolin analyzed the role that listing status played in 4,429 acquisitions by Western European companies over the period 1996 to 2001.[46] They found that acquirers of listed targets earned significant average abnormal returns of –0.38 percent, compared to a 1.48 percent abnormal return for unlisted targets. The Faccio, McConnell, and Stolin results show that the greater returns in private company acquisitions compared to public companies is not just a U.S. phenomenon but rather is a global result.

CASE STUDY: AWARD WINNER FOR WORST M&A COMPANY

In Chapter 5, we discussed the Sprint–Nextel merger and pointed out that it was one of the worst M&A in history. In Chapter 3, we pointed out the AOL–Time Warner merger was probably one of the single worst M&A in history. However, the question remains: Who is the *worst* acquirer in M&A history? The winner of such an award cannot just boast one terrible deal. The winner needs to be able to demonstrate a track record of terrible deals over a long time period as well as an inability to learn from its mistakes. Defined this way, AT&T clearly wins the award.

AT&T long dominated the U.S. telecommunications market and for many years enjoyed a monopoly. Regulators prevented the dominant telecom company from using its cash flows to compete with companies in other industries, such as the computer industry. AT&T was not satisfied being the top U.S. telecom firm as well as one of the leading corporations in the world. It could not wait to enter the exciting computer industry and was therefore willing to walk away from the local telephone business. Thus, in 1984, it agreed to a spinoff of seven regional operating companies: Ameritech, Bell Atlantic, BellSouth, Nynex, Pacific Telesis, Southwestern Bell, and U.S. West. Several of these "Baby Bells" later merged, such as Nynex and Bell Atlantic, which combined to form Verizon, the company that would eventually became one of the largest telecommunications companies in the United States. AT&T shareholders received 1 share in each of these regional companies for every 10 shares they held in AT&T. They also still owned 10 shares in the new AT&T, which would prove to be a company that would engage in some of the more notable merger failures in merger history. Indeed, the surviving AT&T would eventually be acquired by one of its progenies—Southwestern Bell.

(continued)

(*continued*)

The AT&T that emerged from the spinoff had the unenviable track record of conducting some of the worst mergers in history. AT&T proved to be a company that had difficulty learning from its mistakes and would proceed to initiate ever-larger merger blunders. The spinoff of the operating companies allowed AT&T to enter the computer industry, as an antimonopoly consent decree had prohibited it from using revenues from its telecommunications businesses to finance competitive ventures into other industries. AT&T was a technologically advanced company with a bloated cost structure that left it in poor shape to compete in the highly competitive computer industry. When AT&T was unsuccessful with its computer business, it acquired NCR in a hostile acquisition and greatly overpaid after it encountered resistance from the target. Cultural rifts created further problems and, after in 1995, after AT&T had lost much money in the computer business, it started the process of breaking itself up into three parts: (1) AT&T Communications, (2) a company that became Lucent, and (3) a computer company that used the NCR name. So much for its very expensive foray into the highly competitive computer industry. And all the while, the companies it spun off in the 1980s were thriving and consolidating.

Recovering from its wounds, a new management team decided to outdo their predecessors in orchestrating merger flops. AT&T's management envied the growth and profitability of its progenies, such as Verizon. It wished to be able to again offer local phone services (yes, you read that correctly). Unfortunately, while it was once a leader in this business, it had given it all away in the fourth merger wave so as to be able to enter the computer business, in which it failed. The fifth-wave version of AT&T wanted to gain access to local phone markets and believed that two cable targets, MediaOne and TCI, would enable it to accomplish this. It also wanted to be a one-stop shop, offering long distance, mobile, and local telecommunications plus cable for its customers. Readers know to be wary when management is offering customers a one-stop shop. AT&T announced that it was paying approximately $100 billion for its two cable acquisitions. After it bought the companies (rushing the sellers through without doing its own proper due diligence), it discovered that the acquired local cable lines could not support telecommunications services without a major capital infusion. Once again, AT&T blundered in the M&A area— with each blunder being larger than the last one. Not long after the

(*continued*)

deals, AT&T announced it was breaking itself up—again. It is ironic that after this latest M&A debacle and breakup, AT&T was acquired in November 2005 by one of the companies it had previously spun off—SBC. SBC then assumed the AT&T name.

In fairness, the new AT&T, though it can trace its roots back to the AT&T of the 1980s and 1990s, is quite different from its previous incarnation, even if the firm still uses the iconic AT&T name. However, the M&A curse seems to persist. In 2011, AT&T announced its intention to acquire rival T-Mobile. However, it did not do its homework and did not correctly anticipate the opposition of U.S. antitrust regulators. It cancelled the deal by the end of the year and had to pay a huge breakup fee that has been estimated to be in the $4 billion range. This is the largest breakup fee in history. So, once again, AT&T has worked its way back into the M&A history books—always on the wrong side of success. At least they are consistent.

NOTES

1. Ajeyo Banerjee and James E. Owers, "Wealth Reduction in White Knight Bids," *Financial Management* 21, no. 3 (Autumn 1992): 48–57.
2. It is important to note the fact that while some research studies may be dated several years earlier, this does not mean that their findings no longer apply. It is difficult to publish research that uses a similar methodology and reaches the same conclusions as studies published a decade earlier. Generally, only if their findings differ in some significant aspect will journal referees and editors accept a new version of prior research. It is a tougher sell to an academic journal to publish very similar results based upon a similar methodology as several prior studies, but note that they still apply to a later time period. This is not to say that this cannot be done, it is just a tougher sell. Many of these research studies consider the impact of bids over a relatively short-term window, which may be several months before and after a bid. Proponents of the positive effects of mergers contend that it takes many years for the bidder's acquisition plans to come to fruition. Researchers, however, respond that the market has the long-term experience of many prior acquisitions and that it draws on this information when evaluating bids. In addition, it is difficult to conduct long-term studies that filter out the effects of a specific transaction from many events and other transactions that may occur over a longer time period. Nonetheless, there are some that look at various financial measures over an extended time period after deals.

3. Debra K. Dennis and John J. McConnell, "Corporate Mergers and Security Returns," *Journal of Financial Economics* 16, no. 2 (June 1986): 143–187; Paul Asquith, "Merger Bids, Uncertainty and Stockholder Returns," *Journal of Financial Economics* 11 (April 1983): 51–83; Paul Asquith and E. Han Kim, "The Impact of Merger Bids on Participating Firm's Security Holders," *Journal of Finance* 37 (1982): 121–139; and Peter Dodd, "Merger Proposals, Management Discretion and Shareholder Wealth," *Journal of Financial Economics* 8, no. 2 (June 1980): 105–138.

4. Michael Bradley, Anand Desai, and E. Han Kim, "The Rationale Behind Interfirm Tender Offers," *Journal of Financial Economics* 11, nos. 1–4 (April 1983): 183–206.

5. Debra K. Dennis and John J. McConnell, "Corporate Mergers and Security Returns," *Journal of Financial Economics* 16, no. 2 (June 1986): 143–187.

6. P. Raghavendra Rau and Theo Vermaelen, "Glamor, Value and the Post-Acquisition Performance of Acquiring Firms," *Journal of Financial Economics* 49, no. 2 (August 1998): 223–253.

7. Sara B. Moeller, Frederick P. Schlingemann, and Rene Stulz, "Wealth Destruction on a Massive Scale: A Study of Acquiring Firm Returns in the Recent Merger Wave," *Journal of Finance* 60 (April 2005): 757–783.

8. Robert Shiller used this relationship to show that security markets are not perpetually efficient, as some researchers would like to believe. More relevant is that markets can be efficient, which means they respond quickly to new information, but they may not always be rational and often may be incorrect in how they process this new information. They may overreact and then reverse direction. See Robert Shiller, "Do Stock Prices Move Too Much to Be Explained by Subsequent Changes in Dividends?" *American Economic Review* 71 (1981): 421–426.

9. Andrei Shleifer and Robert W. Vishny, "Stock Market Driven Acquisitions," *Journal of Financial Economics* 70, no. 3 (December 2003): 295–311.

10. Nikhil P. Varaiya, "Determinants of Premiums in Acquisition Transactions," *Managerial and Decision Economics* 8 (1987): 175–184.

11. George R. Roach, "Control Premiums and Strategic Mergers," *Business Valuation Review*, June 1998, 42–49.

12. Richard Roll, "The Hubris Hypothesis of Corporate Takeovers," *Journal of Business* 59, no. 2 (April 1986): 197–216.

13. Patrick A. Gaughan, *Mergers: What Can Go Wrong and How To Prevent It* (Hoboken, NJ: John Wiley & Sons, 2005), 75–82.

14. Peter Dodd, "Merger Proposals, Managerial Discretion and Stockholder Wealth," *Journal of Financial Economics* 8 (June 1980): 105, 138.

15. Carol E. Eger, "An Empirical Test of the Redistribution Effect of Mergers," *Journal of Financial and Quantitative Analysis* 18 (December 1983): 547–572.

16. Paul Asquith, "Merger Bids, Uncertainty and Stockholder Returns," *Journal of Financial Economics* 11, no. 1 (April 1983): 51–83.

17. Michael Bradley, Anand Desai, and E. Han Kim, "The Rationale Behind Interfirm Tender Offers: Information or Synergy?" *Journal of Financial Economics* 11, no. 1 (April 1983): 183–206.

18. Nikhil P. Varaiya, "Winners Curse Hypothesis and Corporate Takeovers," *Managerial and Decision Economics* 9 (1989): 209.
19. Paul Malatesta, "Wealth Effects of Merger Activity," *Journal of Financial Economics* 11, no. 1 (April 1983): 178–179.
20. Mathew L. A. Hayward and Donald C. Hambrick, "Explaining Premiums Paid for Large Acquisitions: Evidence of CEO Hubris," *Administrative Sciences Quarterly* 42 (1997): 103–127.
21. Anju Seth, Kean P. Song, and Richardson Pettit, "Synergy, Managerialism or Hubris? An Empirical Examination of Motives of Foreign Acquisitions of U.S. Firms," *Journal of International Business Studies* 31, no. 3 (3rd Quarter, 2000): 387–405.
22. Ulrike Malmendier and Geoffrey Tate, "Who Makes Acquisitions? CEO Overconfidence and the Market's Reaction, *Journal of Financial Economics* 39 (2007): 353–378.
23. Matthew T. Billet and Yiming Qian, "Are Overconfident CEOs Born or Made? Evidence of Self-Attribution Bias from Frequent Acquirers," *Management Science* 54, no. 6 (June 2008): 1037–1051.
24. Nihat Sktas, Eric de Bodt, and Richard Roll, "The Elapsed Time Between Deals" (UCLA Anderson School of Management Working Paper, March 2008).
25. Nihat Sktas, Eric de Bodt, and Richard Roll, "Learning, Hubris and Corporate Serial Acquisitions," *Journal of Corporate Finance* 15, no. 5 (December 2009): 543–561.
26. Max Baserman and William Samuelson, "I Won the Auction but I Don't Win the Prize," *Journal of Conflict Resolution* 27 (1983): 618–634.
27. James Cassing and Richard Douglas, "Implication of the Auction Mechanism in Baseball's Free Agent Draft," *Southern Economic Journal* 47 (July 1980): 110–121.
28. Interestingly, there is a very real connection between M&A and the Texas Rangers. Tom Hicks was the CEO and chairman of the Texas Rangers baseball team. He also was one of the founders of the LBO firm Hicks Muse. The firm was very active in rollups, which as a type of deal often did not turn out well. Hicks Muse got into financial trouble over bad investments made in the telecom and Internet sectors when these sectors were in a bubble and were very overpriced (like the Texas Rangers hiring of Rodriguez). Hicks had to leave the firm.
29. Carol J. Loomis, "The Biggest and Looniest Deal Ever," *Fortune,* June 18, 1990.
30. John Rothchild, *Going for Broke: How Robert Campeau Bankrupted the Retail Industry, Jolted the Junk Bond Market, and Brought the Booming Eighties to a Crashing Halt* (New York: Simon & Schuster, 1991), 202–203.
31. Ibid.
32. Nikhil Varaiya, "The Winner's Curse Hypothesis and Corporate Takeovers," *Managerial and Decision Economics* 9 (1988): 209–219.
33. Alex Edmans, Itay Goldstein, and Wei Jiang, "Takeover Activity and Target Valuations: Feedback Loops in Financial Markets" (University of Pennsylvania and Columbia University Working Paper, unpublished).

34. Claudio Loderer and Kenneth Martin, "Corporate Acquisitions by Listed Firms: The Experience of a Comprehensive Sample," *Financial Management* 19 (1990): 17–33.

35. Ulrike Malmendier and Geoffrey Tate, "Who Makes Acquisitions? CEO Over-confidence and the Market's Reaction," *Journal of Financial Economics* 89 (2008): 20–43.

36. Sara B. Moeller, Frederik P. Schlingemann and Rene M. Stulz, "Firm Size and the Gains from Acquisitions," *Journal of Financial Economics* 73 (2004): 201–228.

37. Ibid.

38. George Alexandridis, Kathleen P. Fuller, Lars Terhaar, and Nicholas G. Travlos, "Deal Size, Acquisition Premia and Shareholder Gains," unpublished paper.

39. Patrick Gaughan, *Mergers and Acquisitions* (New York: Harper Collins, 1991), 173.

40. Kenneth Ferris and Barbara S. Pecherot Petitt, *Valuation: Avoiding the Winner's Curse* (Upper Saddle River, NJ: Financial Times Prentice Hall, 2002), 102–103.

41. For a few references among many potential ones, see Eugene Fama and Kenneth French, "The Equity Premium," *Journal of Finance* 57, no. 2 (April 2002): 637–659; Roger Grabowski and David Ring, "Equity Premium: What Consultants Need to Know About Recent Research," *Valuation Strategies* (September/October 2003): 5–9; Ravi Jagannathan, Ellen R. McGrattan, and Anna Scherbina, "The Declining U.S. Equity Premium," *Quarterly Review of the Federal Reserve Bank of Minneapolis* (Fall 2000): 3–20; and Pablo Fernandez, "The Equity Premium in 150 Textbooks," *IESE Business School Paper*, November 16, 2010.

42. *Ibbotson 2012 Valuation Handbook* (Chicago, IL: Morningstar, 2012).

43. Leonce Bargeron, Frederik P. Schlingemann, Chad J. Zutter, and Rene M. Stulz, "Why Do Private Acquirers Pay So Little Compared to Public Acquirers," *Journal of Financial Economics* 89 (2008): 375–390.

44. Kathleen Fuller, Jeffry Netter, and Mike Stegemoller, "What Do Returns to Acquiring Firms Tell Us? Evidence from Firms that Make Many Acquisitions," *Journal of Finance* 57, no. 4 (2002): 1763–1769.

45. Saeyoung Chang, "Takeovers of Privately Held Targets, Methods of Payment, and Bidder returns," *Journal of Finance* 53, no. 2 (April 1998): 773–784.

46. Mara Faccio, John J. McConnell, and David Stoli, "Returns to Acquirers of Listed and Unlisted Targets," *Journal of Financial and Quantitative Analysis* 41, no. 1 (2006): 197–220.

Patrick A. Gaughan is president of Economatrix Research Associates, Inc., which is an economic and financial consulting firm with offices on Wall Street, New York City, as well as in New Jersey and Miami. He is also a full professor of economics and finance at the College of Business at Fairleigh Dickinson University, where he has taught mergers and acquisitions for the past quarter of a century. Dr. Gaughan is the author and editor of nine books, including the award-winning *Mergers Acquisitions and Corporate Restructurings*, published by John Wiley & Sons.

Index